MW00613869

HANDBOOK ON INTERNATIONAL COMMERCIAL ARBITRATION

Peter Ashford

Ⴔ

JurisNet, LLC

Questions About This Publication

For assistance with shipments, billing or other customer service matters, please call our Customer Services Department at:

1-631-350-2100

To obtain a copy of this book, call our Sales Department:

1-631-351-5430
Fax: 1-631-351-5712

Toll Free Order Line:

1-800-887-4064 (United States & Canada)

See our web page about this book:
www.arbitrationlaw.com

JurisNet, LLC
71 New Street
Huntington, New York 11743
USA

www.arbitrationlaw.com

TABLE OF CONTENTS

TABLE OF CONTENTS

ABOUT THE AUTHOR

Peter Ashford is Solicitor of the Supreme Court and a Partner in the leading United Kingdom firm of Cripps Harries Hall LLP, where he heads the firm's Commercial Disputes and International Arbitration Teams. He has over 20 years of experience in commercial disputes of all types, including High Court, Court of Appeal and House of Lords in England and in international arbitrations before the ICC, LCIA and *ad hoc* tribunals. Mr. Ashford also regularly advises clients on commercial issues, including the drafting of contracts and especially dispute resolution clauses, and he is particularly experienced in complex, high-value claims and acts for many international clients. A frequent writer and speaker on a variety of contentious topics, Peter is a member of the Chartered Institute of Arbitrators and a graduate of Keele University in Law and Economics.

PREFACE

At the risk of adding to the plethora of books on international arbitration, this handbook aims to assist the practitioner, whether lawyer (or counsel) or arbitrator, in some of the practical minefields. The approach is to consider the typical process of an international commercial arbitration and give some guidance and specimen documents. It seeks to guide practitioners through the complex yet fluid maze of international commercial arbitration but practitioners are encouraged to craft a remedy to fit the issues that arise in the case before them. The aim of this work is to aid the efficiency of the arbitral process especially by reducing time and cost. If it makes a modest contribution in that direction it will have served its purpose for as Lord Hoffmann said in *Fiona Trust & Holding Corp v. Privalov* [2007]; *"The parties have entered into a relationship ... which may give rise to disputes. They want those disputes decided by a tribunal which they have chosen, commonly on the grounds of such matters as its neutrality, expertise and privacy, the availability of legal services at the seat of the arbitration and the unobtrusive efficiency of its supervisory law. Particularly in the case of international contracts, they want a quick and efficient adjudication and do not want to take the risks of delay and, in too many cases, partiality, in proceedings before a national jurisdiction."*

The practitioner will undoubtedly need to access other books on specific issues or for further detail on the points covered, as space has not permitted an analysis or deeper analysis of those issues. The Handbook is intended, very much as its name implies, to guide practitioners in good practice as to how to do many of the things that are required to be done in the process of international commercial arbitration.

The Handbook is written with an English bias for two reasons. Firstly, as an English solicitor, English law and procedure are the matters I profess some expertise in. I do not do the same for other laws and users of the Handbook must acquaint themselves with the appropriate laws of the substantive agreement and the seat of the arbitration. I have, however, added foreign cases where I am aware of them and where I consider they add to the points I have sought to make. Secondly, international commercial arbitration is often a compromise between competing national standards. The extremities, especially on, say, discovery, are U.S. and European civil law standards. English law and procedure sits both geographically and jurisprudentially between the two and may be a happy compromise between the extremes.

My thanks go to my partners and colleagues at Cripps Harries Hall LLP for both indulging and supporting me in the writing of this book and to John Fisher of PricewaterhouseCoopers for his comments on the chapter on Damages. As usual all errors remain mine alone. I have stated the law as I believe it to be as of 31 December 2008; any later developments have been included where possible. My thanks also go to my clients who have enabled me to experience the challenge and enjoyment of this field.

Finally, thanks go to my family and to my father who, sadly, will not see the publication of this work but was so encouraging at the early stages and would have been so proud of its completion. Thanks go especially to my wife, without whose love and support this task would have been impossible. This book is dedicated to her.

Tunbridge Wells, England 2009

CHAPTER 1
WHAT CLAIMS MAY BE ARBITRATED

Many international commercial contracts contain clauses submitting future disputes to arbitration and by doing so the parties take the resolution of the dispute outside the scope of the national courts and into a private regime of party autonomy in arbitration.

What can be arbitrated depends on the parties' agreement. The original arbitration clause will define those claims that can and cannot be arbitrated, as stated by Lord Hoffmann in *Fiona Trust & Holding Corp v. Privalov:*[1]

Arbitration is consensual. It depends upon the intention of the parties as expressed in their agreement. Only the agreement can tell you what kind of disputes they intended to submit to arbitration. But the meaning which parties intended to express by the words which they used will be affected by the commercial background and the reader's understanding of the purpose for which the agreement was made. Businessmen in particular are assumed to have entered into agreements to achieve some rational commercial purpose and an understanding of this purpose will influence the way in which one interprets their language … If one accepts that [consensual dispute resolution outside of the national courts] is the purpose of an arbitration clause, its construction must be influenced by whether the parties, as rational businessmen, were likely to have intended that only some of the questions arising out of their relationship were to be submitted to arbitration and others were to be decided by national courts … If, as appears to be generally accepted, there is no rational basis upon which businessmen would be likely to wish to have questions of the validity or enforceability of the contract decided by one tribunal and questions about its performance decided by another, one would need to find very clear language before deciding that they must have had such an intention.

---

[1] [2007] 4 All ER 951, 956 – 957.

Using the same logic, Lord Hoffmann dispensed with earlier distinctions as to whether disputes "arose out of" or "arose under" contracts. The tendency is to have widely drawn clauses that encompass all claims. The inclusion, in contracts, of phrases such as "*any dispute or difference arising out of or in connection with*"[2] has resulted in all disputes being within the scope of the clause.

The law prior to *Fiona Trust* was already in favour of a wide construction. The cases that indicated that there may be a line and that certain matters would fall outside of the scope of the arbitration clause will have to be reconsidered in light of *Fiona Trust*. Even before *Fiona Trust,* fraud was generally accepted to be within the scope of an arbitration agreement (although it depended on the precise words used).[3] Equally, claims in tort — e.g., negligent misrepresentation inducing the other party to enter into the contract and so-called contractual negligence — are typically within the scope of an arbitration clause. Clear words will therefore be required to exclude claims. Plainly, however, there must be a degree of connection between the contractual agreement to arbitrate and the tort, and even a clause referring "all disputes" could not extend to tort claims having no connection to the contract.[4]

This English approach is mirrored in the U.S. For example, in *Moses H Cone Memorial Hospital v. Mercury Construction Corp,*[5] the court held that "any doubts concerning the scope of arbitrable issues should be resolved in favour of arbitration, whether the problem at hand is the construction of the contract language itself or an allegation of waiver, delay, or a like defense to arbitrability." The court reached a similar conclusion in *JJ Ryan & Sons Inc v. Rhone Poulenc Textile SA*[6] and said "The [ICC's] recommended clause which provides for arbitration of "all disputes arising in connection with the present contract" must be construed to encompass a broad scope of arbitrable issues. The recommended clause does not limit arbitration to the literal interpretation or performance of the contract. It embraces every dispute between the

---

[2] It might be said that strictly disputes do not arise "out of a contract" rather out of conflicting views taken by the parties to the contract – *see* Lord Sumner in Produce Brokers Co Ltd v. Olympia Oil and Cake Co Ltd [1916] AC 314, 328.

[3] Heyman v. Darwins Ltd. [1942] AC 356, 378, 392.

[4] In re An Arbitration between Hohenzollern Aktien Gesellschaft fur Locomotivban and City of London Contract Corporation, (1886) 54 L.T. 596.

[5] 460 U.S. 1, 24-25 (1983).

[6] 863 F. 2d 315,324 (4th Cir. 1988).

2

parties having a significant relationship to the contract regardless of the label attached to the dispute." Finally, the Supreme Court confirmed this wide approach in *Preston v. Ferrer*.[7]

This presumption in favour of arbitration is greater where there is an international relationship.[8]

As arbitration is a private dispute resolution system, it is not the appropriate forum for declaring public rights. For example, the question of whether a party has a valid patent is a matter for the State to resolve through its courts and not one for a private tribunal. Disputes as to the existence of such rights are generally regarded as non-arbitrable. Conversely, the infringement or otherwise of the patent and the damages payable for doing so, would be arbitrable.

In commercial arbitration, it is unlikely that the parties will be of unequal power but it is quite possible that a huge conglomerate might be in dispute with a small family company. At first blush, it seems that an arbitration provision would be perfectly enforceable as between such parties. That would undoubtedly be the position in the UK where the impecuniosity of one party does not make an arbitration incapable of being performed.[9] In the U.S., there are provisions that protect consumers and employees[10] but it seems unlikely that they will extend to small commercial concerns. In Germany, there are also instances of courts striking out references to arbitrations in which one party is unable to adequately present its case due to limited resources.[11]

Even if the parties are bound to arbitrate, but they are patently of differing resources, the Arbitral Tribunal will have to balance the duty to do justice as between the parties and the obligation to treat each party fairly and equally. The Tribunal cannot, and should not, favour an under-resourced party but would be entitled to point out issues that have not been raised and ask that they be addressed. If minded to do so, the Arbitral Tribunal should, however, restrict itself to matters that arise

---

[7] 128 S. Ct. 978 (2008).

[8] Deloitte Noraudit A/S v. Deloitte Haskins & Sells US, 9 F.3d 1060, 1063 (2d Cir. 1993).

[9] Pazcy v. Haendler & Natterman GmbH [1981] 1 Lloyd's Rep 302.

[10] *See* Green Tree Fin. Corp v. Randolph, 531 U.S. 79 (2000); Ingle v. Circuit Stores Inc., 328 F.3d 1165, 1179 (9th Cir), *cert denied* 124 S. Ct. 1169 (2004).

[11] The Bundesgerichtshof (III ZR 33/00 9 April 2000) reversed a decision to refer parties to arbitration.

from issues that have already been raised and not embark on a wholesale recasting of the case. Furthermore, it must do so without giving any indication of the merits of the point. That might create, however it is presented, a perception of apparent bias in favour of the weaker party. Equally, a procedure that imposes an unreasonable burden on a weaker party may be oppressive and make the award vulnerable to attack.

If there is an issue over whether a dispute is arbitrable, it could be resolved in three different ways. First, it could be determined by the Arbitral Tribunal as a preliminary issue. A party may raise the issue of arbitrability as one of jurisdiction. Secondly, the party might apply to the national courts of the seat of the arbitration for an injunction to restrain the reference on the basis that the dispute is not capable of determination by arbitration. Thirdly, a party might commence proceedings before a national court to determine the merits of the dispute. The other party may either submit to the jurisdiction of the national court or seek to stay the court proceedings on the basis that there is a valid agreement to arbitrate.

Generally, if there is an effective submission to arbitration, it will prevent the national courts from hearing the dispute.[12] Any challenge to the jurisdiction of the national courts has to be raised promptly so as to avoid a de facto submission to the jurisdiction of the national courts. If a dispute of arbitrability is raised before the Arbitral Tribunal, it should generally be determined as a preliminary issue of jurisdiction.

---

[12] New York Convention Article II.3 and Geneva Convention Article VI.1.

CHAPTER 2
SEPARABILITY

It is well established that the agreement to arbitrate, albeit typically a clause in the larger commercial agreement, is separate and distinct (or severable) from the contract in which it is contained and may survive the failure of the underlying contract. This will apply whether the main contract is avoided, a voidable contract is rescinded or the main contract discharged by performance, frustration or breach.

Section 7 of the English Arbitration Act 1996 provides:

Unless otherwise agreed by the parties, an arbitration agreement which forms or was intended to form part of another agreement (whether or not in writing) shall not be regarded as invalid, non-existent or ineffective because that other agreement is invalid, or did not come into existence or has become ineffective, and it shall for that purpose be treated as a distinct agreement.

To the same effect, Section 4 of the U.S. Federal Arbitration Act of 1925 provides:

A party aggrieved by the alleged failure, neglect, or refusal of another to arbitrate under a written agreement for arbitration may petition any United States district court ... The court shall hear the parties, and upon being satisfied that the making of the agreement for arbitration or the failure to comply therewith is not in issue, the court shall make an order directing the parties to proceed to arbitration in accordance with the terms of the agreement.

There are strong policy reasons underlying this approach, for the parties, when they decided to refer any dispute between them to arbitration, must be taken to have expected the Arbitral Tribunal to have and exercise jurisdiction if the very validity of the main contract were in issue. It cannot be a logical view of the actions of experienced businessmen for them to agree that national courts should first decide whether the contract needs to be rectified or avoided or rescinded and then, if held to be valid, require an Arbitral Tribunal to determine the dispute between them. The "one-stop-shop" of the Arbitral Tribunal determining all issues is the more logical route unless the parties have used clear words to indicate a contrary intention.

The courts of many jurisdictions have recognised that this is the case, for example, in New South Wales,[1] the U.S.,[2] and England.[3]

As Hoffmann LJ explained in *Harbour Assurance Co (UK) Ltd v. Kansa General International Insurance Co Ltd*:[4]

> . . . There will obviously be cases in which a claim that no contract came into existence necessarily entails a denial that there was any agreement to arbitrate. Cases of non est factum or denial that there was a concluded agreement, or mistake as to the identity of the other contracting party suggest themselves as examples. But there is no reason why every case of initial invalidity should have this consequence . . .
>
> In every case it seems to me that the logical question is not whether the issue goes to the validity of the contract but whether it goes to the validity of the arbitration clause. The one may entail the other but . . . it may not . . . saying that arbitration clauses, because separable, are never affected by the illegality of the principal contract is as much a case of false logic as saying that they must be . . . the same is true of allegations of fraud.

Thus, because the agreement to arbitrate is a separate and distinct agreement from the main contract, an attack on an agreement to arbitrate must be either specifically directed at the agreement to arbitrate by, for example, submitting that the arbitration clause (as opposed to the main contract itself) was induced by fraud or by submitting that there was no agreement at all.

If the submission is, for example, that there was no agreement at all, then the national court must determine that before any arbitration can take place, and it will often be appropriate to restrain any reference to arbitration by injunction as needless expense may be incurred in pursuing the reference.[5]

---

[1] Ferris v. Plaister (1994) 34 NSWLR 474 (CA).

[2] Prima Paint Corp. v. Flood & Conklin Mfg. Co., 388 U.S. 395 (1967); Scherk v. Alberto-Cilver Co., 417 U.S. 506 (1974).

[3] Fiona Trust & Holding Corp v. Privalov [2007] 4 All ER 951.

[4] [1993] Q.B. 701.

[5] Albon v. Naza Motor Company Sdn Bhd [2008] Lloyd's Rep 1.

CHAPTER 3
THE PROPER LAW

The agreement to arbitrate can involve the interaction of a number of different laws and it is simply wrong to refer to the arbitration as being governed by one law as might be inferred from clauses in a contract that provide for arbitration as follows:

Any dispute of difference arising out of this agreement shall be referred to arbitration under the Rules of Arbitration of the International Chamber of Commerce. The arbitration shall take place in Paris.

And a governing law clause that provides: "This agreement is governed by English law."

To the uninitiated, it might be thought that only English law might be relevant. In fact, there are many more laws that might be relevant. Confusingly, many of these are described in Latin. Appendix 1 is a list of various laws and corresponding descriptions and meanings. The laws that may have to be considered in an international commercial arbitration include:

1   The law governing the parties' capacity to enter into the main agreement;

2   The law governing the parties' capacity to enter into an arbitration agreement;

3   The substantive law of the contract or obligations in dispute;

4   The law governing the agreement to arbitrate;

5   The law governing the proceedings of the Arbitral Tribunal upon the particular reference;[1] and

---

[1] It is for this reason that it is important to define the seat of the arbitration as that will invariably dictate the law governing the proceedings. Geographical convenience can result in a venue for hearings other than at the seat of the arbitration, and it is wise to include an express provision that "...meetings and hearings can take place in a venue other than at the seat of the arbitration" – *see* paragraphs 18 and 19 of the sample Terms of Reference at Appendix 7.

6   The law governing the recognition and enforcement of the Award (which may involve numerous jurisdictions dependant upon where assets are located).

Laws 1, 2, and 6 above are outside the scope of this work. In practice, laws 4 and 5 are likely to be the same; therefore, there are likely to be two main laws that practitioners and the Arbitral Tribunal will need to consider—those of the seat or place of the arbitration (and in the example above, this would be French law as the arbitration is to take place in Paris) and the substantive law of the contract (in the example above this will be English). If the seat of the arbitration were London rather than Paris, there would, for all practical purposes, be only one law as the law of the seat and the substantive law would be the same.

Another way of looking at the same point is to consider the laws of the two agreements—the agreement to arbitrate and the main agreement. Viewed in this way, the law of the agreement to arbitrate is whatever law the parties have expressly or impliedly chosen[2] and, in the absence of choice, the law most closely connected with the arbitration agreement. That will generally be the seat of the arbitration. Conversely, the law of the main agreement will be the law chosen by the parties (and it will often be chosen) and, in default, the law the Arbitral Tribunal determines applying conflicts of laws rules.

At least three key distinct issues of governing law may arise in international arbitration: the law governing the arbitration agreement itself; the law governing the arbitral procedure, and; the law governing the substance of the dispute. It is outside the scope of this work to consider in detail the rules for ascertaining the governing law and the issues arising, however, a brief mention is required to comment on the implications of the governing law for various purposes.

The importance of the arbitration agreement is that it is the agreement that gives the Arbitral Tribunal its jurisdiction to determine the issues referred to it and, by circular reasoning, it will need to found its jurisdiction on the validity of the arbitration agreement. There is, however, no international consensus on the choice of law rule applicable to an arbitration agreement. The Rome Convention on the Law Applicable to Contractual Obligations 1980 does not apply to arbitration agreements and hence is, at best, only of persuasive authority.

---

[2] It is rare for parties to choose something other than the law of the seat.

The New York Convention provides that the recognition and enforcement of an Award may be refused where "the said agreement is not valid under the law to which the parties have subjected it or, failing any indication thereon, under the law of the country where the award is made."[3]

International developments have had a profound effect on the conduct of international arbitration. The United Nations Commission on International Trade Law Model Law on International Commercial Arbitration ("the Model Law") has had the greatest impact. It has been adopted wholesale as the arbitration law in over forty countries from Azerbaijan to Zimbabwe and including Canada, Singapore, and Germany. Five states in the U.S. have legislation based on the Model Law and England enacted the Arbitration Act 1996 largely based on the Model Law.

The Model Law has provisions to the same effect as the New York Convention. Although this is not a choice of law provision in its true sense, it clearly indicates that the validity of the arbitration agreement is determined under the law of the seat.

The parties can stipulate the law governing the arbitral procedure at the time of the contract and nominate a set of standard rules (whether the UNCITRAL Arbitration Rules, the International Chamber of Commerce Court of Arbitration (ICC), the London Court of International Arbitration (LCIA), or some other rules). If no law is specified in the agreement, the law of the seat of the arbitration will generally govern the arbitral proceedings. The concept of the *lex arbitri* or curial law is not to be equated with the procedural rules for litigation in national courts, although there are similarities. In essence, the procedural law addresses the procedure of the arbitration itself and the potential intervention of the national courts. Included in the rules of procedure for the arbitration, there are provisions relating to, for example, discovery and, therefore, it is the law governing the arbitral procedure (normally the law of the seat of the arbitration) that will govern discovery obligations.

The law governing the arbitration agreement itself is of great practical importance. The agreement to arbitrate will typically be an integral part of a larger contract but nevertheless forms a separate and distinct agreement. Accordingly its validity, scope, and interpretation fall

---

[3] Article V (1)(a).

to be considered separately from that of the main contract and its status is normally unaffected by the invalidity or avoidance of the main aspects of the contract. In essence, the scope and interpretation of the arbitration agreement is governed by its applicable law, being the law expressly or impliedly chosen by the parties or, in the absence of such choice, the law most closely connected with the arbitration agreement. This will typically be the "law of the seat of the arbitration" (often known as "*lex abitri*").

That said, the law governing the substance of the dispute, the substantive or "proper" law, has an important part to play in the arbitration. The substance of the dispute will be governed by the law chosen by the parties—in a manner they chose to have it determined—and, in default, will be determined by the Tribunal in accordance with the rules of the conflict of laws.

The substantive law determines what facts are in issue, but questions as to the admissibility of evidence are governed by the *lex arbitri*. So, for example, a document may be received in evidence under the *lex arbitri* notwithstanding it would be inadmissible under the substantive law. Furthermore, extrinsic evidence relating to a contract may prove to be inadmissible for one purpose but admissible for another. Documents sought to be adduced as an aid to interpretation are admitted under the substantive law. Conversely, documents that seek to add, vary, or contradict the terms of a contract are matters of evidence and, in general terms, are governed by the *lex arbitri*.

It can thus be seen that, in instances where the laws governing the procedure of the arbitration and the substance of the dispute are different, extremely complex issues can arise. Notwithstanding this, many arbitration clauses deliberately choose different laws for each, perhaps out of a sense of neutrality. Particular care needs to be taken to ensure that arbitration clauses that provide for different laws on procedure and substance do so advisedly and not simply out of some misplaced sense of convenience for the location of the arbitration.

The law governing the procedure of the reference itself can, in the very broadest sense, be equated to procedural rules that might govern litigation before national courts but that is a gross simplification. It covers two concepts; firstly, the internal procedure of the arbitration encompassing the commencement of the reference, the appointment of the Arbitral Tribunal, written pleadings, provisional measures, evidence, hearings, and the award itself. Secondly, it covers external intervention by national courts either supporting the process or supervising it. Examples of the former are appointing members of the Arbitral Tribunal in the absence of agreement and, of the latter, challenging the award. Very often, the first concept (the internal procedure) is agreed to be a set of rules from one of the major institutions such as the ICC, LCIA, or AAA. The second concept (external support and supervision) is invariably sourced from national laws.

It is not unusual for the parties to expressly choose either general principles of contract law or equity or even to permit the Arbitral Tribunal to act as *amiable compositeur*—that is, to permit the arbitrators to decide the dispute according to the legal principles they believe to be just—without being limited to any particular national law, to disregard legal technicalities and strict constructions).[4] The approach to equity provisions such as determining the issues "according to an equitable rather than a strictly legal interpretation" may well depend on the person (and, in particular, his nationality or legal education) considering the provision. The approach of the English Court of Appeal in *Eagle Star Insurance Co Ltd v. Yuval Insurance Co Ltd*[5] was:

> I do not believe that the presence of such a clause makes the whole contract void or a nullity. It is a perfectly good contract . . . . the clause seems entirely reasonable . . . it only ousts technicalities and strict constructions. That is what equity did in the old days, and it is what arbitrators may properly do today under such a clause.

Others from a civil jurisdiction may regard it with greater freedom to craft a remedy. In some common law jurisdictions, it was only possible to have a recognised system of law as the proper law, indeed that was the position in England prior to the Arbitration Act 1996. The 1996 Act changed that and Section 46(1)(b) of the Act enables parties to choose

---

[4] *"Amiable compositeur"* clauses are expressly permitted by art. 28(3) of the Model Law, as well as in domestic and international procedures. *See, e.g.,*, the New Code of Civil Procedure (France), arts. 1474, 1495, and 1496, and the Québec Code of Civil Procedure, art. 944.10. *See also* Art. 1054(2) of the Netherlands Arbitration Act; Art. 182 of the 1987 Swiss Law on Private International Law; Art. 28(1) of the 1993 Russian Law on International Commercial Arbitration; Art. 834(1), Part I, of the Italian Code of Civil Procedure; § 1051(1) of the German Code of Procedure, and; the U.K. *Arbitration Act 1996*, c.23, sect. 46 (1)(b).

[5] [1978] 1 Lloyd's Rep 357.

principles other than the law of a country as the basis on which the dispute is to be decided by the arbitrators. Section 46 provides as follows:

1) The arbitral tribunal shall decide the dispute—

    (a) in accordance with the law chosen by the parties as applicable to the substance of the dispute, or

    (b) if the parties so agree, in accordance with such other considerations as are agreed by them or determined by the tribunal.

(2) For this purpose the choice of the laws of a country shall be understood to refer to the substantive laws of that country and not its conflict of laws rules.

(3) If or to the extent that there is no such choice or agreement, the tribunal shall apply the law determined by the conflict of laws rules which it considers applicable.

This follows Article 28 of the Model Law:

(1) The arbitral tribunal shall decide the dispute in accordance with such rules of law as are chosen by the parties as applicable to the substance of the dispute. Any designation of the law or legal system of a given State shall be construed, unless otherwise expressed, as directly referring to the substantive law of that State and not to its conflict of laws rules.

(2) Failing any designation by the parties, the arbitral tribunal shall apply the law determined by the conflict of laws rules which it considers applicable.

(3) The arbitral tribunal shall decide *ex aequo et bono* or as *amiable compositeur* only if the parties have expressly authorized it to do so.

(4) In all cases, the arbitral tribunal shall decide in accordance with the terms of the contract and shall take into account the usages of the trade applicable to the transaction.

The "law" that may be chosen under section 46(1)(a) or that may be applied under section 46(3) must be the law of a country. By contrast, section 46(1)(b) allows the parties the freedom to apply a set of rules or principles which do not in themselves constitute a legal system.

Such a choice may thus include a non-national set of legal principles—e.g., the 2004 UNIDROIT Principles of International Commercial Contracts[6]—or, more broadly, general principles of commercial law or the *lex mercatoria*.

The distinction made in section 46 between "law," being the law of a country, and "other considerations" is consistent with the common law position.

---

[6] The text of the principles can be found at www.unidroit.org.

CHAPTER 4
CONDITIONS PRECEDENT TO A REFERENCE

Dispute resolution clauses are becoming increasingly more sophisticated and are typically now in a tiered form with parties "obliged"[1] to perhaps meet at an operational level, then at a senior management level and, thereafter, mediate and only then pursue arbitration.

The status of a reference commenced in breach of such a clause raises important questions of both substantive jurisdiction and costs.

If the clause is construed as a true condition precedent—i.e., the right to refer a dispute to arbitration is truly conditional upon compliance with the lower "tiers" of the dispute resolution process—then any reference commenced before full compliance with the lower tiers should never have existed. It may be tempting to stay the reference so as to permit the lower "tiers" to be complied with but that is to ignore the plain breach of contract that the referring party has committed. The innocent respondent has no adequate remedy in damages—the particular constitution of the Tribunal might well, perhaps almost inevitably, not be replicated in a properly constituted Tribunal after the lower "tiers" had been complied with. Moreover, the earlier "tiers" might have resulted in a settlement that would have made the reference a nullity—it should never have existed.

Equally, a referring party may be facing limitation problems that necessitate commencing the reference. On the basis that the party would have had plenty of time and must have known of the contractual provisions, it has only itself to blame and the maxim that a party cannot take advantage of its own breach of contract may come into play. Some clauses may permit proceedings to be commenced for urgent protection or injunctive relief.

A. Conditions Precedent

An arbitration agreement may provide that any dispute may be arbitrated only after the occurrence of some specified event. The clause may stipulate that some aspect of the subject matter of the contract must be performed prior to the commencement of the arbitration.

---

[1] The degree of obligation is of vital importance as will be seen.

Alternatively, the contract may provide that, before submitting disputes to arbitration, the parties should strive to settle their differences through any of a number of dispute resolution processes, which may include negotiation, conciliation, adjudication by an expert, mediation, or myriad other processes. Arbitration represents the final port of call. Multi-layer dispute resolution clauses are becoming increasingly common in international commercial transactions.

If a claimant has fails to comply with a pre-arbitration clause and therefore commences the arbitration prematurely, then the consequences can be serious.

B. Requirement to Negotiate: Is the Term Enforceable?

If a respondent alleges that a claimant has not complied with pre-arbitration provisions contained in the parties' agreement, then the claimant may seek to argue that the pre-arbitration provisions are not enforceable and so do not constitute a bar to proceeding to arbitration.

The Arbitral Tribunal should first evaluate the precise wording of the term to ascertain whether it is merely permissive, or whether it imposes a mandatory requirement for pre-arbitration negotiations or ADR. If the term is merely permissive, then a party is clearly under no positive obligation to comply before commencing arbitration.

If the term is mandatory, it may be argued that it is so vague as to be unenforceable. For example, nebulous stipulations requiring parties to undertake "good faith" settlement negotiations are not uncommon, but such terms have been found to lack sufficient certainty for a respondent to rely on them. A term providing that the parties: "shall strive to settle [disputes] amicably" prior to submitting to arbitration has been found by the English High Court to be unenforceable.[2] Similarly, it has been said that an agreement which requires parties to "attempt in good faith to resolve the dispute or claim" will be unenforceable because the court would not have sufficient objective criteria to decide whether the parties had complied with the condition or not.[3] This traditional view of the law[4]

---

[2] Paul Smith Ltd. v. H & S International Holding Inc. [1991] Lloyd's Rep. 127, 131 and Walford v. Miles [1992] 2 AC 128.

[3] Cable & Wireless plc v. IBM UK Ltd [2002] EWHC 2059 (Comm), 1326.

[4] In English law, it has historically been an established principle that an agreement to negotiate cannot be enforced in English law; *see* Courtney & Fairburn Ltd. v. Tolaini

is under some attack in England. Most recently the Court of Appeal in *Petromec v. Petroleo Brasileiro*[5] held that provisions to negotiate additional costs in good faith were enforceable. The traditional approach was distinguishable because, in *Petromec,* there was a concluded agreement and the agreement to negotiate in good faith was an express provision in the agreement drawn up by highly skilled lawyers. To say that such a provision was unenforceable would, the court said, make a mockery of the provision.

The Australian courts have taken a similar approach, holding that an obligation to negotiate in good faith can be sufficiently certain to give rise to a binding obligation if it is expressed in particular terms and is sufficiently precise as to the procedure to be followed.[6] The German Federal Supreme Court has upheld a clause whereby the parties agreed to try to resolve disputes by negotiations before commencing litigation and stated that the parties must co-operate in the agreed settlement process.

Those favouring a strict compliance with the different tiers of dispute resolution will find comfort in the words of Lord Mustill in *Channel Tunnel Group Ltd v. Balfour Beatty Construction Ltd:*[7]

> Those who make agreements for the resolution of disputes must show good cause for departing from them . . . Having promised to take their complaints to the experts and if necessary to the arbitrators, this is where the appellants should go. The fact that the appellants now find their chosen method too slow to suit their purposes is to my way of thinking quite beside the point.

C. If a Term Requiring Negotiation Is Enforceable, How Far Will the Tribunal Enquire as to Whether the Parties Have Fulfilled the Requirements of the Term?

Tribunals have traditionally taken a practical approach to conditions precedent requiring negotiation. Such clauses are put into contracts to try to avoid the expense of formalised dispute resolution, not to deny a party

---

Brothers (Hotels) Ltd [1975] 1 WLR 297, cited with approval in Cable & Wireless plc v. IBM UK Ltd [2002] EWHC 2059 (Comm).

[5] [2005] EWCA Civ 891.

[6] Aiton Australia Pty Ltd v. Transfield Pty Ltd [2000] ADRLJ 342.

[7] [1993] AC 334.

that has a genuine grievance its strict legal rights if the condition has not been complied with. Further, there will be situations in which the parties are at loggerheads and negotiations are likely to prove fruitless. In such situations, the Tribunal will often look to the purpose of the condition precedent, and should not enquire too deeply into the content of the negotiations, merely looking to whether the formal requirement to approach negotiation has taken place.

D. Requirements to Submit to Pre-Arbitration ADR

In a multi-layered dispute resolution clause, a first tier requirement to negotiate may be followed by a second tier requirement to mediate or undergo another formal ADR process such as adjudication or conciliation prior to the final tier of arbitration.

As with the approach to negotiation, where the contract provides sufficient detail of the pre-arbitration ADR process to be undertaken so that the Arbitral Tribunal can objectively assess whether the term has been complied with or not, the term may be enforceable.

The English courts have upheld a condition precedent which required parties to attempt to resolve disputes "through an ADR procedure as recommended by [CEDR]."[8] The court found that resort to this institution and compliance with a procedure recommended by it was a stipulation of sufficient certainty that the court could readily say whether the condition had been complied with or not. The court went further, stating that to refuse to enforce contractual references to ADR on the grounds of intrinsic uncertainty would be to fly in the face of the English Civil Procedure Rules, one of whose premises is that parties should be encouraged to negotiate their disputes before submitting to formal dispute resolution procedures. Contractual references to ADR which do not identify the procedure to be used will not necessarily fail to be enforceable by reason of uncertainty:[9]

The English courts should nowadays not be astute to accentuate uncertainty (and therefore unenforceability) in the field of dispute resolution references.

---

[8] Cable & Wireless plc v. IBM UK Ltd [2002] EWHC 2059 (Comm) at 1326.

[9] Holloway v. Chancery Mead Limited [2007] EWHC 2495 (TCC).

The German courts have also compelled compliance with conciliation proceedings in a pre-litigation context.[10]

Further, national courts may insist on compliance with the condition precedent before they will compel arbitration. The U.S. courts have held that a party to an agreement which requires mediation prior to commencing arbitration cannot compel arbitration under the Federal Arbitration Act without first complying with the condition precedent.[11]

It should be remembered, however, that submission to ADR or undertaking settlement negotiations clearly requires the participation and co-operation of both parties. It would be inequitable for a respondent to refuse to participate in such a process and then rely on its non participation as evidence that a condition precedent had not been complied with and that arbitration should not proceed. The English courts have developed a general principle that when one party (A) is prevented from performing a contractual condition because of the fault of another party (B), then A will be excused his performance[12] and the arbitration may commence.

E. Consequences of Non-Compliance with a Pre-Arbitration Condition

If the tribunal decides that a condition precedent has not been complied with, what is the status of an arbitration commenced in breach of such a term? There are three possibilities often canvassed, each of which has its supporters:

1. The tribunal has no jurisdiction until the condition precedent has been complied with

According to the school of thought of supporters of this position, the Arbitral Tribunal has no jurisdiction until the pre-arbitration conditions have been complied with. The Tribunal will not only be unable to deal with the parties' dispute at this stage but, it is sometimes argued, would not be properly constituted and would have to be reconstituted at some time in the future when the condition precedent had been met. A tribunal

---

[10] Decision of the Bundesgerichtshof of November 18, 1998; VIII ZR 344/97; Decision BGH reported in (1984) Neue Juristiche Wochenschrift; both cited in Jolles "Consequences of Multi-tier Arbitration Clauses: Issues of Enforcement" (2006) 72 Arbitration 4 at 329, at 332.

[11] HIM Portland v. DeVito Builders, Inc., 317 F.3d 41 (1st Cir. 2003).

[12] Miguel Mico (London) Ltd v. H Widdop & Co Ltd [1955] 1 Lloyd's Rep 491.

that had been convened only to find that it lacked jurisdiction would need to be disbanded, with the attendant costs consequences. Quite possibly, the arbitrators chosen by the party to constitute the tribunal would then be ruled out for participation in any tribunal re-constituted after the pre-arbitration condition had been complied with.

The implication for a party who has ignored, or imperfectly complied with the condition precedent is that he will have to first jump through the hoops of compliance with the pre-arbitration tiers and then recommence the arbitration. Where the party is up against a tight limitation period, the delay caused by compliance may mean that he cannot recommence the arbitration prior to the expiry of the limitation deadline. His remedy for the substantive breach of contract would be statute-barred. The English courts have upheld a condition precedent to litigation which had this effect.[13]

To state that the Tribunal has no jurisdiction at all, until the condition precedent has been complied with, produces some further consequences, not the least of which is that it will not have jurisdiction to police the condition precedent itself. Thus, parties that have included an arbitration clause in their contracts and thereby seek to preclude litigation in the national courts will find that they need to bring an action before those very courts in order to establish whether the term has been complied with or not. It is unlikely that parties intend that this passing of the ultimate jurisdiction over their affairs from the national courts to the tribunal should occur only after any earlier tiers of the dispute resolution clause have been complied with, or that, in the event that one of the parties does not comply with pre-arbitration conditions, the national courts, and not the tribunal, should decide disputes between the parties. A better view, therefore, must be that the Tribunal has jurisdiction, at least to decide on whether the condition precedent has been complied with.[14] Similarly, the question of whether the arbitration agreement contains an enforceable condition precedent should be one for the tribunal to be decided in accordance with the principle of *Kompetenz-Kompetenz*.

---

[13] Harbour and General Works Ltd. v. Environment Agency [2000] 1 WLR 950.

[14] That the tribunal has jurisdiction is clearly envisaged by the UNCITRAL Model Law, Article 13 of which requires that a tribunal must give effect to pre-arbitration conditions, thereby implying that it has authority to take at least procedural actions in relation to the dispute.

2. *The tribunal has jurisdiction, but will not hear the substantive claim until the condition precedent has been complied with*

Assuming that the Tribunal has jurisdiction, it must then decide the procedural question of how to deal with an arbitration that it finds has been commenced prematurely. Should it refuse to accept the claimant's request for arbitration and require him to recommence the arbitration later, or should it accept the notice of arbitration and treat the arbitration as having been commenced, but held in suspense or stayed until the condition precedent is complied with? In both these instances, the tribunal will not consider the substantive merits of the claim until the pre-arbitration conditions have been complied with.

To refuse to accept the request for arbitration is the logical outcome of applying many standard dispute resolution clauses. The approach has the advantage that it appears to respect party autonomy since the tribunal will enforce the bargain into which the parties freely entered. This consideration was clearly paramount with the House of Lords in their decision in the *Channel Tunnel* case.[15]

However, if the request for arbitration is not accepted, the consequences for the claimant may be very harsh, especially if he is up against a limitation deadline. His time to commence an action may expire, and his substantive right of redress be extinguished, as he is compelled to participate in one or more pre-arbitration tiers of dispute resolution. Where no timetable has been prescribed for the completion of the pre-arbitration procedures, and where the respondent has dragged his feet, the danger for the claimant is particularly acute. Additionally, because there would be no pending action before the tribunal, it might be easier for one of the parties to engage in forum shopping and to commence litigation elsewhere than would be the case if the action were pending but stayed, in which case a plea of *lis alibi pendens* could be entered on behalf of the party seeking to enforce the arbitration agreement.

Where a refusal to accept the request to arbitrate would lead to undue hardship for one of the parties, the tribunal may be assisted by looking to the purpose of the dispute resolution clause and of any condition precedent. Pre-arbitration dispute resolution provisions are often included in contracts in the hope that they will avoid the expense of a formalised dispute resolution process and encourage the preservation of business relations through an initial resort to consensual problem solving

---

[15] *Supra*, note 7.

rather than adversarial dispute resolution. The purpose is not to deny any party the right to determination of his substantive grievances, and such a result may in fact be totally against what the parties would have intended if the situation were put to them at the time of contracting. It might also be argued that the party autonomy based rationale for refusing to accept the request for arbitration is weakened in cases in which the conditions precedent are contained in standard form contracts (although a logical extension of this argument might call into question the validity of the arbitration agreement itself).

The alternative course is for the tribunal to accept the request for arbitration but state that the arbitration is merely in suspense until the condition precedent has been complied with. This would have the effect of stopping the clock running on any limitation period. Any risk of substantive injustice to the parties is thereby eliminated.

The English courts have rejected this approach, finding that the effect of failure to comply with a condition precedent is that the reference to arbitration was invalid, and that the argument that the arbitration was in suspense until such times as the condition precedent was complied with would make a "mockery" of the contractual provisions.[16]

3. The Tribunal has jurisdiction and will hear the substantive issues even though the pre-arbitration condition has not been complied with

As an alternative, the Tribunal may chose to treat the breach of the pre-arbitration condition as merely a breach of contract which has no procedural implications for the conduct of the arbitration. The Tribunal will hear the substantive issues immediately, even though the pre-arbitration condition has not been complied with. The respondent's remedy for the claimant's breach of the pre-arbitration condition would be contractual. A party's damages in such a situation will be hard to quantify in financial terms and he may fail to recover any damages as a result.

Such an approach flies in the face of the principle of party autonomy. The parties have agreed to settle disputes in a certain way and as a matter of policy the Tribunal should not assist one party unilaterally to dispense with the contractual provisions. Furthermore, the tribunal's authority, which is based on the parties' consent, may be undermined if it refuses to

---

[16] J.T. Mackley & Company Limited v. Gosport Marina Limited [2002] EWHC 1315 (TCC).

compel compliance with other consensual processes stipulated in the agreement.

While it may be appropriate to hold the parties to a pre-dispute resolution tier, the practical benefit of doing so will depend on the content of the pre-arbitration process itself. A process which involves determination by an expert, for example, may prove more profitable than compelling a recalcitrant party to negotiate in good faith. The fact that one of the parties has ignored the condition precedent in the first place may indicate a lack of confidence that the process stipulated, which may be costly and time consuming, will succeed. The effect of complying with a condition precedent may be to delay, perhaps substantially, the award of redress to the wronged party. Although he may be adequately compensated by interest on the damages eventually awarded, this will not always be the case, for example, where lack of cashflow to a business caused by late payment of contractual dues, eventually ordered by the arbitrators, means that the business is damaged.

If it appears to the arbitrators that strict adherence to a pre-arbitration condition would be unproductive or even counterproductive, then the best course may be to seek the parties' consent to waive the condition precedent.

F. Counterclaims

There is some question as to whether a counterclaim should be subject to a contractual condition precedent that would involve the same steps to be taken as would be necessary for a claim. In many cases, both the claim and counterclaim will be at issue before the request for arbitration is filed, but it may not always be the case. If a respondent raises a counterclaim only after the arbitration has been commenced, it will cause more delay if these claims must be subjected to the condition precedent.

G. Costs

In addition to the jurisdictional issue, there will be costs consequences for the Tribunal to address. There is an argument that a party who deliberately ignores an agreed dispute resolution clause should bear the costs, and quite possibly all of the costs, of the other party.[17]

---

[17] Tribunals may find some guidance from the approach of the English court in A v. B (No. 2) [2007] 1 Lloyd's Rep. 358. This was a case in which claims were made in the

It is also possible that the tribunal may take account of a failure to comply with a non-binding pre-arbitration dispute resolution clause when deciding who should bear the costs of the reference.

A counter-argument is that, if the Arbitral Tribunal has no jurisdiction, it has no jurisdiction to make any award as to costs. The response to this is likely to be that the parties consented to the Tribunal determining whether jurisdiction existed and certainly if both sought costs awards t can be inferred that they also, bestowed upon the Tribunal the authority to award costs.[18]

Alternatively, costs incurred in a reference where the Tribunal had no jurisdiction might be recoverable in a subsequent reference. An English court allowed costs incurred in an action in New York, commenced in breach of an exclusive jurisdiction clause in favour of England, to be recovered in a new action in England.[19] By parity of reasoning, the same should apply to costs incurred in defending a reference when there had been no compliance with a condition precedent.

It is clear that a party that wishes to be sure that the arbitration has been validly commenced and that the Tribunal has jurisdiction is wise to ensure compliance with any condition precedent.

H. Form of Award

If the Arbitral Tribunal determines that a condition precedent is not met it should so declare and render the award.[20]

Barbadian court in contravention of an agreement to arbitrate. The court had previously found that the party that brought the court proceedings was in breach of the agreement to arbitrate and that the court proceedings should be stayed. On the question of costs, the English Court found that where there was a breach of a clause compelling arbitration (that could be said to be analogous to a breach of a condition precedent in an arbitration agreement), the party in breach should usually pay the other party's costs on an indemnity basis. If recovery was limited to the standard basis, then there would necessarily be a part of its cost that the innocent party could not recover. There was no policy consideration that could support the innocent party having to recover the remainder of its costs as damages for a breach of the arbitration agreement.

[18] That has been found to occur in relation to statutory adjudication in England – a scheme for resolving disputes without the ordinary English (loser pays) costs consequences: Nolan Davis Ltd v. Steven Catton (February 2000 – unreported) and *see also* Linnett v. Halliwells LLP [2009] EWHC 319 (TCC).

[19] Union Discount Co Ltd v. Zoller [2002] 1 WLR 1517.

[20] A model for the formal part of the award is at Appendix 2.

CHAPTER 5
GETTING STARTED

A. Preliminaries before Getting Started

International commercial arbitration is an established method of dispute resolution in the international business community. To those involved with such arbitrations on a regular basis, there are established methods of working within the broad flexibility of the various institutional rules and still more so in *ad hoc* arbitrations. To the novice, it might appear that there are nuances and procedures that are obscure and opaque.

In practice, although not an area the uninitiated should venture without proper research and representation, the international arbitration community is both friendly and supportive. Although arbitrators are not there to protect parties from themselves, they will usually seek to steer the novice in the right direction.

When presented with a dispute, there are a number of preliminary matters such as the identification of the proper law and the seat of the arbitration that must be addressed from the outset.

B. The Request, Answer and Terms of Reference

All of the major institutional rules provide for an international commercial arbitration to be initiated by filing a request for arbitration with the institution. The form and content of the request will naturally vary from institution to institution but the broad outline and substantive content is fairly uniform. Clearly, regard must be had to the precise rules and requirements. Counsel from a civil law jurisdiction tend to draft a more comprehensive request whereas those from a common law jurisdiction tend to draft perfunctory requests.

The request, together with the appropriate number of copies, is sent to the institution and, for some institutions, a copy must be sent simultaneously to all other parties. Invariably, a fee must be sent with the request.

When an arbitration is commenced can be crucial for limitation purposes. Jurisdictions that have limitation provisions usually apply those limitation provisions to arbitration. For example, §13 of the English Arbitration Act 1996 expressly applies the Limitation Acts to arbitral proceedings. Section 14 of the same Act stipulates that the parties are free to agree on what will constitute the commencement of an arbitration and provides for default rules for cases in which there is no agreement.

Institutional rules may establish when the arbitration is commenced. For example, Article 4(2) of the ICC Rules and Article 1.2 of the LCIA Rules provides that the date of receipt of the request by the institution is the date of commencement of the arbitration.

A sample Request for Arbitration under the ICC Rules is set out at Appendix 3. It can be adapted as necessary for other institutional rules.

Most institutional rules also contain provisions governing the Respondent's "Answer" or "Response" to the Request. The ICC Rules provide for an "Answer" within thirty (30) days of receipt of the request (Article 5), and the LCIA Rules provide for a "Response" within the same period (Article 2).

A sample Answer in accordance with the ICC Rules is set out at Appendix 4. Again it can be adapted as necessary for other institutional rules.

The ICC Rules provide for the possibility of a Reply (Article 5[6]) but the LCIA rules do not. The ICC Rules do not make any formal requirements for the Reply.

The Request and Answer (or Response) and Reply may provide a sufficient "agenda" for an evidential hearing but more often the parties will wish to expand their respective positions by more formal pleadings. These can be known as memorials, briefs, or statements of case. Whatever the name, the function of the pleadings is to define the issues that are in dispute. Formal requirements for pleadings that would apply in court proceedings do not apply at all or at least with the same vigour as they would in court proceedings. For example, in England the general rule is that only facts and not evidence or law are pleaded whereas it is very common to see both evidence and law pleaded in arbitration pleadings.

The main exception to the relatively relaxed view taken of pleading is for allegations of dishonesty and fraud. Such allegations are, thankfully, relatively rare but when pleaded ought to be pleaded with great detail and particularity. Counsel should not plead fraud "*unless he has clear and sufficient evidence to support it*"[1] as to do so may have professional consequences for the counsel concerned. These issues are discussed further in Chapter 13.

---

[1] Associated Leisure Ltd v. Associated Newspapers Ltd [1970] 2 QB 450, 456.

CHAPTER 6
PARTIES AND INTERNATIONAL COMMERCIAL ARBITRATION

The potential parties to any arbitration are the signatories to the underlying contract. It is their signature to the contract that signifies their agreement to have their disputes resolved by an arbitral tribunal and not by national courts. Sometimes when a dispute arises it appears that the "correct" party is not a signatory to the contract either because it is a non-signatory who has suffered the loss, is the true wrongdoer or the signatories are of insufficient means to justify being pursued. So starts the search for a theory to join a non-signatory.[1]

Equally, one of the main disadvantages of arbitration, in general (and international commercial arbitration is no different), is the restrictions imposed on who can be a party. In a typical contractual relationship of employer, main contractor, and sub-contractor, there will be two contracts: one between employer and main contractor and a second between main contractor and sub-contractor. If the employer-main contractor contract has an arbitration provision but the main contractor-sub-contractor does not, there is a real risk that the disputes might be decided in different forums. This can lead to inconsistent results and consequent hardship. For example, if the employer pursues a claim against the main contractor on the basis of poor workmanship for works undertaken by the sub-contractor, the sub-contractor can normally resist being joined to the arbitration on the grounds that it has not agreed to submit its disputes to arbitration, and can insist on any claim being resolved through national courts. Furthermore, the sub-contractor will not be bound by the findings of the Arbitral Tribunal. Therefore, if the employer succeeds against the main contractor, there is no guarantee of success by the main contractor against the sub-contractor as the different forums may reach different conclusions on the facts and the law. The involvement of any non-signatory party may result in the exclusion of a dispute from the agreed arbitration. In the Australian case of *Paharpur Cooling Towers Ltd v. Paramount (WA) Ltd*[2] the court refused to stay

---

[1] Various theories can be advanced for joinder, for example, in Thomson-CSF v. American Arbitration Association, 64 F.3d 773, 776 (2d Cir. 1995) the court considered (and rejected on the facts) five theories for joinder: (i) incorporation by reference (ii) assumption (iii) agency (iv) veil-piercing / alter ego and (v) estoppel.

[2] [2008] WASCA 110.

proceedings on a bill of exchange as a non-signatory to the arbitration agreement was a party to the bill.

In respect to considering the joinder of third parties, arbitration is crucially different from litigation in national courts for two main reasons. First, the very nature of the arbitral process whereby parties agree to have *their* disputes resolved by a contractual mechanism, does not involve non-parties. Second, part of that contractual mechanism inherently involves the choice of the constitution of the Arbitral Tribunal. A proposed new party may have no opportunity to exercise the right to be involved in the choice of the members of the Tribunal.

Against this background, the ability to join parties needs to be considered. That will invariably be a function of the arbitration clause itself (and the parties to the arbitration clause), national law, and the institutional rules governing the reference. The latter will be considered first and, thereafter, national law.

A. The ICC Rules

The ICC Rules are regarded as one of the most restrictive sets of institutional rules for the joinder of parties. The starting point is Article 4(3)(a) that provides: "The Request shall . . . contain . . . the name . . . of each of the parties." This provision has been used to argue that it enables the Claimant to name the parties to "its" reference and that no other provision of the Rules permits the naming of other parties.[3] That is, effectively, a bar to the Respondent seeking to join additional parties whether for an indemnity, contribution, or by way of counterclaim.

Similarly, Article 4(6) does not permit consolidation unless the parties to the two separate references are identical and the Terms of Reference have not been signed. After the Terms of Reference have been signed, the procedure in Article 19 applies, albeit it is extremely unlikely that it can be used to permit the joinder of additional parties. The author does have experience in the consolidation of two ICC references with non-identical parties albeit that the joinder in that instance was by consent.[4]

---

[3] *See generally* Anne Marie Whitesell & Eduardo Silva-Romero, *L'arbitrage à pluralité de parties ou de contrats: l'expérience récente de la Chambre de Commerce Internationale* 2003 BULL. CCI SUPPLÉMENT SPÉCIAL 7, 10.

[4] ICC Cases 13643 and 13711.

The generally restrictive approach of the ICC is illustrated by ICC Case 5625 decided in 1987. The Tribunal restricted the parties to those named in the original Request, reasoning that the only way in which one can become a party is by means of an Article 3 Request that identifies the Claimants and Respondents; there is no discretion to add parties. This award was included in an ICC publication entitled *Multi-Party Arbitration* in 1991 by which the ICC appeared to endorse the reasoning.

This strict approach has been criticised and a modest softening of position has occurred in recent years. The ICC Court now permits Respondents to join additional parties if three conditions are satisfied:

- The additional party is a signatory to the arbitration clause upon which the reference is founded (it is insufficient if the new party was involved in the negotiation or performance of the contract);
- The Respondent must raise claims against the new party; and
- The new party must either have a full opportunity to participate in the constitution of the Arbitral Tribunal or consent to any existing Tribunal.

Anything beyond this requires the consent of all parties.

B. The LCIA Rules

In contrast, Article 22.1(h) of the LCIA Rules permits the Tribunal to join one or more parties on the application of any existing party subject to (written) consent from the proposed new party. That authority is subject to the parties agreeing that the Arbitral Tribunal does not have that power and is conditional upon all existing parties having a reasonable opportunity to state their views. Like all powers, it is discretionary and factors such as the nature of the proposed claim against or by the new party, its relationship to the existing matters in the reference, and the state of the existing reference (specifically how far it has progressed) are all matters that will be taken into account. There is, however, little reported use of this provision.

C. Other Rules and *Ad Hoc* Arbitrations

Neither the UNCITRAL Rules nor the AAA Rules have any provisions regarding additional parties. The Swiss Rules of International

Arbitration have wider powers to join new parties[5] and encompasses both a third party wishing to be joined and a party wishing to join a third party. In both cases, the joinder is possible without further consent but it is a discretionary power to be exercised after consulting all parties. The Rules of the Netherlands Arbitration Institute[6] and the Court of Arbitration for Sport[7] expressly authorise intervention and joinder but both require the consent of all parties.

Where there are no institutional rules, the preponderance of opinion is that parties should, in principle, be permitted to apply to join any additional party provided they were parties to the original arbitration agreement. Clearly, factors such as the commonality of issues and the progress of the existing reference will be factors for the Arbitral Tribunal to consider in deciding whether, based on the facts, to permit joinder.

D. National Laws

With the notable exception of the arbitration statutes of the Netherlands,[8] Belgium,[9] Iran,[10] and Italy,[11] national laws are silent on the joinder of new parties. All of the laws require the consent of the existing parties and the new party. Any consent must be real, so a mere signature induced by fraud or duress may be insufficient consent. Conversely, a signature is often not required.[12] As with consent, joinder would be likely in any event, it might be thought that the national laws add little.

In the U.S., the Federal Arbitration Act is silent and the state laws of, for example, New York, California, Texas and Florida are likewise

---

[5] Article 4(2).

[6] Article 41.

[7] Article 41.4.

[8] Article 1045, Netherlands Arbitration Act, 1986.

[9] Article 1696 *bis,* Belgian Judicial Code.

[10] Article 26, Iranian International Commercial Arbitration Act, 1997.

[11] Legislative Decree 40/2006.

[12] The laws of the U.S. require a written provision albeit not signed (§2 Federal Arbitration Act) as do England (§5(4) Arbitration Act 1996), and France (Article 1443 French Code of Civil Procedure). Switzerland permits agreement by text (Article 178 Swiss Private International Law) and New Zealand permits oral agreements (7 Schedule 1 Arbitration Act 1996).

silent, although all but the former have provisions for consolidation.[13] In early U.S. cases, the courts held that they could order consolidation but after several Supreme Court decisions this approach was modified to an emerging consensus that the courts could only order consolidation if there was evidence that the parties agreed to consolidation.[14] Similar to English law the fifth, sixth, eighth, ninth, and eleventh U.S. circuits all held that the agreement had to be express. In contrast in the first, third, and seventh circuits, the courts held that the consent did not have to be express.

Notable exceptions to this orthodox approach are to be found in cases that appear to permit the extension of arbitration clauses to other companies in the same group or companies that actually perform obligations. France, and to a lesser extent Switzerland and Germany, have a more relaxed approach. In the French case *SMABTP v. Statinor,*[15] the liberal approach was expounded: "the arbitration clause inserted in an international contract has self-standing validity and effectiveness which requires that its application be extended to parties which are directly implicated in the performance of the contract and in the dispute that may arise therefrom as long as it is established that their situation and their activities give rise to the presumption that they were aware of the existence and the scope of the arbitration clause, even though they were not signatories of the contract which provides for it." There is similar language in a case[16] in the Swiss Federal Supreme Court.

E. Intervention as *Amicus Curiae*

There is little scope for the intervention as *amicus* in a typical commercial contract reference. The same cannot be said for investment disputes in which issues of wider public interest arise. Indeed Rule 37 of the ICSID Arbitration Rules expressly acknowledges the possible receipt of *amicus* briefs (although not attendance at hearings without consent).

---

[13] CAL. CODE OF CIVIL P. §§1281.3, 1297.272; TEX. CIV. PRAC. & REM. CODE §172.173 (both court-ordered consolidation) and FLA. STAT. § 684.12 (tribunal-ordered consolidation).

[14] The agreement can be inferred from the text of the contract as well as express. *See* Connecticut Gen Life Ins v. Sun Life Assurance, 210 F.3d 771 (7th Cir. 2000).

[15] Cour d'appel de Paris 22 March 1995.

[16] X s.a.l., Y s.a.l. et A c/ Z s.a.r.l. et Tribunal Arbitral CCI, BGE 129 III 727.

The introduction of Rule 37 followed a number of decisions where *amicus* briefs had been received.[17]

F. Group Companies

In some jurisdictions there is the "group of companies doctrine". This is most notably present in France. Under French law, in accordance with a case law inaugurated in *Dow Chemical v. Isover-Saint-Gobain*,[18] a parent company will be deemed to be bound by an arbitration agreement entered into by one of its subsidiaries if the parent company appears to be chiefly concerned by the contract and any disputes that may arise in its connection: the parent and the subsidiary and "one and the same economic reality." It is generally accepted that the shareholder must be involved both with the formation of the contract and its performance. The doctrine has been widely applied in arbitral proceedings but has been rejected in England if there is "a mere legal or commercial connection."[19] When considering the lifting, or piercing, of the veil the applicable law for the law of the place of incorporation is likely to be the appropriate law to consider. The U.S. Restatement of Conflicts of Law §307 (1971) provides that the "local law of the state of incorporation will be applied to determine the existence and extent of a shareholder's liability to the corporation . . . to its creditors for corporate debts." The same applies in France and Switzerland.

G. Other Exceptions to "New" Parties

Notwithstanding the apparent restrictive nature of the ability to join new parties, it does not mean that parties whose names do not appear in the arbitration agreement cannot be parties to a reference. In light of the

---

[17] NAFTA investment dispute arbitrations (Methanex Corp. v. USA (2001) and United Parcel Service of America v. Government of Canada (2001)) and ICSID decisions (Aguas Argentinas etc v. Argentine Republic (2005) and Aguas Provinciales etc v. Argentine Republic (2006)). The Tribunals based their power to receive amicus briefs on the general powers to conduct proceedings as it sees fit—specifically in the cases in point. Article 15(1) of the UNCITRAL rules and Article 44 of the ICSID Convention.

[18] ICC Case No. 4131 (Dow Chemical) (1982) (France).

[19] *See* City of London v. Sancheti [2009] 1 Lloyd's Rep 117. The exceptions to this rule will be where the parent has control over the subsidiary for illegitimate purposes or otherwise uses the corporate structure to conceal a legal impropriety (Adams v. Cape Industries PLC [1990] Ch 433) or where there is fraud (Jones v. Lipman [1962] 1 WLR 832).

U.S. Supreme Court decision in *Green Tree Financial Corp. v. Bazzle*[20] that arbitrators (rather than courts) can decide whether arbitration clauses, silent on the point, permit class actions, there is plainly scope for enormous "non-party"[21] references. There are six main situations in which parties not named might become parties under English law and similar situations may arise under other national laws:

1. Agency

If an agent makes a contract for its principal (whether disclosed or undisclosed) or a trustee makes a contract for a beneficiary, the principal is throughout a party to the contract and can sue and be sued. Both the agent and the principal can sue but they have different causes of action and at some stage an election is required.[22] The agent may, in some jurisdictions, be able to benefit from the arbitration agreement and commence a reference.[23] The agency contract will be governed by the laws relevant to that agency contract and these may be different from both the law of the agreement to arbitrate and from the substantive law of the contract.[24]

2. Succession by operation of law

Under various mechanisms, by operation of law, the proper party succeeds to the rights of the named party. This can occur, for example, when a person dies and personal representatives are appointed or when a liquidator adopts a contract and seeks to enforce it.

3. Novation

Although there can be statutory novations, the more likely is a contractual novation whereby the original parties to a contract agree that a new party will replace one of the original parties. In this instance, the

---

[20] 539 U.S. 444 (2003).

[21] In the sense that each member of the claimant class will have a separate arbitration agreement but will probably not find it economical to pursue individually, by pursuing by class the aggregate claim will make it economic particularly by being able to engage counsel to act.

[22] Leif Hoegh & Co v. Petrolsea Inc [1992] 1 Lloyds 45.

[23] Arnold v. Arnold Corp, 920 F.2d 1269, 1282 (6th Cir. 1990).

[24] Total Soc It Pa v. Achille Lauro (1979) IV Yearbook of Commercial Arbitration 284.

position of the substituted party is the same as if it had been a party to the contract from the outset and it must accordingly arbitrate rather than litigate.

4. Assignment

The presence of an arbitration clause does not prevent a party assigning its rights to claim and the assignee must enforce its claims by arbitration unless the arbitration clause makes it clear that it is personal to the original contracting parties—it is unlikely to do so. For a legal assignment, the assignee may maintain an arbitration in its own name,[25] the assignor can arbitrate but will recover nothing. In the *French case HGL v. Blue Sky Marketing Ltd* the court held that "in a chain of contracts that transfer property rights, an arbitration clause is automatically transferred as an ancillary element of the right of action, which itself an ancillary to the substantive rights transferred by the agreement."[26] Both assignor and assignee should join in where the assignment is equitable. It must be remembered that the benefit of a contract can be assigned and the burden only assigned with consent.

It makes no difference if the benefit of the whole contract is assigned or merely a claim arising under it.[27] The assignment does not make the assignee automatically a party to the reference—it must furthermore submit to the jurisdiction of the Arbitral Tribunal.[28]

5. Estoppel

It seems conceptually possible for the doctrine of estoppel to apply so as to preclude a party from denying that it is or has become a party to an arbitration agreement. If so, it would be precluded from denying the right of the other party to commence proceedings against it. There would have to be either a representation relied upon to its detriment (a promissory estoppel) or an agreed common assumption (an estoppel by convention). In either case, there would have to be clear evidence.

---

[25] Schiffahrtsgesellschaft Detlev van Appen v. Voest Alpine Intertrading [1997] 2 Lloyd's Rep 279, 287.

[26] Cass. Civ. 1ère 9 January 2008 07-12.349.

[27] Rumput (Panama) SA v. Islamic Republic of Iran Shipping Lines [1984] 2 Lloyd's Rep 259.

[28] Charles M Willie & Co (Shipping) Ltd v. Ocean Laser Shipping Ltd [1999] 1 Lloyd's Rep 225, 241 – 3.

6. *Contracts (Rights of Third Parties) Act 1999*

This is an English Act that permits a non-party to a contract to enforce a term of the contract expressly or impliedly for its benefit.[29] It applies to all contracts made after 11 May 2000 and might apply to, for example, a group company contracting for the benefit of all members of its group. Any similar legislation that may exist in other jurisdictions would permit non-parties to claim.

---

[29] The Act was used in Nisshin Shipping Co Ltd v. Cleaves & Co Ltd [2004] 1 Lloyd's Rep 38 to permit the recovery of commission due to chartering brokers.

CHAPTER 7
ARBITRAL INDEPENDENCE

The choice of the members of the Arbitral Tribunal is one of the most, if not the most, important decision taken in the tactical and procedural stage of the reference. The pool from which international arbitrators are selected is both large and small. In theory, anyone can be an arbitrator as there are generally no formal qualifications. In practice, the vast majority of international arbitrators have a legal background or training and a relatively small number of arbitrators undertake the vast majority of arbitrations.

Therefore, a party may have been adjudged by an arbitrator before, a party may have appointed the same arbitrator before, counsel may have appointed the same arbitrator before, or the arbitrator may have some knowledge or affiliation with a party to the arbitration. This is more often the case in specialised fields in which the pool of suitably experienced and skilled arbitrators may be limited.

The twin issues of conflicts of interest and apparent bias arise in relation to arbitrator appointments in this context. There is a tension between party autonomy (the right for the parties to "agree on the procedure to be followed by the arbitral tribunal in conducting the proceedings")[1] and the duty of the arbitrator to act fairly and to avoid any appearance of impropriety (albeit there is not the same "audience" in arbitration).

The ability of a party to appoint one of the decision-makers prompts the parties to seek to appoint an arbitrator who has some disposition to favour the party appointing him, not in an overt and biased way, but because the arbitrator may have a shared cultural background, and as discussed later, he may be predisposed towards extensive discovery that a party sees as important to prove its case. Provided this predisposition does not become bias or prejudice, it is an inevitable feature of party-appointed arbitrators. The concept of party-appointment can often create considerable confusion and concern for the parties unsure what influence is being exercised "behind the scenes" or still worse construing a legitimate question or comment as evidence of partiality.

---

[1] Article 19(1) of the UNCITRAL Model Law.

It is not the role of a party-appointed arbitrator to advocate the cause of the party appointing him before the other members of the Tribunal. Rather he can ensure that the entire Arbitral Tribunal understands the case that is advanced by his appointer although this role is far from universally accepted. It is universally accepted that there can be no private communications by a party with its party-appointed arbitrator, at least after the Tribunal is fully appointed. Some take the view that although communication cannot take place after the Tribunal is fully constituted, it is permissible, indeed desirable, to communicate with the party-appointed arbitrator in the selection of the chairman or president. Undoubtedly, the party-appointed arbitrator may have views as to who would make a suitable chairman. It is suggested that if a party proposes to so communicate with its party-appointed arbitrator, it should communicate that to the opposing party. Ideally the parties would agree what dialogue each party might have with its party-appointed arbitrator and also whether the two party-appointed arbitrators should themselves confer so as to agree upon a chairman. Transparency in such matters has everything to commend it and nothing detrimental. This does not imply that the communications with the party-appointed arbitrator should themselves be disclosed but rather that the intent to have those communications should be agreed upon and the process should be transparent.

The role of the party-appointed arbitrator may extend to a public indication that there are aspects of the case of his appointing party where the Tribunal needs further assistance. He might do so by a well-timed comment or question at an evidential hearing or he might explain the argument to the other Tribunal members so as to ensure that the propositions of fact and law advanced by his appointing party have been fully and properly considered during their deliberations. The key touchstone will be whether the arbitrator can operate with impartiality and independence. The usual issue will not be actual bias (which under any system of law would be grounds for disqualification) but the appearance of facts that give rise to an impression of bias. The circumstances of each case must be considered carefully for it is not only financial interests that may be relevant. Furthermore of equal relevance is the relationship of an arbitrator to a party or even a non-party connected to a party. In the English case of *R. v. Bow Street Metropolitan Stipendiary Magistrate Ex p. Pinochet Ugarte (No.2)*,[2] the court was

---

[2] [2000] 1 A.C. 119.

concerned with the extradition of former President Pinochet to face charges of crimes against humanity. Amnesty International was permitted to intervene in the court proceedings. Lord Hoffmann had been a director of Amnesty's charity and he sat on the appeal. That was sufficient direct relationship to amount to automatic disqualification as Amnesty, as an intervenor, became a party and Lord Hoffmann effectively sat as a judge in his own cause.

There is no doubt that, in some jurisdictions, the test of partiality is different in courts and in arbitration. In the U.S., judges can be disqualified "in any proceeding in which his impartiality might reasonably be questioned"[3] whereas in an arbitration, an arbitrator can only be disqualified in cases in which a reasonable person, considering all of the circumstances, "would have to conclude" that the arbitrator was partial to one side.[4] In reaching that conclusion of arbitrator bias, the court found that "the standard of 'appearance of bias' . . . too low" and "'proof of actual bias' too high."

Conversely, in England the same test is applied to judges as it is to "justices or members of other inferior tribunals, or with jurors or with arbitrators."[5] The test applied is, having regard to all relevant circumstances, that "there was a real danger of bias on the part of the relevant member of the tribunal . . . in the sense that he might unfairly regard . . . with favour, or disfavour, the case of a party to the issue under consideration by him . . . ."[6] Similarly, in *Porter v. Magill,* the test was framed as "whether the fair-minded and informed observer, having considered the facts, would conclude that there was a real possibility that the tribunal was biased."[7] Indeed in *AT&T v. Saudi Cable Company,*[8] the court said "it would be surprising if a lower threshold applied to arbitration than applied to a court of law. The courts are responsible for the provision of public justice. If there are two standards I would expect a lower threshold to apply to courts of law than applies to a private tribunal whose 'judges' are selected by the parties. After all, there is an

---

[3] Apple v. Jewish Hosp. & Med. Ctr., 829 F.2d 326, 332 – 33 (2d Cir. 1987).

[4] Morelite Constr. Corp v. New York City Dist. Council Carpenter Benefits Fund, 748 F.2d 79 (2d Cir. 1984).

[5] R v. Gough [1993] AC 646, 669 – 670.

[6] *Id.*

[7] [2002] 2 AC 357, 494.

[8] [2000] 2 Lloyd's Rep 127.

over-riding public interest in the integrity of the administration of justice in the courts." In Australia and South Africa, as well as in the European Court of Justice, the "reasonable suspicion" or "reasonable apprehension" test is applied.

The proper understanding of the role of a party-appointed arbitrator is vital not only to addressing cultural and other expectations, but also to addressing the position of multiple parties (and especially additional parties added to the reference). If a Claimant pursues three Respondents, it may well be that the Claimant has one party-appointed arbitrator and the three Respondents have appointed one arbitrator between them. If the three Respondents have different defences, arguments, and counsel, agreeing on one party-appointed arbitrator may be problematic, at best, but even if the Respondent parties are able to concur they will have a share in the Respondent-nominated arbitrator, whereas the Claimant will have exclusively appointed its arbitrator.

The potential for the appearance of unfairness (and potentially bias) is self-evident in these circumstances. The solution may well be for the institution to appoint all the members of the Tribunal in such circumstances.

These issues arise at the very earliest stage. Potential arbitrators are now often interviewed for potential appointments. The Chartered Institute of Arbitrators have issued guidance[9] to address concerns over the interviewing process. The guidance promotes transparency and openness. Generally, brief questions as to experience, expertise, language proficiency, availability and possible conflicts, are permitted. The specific issues to be raised in the arbitration must not be discussed.

When the parties have appointed their arbitrators, the Chairman must be appointed. The premise of the ICC Rules is that the ICC Court will appoint the Chairman[10] and this is only displaced if the parties agree upon either a joint nomination or an alternative method of appointment – e.g., that the party-appointed arbitrators should seek to agree on a chair. If this is the case then, for the reasons given above, it is wise to agree upon the extent to which the party may communicate with its party-appointed arbitrator for such a purpose. The LCIA Rules do not contemplate anything other than an LCIA Court appointment.[11]

---

[9] Practice Guidance 16, The Interviewing of Prospective Arbitrators.

[10] Article 8(4) of the ICC Rules.

[11] Article 5.6 of the LCIA Rules.

The UNCITRAL Arbitration Rules provide for the party-appointed arbitrators to agree on a chair and in default of agreement, the appointing authority should do so.[12] The AAA Rules provide for party-appointed arbitrators to agree, or the parties themselves, and in default, the AAA will nominate the chair.[13] A specimen letter to approach a possible chairman is set out at Appendix 5.

The *IBA Guidelines on Conflicts of Interest in International Arbitration (2004)* provide a wealth of good sense when issues arise. The Guidelines have lists of examples of "justifiable doubts as to the arbitrator's impartiality and independence" (so-called "Red List" items); matters that "in the eyes of the parties may give rise to justifiable doubts as to the arbitrator's impartiality and independence" (so-called "Orange List" items) and "situations where no appearance of, and no actual, conflict of interest exists" (so-called "Green List" items). The Red List items are divided into waivable and non-waivable items. For the former (and for the Orange List items), there must be full disclosure by the proposed arbitrator. For the Red list items, the parties must expressly state their willingness to have the person as arbitrator, for the Orange List lack of objection after the disclosure is a deemed acceptance. Because certain Red List items are non-waivable, there is no disclosure obligation and, similarly, there is no disclosure obligation for Green list items as they are matters not considered to be a conflict.

The lists are non-exhaustive and support statements of principle none of which might be considered controversial. The IBA Guidelines principles start with impartiality and independence (Principle 1) and move to not accepting or refusing to continue if there are doubts as the ability to be impartial and independent (Principle 2); disclosure if he/she considers himself/herself impartial and independent but recognises that another view might reasonably be held (Principle 3); the ability of the parties to waive apparent conflict (Principle 4); not applying to non-neutral arbitrators as some rules permit (Principle 5); extend to other relationships indirect relationships an arbitrator may have (Principle 6) and the duty on the parties and the arbitrator to make reasonable enquiries (Principle 7).

---

[12] Articles 7(1) and 7(3) of the UNCITRAL Arbitration Rules.

[13] Rule 13(b) of the AAA Rules.

It is hopefully clear that disclosure is of potentially vital importance. As was said in the U.S. case of *Commonwealth Coatings Corp. v. Continental Casualty Co.*:[14]

> [A]rbitrators are not automatically disqualified by a business relationship with the parties before them if both parties are informed of the relationship in advance, or if they are unaware of the facts but the relationship is trivial." However, "arbitrators must take steps to ensure that the parties are not misled into believing that no nontrivial conflict exists. If therefore follows that where an arbitrator has reason to believe that a nontrivial conflict might exist, he must (1) investigate the conflict (that may reveal information that must be disclosed under *Commonwealth Holdings*) or (2) disclose his reasons for believing there might be a conflict and his intention not to investigate.[15]

If an arbitrator accepts an appointment and subsequently becomes impartial or is no longer independent, plainly he must resign his appointment. If an arbitrator resigns without good reason—which generally is not permitted, although the parties may accept the inevitable rather than try to compel the arbitrator to serve—he may disentitle himself to any fee and incur a liability to the parties.[16]

---

[14] 393 U.S. 145, 149 (1968).

[15] Applied Indus. Materials Corp. v. Ovalar Makine Ticaret ve Sanayi, 492 F.3d 132 (2d Cir. 2007).

[16] *See* the English Arbitration Act 1996 §25; French New Code of Civil Procedure §1462; Italian Code of Civil Procedure §813 and Netherlands Code of Civil Procedure §1029(2).

CHAPTER 8
DUTIES AND OBLIGATIONS OF THE ARBITRAL TRIBUNAL

The duties and obligations of the Arbitral Tribunal are to be found primarily in the arbitration agreement and, by incorporation, in any institutional rules. These will be supplemented by the national laws of the seat and, as applicable, common law principles. The Tribunal will also have to observe ethical standards although these may replicate many of the primary sources.

Several common themes emerge from agreements, rules, and laws.

A. Acting Fairly and Impartially

This duty is a feature of nearly all modern legislation.[1] It is considered to be a feature of the UNCITRAL Model Law (albeit it does not use the words "impartial" or "fair") because the treatment of the parties "with equality" and that the requirement that "each party shall be given a full opportunity of presenting his case" are considered to be equivalent to principle of impartiality and fairness.

The concept of "fairness" entails fairness to both sides.[2] Principles may conflict. For example, many rules will have an obligation to determine the reference with expedition and yet a party may wish to adduce further submissions, argument, and evidence that may defeat that aim. This may also conflict with a duty to allow a party to fully present its case. Inevitably, a balance must be struck to ensure that the procedure is kept under control.

Perhaps the foremost duty in this connection is that of equality and permitting a party to fully present its case.[3] The equality rule permits both parties to have the same opportunity and this can result in, for

---

[1] This is reinforced by institutional rules such as ICC Rules §15(2); UNCITRAL Rules §15(1); AAA International Arbitration Rules §16(1), and; LCIA Rules §14(1).

[2] Corporación Transnacional de Inversiones SA de CV v. STET International (1999) 45 OR (3d) 183 (Ont SCJ) affirmed (2000) 49 OR (3d) 414.

[3] For example, the UNCITRAL Arbitration Rules Art. 15 provide that the arbitral tribunal can conduct matters as it sees fit "provided that the parties are treated with equality and that at any stage of the proceedings each party is given a full opportunity of presenting its case." ICC Rules 14.1 and 15 are to much the same effect.

example, the refusal of a Reply brief or submission on the basis that it would give one party two submissions and the other only one.

In *Parsons & Whittemore Overseas Co v. Société Générale de l'Industrie du Papier,*[4] the court refused to set aside an award where the Arbitral Tribunal had refused to postpone a hearing when a party was unable to secure the attendance of a witness. The court held that this did not amount to an inadequate opportunity to present its case under the due process requirements of the New York Convention. The same result was achieved in *Iran Aircraft Industries v. AVCO Corp.*[5]

B. Acting with Due Care

Two views of the nature of the relationship between the arbitral tribunal and the parties exist. Broadly, civil law countries regard the relationship as contractual and common law countries regard it as quasi-judicial. In the former, there are remedies for some breaches of contract — some restricted to gross negligence.

Such duties as may be owed are obscured by arguments of immunity but an arbitral tribunal appointed in a civil law jurisdiction might well seek contractual immunity and/or an indemnity for such liability as may arise.

C. Independence and Impartiality

Different national laws either include or omit a duty of independence. In England, the duty of independence was deliberately omitted as the features of what might be described as features of independence were felt to be better described as impartiality but there is undoubtedly a duty of independence as discussed in Chapter 7.

The essence of impartiality is the ability to determine the dispute objectively[6] and that is a question of fact. It does not amount to a lack of partiality if an Arbitral Tribunal forms, and even expresses, a provisional view on the merits provided the Tribunal is genuinely open to a change of heart.[7]

---

[4] (1976) I Yearbook of Commercial Arbitration 205.

[5] 980 F.2d 141, 145-6 (2d Cir. 1992).

[6] Société Philipp Brothers v. Société Drexel Burnham Lambert (1990) Rev Arb 497.

[7] Ballantine Books Inc v. Capital Distrib. Co., 302 F.2d 17, 21 (2d Cir. 1962).

D. Duty to Act with Due Diligence

There can be little doubt that an arbitral tribunal is obliged to act with reasonable expedition. Indeed, the Model Law permits the termination of the appointment of the arbitrator if he/she "fails to act without undue delay."[8] Some institutional rules, for example, the ICC Rules, provide for specific time limits for the Award.

E. Completing the Reference and Issuing an Award

The obligation to make and issue an award is included in both some national laws and institutional rules.[9]

F. Specific Duties

Under an ad hoc submission to arbitration, the parties may seek to impose specific obligations on the appointed arbitral tribunal. Any prospective arbitrator should carefully check for unreasonable obligations or obligations, perhaps as to the prompt delivery of an award, that he cannot comply with.

Specific institutional rules may provide for specific steps. For example, the ICC Rules provide for the Tribunal to draw up terms of reference and submit the award to the ICC Court for scrutiny.

---

[8] Article 14.

[9] *See, e.g.,* ICC Rules §24(1).

CHAPTER 9
PRELIMINARY MEETING

The first preliminary meeting is a vital stage in the proper administration of the reference. It is often the first opportunity for members of the Arbitral Tribunal to meet face-to-face; for the parties to meet each other since the dispute took on its formal dispute resolution process started; for counsel and the parties to meet each other and the members of the Tribunal. The attendance of appropriate senior representatives of the parties at the preliminary meeting is a matter of some debate; some practitioners favour it and others not (those in the latter camp consider it avoids grandstanding by counsel), but the clearly preferable view is in favour of attendance. Whilst there is unlikely to be any resolution of issues at the meeting by the Tribunal—the purpose of the meeting being procedural rather than substantive—nevertheless, the attendance of senior representatives enables a better understanding by those representatives of the issues, time and cost of the process which may itself promote settlement.

An agenda of items to be raised at the first meeting will often be circulated by the Chairman. A sample of such an agenda is attached at Appendix 6.

By the very nature of international arbitration the parties and their counsel may be from different jurisdictions with quite different expectations of the process of resolving disputes by arbitration. Equally, the experience of the parties and their counsel may be very different; the seasoned campaigner may come up against the young rookie.

Some issues that may require specific mention, discussion, and resolution are discussed below. They all derive from potentially diametric views that the parties and their counsel may have to the approach that ought to be adopted and the issues raised are designed, so far as possible, to dispel potential misunderstandings.

The UNCITRAL Notes on Organizing Arbitral Proceedings are a useful source of guidance. Whilst they do not pretend to provide all the answers, they do pose most of the questions and a study of the Notes is a helpful reminder of the issues that can arise.

Some of the issues that may merit specific discussion and elaboration so as to avoid ongoing confusion are as follows:

A. Pleadings

The "look and feel" of pleadings is of course a matter for the individual pleader but some discussion, for example, as the extent that the Arbitral Tribunal would find the pleading of evidence helpful or unhelpful; the extent to which documents should be attached and whether propositions of law might all remove differing perceptions as to what each party might receive from the other and what the Tribunal might find of assistance. It is unlikely that the Tribunal would consider it appropriate to make an order as to such matters as the format of pleadings is very much a matter of style and the parties should, within reason, be permitted to present the case as they wish. Clarity of expectation is, however, likely to be helpful.

B. Discovery

These issues are discussed in greater detail in the chapters on discovery but issues of the production of all documents whether helpful or not and the approach to e-discovery are issues that could properly be raised.

C. Evidentiary Hearing and Cross-Examination

In some jurisdictions witnesses that are directly related to a party— e.g. directors or owners of a corporation—are considered of little assistance (or credibility) as opposed to neutral witnesses—e.g. bystanders or expert witnesses—while other jurisdictions expect that such directly related witnesses not only will give evidence but that they are likely to be the witnesses with the most material evidence. Others will see it as entirely proper for all witnesses to have the same weight. Equally, some jurisdictions see cross-examination as an affront but most Tribunals will expect it and accept it as the more likely route to the truth. Some Tribunals may wish to question witnesses themselves in advance of any questioning by the parties or prefer that all questions are put through the Tribunal—this can be very cumbersome and is best avoided. The parties are likely to have a better understanding of the issues and are better situated than the Tribunal to raise the relevant questions without significant preparation. Again, it is a matter of managing expectations.

Whether witnesses are sworn or must otherwise affirm the truth of their evidence is another matter upon which expectations may differ. Some will expect only a judge to have the ability to administer an oath.

Furthermore, whether witnesses should be present solely for their own evidence and should withdraw at other times (when other witnesses are giving evidence) is a matter of differing opinion. Some Tribunals will prefer the witness to not see other witnesses give evidence so that their evidence is not tainted by what a prior witness may have said. Other Tribunals will be willing to have all witnesses present throughout the proceedings so that any ambiguity in the evidence may be cleared up.

D. Summary

Properly organised and handled, the preliminary meeting can be a vital opportunity for the parties and their counsel to meet, the Arbitral Tribunal to meet both the parties and counsel, and for some ground rules to be established. The parties can build trust and understanding with the Tribunal and can begin the process of understanding how best to present a case to the particular Tribunal.

CHAPTER 10
TERMS OF REFERENCE AND LISTS OF ISSUES

ICC Rules provide that the terms of reference shall be in writing and signed by the Tribunal and the parties. Generally, the other institutional rules do not have this stage. In ICC cases, this is done at an early stage on the appointment of the Arbitral Tribunal. Indeed, Article 18 of the ICC Rules makes it clear that it is the first function of the Tribunal: "As soon as it has received the file from the Secretariat, the Arbitral Tribunal shall draw up ... a document defining its Terms of Reference." Formal requirements as to what needs to be included are set out in Article 18. Invariably, the Terms are drawn from the Request for Arbitration and the Answer (and any Reply) although in forming the Terms of Reference, the Arbitral Tribunal may call for a "position summary" from the parties. This should summarise the Request and any Reply (for the Claimant) or Answer (for the Respondent) as the case may be. Alternatively, if the Request, Answer, and Reply are short, it may be possible to incorporate them wholesale into the terms of reference. It follows from this that the detailed written pleadings will not normally have been produced at this stage.

A sample set of Terms is at Appendix 7.

One of the key requirements is that the Terms of Reference should include "*unless the Arbitral Tribunal considers it inappropriate, a list of issues to be determined.*"[1] Unless a list of issues is included, the Terms of Reference are "what" is to be decided whereas a true list of issues whilst being "what" is as much "how" something will be decided.

In contrast to the ICC procedure, where the list of issues is prepared after the Request for arbitration and Answer but before detailed written pleadings, a list of issues prepared after the detailed written pleadings can be a very useful tool. This is the practice under the Arbitration Rules of the Singapore International Arbitration Centre (SIAC Rules). Rule 17 provides that:

(1) Within 45 days following completion of the submission of the written statements ... the Tribunal shall on the basis of the parties' written statements and in consultation with the parties proceed to draw up a document defining the issues to be

---

[1] Article 18(1)(d).

determined ...(4) The Memorandum of Issues ... defines the issues that the Tribunal shall decide in its award.

Of course, a list done before written pleadings (indeed any list) can be updated and refined after written pleadings.[2]

A properly formulated List of Issues drawn up not only in consultation with the Arbitral Tribunal but with active management could well become the keystone to the proper management of all substantial references. A real effort needs to be made to move away from lists that are often either too short and general or too long and then often fail to distinguish between key issues and sub-issues. Such lists are often not much use to the Arbitral Tribunal. However they are drawn up a proper List of Issues should be the key working document in all substantial references and potentially all references.

The List of Issues should be based on the written pleadings of the parties and, once finalised, should be the basis on which decisions are made about the breadth and depth of disclosure, the provision of witness statements, what experts will be permitted, and on what issues and, ultimately, the way in which any evidentiary hearing is conducted.

For all but the most complex cases, the List of Issues should be ten pages or less in length, and once the List of Issues has been produced, the written pleadings will have only secondary importance. They would only need to be referred to if there is a doubt about the accuracy of the List of Issues or to confirm a party's position with respect to a particular issue.

The List of Issues should not be confused with the Terms of Reference albeit that Terms may include issues. A List does not, or ought not, seek to define the jurisdiction of the Tribunal. It should be a tool to assist the proper administration of the reference and not be a impediment to it by parties being overly concerned that in drafting a List they might be restricting the jurisdiction of the Tribunal.

A sample List of Issues based on the responsive pleadings at Appendix 10, is at Appendix 8.

---

[2] Article 19 of the ICC Rules provides that, after the Terms of Reference have been signed, no new claim falling outside of the Terms can be made without the consent of the Arbitral Tribunal. A refinement of the list of issues ought not to involve new claims, but if it does it may require consent.

CHAPTER 11
SECRETARIES

The use by members of the Tribunal of a secretary is now common and does much to promote the smooth and efficient functioning of the Arbitral Tribunal. Broad statements about the role of secretaries are relatively easy to frame but, at the margins, it becomes more difficult. For example, it is uncontroverted that a secretary should not be involved in the decision-making process; however, it is less clear is where that process begins and ends. Equally, it is uncontroverted that the secretary should undertake clerical tasks such as maintaining a master file or record; however, functions such as summarising the parties' submissions or research are sometimes controversial. For these reasons, the Arbitral Tribunal should be at pains to ensure there is the highest degree of clarity of the role that the secretary will fulfil for the Arbitral Tribunal in order that the parties give an informed consent to the appointment and function of the secretary.

Institutional rules generally make no comment on the appointment of a secretary. The exception, however, appears to be Article 15(5) of the Swiss Rules of International Arbitration that provides *"The arbitral tribunal may, after consulting with the parties, appoint a secretary."*

The ICC has issued a Note[1] containing guidance on the appointment of secretaries. The Note provides that:

> The duties of the administrative secretary must be strictly limited to <u>administrative tasks</u> . . . Such person must not influence in any manner whatsoever the decisions of the Arbitral Tribunal.

> In particular, the administrative secretary must not assume the functions of an arbitrator, notably by becoming involved in the decision making process of the Tribunal or expressing opinions or conclusions with respect to the issues in dispute.

The UNCITRAL Rules are similarly silent but the UNCITRAL Notes on Organizing Arbitral Proceedings do have some very sound

---

[1] Note from the Secretariat of the ICC Court Concerning the Appointment of Administrative Secretaries by Arbitral Tribunals, 6(2) ICC Int'l Court of Arbn. Bull. 77 (1995).

guidance reflecting the tensions that exist in the arbitration community. Articles 26 and 27 provide:

26. Administrative services might be secured by engaging a secretary of the arbitral tribunal (also referred to as registrar, clerk, administrator or rapporteur), who carries out the tasks under the direction of the arbitral tribunal. Some arbitral institutions routinely assign such persons to the cases administered by them. In arbitrations not administered by an institution or where the arbitral institution does not appoint a secretary, some arbitrators frequently engage such persons, at least in certain types of cases, whereas many others normally conduct the proceedings without them.

27. To the extent the tasks of the secretary are purely organizational (e.g. obtaining meeting rooms and providing or coordinating secretarial services), this is usually not controversial. Differences in views, however, may arise if the tasks include legal research and other professional assistance to the arbitral tribunal (e.g. collecting case law or published commentaries on legal issues defined by the arbitral tribunal, preparing summaries from case law and publications, and sometimes also preparing drafts of procedural decisions or drafts of certain parts of the award, in particular those concerning the facts of the case). Views or expectations may differ especially where a task of the secretary is similar to professional functions of the arbitrators. Such a role of the secretary is in the view of some commentators inappropriate or is appropriate only under certain conditions, such as that the parties agree thereto. However, it is typically recognized that it is important to ensure that the secretary does not perform any decision-making function of the arbitral tribunal.

There is common ground that the actual decision should be taken by the arbitrators alone. If there is any appearance of involvement of the secretary in the decision-making process, the Award may be vulnerable. In *Campagnie Honeywell Bull SA v. Computación Bull de Venezuela,*[2] the losing party sought to set aside an award on the basis of a lack of due

_____

[2] Cour d'Appel (Paris) 21 June 1990, 1991 Rev. Arb. 96, 100.

process and equal treatment because of the secretary's presence at and alleged interference with an oral hearing. The Court dismissed the application finding that the Arbitral Tribunal was permitted to appoint a secretary and that the losing party had not proved the alleged interference.

This cardinal principle of decision-making is reflected by the AAA's Code of Ethics that provides, in Canon V, that an arbitrator "should not delegate the duty to decide to any other person." Canon VI recognises that an arbitral tribunal is not, however, expected to do everything itself: "An arbitrator may obtain help from an associate, a research assistant or other persons in connection with reaching his ... decision if the arbitrator informs the parties of the use of such assistance and such persons agree to be bound by the provisions of this Canon."

ICSID arbitrations have a secretary but that person assists the Secretary-General rather than the Arbitral Tribunal. The WTO has legal officers who have a much wider range of responsibilities which should not be considered applicable to a typical international commercial arbitration.

The ICC Note has its critics for limiting party autonomy. The reasoning is that, if the parties, in consultation with the Arbitral Tribunal, decide that the secretary should, for example, prepare factual summaries or draft the procedural section of the Award, they should be able to do so. The argument to the contrary is that the parties have appointed the members of the Tribunal to decide their dispute and, therefore, they alone should do so. If, to assist the members of the Tribunal a secretary is appointed, it is much safer and easier to have the purely administrative tasks spelled out for the secretary rather than have "mission creep" where, in the process of the reference and especially the deliberations of the Tribunal members, the parties are not sure exactly what role the secretary might undertake. The AAA Code equally has its critics for merely "informing" the parties of the role of the secretary and not obtaining their consent. The UNCITRAL Note reflects the current differing views.

Whilst a secretary can be appointed at any stage, there is much to be said to making the appointment at an early stage. It gives the secretary the opportunity to become familiar with the documents on the record and form a relationship with the parties that will serve well when the evidentiary hearing arises. That being said, the tribunal might consider the reference to be relatively straightforward and find that there is no need for a secretary; however, when the documents are disclosed or witness statements served, it could become apparent that the scale was quite different from the initial perceptions. In that event, it is quite proper to raise the issue of an appointment of a secretary at a late stage.

The background and qualifications of the secretary are matters for the tribunal to decide. Normally, a secretary is not simply a typist and more often will be junior attorney or lawyer and often at the same firm as the chairman (if he is in practice). Clearly, the secretary should have no conflict of interest and should be independent and impartial. The role can be very useful in giving invaluable experience to the aspiring arbitrator. The hourly rate of the secretary usually is (and indeed should be) substantially lower than that of the members of the tribunal so that tasks performed by the secretary show a marked cost saving notwithstanding that there is an additional person being billed. Very experienced practitioners should be avoided. Although their experience might be of considerable value to the Arbitral Tribunal the perception is likely to be that an experienced practitioner would, however subconsciously, influence the members of the Arbitral Tribunal.

The payment or remuneration of the secretary can be controversial. The practice of the ICC is for the Arbitral Tribunal to pay the secretary from the aggregate fee allowed for the Tribunal. As the fee is calculated on the basis of a function of the amount in dispute, there can be sufficient over and above the equivalent fee on an hourly basis to absorb the expense. The LCIA and Swiss Rules of International Arbitration provide for the fees of the secretary to be paid in addition as an expense but these rules remunerate the members of the Arbitral Tribunal on an hourly basis. Certainly, where the members of the Arbitral Tribunal are remunerated on an hourly basis, a strong case can be made for the secretary to be paid in addition. With ICC arbitrations and any others where the fee is a percentage of the amount in dispute, there may be a basis for paying from the aggregate fee, and that should be the starting point. In some low value cases that are especially "heavy" there may be a case for remunerating the secretary in addition to the fee for the Arbitral Tribunal.

Some common threads can be drawn from the various publications and guidance:

- The secretary has no role in decision-making;
- The secretary can make the process more efficient and faster by performing administrative functions;

- There should be full disclosure of the proposed appointment of and of role of the proposed secretary;
- There should be consent to the appointment and role of the secretary;
- The secretary should meet the same standards of independence an impartiality as a member of the arbitral tribunal;

A sample of a letter proposing appointment of a secretary is at Appendix 7. The purpose is to disclose fully to the parties the proposed appointment, who the proposed secretary is, and the role or function he/she will perform. The aim of the sample letter is to obtain an informed consent from the parties. The draft provides for the parties to have the opportunity of jointly commenting. This aims to avoid one party from having to object whilst the other agrees—carrying with it the impression that the objection party might be seen as unhelpful or worse. Equally the precedent provides for the parties to suggest alternatives to the proposal. It is unlikely that a change in the identity would be proposed but, if the proposed secretary were too experienced, the parties might wish to propose an alternative (not necessarily by name but by qualification or experience). Equally, the parties might wish to exclude from the remit of the secretary, the ability to summarise the parties' submissions or evidence and indicate to the Arbitral Tribunal that if it wanted a summary the parties would provide it.

Through an open dialogue the parties and Arbitral Tribunal should be able to agree a sensible way forward to the appointment of a secretary. If there is stalemate the sample letter reserves to the Arbitral Tribunal the right to proceed as it sees fit. If such a power is used the Arbitral Tribunal should be very wary of having the secretary perform greater functions than the parties have agreed unless they rely upon some express power to do so. Any Award might be vulnerable to being challenged if the secretary performs functions not agreed by the parties either by agreeing some institutional rule or by specific agreement during the reference.

CHAPTER 12
REPRESENTATION

One of the main advantages of international arbitration is that practitioners experienced in the field can practice overseas as the laws of the jurisdiction of the seat may not be relevant or applicable or, where relevant, either local counsel may be engaged or the experienced practitioner can be advised by local counsel.

In many jurisdictions this does not create a problem, however, this is not universally the case. This was particularly so in Hong Kong in the late 1980s, prompting a clarification that non-local counsel could appear in local arbitrations.[1]

In England, there are generally no problems with foreign counsel appearing before Arbitral Tribunals. Sections 20 – 25 of the English Solicitors Act 1974 prohibit non-solicitors from engaging in certain activities. Whilst none are likely to be required in the normal conduct of an arbitral reference, foreign counsel, in general, should not act as a solicitor in relation to any court proceedings.

In the U.S., the high water point was *Williamson v. John D Quinn Construction Corp.*[2] In this case, the court held that representing a party in arbitration does not amount to the practice of law and, hence, foreign counsel were permitted to represent parties in arbitration proceedings in the U.S.—this was due to the relative informality of the proceedings. New York law seems fairly clear on this point (permitting foreign lawyers to do so) but the same cannot be said for other states. California,[3] Arizona[4] and Florida[5] laws prevent foreign lawyers from conducting international arbitrations in those states.

---

[1] The position is now clarified by Section 2F of the Arbitration Ordinance which expressly provides that representation and preparation of arbitration proceedings may be conducted by persons who are not legally qualified except where it is done in connection with court proceedings arising out of an arbitration agreement or arbitration proceedings.

[2] 537 F. Supp. 613 (S.D.N.Y. 1982), affirmed by Siegel v. Bridas Sociedad Anónima Petrolera, Industrial y Comercial, 1991 U.S. Dist LEXIS 11455 (S.D.N.Y. 1991).

[3] Birdbrower, Montalbano, Condon & Frank PC v. Superior Court, Santa Clara County, 949 P.2d 1 (Cal. 1998).

[4] In the Matter of a Former Member of the State Bar of Arizona, Frederick C Creasy, Jr., Respondent, 12 P.3d 214 (Ariz. 2000).

Counsel need to be cautious about representing parties in arbitrations in foreign jurisdictions even if local counsel are employed as well, especially as unauthorised practice of law can carry criminal sanctions.

---

[5] Florida Bar v. Rapoport, 2003 Fla. LEXIS 250, 2003 Fla L Weekly S. 174 (Feb. 20, 2003).

CHAPTER 13
WRITTEN PLEADINGS

In some arbitrations, the Request for Arbitration and the Answer will provide a sufficient "agenda" for the evidentiary hearing, or even the Final Award itself. Such cases will, however, be rare. The primary purpose of the Request and Answer is to facilitate the identification of suitable arbitrators and their appointment and to provide suitable directions. In ICC arbitrations, they also form the basis of the drafting of the Terms of Reference.

In the considerable majority of cases, one of the early directions will be for more comprehensive written pleadings. Confusingly, these can be known by a variety of names: memorials,[1] briefs, statements of case and defence,[2] and statements (or points) of claim and defence.[3] Unless Rules specifically provide for the name of the pleading (and most notably the ICC Rules do not provide for further pleading[4] beyond the Request and Answer still less the name any pleading should have), practitioners may use any term they are comfortable with.

The purpose of the written pleading can also be very different as the understandings of practitioners from different jurisdictions can be very different. By way of illustration, the contrasting pleading requirements of U.S., German, and English pleading in national court cases demonstrates the differing cultures and, hence, counsel and party expectations.

A. U.S. Procedure

In the U.S., there are different pleading requirements in Federal and state courts.[5] In Federal courts, the rule is for so-called "notice pleading," designed merely to give notice of the nature of and basis for the claim:

---

[1] The terminology of the ICSID Rules: Rule 31.

[2] The terminology of the LCIA Rules: Article 15.

[3] The terminology of the UNCITRAL Rules: Articles 18 and 19 and ICDR Rules: Article 17.

[4] It is, however, extremely common in ICC Arbitrations to do so.

[5] Many states, however, have adopted Federal standards.

A pleading that states a claim for relief must contain:

(1) A short and plain statement of the grounds for the court's jurisdiction, unless the court already has jurisdiction and the claim needs no new jurisdictional support;

(2) A short and plain statement of the claim showing that the pleader is entitled to relief; and

(3) A demand for the relief sought, which may include relief in the alternative or different types of relief.[6]

The Federal system of notice pleading is intended to be brief and the pre-trial discovery process bears the burden of filling in details giving rise to the importance attached to discovery in the U.S. The pleading must be signed, and the signature operates to regulate spurious claims:

By presenting to the court a pleading . . . an attorney . . . certifies that to the best of the person's knowledge, information, and belief, formed after an inquiry reasonable under the circumstances:

(1) it is not being presented for any improper purpose . . . ,

(2) the claims, . . . are warranted by existing law or by a nonfrivolous argument for extending, modifying, or reversing existing law or for establishing new law;

(3) the factual contentions have evidentiary support or, if specifically so identified, will likely have evidentiary support after a reasonable opportunity for further investigation or discovery; and

(4) the denials of factual contentions are warranted on the evidence or, if specifically so identified, are reasonably based on belief or a lack of information.[7]

In contrast, New York State law obliges a party to plead particular facts that support a specific cause of action (so-called "code pleading") and provides:

---

[6] Rule 8 Federal Rules of Civil Procedure 2007.

[7] Rule 11 Federal Rules of Civil Procedure 2007.

Statements in a pleading shall be sufficiently particular to give the court and parties notice of the transactions, occurrences, or series of transactions or occurrences intended to be proved and the material elements of each cause of action or defense.[8]

Under New York law, a defective or insufficient pleading is met by a "bill of particulars" that seeks additional information.

B. German Procedure

Pleadings are not very technical in Germany, but they are very carefully prepared and lengthy. Due to the prominent role played by a judge in German court cases, the objective is not merely to define issues but to convince and persuade the judge. Facts may be stated in great detail; evidence by which the facts may be proven is fully set out; documents relied upon are attached; law is pleaded and what might be considered peripheral points are laboured for fear of overlooking something that the judge may consider important. Oral hearings are required but are quite perfunctory so the detail of the written pleading is important.

C. English Procedure

In England, pleadings must contain "a concise statement of the facts on which the claimant relies."[9] The object of pleadings is to define, with clarity and precision, the issues or questions which are in dispute and are be determined by the court; to require each party to give fair and proper notice of the case that has to be met by its opponent; to inform the court of the precise matters in issue between the parties and, finally, to provide a record of the issues raised and decided so as to prevent re-litigation of matters already determined.

Similar to the U.S., pleadings before English courts must be signed with a "statement of truth." The statement is "a statement that . . . the party putting forward the document . . . believes the facts stated in the document are true."[10] Making a false statement is contempt of court.[11]

---

[8] New York Civil Practice Law and Rules §3013.

[9] Civil Procedure Rules, Rule 16.4.

[10] Civil Procedure Rules, Rule 22.1.

[11] Civil Procedure Rules Rule 32.14.

The verification of the claim put forward in either the English or U.S. manner is not a feature of international arbitration but it is conventional for counsel who have drafted and submitted a written pleading to sign it nonetheless. The written pleading will form part of the record of the reference and, if the Arbitral Tribunal finds that a party has put forward a case without any genuine belief in its contents, that will, no doubt, count severely against the party doing so.

D. Controlling the Prolix Pleading

Whether the U.S. "short and plain statement" or the English "concise statement," it is clear that national court pleadings are intended to be crisp and perfunctory. The scope to argue, encompassing evidentiary and legal arguments, is greater in arbitration so it is quite possible that the length will be greater. Nevertheless, the Arbitral Tribunal may well wish to encourage (or even direct) that the written pleadings are of a limited length and are as concise as possible.

First, this can be done by a specific direction to limit length and, second, by requiring the pleading to be responsive by building a master or amalgamated pleading. This is typically done by the defence document repeating the claim and responding to it. An example of a direction from the Arbitral Tribunal is at Appendix 8 and a sample responsive or amalgamated pleading is at Appendix 9. The claim is set out in the consolidated claim and defence as paragraphs prefaced by "C" and the defence set out immediately below with paragraphs prefaced by "D," A reply could be incorporated prefaced by "R." Although this could be done in tabular form along the lines of a Scott or Redfern schedule, the length and narrow columns may make this impractical. Following these guidelines may make a consolidated pleading that is considerably easier to work with not only for all parties and their counsel but also for the members of the Arbitral Tribunal.

E. Drafting

It is not possible to provide any precedent for a written pleading as the potential for different styles and the infinite variety of facts that give rise to claims are too varied to make any precedent worthwhile. Nevertheless, there are some basic rules of structure that might guide the practitioner.

The first guiding rule is to tell the factual story. Telling the story involves setting out the material facts. What is material is what it is necessary to establish in order to succeed on the claim (or defence) and to get the remedy sought. The second guiding rule is to tell the factual story in a logical order and this will invariably be chronologically.

The chronological factual story should focus on the necessary ingredients for the successful claim. They may need to be linked by non-essential factual links to make the whole story hold together.

The framework is likely to be fairly standard and adhering to a conventional layout will assist the Arbitral Tribunal as they will be expecting to see the written pleading presented in this way and assisting the Tribunal is helpful to that party that does so.

The conventional framework is as follows:

- Parties – in this section explain who the parties are and the nature of their business, consider introducing the key players in the factual account;[12]

- Contract – explain the contract by date and parties and annex a copy;

- Terms – set out the terms/clauses of the contract that are relied upon and, in the context of the contract, what rights, duties and obligations the parties had. Start first with express terms and later include implied terms (if any);

- Knowledge – if the knowledge of one party is material, set out both what that party knew and how it was known to the party;[13]

- Breach of the contract – this is likely to be most extensive factual area and should explain what the other party has not done, did defectively, or negligently. This should be referenced back to the terms of the contract[14] so if the breach relates to a term that is not

---

[12] For example, "A is a company incorporated under the laws of England having its registered office at [address]. A is involved in the manufacture and sale of [products]. A operates from various locations throughout the world although its office at [address] is the most relevant for the matters in this reference. A was represented in the matters giving rise to this reference by B who was managing director and was a main board member and C who was a sales director who although on the operational board was not on the board of directors."

[13] Knowledge can be important, for example, as to what damages can be recovered.

[14] For example: "In breach of the obligation in clause [x] of the Agreement set in paragraph [y] above, D failed to . . . "

pleaded re-visit the Terms section. Use this section to set out the claimant's actions.[15]

- Causation, Loss and Damage – explain what the consequence was of the breach and the monetary result. If there is one chain of causation that applies to all elements of the loss, a separate paragraph or section might be the most convenient manner of setting it out before setting out the loss and damage. If the causation differs for each category or head of loss and damage, it may be preferable to set out the causation and loss and damage separately in relation to each category or head of loss.

- Interest – claim interest on the loss and damage. This should include whether the claim is for contractual or statutory interest and, if claimed pursuant to mercantile custom, the facts relied upon for that custom and the entitlement must be pleaded. The calculation should be set out or the principles upon which it is to be calculated set out such as rate, whether compound (and if so the rests) or simple and the period over which it is calculated

- Remedies sought – explain precisely what you want the Arbitral Tribunal to decide and award

F. Evidence

The question of whether to include evidence with the pleading is a matter of judgment. It can add considerably to the volume of material before the Arbitral Tribunal. If the decision is made to include evidence, the issue is then whether to include it in the pleading or attach it to the pleading. The latter is generally preferable. If the directions contemplate the exchange of statements from witnesses, it is probably unwise to disclose the evidence in advance. However, if it is particularly powerful, the argument in favour of leaving it to the evidence stage might be outweighed by the impact it could potentially have at an early stage to either prompt settlement or colour the minds of the Arbitral Tribunal.

---

[15] This might be where the claimant's performance is a condition precedent to the performance of the respondent's obligations; the claimant is claiming expenditure incurred in performance or where the claimant is claiming back his performance as a restitutionary remedy.

G. Law

The legal consequence is often helpfully identified. Where there is any doubt that an opponent or the Arbitral Tribunal might be in doubt as to the legal effect it is probably preferable to plead the legal consequence especially if dealing with parties and counsel from different jurisdictions. If foreign law is relevant it should be set out and the conclusions deriving from it also set out.

H. Fraud

In most jurisdictions certain types of claims need to be pleaded with particular care or formality. The most obvious of these is a claim for fraud or other dishonesty. The Federal Rules of Civil Procedure provide:

> In alleging fraud or mistake, a party must state with particularity the circumstances constituting fraud or mistake. Malice, intent, knowledge, and other conditions of a person's mind may be alleged generally.[16]

In England the Civil Procedure Rules provide:

> The claimant must specifically set out the following matters in his particulars of claim where he wishes to rely on them in support of his claim: . . . any allegation of fraud . . . the fact of any illegality . . . [17]

Because of the seriousness of the allegation, it is good practice to make any such allegations advisedly and with specificity.

I. *Res Judicata*

If a dispute has already been determined, a claim may be subject to the defence of *res judicata*. This defence is expressly recognised by a number of civil law jurisdictions in relation to arbitral awards.[18]

---

[16] Rule 9 Federal Rules of Civil Procedure 2007.

[17] Civil Procedure Rules Rule PD 16 para. 8.2.

[18] France: §§1476 and 1500 of the New Civil Code of Civil Procedure; Belgium: §1703 of the Code of Civil Procedure; Germany: §1055 of the Code of Civil Procedure; Austria: §594 of the Code of Civil Procedure; the Netherlands: §1059 of the Code of

Whilst the defence of *res judicata* is well-recognised in common law jurisdictions, it is generally confined to courts of competent jurisdiction. In arbitration, as the strict provisions of *res judicata* are not available in common law jurisdictions, the practice is to rely upon either cause of action estoppel or issue estoppel. In the U.S., these are referred to as issue preclusion and claim preclusion. Cause of action estoppel relies upon a party being precluded from relitigating the same cause of action that gave rise to an earlier final decision, including all claims and defences that were raised in the earlier proceedings. Issue estoppel precludes the relitigation of issues raised in earlier proceedings even if the precise causes of action are different.

If an Arbitral Tribunal is called upon to determine whether the wide concept of res judicata applies—whether categorised under civil or common law—it should consider whether the parties are the same, the subject matter is the same, and the legal basis is the same. Even if a prima facie case of res judicata is made out, it does not necessarily result in an Arbitral Tribunal having to decline jurisdiction. A decision of a court other than that of the seat of the reference does not automatically result in a full res judicata. A national court's decision that has no international consequence is merely a fact to be taken into account consistent with the laws governing the reference.

If there is a prior Award, the same issues of cause of action estoppel and issue estoppel may arise. If the Award is between different parties, there may nevertheless be a connection through the contractual chain. Good practice dictates that due regard should be had to any earlier decision of another Tribunal but the second Arbitral Tribunal should reach a decision based on the evidence and submissions directed to it. One fact that may be proved to it is the finding of an earlier Tribunal but the second Tribunal is not bound by the earlier decision.

J. Set-Off

Set-off can be a vital part of any pleading. As demonstrated in Chapter 14, a transaction set-off amounting to a true defence can be a vital part of the reference. It is conventional to have the formal defence

---

Civil Procedure; Switzerland: §190 of the Code of Private International Law; Spain: §43 of the Arbitration Act and Italy: §829.8 of the Code of Civil Procedure. *See also* generally Associated Electric and Gas Insurance Services v. European Reinsurance of Zurich [2003] 1WLR 1041.

to the matters raised in the claim and, thereafter, the set-off[19] and, finally, any counterclaim.

K. Presentation

As an aid to presentation, the pleading should have numbered paragraphs (and sub-paragraphs as necessary). Abbreviations and definitions should be used with either a definition section at the beginning or a glossary as an appendix. These should be non-contentious and non-confrontational to encourage common usage by all parties. It is generally helpful to have each paragraph or sub-paragraph containing only one allegation or contention. Headings are often helpful to break up the pleading into distinct sections and schedules and appendices are helpful to contain lengthy particulars of allegations or for detailed material. If a long quote is desired, it can be easier to attach the document or have the quote in a schedule or appendix.

---

[19] The typical wording of the set-off paragraph is: "The Respondent will seek to set-off so much of its counterclaim as may be necessary to extinguish or diminish the claim."

CHAPTER 14
SET-OFF

One of the most complex areas of arbitrability and one that arises often in practice is the question of set-off. In very many cases the claims advanced in the reference (whether by claim or counterclaim) will be plainly within the scope of the arbitration agreement, especially in light of the wide interpretation of the arbitration agreement. Situations will arise, however, when claims may (at least arguably) not be within the scope of the arbitration agreement.

In considering this area, it is important to have in mind two key factors:

1. What has been referred to arbitration and hence what jurisdiction the Arbitral Tribunal has, and;

2. Whether any cross- or counter-claim amounts to a true set-off in law.

Most arbitration agreements and institutional rules make no comment on this area. Broadly, the parties are entitled to bring whatever claims they wish provided they are within the scope of the broad arbitration clause. The notable exception to this is the UNCITRAL Rules. Article 19(3) provides:

> In his statement of defence ... the respondent may make a counter-claim arising out of the same contract or rely on a claim arising out of the same contract for the purpose of a set-off.

This Article has been considered by the English courts in *Econet Satellite Services v. Vee Networks*[1] in which the court held that:

> ... the plain and ordinary meaning of article 19(3) is that a respondent may raise a set-off ... only if it is founded on a claim arising out of the same contract as that on which the claimant's claim is based ... this meaning is not contrary to commercial common sense, for, as in this case, the contract relied upon for the set-off might be subject to an entirely different arbitration

---

[1] [2006] 2 Lloyd's Rep 423, 427.

regime and governing law and it may well be that the set-off exceeds the primary claim, in which case there will in any event have to be a separate arbitration to establish entitlement to the balance.

Exceptionally, institutional rules provide the other way with an enlarged right of set-off. For example, the Swiss Rules of International Arbitration provide in Article 21-5:

> The arbitral tribunal shall have jurisdiction to hear a set-off defence even when the relationship out of which the defence is said to arise is not within the scope of the arbitration clause or is the object of another arbitration agreement or forum-selection clause.

In court proceedings in most jurisdictions, it is permissible to bring counterclaims and cross-claims against a claim. Set-off is traditionally regarded as either "independent" or "transactional." Independent set-off does not require any relationship between the transactions out of which the claims arise. Conversely, transaction set-off arises out of the same transaction or transactions that, whilst different, are so closely related that they should be considered as if the same transaction.

Most jurisdictions favour permitting transaction set-off, notwithstanding that there is an express choice of another dispute resolution mechanism or jurisdiction.[2] That does not mean that the cross-claim can be advanced and any excess recovered—it only permits the advancement of the set-off as in law that usually amounts to a defence. There is nothing new in that proposition. As long ago as 1841, the concept of an abatement as a set-off—or in the US, "recoupment"[3]—and, hence, a defence was recognised. In *Mondel v. Steel*[4] the court said:

---

[2] *See, e.g.,*, the English case of Gilbert-Ash v. Modem Engineering [1973] 3 All ER 195 wherein the House of Lords permitted a claim that was the subject of an arbitration agreement to be advanced as a defence to a debt action. *See also* Meeth v. Glacetal (Case 23/78) [1978] ECR 2133 wherein the European Court permitted a German buyer sued for the price by a French seller in a German court to advance as a defence to the German action, delays and defaults notwithstanding that any claim against the French supplier was, by the contract, only to be sued in its own jurisdiction.

[3] Bull v. United States, 295 U.S. 247 (1935).

[4] (1841) 8 M &W 858, 870.

It must however be considered, that in all these cases of goods sold and delivered with a warranty, and work and labour, as well as the case of goods agreed to be supplied according to a contract, the rule which has been found so convenient is established; and that it is competent for the defendant, in all of those, not to set off, by a proceeding in the nature of a cross-action, the amount of damages which he has sustained by breach of the contract, but simply to defend himself by showing how much less the subject-matter of the action was worth, by reason of the breach of contract; and to the extent that he obtains, or is capable of obtaining, an abatement of price on that account, he must be considered as having received satisfaction for the breach of contract, and is precluded from recovering in another action to that extent; but no more.

In common law countries, the transactional set-off is a substantive defence at law whereas the independent set-off is a matter of procedural convenience albeit resulting in a reduction or extinction of the claim.

Transactional set-off is available in many situations, including to the purchaser of goods that are defective, against a claim for the purchase price; for a charterer of a ship for the delayed delivery of the vessel against the price for the hire, and to a tenant for breaches of the tenancy agreement against a landlord claiming rent.

Independent set-off is altogether different. The policy reasons to have disputes heard together are not so strong for independent set-off. The only requirements for independent set-off are that the cross-claim must both be due and payable and either liquidated or capable of being quantified by reference to ascertainable facts which do not, in their nature, require estimation or valuation. As the court said in the English case of *Aecta Refining & Manufacturing v. Exmar:*[5]

Independent set-off enables the parties to have their various disputes tried in one action instead of two or more. But since they are ex hypothesis unrelated to each other, this is a modest advantage. It is not essential to the fair determination of the dispute, as it will usually be in the case of transaction set-off. As a policy it seems to me to be outweighed by the desirability of

---

[5] [1994] 1 WLR 1634.

giving effect to an agreement to submit a particular dispute to arbitration or the jurisdiction of a foreign court.

As arbitration is consensual, it prevents the Arbitral Tribunal from having jurisdiction over disputes that are outside the scope of the agreement to arbitrate. Whether any particular dispute is within the scope of an arbitration agreement will depend upon a proper analysis of the agreement. It may well be that a cross-claim is outside the scope of an arbitration agreement yet, if it is capable of being a transactional set-off, it can be used as a defence and, hence, can be arbitrated even if the claim sought to be set-off has an entirely separate dispute resolution provision—i.e., one other than the arbitration provision for the claim.

Even if the claim is undisputed an arbitrable cross-claim may amount to a true defence resulting in nothing being due. The same applies even if the cross-claim is non-arbitrable as being on its face outside the scope of the arbitration agreement—provided it amounts to a defence, it can be advanced as such irrespective of the dispute resolution, mechanism, and jurisdiction provisions. It seems from *Econet Satellite Services* that the cross-claim can be advanced as a defence and, to the extent that the cross-claim exceeds the claim, it cannot be recovered in the arbitration as that would be to defeat the dispute resolution mechanism and jurisdiction provisions. Although it may give rise to a duplication of proceedings, the respondent would have to commence a claim under the dispute resolution provisions governing the cross-claim and give credit for the amount found to be necessary to extinguish the claim.

CHAPTER 15
INTERIM MEASURES

Tribunals, however constituted, will have some powers to grant interim measures. The precise extent of those powers may depend on the terms of the arbitration agreement, the institutional rules (if any) under which the reference is conducted, and the laws of the seat.[1] A typical institutional rule is Article 23 of the ICC Rules: "Unless the parties have otherwise agreed . . . the Tribunal may, at the request of a party, order any interim or conservatory measure . . . The Arbitral Tribunal may make the granting of any such measure subject to appropriate security being furnished by the requesting party . . ."[2]

The purpose is, however, clear. It is to ensure that the status quo between the parties remains pending the final award. These temporary measures are designed to hold the position: to "preserve a factual or legal situation so as to safeguard rights the recognition of which is sought from the court having jurisdiction as to the substance of the case."[3]

In cases of real urgency, the fact that a Tribunal has not been appointed is an obvious impediment to the granting of any relief. The appointment of the entire Tribunal can take some considerable time and valuable opportunities can be lost whilst there is no Tribunal to make a decision. This lacuna is addressed in a number of ways. Some institutions have developed procedures to have someone appointed who can make decisions. The ICC has its Rules for Pre-Arbitral Referee Procedure which provide for the appointment of a referee within eight days and a decision/order within thirty days of receipt, by the referee, of the file. The problem with this ICC solution is that the Rules must be specifically agreed to either in the original agreement or on an ad hoc basis.

The ICDR addressed this by incorporating a new rule within the existing body of Rules: the new Rule 37 of the ICDR International Rules.

---

[1] Note, however, that the English Arbitration Act 1996 has a restrictive approach towards permitting the parties to confer jurisdiction on the Tribunal and having limited default powers; §38 AA 1996.

[2] *See also* Article 39, ICSID Rules; Article 26, UNCITRAL Rules; Section 20, DIS Rules; Article 21, AAA Rules; Article 25, LCIA Rules; Rule 24j, SIAC Rules; Article 32, Stockholm Rules, and; Article 26, Swiss Rules.

[3] Van Uden Maritime BV v. Kommanditgesellschaft in Firma Deco-Line C391/95 [1988] ECR I-7091, 7133.

This provides for emergency relief before the constitution of the Tribunal. In cases of demonstrable need, the right to emergency relief was accordingly established. Rule 37 requires notice of the nature of the emergency relief sought, the reasons why it is sought on an emergency basis, and the reasons why the applicant believes it is entitled to emergency relief. The ICDR appoints, within one business day (with truncated timeframes for challenge). The emergency arbitrator is to establish a timescale for evidence within two business days. In contrast to the ICC Referee, the ICDR emergency arbitrator is entitled to issue an order or render an award. Any decision may be made conditional upon—e.g., security—and any order or award may be reviewed for "good cause." The authority of the emergency arbitrator ends on the appointment of the Tribunal member(s) who may review, modify, or vacate the decision.

Notwithstanding what might appear to be a most useful jurisdiction, it is little used although there is some evidence of an increasing uptake in the use of such applications. In some cases, national law provides a route.[4] Indeed, in some countries, national law provides that only the national courts can grant interim measures.[5] Article 17 of the UNCITRAL Model Law provides:

> Unless otherwise agreed by the parties, the arbitral tribunal may, at the request of a party, order any party to take such interim measure of protection as the arbitral tribunal may consider necessary in respect of the subject matter of the dispute. The arbitral tribunal may require any party to provide appropriate security in connection with such measure.

The problem may, however, not be in persuading the Tribunal to make an order for an interim measure but in the enforcement of that order. The ICC Rules make it clear that the decision may be either an order or an award: "Any such measure shall take the form of an order, giving reasons, or of an Award, as the Arbitral Tribunal considers appropriate."[6]

---

[4] *See, e.g.*, §44 English Arbitration Act 1996 and §145 French New Code of Civil Procedure.

[5] *See, e.g.,* both Italian and Greek law so provides.

[6] Article 23.

Any decision by a national court is necessarily an interim decision pending the formation or determination by the Arbitral Tribunal.[7] The Arbitral Tribunal is free to reach its own determination on the merits unconstrained by the interim decision of the national court.

Any application to national courts has to be on the basis of urgency and perceived irreparable harm.

One of the more frequently requested (and granted) forms of interim relief is the preservation of assets, not only those assets that are the subject matter of the dispute. A typical order might be to prevent a respondent from disposing of assets such that they are available for enforcement of any award. Typically, a respondent might be restrained from disposing of bank balances as part of an order preventing the disposal of assets. An arbitral tribunal has no jurisdiction over banks and the order will be of limited effect unless the bank agrees to be bound by the order of the Tribunal. Thus, an order from a national court may be necessary. Any order preventing the disposal of assets does not create any form of charge or priority over those assets.[8] The English courts are, probably, at the forefront of the freezing of assets but the courts of British Columbia have also secured assets pending a final award[9] as, indeed, have the courts of the U.S.[10]

A. Summary Judgment

A distinct sub-set of an interim measure is an application for summary judgment or at least the summary disposal of an issue or issues. This can at its highpoint be very similar to the procedures available in many common law jurisdictions to summarily determine that a claim (or a defence) is either bound to succeed or fail.[11] But it can encompass a much wider range of potential decisions. It can include:

---

[7] Amco Asia v. Indonesia, (1985) 24 ILM 1022, 1026.

[8] Re Swissair Schweizerische Luftverkehr-Attiengesellschaft; Flightline v. Edwards, [2003] 1 WLR 1200.

[9] Trade Fortune Inc v. Amalgamated Mill Supplies Ltd (1995) XX Ybk Comm Arbn 277.

[10] Carolina Power and Light Co v. Uranex, 451 F. Supp. 1044 (N.D. Cal. 1977), cf. McCreary Tire and Rubber Co v. CEAT SpA, 501 F.2d 1032 (3d Cir. 1974).

[11] The practice of national courts may be a poor guide, in this instance, as national courts have an appeal structure that can prevent injustice. An Arbitral Tribunal's award is generally not susceptible to challenge. Regard should also be had to possible enforcement

- Bifurcation (or trifurcation) on issues such as liability and quantum (to quote the most common) or on jurisdiction or applicable law. The common feature is that a decision on one may preclude the need to proceed with the others—for example if the Tribunal finds it has no jurisdiction that necessarily brings matters to an end—likewise for a decision on liability—if there is no liability, it makes it unnecessary to consider quantum.

- Determination of an issue or issues. A contract might have been determined on grounds of both dishonesty and misrepresentation. A finding on one ground might make the other unnecessary to determine.

- A true summary judgment with a consideration of the overall merits based on written evidence not tested by cross-examination and submissions on the law. In general terms, this will have to assume the facts in favour of the party against whom the summary judgment is sought.

The right to act in these ways is rarely specifically dealt with in institutional rules[12] but there are usually wide provisions enabling Tribunals to act in a manner they consider appropriate. National law may bestow authority to act in this manner.[13] The Preamble to the IBA Rules for the Taking of Evidence in International Commercial Arbitration provides that: "Each Arbitral Tribunal is encouraged to identify to the Parties, as soon as it considers it to be appropriate, the issues that it may regard as relevant and material to the outcome of the case, including issues where a preliminary determination may be appropriate."[14]

For example, the Model Law, in Article 19, provides for the Tribunal to conduct the reference in such manner as it considers appropriate

---

difficulties if the country where the award may have to be enforced would raise a due process objection.

[12] The most specific rule is probably ICSID Article 41(5) that permits a party to object to a claim that is "manifestly without legal merit"; AAA Rule 32 permits the Tribunal to direct the parties to focus on specific issues, and JAMS Rule 16 permits a motion for summary disposition with a norm of no oral argument.

[13] In some jurisdictions, domestic procedure does not recognise summary disposal—e.g., France, Italy, China, and Korea. Indeed many U.S. jurists would be distrustful of a process without an oral hearing in the fullest sense.

[14] Preamble 3.

(but equally provides, in Article 18, for the parties to have a "full" opportunity to present its case which is inconsistent with a summary determination). This is essentially the struggle; for the Tribunal to fulfil the objectives of efficiency, cost saving, and expedition, all militate in favour of summary disposal of weak claims or defences. There must, however, be equal treatment of the parties and especially the right to present the case fully. Balancing those objectives, whilst difficult, is possible. However, an Arbitral Tribunal, assuming all disputed facts in favour of the party against whom summary disposal is sought, and thus leaving open only questions of law can and it is suggested should give that party a full and proper opportunity to present its case and nevertheless be ready to determine issues summarily.

In the U.S., notwithstanding that the law and procedural rules in the national courts do not recognise summary disposal, the Court of Appeal in California has twice said that arbitrators may proceed in this way.[15] The opposite result occurred in an Oklahoma court that vacated an award on the basis of a lack of a fair hearing.[16]

---

[15] Schlessinger v. Rosenfeld, 40 Cal. App. 4th 1096 (1995) and Sherrock Brothers Inc. v. DaimlerChrysler Motor Co. LLC, 260 Fed. Appx. 497 (3d Cir. 2008).

[16] Prudential Secs. Inc. v. Dalton, 929 F. Supp. 1411 (N.D. Okla. 1996).

CHAPTER 16
PROCEDURAL AGREEMENTS AND PARTY AUTONOMY

A cardinal principle in international commercial arbitration is party autonomy. Essentially, it is the right of self-determination—as Article 19(1) of the UNCITRAL Model Law provides: "Subject to the provisions of this Law, the parties are free to agree on the procedure to be followed by the arbitral tribunal in conducting the proceedings."

Leaving to one side theoretical rather than practical problems, before a dispute has arisen the parties are generally free to agree on whatever dispute resolution system they wish. National laws may prohibit clearly one-sided agreements from surviving. For example, in England, §33 of the Arbitration Act 1996 provides that "The Tribunal shall . . . act fairly and impartially . . . giving each party a reasonable opportunity of putting his case and dealing with that of his opponent . . ." So if an arbitration clause purported to give only one side the opportunity of addressing the arbitrator, such provision would be invalid.[1] The parties also cannot agree on something that is fundamentally inconsistent with the laws of the seat of the arbitration.[2]

The more practical issue is the extent to which the parties can agree on something that is patently excessive or appears to the Arbitral Tribunal unreasonable or unnecessary. In considering this, the relationship between the Arbitral Tribunal and the parties needs to be considered. The proper analysis appears to be that "The arbitration agreement is a bilateral contract between the parties to the main contract. On appointment the arbitrator becomes a third party to that arbitration agreement, which becomes a trilateral contract.[3] Under that trilateral contract, the arbitrator undertakes his quasi-judicial functions in consideration of the parties agreeing to pay him remuneration. By accepting appointment, the arbitrator assumes the status of a quasi-judicial adjudicator, together with all the duties and disabilities inherent in that status."[4] Whilst perhaps correct, the point needs a little further explanation. It cannot be right that the Arbitral Tribunal becomes a party

---

[1] Jakob Boss Söhne KG v. Federal Republic of Germany, Application No 18479/91.

[2] Hebei Import & Export Corp v. Polytek Engineering, (1999) XXIVa Ybk Comm Arbn 652.

[3] *See* Cie Européene v. Tradax [1986] 2 Lloyd's Rep 301.

[4] K/S Norjarl A/S v. Hyundai Heavy Industries Co Ltd [1991] 1 Lloyd's rep 524.

to the arbitration agreement for all purposes for, if there were a subsequent dispute, it could not be sensibly argued that the same Arbitral Tribunal must determine it. The proper analysis seems to be that, when a particular dispute arises and is referred to arbitration, a contract comes into existence between the parties and the Arbitral Tribunal which includes the terms of the arbitration agreement.

It follows from the fact that the Arbitral Tribunal is a party to the arbitration agreement that the parties cannot change the terms of the arbitration agreement without the consent of the Arbitral Tribunal. Nevertheless, whilst not changing the arbitration agreement, the parties should still, in principle, be able to agree on procedural matters as the reference progresses because to do so would not normally change the basic arbitration agreement to submit disputes to determination by arbitration. This will be so unless the arbitration agreement itself contains procedural matters or the parties' procedural agreement infringes upon some express or implied term of the arbitration agreement. The express terms will include any institutional rules and the most obvious potential inference is that the parties would agree upon a reasonable procedural timetable or, conversely, would not agree to something unreasonable.

ICC Rules provide for party autonomy in Article 15(1) which provides: "The proceedings before the Arbitral Tribunal shall be governed by these Rules and, where these Rules are silent, by any rules which the parties or, failing them, the Arbitral Tribunal may settle on . . ." The hierarchy of rule is, accordingly, the ICC Rules, the parties' agreement, followed by determination by the Arbitral Tribunal. As other ICC Rules provide for procedural matters, the parties' agreement is subject to those Rules. Specifically, Article 18 obliges the Arbitral Tribunal to draw up the Terms of Reference. These are to include "particulars of the applicable procedural rules . . .", however, this is usually satisfied by general statements and an agreement that the IBA Rules on the Taking of Evidence in International Arbitration (1999) shall serve as guidelines for the Arbitral Tribunal.

More specifically, Article 18(4) provides that: "When drawing up the Terms of Reference, or as soon as possible thereafter, the Arbitral Tribunal, after having consulted the parties, shall establish in a separate document a provisional timetable . . ." It follows from the "consultation" with the parties that, even were the parties to agree, the ultimate right of veto and, hence, power rests with the Arbitral Tribunal. It follows that even were the parties to agree a ten-year timetable, the Arbitral Tribunal could direct something otherwise. The same logic would apply to any variations to the timetable. This has obvious sense for, if the parties agreed an evidentiary hearing would take place on a particular date, it might be inconvenient to the Arbitral Tribunal and it could not be forced into those dates merely on the basis of the whim of the parties.

The position is similar under LCIA Rules. Article 14 provides that: "The parties may agree on the conduct of their arbitral proceedings . . . consistent with the Arbitral Tribunal's general duties at all times . . . to act fairly and impartially . . . and . . . to adopt procedures suitable to the circumstances of the arbitration, avoiding unnecessary delay or expense, so as to provide a fair and efficient means for the final resolution of the parties' dispute." It follows that, if the Arbitral Tribunal finds that a procedural agreement by the parties did not suit the circumstances of the arbitration or caused unnecessary delay or expense, it would be entitled to override the parties' agreement.

Arbitral Tribunals are clearly going to be loath to overrule the parties whose reference it is and who probably know the dispute better than the Arbitral Tribunal. No doubt the Arbitral Tribunal would question the wisdom of a course of action and encourage the parties to reconsider the position. Most rules and national laws have some reference to conducting the reference expeditiously. In considering the parties procedural agreement, the Arbitral Tribunal will no doubt have this in mind together with any other obligations and duties on the Tribunal, their own availability in the future, and whether any evidentiary hearing is likely to be affected by any change to the timetable. Equally, why the parties have reached an agreement can be very significant. For example, the parties' need for time to mediate or negotiate would generally be a good reason for extending the timetable whereas indolence by the parties' counsel may be less persuasive.

CHAPTER 17
GIVING DISCOVERY

Documentary discovery is part of the process of presenting evidence. Evidence is, of course, essential for any tribunal to make findings of fact. The principal purpose of documentary discovery is to assist the parties in ascertaining the existence of documents, the whereabouts of those documents and, hence, details and facts relevant to the claims and defences in issue in the reference.

In common law jurisdictions (which are essentially adversarial), the judge will seek to ensure that the rules of evidence are adhered to, hear the evidence (which is effectively left to the parties to present as they wish), seek to ensure "fair play" and, thereafter, render a decision or judgment. In contrast civil law jurisdictions are not bound by the strictures of the rules of evidence that common law jurisdictions are. Judges generally take a more active role but, as each civil law jurisdiction has a different procedure, it is unsafe to generalise especially as civil law jurisdictions may have state as well as federal law.

In presenting evidence to a tribunal (whether national court or arbitral tribunal), documentary evidence is often a key part of the overall evidence. As international arbitration is an alternative to litigation in national courts, it follows that the practices of those national courts do not have to be followed in arbitration. It follows that the procedures applicable in the national courts of one or more of the counsel representing the parties or the practices familiar to one or more counsel representing the parties should not be followed unless the Tribunal is satisfied that they are appropriate to the facts of the reference. However, there remains the need to ensure that the parties have had a full and fair opportunity of presenting their case and this is often dependant on proper discovery eliciting key documents. Admittedly the "smoking gun" is rarely found through the process of discovery but some "bullets" or "bombs" are not uncommon. Documents are often perceived as a more accurate guide to the truth and do not have the disadvantage of conflicting oral evidence on to disputed facts. For this very reason cross-examination is not regarded as a reliable route to the truth by civil lawyers. Trial, in large part by documents, can also be less time-consuming than conventional oral hearings as extensive examination and cross-examination are avoided. The absence of oral testimony can likewise be unsatisfactory where there are relevant issues of disputed fact not addressed by documents. The manner in which any trial proceeds has to be managed so as to ensure that the process does justice between the parties.

As discovery is often perceived as such an important issue especially by common law lawyers (and some clients), it can be one of the most hard-fought and difficult of the issues that arbitral tribunals have to address in international commercial arbitration. The fact that parties and arbitrators may come from different cultures and different systems of law results in very different perceptions of how the arbitration should be conducted and justice achieved. This and the following chapters seek to address documentary discovery (to the exclusion of the wider issues of discovery that may be familiar to U.S. lawyers where the concept encompasses depositions, interrogatories, admissions, and the like).

Those from civil law regimes may not be as familiar with or at least have experience of, the concept of production of "documents both favourable and unfavourable" under compulsion, rather they will be used to the limited production of documents relied upon. Those from common law jurisdictions will have varying experiences of discovery although at the heart of all systems will be an obligation to produce documents relevant to the issues in dispute (whether or not they are favourable to the disclosing party's case).

It is for these reasons that the choice of the constitution of the Arbitral Tribunal—both the party-appointed member(s) and the chairman—can be very important to the parties. Those seeking extensive discovery will seek a common law lawyer with an "aggressive" or U.S. background. Those not wanting extensive discovery may seek a lawyer from a civil law jurisdiction or even a non-lawyer.

The differing laws that can apply to international arbitration especially the interaction of the proper law and of the arbitration will be especially relevant for matters such as privilege. In the English case of *Bourns v. Raychem No 3*[1] there had been a limited waiver of privilege in certain documents for the purpose of assessing the amount of costs that a party had to pay. The party receiving the documents wanted to use them in U.S. proceedings to show that proper discovery had not been given in the U.S. proceedings. The court said:

> U.S. law and practice is for the U.S. courts. However it cannot be right that under English law privileged documents and the

---

[1] [1999] 3 All ER 154.

information in them should be used in breach of privilege just because the party claiming privilege has allegedly not complied with an obligation of U.S. practice in the U.S. proceedings. In the present case the documents, which by their nature were privileged, were produced . . . in circumstances where the privilege was waived only for [specific] purposes . . . That is the only purpose for which they can be used under English law. To suggest . . . that to enforce that restriction amounts to interference with U.S. court proceedings is wrong.[2]

Although this was a case in an English domestic court, it shows that the question of whether a document is privileged under English law is to be determined by English law and that foreign law is irrelevant. The confusing point for the unwary practitioner is that privilege has long been described to be a substantive, rather than a procedural, right.[3] Questions of substantive rather than procedural rights may not sit exactly with the distinction between the law governing the arbitral procedure and the law governing the substantive dispute. Practitioners should approach pre-conceived ideas of substance and procedure with care as the laws of the arbitral procedure and the substantive dispute may not draw the same distinction.

A. Whether and, If So, What Discovery

Nearly all international arbitrations have some provisions for discovery. It is well-known that wide-ranging pre-trial procedures are available in the U.S. for obtaining oral and documentary discovery from parties and non-parties. In contradistinction, the concept of discovery beyond producing documents relied upon, even as between immediate parties to litigation, is almost unknown in civil law systems. Other jurisdictions take a position somewhere in-between.

Mutual discovery in arbitration is generally perceived as being in the public interest in that it promotes settlement by enabling parties to accurately evaluate strengths and weaknesses, discourages gamesmanship, reduces the risk of a party being taken by surprise (trial by ambush),

---

[2] *Id.* at 168.

[3] *See* Lord Hoffmann in *R. (Morgan Grenfell & Co Ltd) v. Special Commissioner of Income Tax,* [2003] 1 AC 563, 606 (finding that a legal professional privilege was "*a fundamental human right long established in the common law.*").

promotes the efficient use of trial time, promotes justice by disclosing favourable and unfavourable material, and enables the Arbitral Tribunal to decide the case in light of contemporary documentary material (which is often more valuable than oral testimony and forms the basis for testing, by cross-examination, the oral testimony that is received). This is in accord with, for example, the fourth preamble to the IBA Rules on Taking Evidence in International Commercial Arbitrations ("IBA Rules") that provides: "The taking of Evidence shall be conducted on the principle that each Party shall be entitled to know, reasonably in advance of any Evidentiary Hearing, the Evidence on which the other Parties rely." The IBA Rules are the reference point for reasonableness in discovery (and indeed all matters relating to evidence) and full regard should be had to the provisions of the Rules.[4]

The ICC Publication "Techniques for Controlling Time and Costs in Arbitration"[5] provide for the production of documents relied upon and requests to produce.[6]

The IBA Rules also provide for the disclosure of documents relied upon (Article 3(1)) with recourse to requests to produce additional documents. This process is rapidly becoming the standard direction for international commercial arbitration. Any such request must be for "relevant and material" documents (Article 3(3) (b)). However, many documents may fall within this definition and thus discovery may be fairly extensive. Opponents to such broad discovery point to its overly intrusive nature, its potential to be time consuming, dilatory, expensive, and susceptible to abuse by the parties. At its worst, it can distract from the substantive issues and become an all-consuming battle.

Nevertheless, orders for discovery are now the rule rather than the exception. The general practice in international commercial arbitration is to limit discovery to those documents that are both: 1) relevant to the issues in dispute, and; 2) necessary for the proper resolution of those issues. This is often done in a two-stage process reflected, for example, by the IBA Rules, of a party producing the documents it intends to rely upon and giving the opposing parties the opportunity to request

---

[4] There is also much good practice in the International Institute for Conflict Prevention and Resolution's Protocol on Disclosure of Documents and Presentation of Witnesses in Commercial Arbitration available to download at www.cpradr.org.

[5] ICC Publication 843.

[6] §§53 - 55.

additional discovery. Where issues arise in respect to the extent or degree of discovery, the tribunal will normally take a proportionate path, limiting discovery to that necessary in the context of the size, scope, and monetary value of the dispute and relative significance of the evidence to the dispute as a whole.

It is suggested that the better route is for the parties to produce what they think is required rather than the Arbitral Tribunal trying to dig for information. The parties will, of course, know the dispute better than the Tribunal and considerable time and cost will be saved by the parties doing the discovery themselves. This should not prevent the Arbitral Tribunal from itself requesting documents that it considers material and might have been overlooked by the parties.

An order for discovery might not be clear enough to enlighten the parties as to precisely what they are being obliged to submit. It may be helpful to consider documents as falling into four categories:

1. The parties' own documents, which they rely upon in support of their own contentions in the proceedings;

2. Adverse documents of which a party is aware and which, to a material extent, adversely affect his own contentions or support another party's contentions;

3. Documents that do not fall within categories (1) and (2) but are part of the "story" or background, including documents which, though relevant, may not be necessary for the fair disposal of the reference, and;

4. Train of inquiry documents; these are documents that may lead to a train of inquiry enabling a party to advance his own contentions or damage that of another party.

Appendices 13 to 15 are sample orders for discovery that might guide Arbitral Tribunals in making procedural orders for discovery. Appendix 13 is a sample of an order for full discovery that is intended to cover all four categories and is an extensive requirement that will put the parties to considerable cost (which may well be justified). Appendix 14 is intended to cover categories (1) and (2) and Appendix 15 category (1) only. It is the category (3) documents that will cause the most concern to common law lawyers if Appendix 14 is used. The line between relevant background documents and materially adverse documents or indeed documents needed to be relied upon to tell the whole story, is a fine one.

Common law lawyers are still likely to include category (3) documents in giving discovery under an Appendix 14 order. Finding an effective means of discouraging that may be difficult.

Arbitration may involve the analysis of detailed records of transactions or otherwise involve considerable repetitive material. For example, detailed accounting records comprising orders, delivery notes, invoices, and credit notes. Often it will be possible to limit discovery by reference to a sample. The sample can be by reference to a time period (for example, taking every other month); author and recipient (for example, taking only the documents of the key protagonists); subject matter (for example, only those documents concerning or excluding a particular subject matter); location (for example, certain offices or computer servers) and nature (for example, excluding faxes that were duplicated by confirmatory letter). Appendix 16 is a sample order for limiting discovery. Arbitral Tribunals are likely to find it necessary to leave the parties to agree the limiting process based on their knowledge of likely methods of limiting on the facts of the particular case. Where assistance is sought from the Arbitral Tribunal, the party seeking assistance is likely to have to explain in detail why the proposed limitation is fair and reasonable.

National courts will generally not interfere to increase the scope of any discovery ordered by the Arbitral Tribunal.[7]

B. The Applicable Rules for Discovery

As we have seen, the parties may well have chosen institutional rules to govern their obligations to give discovery. If not, the law of the seat of the arbitration will dictate the obligation. The specific authority to order discovery will usually derive from a specific institutional rule either expressly or by implication or from the inherent mandate to establish the facts (not least so as to ensure that the award is properly enforceable). Nevertheless, the rules will invariably permit the Arbitral Tribunal to exercise a discretion whether, and if so how, to address discovery.

A comparison of the discovery provisions of the major rules is set out in Appendix 17. The most commonly applied rules provide for discovery as follows:

---

[7] Coastal States Trading v. Zenith Nav., SA, 446 F. Supp. 330 (S.D.N.Y. 1977), but a US court may intervene in exceptional circumstances: *see* Recognition Equip. v. NCR Corp., 532 F. Supp. 271 (N,D, Tex, 1981).

1. ICC Rules

Article 20 provides: "The Arbitral Tribunal shall proceed within as short a time as possible to establish the facts of the case by all appropriate means . . .".

2. UNCITRAL Arbitration Rules

Article 24(3) provides: "At any time during the arbitral proceedings the arbitral tribunal may require the parties to produce documents, exhibits or other evidence within such period of time as the tribunal shall determine."

3. LCIA Arbitration Rules

Article 22(1) provides: "Arbitral Tribunal shall have the power . . . to order any party to produce to the Arbitral Tribunal, and to the other parties for inspection, and to supply copies of, any documents or classes of documents in their possession, custody or power which the Arbitral Tribunal determines to be relevant . . .".

4. American Arbitration Association Commercial Arbitration Rules

Rule 21 provides: "At the request of any party or at the discretion of the arbitrator, consistent with the expedited nature of arbitration, the arbitrator may direct . . . the production of documents and other information . . .".

5. ICDR International Arbitration Rules and Swiss Rules of International Arbitration

These rules have no specific provision for discovery although the ICDR has issued guidelines for arbitrators.[8] The guidelines provide for the exchange of documents relied upon with the ability to request additional documents. Those pursuing disputed requests will have to justify the time and expense of the request and the Tribunal may allocate the costs of compliance between the parties as it sees fit.

It can be seen that the rules generally do not contain any specific meaningful provisions on discovery or any mechanism that the Arbitral Tribunal might adopt. Many of the orders for discovery made are within

---

[8] ICDR Guidelines for Arbitrators Concerning Exchanges of Information, effective for all cases commenced after 31 May 2008.

the general discretion of the Arbitral Tribunal and the general obligation to afford the parties equal treatment and the right to fairly present a case. This is intentional. The general themes are common to nearly all institutional rules. The freedom to craft remedies based on the particular facts giving rise to the arbitration is to be welcomed, for the draftsmen of contracts cannot foresee the nature and extent of disputes that may arise, nor can the draftsmen of institutional rules. The ability of experienced Arbitral Tribunals to craft remedies consistent with the background, expectations, and demands of the parties and their knowledge of the actual dispute and the amounts involved is a route preferable to prescribed and regimented rules. It enables flexibility dependant on whether the dispute is essentially fact based (when extensive discovery may be required) or an issue of law (where limited or no discovery may be appropriate). Further, given the consensual nature of arbitration, the parties may always agree upon some mechanism that the Arbitral Tribunal will invariably confirm by way of a procedural order reflecting the parties' agreement.

C. IBA Rules on the Taking of Evidence in International Commercial Arbitration (IBA Rules)

The current 1999 Rules replace the 1983 Rules and were necessary to reflect the evolving practice of taking evidence in international arbitrations over the sixteen years that the 1983 Rules existed. Because the various other institutional rules are so vague as to the manner and extent of discovery (see table at Appendix 17), parties often adopt the IBA Rules — or at least provide that they serve as guidelines for the Arbitral Tribunal (in accordance with paragraph 2 of the preamble to the IBA Rules) — either in the arbitration agreement itself, the terms of reference, or in the first procedural order. Even if not formally adopted or incorporated as "guidance", the IBA Rules are often considered authoritative in resolving issues of evidence that may arise under other institutional rules. In addition, there is significant authoritative guidance in the 2006 ICC publication entitled *Document Production in International Arbitration*.

Article 3 of the IBA Rules provides for the discovery of documents. Specifically, Article 3(1) provides for the submission of available documents relied upon within the time ordered by the Arbitral Tribunal. The purpose of this Article is to compel the parties to bring forward evidence that supports their case and to enable the opposing party to review and rebut the evidence and not be taken by surprise. It is not intended to limit the ability to produce further documents such as memorials, witness statements, and expert reports, although the latter is to be discouraged in the spirit of enabling both parties a fair opportunity of addressing the other's evidence. Article 3(1) is to be contrasted, for example, with Rule 26(a)(1)(B) of the U.S. Federal Rules of Civil Procedure. The latter requires the production of all documents that a party "may" use to support its claims. The IBA Rules' inclusion of the term "does use" indicates an intentional differentiation from U.S. procedure.

Article 3(2) provides for the submission of a "Request to Produce". The Request to Produce shall contain detail sufficient to identify the document, or a "narrow and specific" category of documents of which discovery is sought, "a description of how the requested documents are relevant and material to the outcome of the case", and a statement that they are not in the possession, custody, or control of the requesting party but are believed to be in the possession, custody, or control of the other party.[9] The remainder of Article 3 deals with the process for determining disputes and allied matters. This provision in the IBA Rules was a marked departure from the 1983 Rules, where internal documents were effectively excluded from production. Similarly, categories of documents were excluded from Requests to Produce rather specific documents had to be identified. It is now appreciated how important internal documents can be and how difficult it is to restrict requests to specific documents.

The key factors that the Arbitral Tribunal is likely to consider when reviewing a request for discovery are whether a request is for a "narrow and specific" category and the conceptual problem that notwithstanding that a request could be framed for a "narrow and specific" category, it might still produce a large volume of material. Ultimately, this is an issue that the Arbitral Tribunal may have to adjudicate and the constitution of the Tribunal may be key in their decision. Specifically whether they have a common law or civil background may predispose them to grant extensive discovery or limited or no discovery and an application for additional discovery may be influenced by that background.

This formulation in the IBA Rules was a compromise between the civil and common lawyers and the Working Party drafting the Rules reported: "The vigor with which the issues were debated demonstrated that the question of document discovery is the key area in which practitioners from common law and civil law countries differ."

---

[9] Article 3(3).

It is clear that, for discovery under the IBA Rules, the documents must be both "relevant and material." This can be contrasted with the U.S. Federal Rules of Civil Procedure that permit parties to "obtain discovery regarding any matter, not privileged, that is relevant to the claim or defense of any party." In practice, these words are widely construed and thus it is clear that the IBA Rules are not as wide as U.S. Federal practice. The word "material" is clearly an attempt to delimit the relevance from being too fanciful or remote. It resonates to the test set out by the Court of Appeal in the English case of *O. Co. v. M. Co.*:[10]

> The [wide relevance] principle was never intended to justify demands for disclosure of documents at the far end of the spectrum of materiality . . . The excessively wide application . . . of [the] formulation of relevance has probably contributed more to the increase of the costs . . . than any other factor other than the development of the photocopying machine . . . the document or class of documents must be shown by the applicant to offer a real probability of evidential materiality in the sense that . . . [it] can be expected to yield information of substantial evidential materiality to the pleaded claim and the defence to it . . . .

The IBA Rules also address the degree of relevance and materiality: article 9(2)(a) excludes from production documents lacking "sufficient relevance or materiality," reinforcing that both relevance and materiality are required and that it must be more than illusory.

The words "possession, custody or control" in Article 3(6) will also be familiar to U.S. lawyers from the Federal Rules of Civil Procedure. Equally, they will be familiar to English lawyers conversant with the rules of procedure pre-1999 when the concept of possession, custody, or power was used. It is suggested that there is no meaningful difference between the English concept of "power" and the U.S. concept of "control" especially as the former was interpreted as meaning those documents which, whilst not in the possession, or custody of a person, he had the right to obtain them. This equates to the generally understood concept of "control". Nevertheless, it is clumsy wording and the more modern English concept of "control"—i.e., being in physical possession or having a right to possess, inspect, or copy—is probably a neater and more precise descriptor. It is this definition that is used in Appendices 12 and 13.

---

[10] [1996] 2 Lloyd's Rep. 347, 350 -1.

CHAPTER 18
DISPUTES ON THE EXTENT OF DISCOVERY GIVEN

Whatever discovery is given, and however carefully the Arbitral Tribunal is in the formulation of the order for discovery, one or more of the parties is often dissatisfied with the discovery given by the other. The Arbitral Tribunal will generally encourage parties to resolve these disputes between themselves in accordance with the party autonomy principle. If the parties are unable to agree, the Arbitral Tribunal will have to assist. The upshot of this will be a procedural order but Tribunals will often convene a meeting or hearing at which indications and express statements of principle may be given to guide the parties, allowing them to break and see if detailed points can be resolved. If agreements or stipulations can be reached, then they can be recorded in a procedural order by consent. The Tribunal can adjudicate any remaining issues with, hopefully, the issues at the very least clarified by the parties' attempts to agree.

If determination is required a so-called "Redfern Schedule" can be used. This is a variation on a Scott Schedule[1] and is simply a convenient method of setting out the dispute. The Schedule can be adapted to suit the circumstances of the case but will generally have, in the first column, the document or category sought; in the second, the justification for the request; in the third, the requested party's reasons for refusing the request, and a final column, for the Tribunal to record its decision. Clearly, additional columns can be inserted between the third and final column to record rebuttal contentions.

Appendix 18 is a sample procedural order that an Arbitral Tribunal might make either at the outset with a general order for discovery or when specific issues become apparent. It uses the tabular form approach.

The full Tribunal usually resolves disputes on discovery as one or more of the parties may perceive that the discovery issues will have an important impact on the resolution of the dispute. In some cases, for example, where there is a legally qualified Chairman with the other members from a technical or industry background, it might be preferable

---

[1] A method used in English cases to set out rival contentions on technical or detailed issues in tabular form, it is much used in building disputes to show disputes on an item-by-item basis and concluding with a column for the judge to put his decision.

that the Chairman decide discovery issues alone. A composite sample of an order is at Appendix 19.

Whatever the decision-making process, the touchstone of "relevance and materiality" is highly likely to govern the discovery process. The ICDR has issued guidance to Arbitrators on the "Exchanges of Information". That guidance stresses the need for maintaining "efficiency and economy" without "unnecessary delay and expense while at the same time balancing the goals of avoiding surprise, promoting equality of treatment, and safeguarding each party's opportunity to present its claims and defenses fairly."

The cost incurred in any request will inevitably be a matter in the balance in determining the response. The Guidance continues: "the tribunal shall require a requesting party to justify the time and expense that its request may involve, and may condition granting such a request on the payment of part or all of the cost . . . "

A. Categories of Documents

Discovery is, and more particularly requests for discovery are, often given by reference to a category or class of documents. When giving discovery the purpose of listing is two-fold. First, to record what has been discovered should that become relevant, and second, to enable the other parties to determine what it requires copies of—this is the more so where parties are paying for copies and the discovery is voluminous.[2] Generally, listing evidence by category or class is accepted practice. Many jurisdictions do not require lists and simply move directly to the provision of copies. Where there is a considerable quantity of evidence, the provision of such a list is rarely a significant cost and it presents the advantage of enabling parties to identify and demonstrate (if need be) what evidence has been discovered and possibly save costs and time in future copying.

An issue may arise where a party seeks additional discovery by reference to a category or class. The requesting party may wish to discover documents it has difficulty in specifying with any accuracy. This is the more so where it relates to actions in which the requesting party was not involved. The party against whom the discovery is sought

---

[2] If one party discloses documents that are common to all parties, it may be considered unnecessary to obtain copies – but there are risks in not doing so as the other copies of a document may have been, for example, annotated.

may wish to know precisely what it should search for and to have considerable specificity so as to limit the scope of what has to be given. The typical request for "all documents being, evidencing, relating to, touching upon or concerning" an issue, without limitation in subject matter, time and interlocutors, is difficult to search for and produce. There is a fine but important distinction between an incoherent and non-specific categorisation and a detailed narrow and specific description. Albeit in another context, Lord Fraser in *Sedgwick Group v. Johns-Manville Fibreboard Corp.*[3] said that the words "separately described" were intended to rule out a compendious description of several documents provided that the exact document in each case is clearly indicated:

> "Monthly bank statements for the year 1984 relating to his current account" with a named bank would satisfy the requirements of specificity, provided that the evidence showed that regular monthly statements had existed during the year and were likely to be still in his possession. But a general request for "all bank statements for 1984" would in my view refer to a class of documents and would not be admissible.

This is a specific restriction for a specific statute but the degree of specificity required for a witness to bring documents under a subpoena has been described as intending to avoid a situation where "a defendant calls for disclosure of numerous substantial files with the intention of going through all of them in the hope of procuring a benefit which is speculative at best and based on . . . assumption . . . ."[4] These are the extreme of calls for specificity and are designed to protect the innocent witness and illustrate that wide categories or classes can be unreasonable. A slightly different test is likely to be applied to discovery but the sentiment of limiting wide categories or classes in favour of specificity remains. Arbitral Tribunals will be vigilant to ensure that requests are not so voluminous, broad or repetitive as to place an unreasonable burden on the requested party.

Good practice dictates that a category or class is limited, if at all possible, by time period, author, recipient, subject matter, location, and nature of document. For example, a request for "all documents being,

---

[3] [1985] 1 WLR 331, 338.

[4] Wakefield v. Outhwaite [1990] 2 Lloyds Rep 157, 164.

evidencing, relating to, touching upon, or concerning communications between A and B" is likely to be perceived as too wide whereas "all emails and letters between A (acting by its employees C, D, or E) to B (acting by its employees F, G, or H) in the period from J to K relating to L, together with any documents attached or enclosed, located in the paper files in the offices at M, or on the computer servers at M, and containing one of more of the following words N, P or Q" is plainly going to have far greater prospects of success before an Arbitral Tribunal.

The Guidance to Arbitrators published by the ICDR concerning Exchanges of Information refers to: "Requests for documents maintained in electronic form should be narrowly focussed and structured to make searching for them as economical as possible." Clearly a focussed approach has better prospects of success.

B.   Adverse Inference and Consequences of Failure to Produce

Most organisations participating in arbitration would not object to the proposition that if a party is required to produce a document on discovery and refuses to do so, it is likely to be because the document harms the case or credibility of the party who ought to have produced it. Article 9(4) of the IBA Rules provides that if a party "without satisfactory explanation" fails to produce a document, the Arbitral Tribunal may infer that such document would be adverse to the interests of that party. The first point to note on this rule is that the Tribunal may draw the inference—it is a matter of discretion and clearly one that can be avoided by providing a satisfactory explanation. If no proper explanation is advanced, the Tribunal has the discretion to infer that the document is adverse to the party. Note it does permit of a wider inference that, for example, the party is generally lying.

The drawing of an inference may be relatively straightforward when the failure to produce relates to a single document—e.g., a note of a meeting at which the parties were both present. The inference to be drawn is that the party's account of events of that meeting is not to be accepted. Far greater difficulties arise if the failure relates to a meeting at which one party was not present—e.g., a board meeting of one of the parties. It may be exceptionally difficult to draw any inference in those circumstances and still more so in relation to a category of documents, some of which might be positive and others negative to a particular point. For example, if the issue was the infringement of some intellectual property right and the category of documents was those evidencing sales in breach of another's intellectual property rights, what can the Tribunal properly infer? Did the party sell 10,000 or 10,000,000 articles? These issues might, however, be tackled in other ways, for example, either by assessing the impact of lost sales on the owner of the intellectual property right and inferring it was all due to the actions of the infringer, or, discovery of the costs of purchase of the materials to make the infringing article. Both may be inaccurate but the party infringing and not producing the sales documents is not in a position to complain. The absence of such material could form the basis for the Tribunal to find that a prima facie case, not necessarily discharging the burden of proof, but which, aided by the adverse inference could be drawn from the absence of material, could tip the party seeking to prove a fact over the burden of proof threshold.

Article 9(4) does not state whether the Arbitral Tribunal is required to inform the parties of the inference it proposes to draw, in order that the affected party can seek to rebut it. This may raise issues of due process which may, in turn, affect the enforceability of the award. Generally, it is likely that an Arbitral Tribunal will be hesitant to draw an adverse inference unless the following are established:

- The documents are plainly relevant and material to the proceedings – some commentators put it as high as "essential to the disposition of the case,"

- The documents are in the control of the requested party,

- The claim or defence upon which the inference might be drawn is established at a prima facie level, even in the absence of the requested document,

- No satisfactory explanation is provided, and

- Sufficient time and opportunity have been given to produce.

This goes slightly further than Article 9(4), especially as Article 9(4) permits an inference simply on the basis of not objecting in time. Arbitral Tribunals will generally be reluctant to draw an inference on that ground alone. It is perhaps the prima facie element that gives the most safeguards and is the element not appearing in Article 9(4). It is generally unwise for an Arbitral Tribunal to rely on the total absence of evidence bolstered by an adverse inference to found the basis of an award. However, where the existing evidence discloses a prima facie case, albeit lacking the required degree of proof to satisfy the evidentiary burden, the absence of documents, from which an adverse inference might be drawn, may well amount to sufficient evidence for an award.

If an independent witness, not being in the employ of any of the parties, attends (other than under a subpoena requiring the production of documents) and gives evidence, he may be questioned about documents that he has. As the Tribunal will generally have no jurisdiction over non-parties to the arbitration, the Tribunal will generally not require or order the witness to produce documents. Therefore, adverse inferences should not be drawn against the party tendering the witness, as it will generally be outside the power or control of that party to compel the witness to produce documents. However, the weight that the Tribunal attaches to that evidence may well be affected by the absence of documentary support.

Article 4(11) of the IBA Rules provides that the Arbitral Tribunal can order a party to provide (or use its best efforts to provide) a witness for testimony. No mention is made of documents. This provision can be contrasted with Article 3(9) that authorises the Arbitral Tribunal to request (note not order) a party to produce documents. This provision is not restricted to documents in the possession, custody, or control of the party. There seems no reason, in principle, why a narrow and specific request could not be made for documents to be produced at the same time as a party is ordered to provide for the attendance of a witness. If a party objects to the request, the Arbitral Tribunal can consider whether to make an order based on the principles in Article 3(6).

CHAPTER 19
CONFIDENTIALITY AS A GROUND FOR RESISTING DISCLOSURE

One of the main attractions of arbitration is the ability of parties to resolve disputes outside of the glare of the publicity that might arise in litigation before national courts. This does not, however, address the concerns that discovery may create in terms of revealing commercially or technically sensitive material to the opponent in arbitration. Further, such concerns are unlikely to be assuaged by the inherent confidentiality of arbitration which prevents the use of discovery documents for any ulterior purpose. Once the "cat is out of the bag," it is difficult to put it back in, not so much in terms of preventing use but in removing or preventing the use of the knowledge derived from the documents.

Equally one party may have the documents of a stranger to whom he owes duties of confidentiality. Under English law, confidentiality is no answer to a request for discovery as Lord Wilberforce in the House of Lords said in *Science Research Council v. Nasse:*[1]

> There is no principle in English law by which documents are protected from discovery by reason of confidentiality alone. But there is no reason why, in the exercise of its discretion to order discovery, the tribunal should not have regard to the fact that documents are confidential, and that to order disclosure would involve a breach of confidence . . . the tribunal may have regard to the sensitivity of particular types of confidential information, to the extent to which the interests of third parties . . . may be affected by disclosure, to the interest . . . in preserving the confidentiality of personal reports, and to any wider interest which may be seen to exist in preserving the confidentiality . . .

It remains a matter of discretion and, as the Lord Diplock said in the House of Lords in *D v. NSPCC:*[2]

> The fact that information has been communicated by one person to another in confidence, however, is not of itself a sufficient

---

[1] [1980] AC 1028, 1065.

[2] [1977] AC 171, 218.

ground for protecting from disclosure in a court of law the nature of the information or the identity of the informant if either of these matters would assist the court to ascertain facts which are relevant to an issue upon which it is adjudicating . . . The private promise of confidentiality must yield to the general public interest that in the administration of justice truth will out, unless by reason of the character of the information or the relationship of the recipient of the information to the informant a more important public interest is served by protecting the information or the identity of the informant from disclosure in a court of law.

To address the great potential for confidentiality issues, the English courts create remedies to address the potential for wrongdoing, whether by redacting (blanking out) sensitive parts of a document or by restricting those who can see and use a document—potentially to the lawyer and not the client.

Article 9(2)(e) of the IBA Rules permits the Arbitral Tribunal to exclude from discovery any document of "compelling" commercial or technical confidentiality. If an Article 9(2) objection is taken on the grounds of confidentiality, the Arbitral Tribunal can appoint an independent expert under Article 3(7) to review the document and report on the objection. The procedure applies equally to privilege or political or institutional sensitivity.

These procedures do not appear to address duties to a stranger of, say, a personal nature although documents such as these are unlikely to be "relevant and material" in an international commercial arbitration. To the extent that they are, the Arbitral Tribunal can balance the competing private interest of confidentiality with the public interest in the administration of justice. Furthermore, Article 9(3) permits the Arbitral Tribunal to make case specific arrangements to protect confidentiality.

Other mechanisms can be used to address confidentiality—most notably, protective orders borrowed from the Federal Rules of Civil Procedure that effectively amount to declaratory relief that a party need not give discovery for reasons of confidentiality—although the procedure can also be used in any situation where the discovery would be oppressive, unduly burdensome or expensive.

One specific aspect of confidentiality is a party's insurance coverage. In England, the orthodox view is that a party need not disclose insurance provisions, not necessarily because they are confidential, but because they are irrelevant to the dispute. This is reflected in the judgment in *West London Pipeline and Storage v. Total UK*[3] wherein the court refused to follow an earlier decision ordering the disclosure of insurance arrangements,[4] and instead, directed that the scope of disclosure be limited to documents relevant to matters in issue in the proceedings.

The same cannot be said for the U.S. where, in court proceedings, insurance documents are required to be disclosed. The Federal Rules of Civil Procedure §26(a)(1)(A)(iv) provides:

> Except as exempted by Rule 26(a) (1) (B) or as otherwise stipulated or ordered by the court, a party must, without awaiting a discovery request, provide to the other party . . . (iv) for inspection and copying . . . any insurance agreement under which an insurance business may be liable to satisfy all or part of any possible judgment in the action or to indemnify or reimburse for payments made to satisfy the judgment.

Clearly, the issues may require careful consideration. In principle, the insurance cover would appear to be irrelevant to the issues to be determined and disclosure is not necessary for the proper determination of the issues referred for determination and Tribunals should exercise care before ordering the disclosure of insurance arrangements.

---

[3] [2008] EWHC 1296.

[4] Harcourt v. FEF Griffin [2008] Lloyd's Rep. I.R. 386.

CHAPTER 20
CONFIDENTIALITY AND SUBSEQUENT USE

Arbitration is inherently confidential in most jurisdictions notably Hong Kong, England, France, and Switzerland. As the court said in *Russell v. Russell:*[1]

> As a rule, persons enter into these contracts with the express view of keeping their quarrels from the public eyes, and of avoiding that discussion in public, which must be a painful one, and which might be an injury even to a successful party to the litigation, and most surely would be to the unsuccessful.

In other jurisdictions, there remain exceptions to the general theme of confidentiality for example in Australia, U.S., and Sweden. The Australian decision of *Esso Australia Resources v. Plowman*[2] is perhaps the most significant as it rejects an implied confidentiality but accepts the possibility of an express confidentiality. It accepts that arbitration is private in the sense that the public is not admitted to the proceedings, and that documents produced under compulsion are subject to a duty to be used solely for the purposes of the arbitration,[3] but all other aspects of confidentiality were rejected.[4] This was a significant decision from Australia's highest court. It is, however, not alone in common law jurisdictions. In *United States v. Panhandle Eastern Gen,*[5] a U.S. Federal District Court held that confidentiality does not necessarily attach to documents obtained in arbitration; on the facts the defendant was not entitled to withhold documents generated in a Swiss ICC arbitration.

---

[1] (1880) 14 Ch D 471, 474.

[2] [1995] 183 CLR 10.

[3] *See also* The Eastern Saga [1984] 2 Lloyd's Rep 373, 379: "The concept of private arbitrations derives simply from the fact that the parties have agreed to submit to arbitration particular disputes between them and only between them. It is implicit in this that strangers shall be excluded from the hearing and conduct of the arbitration and that neither the tribunal nor any of the parties can insist that the dispute shall be heard or determined concurrently with or even in consonance with any other dispute, however convenient that course may be to the party seeking it and however closely associated with each other the disputes in question may be."

[4] Institutional rules recognise the same privacy: LCIA §19.4; ICC §21.3; WIPO §53(c); UNCITRAL §25.4.

[5] 118 F.R.D. 346 (D. Del. 1988).

There is, however, some contrary authority in the U.S. from the Texas Court of Appeals in *Rutherfords v. Blanks*[6] concerning the confidentiality of the Arbitral Tribunal's deliberations.

In England, the thinking behind the implied obligation of confidentiality is influenced by the corresponding court rule that a party may only use a document disclosed for the purposes of the proceedings in which it has been disclosed.[7] As it is a matter of the implied agreement of the parties, it must logically follow that disputes as to any limits of the obligation are a matter for the arbitral tribunal rather than national courts provided, of course, that the tribunal remains constituted.[8]

The Australian Court's reasoning was followed in the Swedish case of *Bulgarian Foreign Trade Bank v. A.I. Trade Finance*[9] in which a party's right to disclose information about the arbitration was recognised and there was held to be a distinction between a mutual understanding of confidentiality and a legal duty of confidentiality:

> The real meaning of [the secrecy associated with arbitration proceedings], as compared with judicial proceedings, is instead that the proceedings are obviously not public, i.e., that the public does not have a right of insight by being present at the hearing or having access to documents . . . a party in arbitration proceedings cannot be deemed to be bound by a duty of confidentiality unless the parties have concluded a separate agreement . . . .

On the contrary, English law is tolerably clear that arbitration is inherently confidential. Indeed, this is one of the reasons for the popularity of English law in arbitration agreements. As the English Court of Appeal described it in *Dolling–Baker v. Merrett:*[10]

> As between parties to an arbitration, although the proceedings are consensual and may thus be regarded as wholly voluntary, their very nature is such that there must . . . be some implied obligation on both parties not to disclose or use for any other

---

[6] No. 04-95-00770-CV, 1996 Tex. App. LEXIS 2578 (Texas Ct. App. June 28, 1996).

[7] The current rule is Civil Procedure Rule 31.22.

[8] Michael Wilson v. Emmott, [2008] 1 Lloyd's Rep 616.

[9] Swedish Supreme Court, 27 October 2000, Case No T 1881/99 *reproduced in* 2 Stockholm Arbitration Report 137 (2000).

[10] [1990] 1 WLR 1205, 1213.

purpose any documents prepared for and used in the arbitration, or disclosed or used in the arbitration, or transcripts or notes of the evidence in the arbitration or the award—and indeed not to disclose in any other way what evidence had been given by any witness in the arbitration—save with the consent of the other party, or pursuant to an order or leave of the court.

These very limited exceptions to the rule were reaffirmed in *Ali Shipping Corp v. Shipyard Trogir*[11] as being; i) consent; ii) order, or leave, of the court, and additionally; iii) necessity to protect legitimate interests of the arbitrating party vis-à-vis a third party.[12] These exceptions were accepted and acknowledged in *Michael Wilson v. Emmott*[13] (and extending it to the public interest or interests of justice) and largely mirrors the duties in a banker-customer relationship: *Tournier v. National Provincial and Union Bank of England.*[14]

The confidentiality extends to preventing strangers from inspecting the court file to discover the contents of confidential arbitration documents unless there are overriding "interests of justice" that require disclosure.[15] This body of English case law has been considered of doubtful assistance where there was an express provision of confidentiality as, in that event, it was that provision that took precedence over any implied duty.[16] The Privy Council in *Associated Electric* went further, however, and doubted the approach taken. It said the approach ran the risk of confusing privacy and confidentiality and failed to distinguish between the different types of confidentiality that might attach to different documents:

> Commercial arbitrations are essentially private proceedings and unlike litigation in public courts do not place anything in the public domain. This may mean that the implied restrictions on

---

[11] [1999] 1 WLR 314 (it arises as a matter of law); *id.* at 326.

[12] This may include the establishment or protection of an arbitrating party's rights against a third party or defending a claim by a third party. Hassneh Insurance Co of Israel v. Mew, [1993] 2 Lloyd's Rep 243.

[13] [2008] 1 Lloyd's Rep 616.

[14] [1924] 1 KB 461 (CA).

[15] Glidepath BV v. John Thompson, [2005] 2 Lloyd's Rep 549.

[16] Associated Electric & Gas Insurance Services v. European Reinsurance Company of Zurich, [2003] 1 WLR 1041.

the use of material obtained in arbitration proceedings may have a greater impact than those applying in litigation. But when it comes to the award, the same logic cannot be applied. An award may have to be referred to for accounting purposes or for the purpose of legal proceedings . . . Generalisations and the formulation of detailed implied terms are not appropriate . . . [17]

This oblique reference to a greater and public interest was also considered in *London & Leeds Estates v. Paribas (No 2)*[18] but note that institutional rules generally provide for the award to be confidential.[19]

The public interest exception was recognised in *Esso Australia Resources v. Plowman.*[20] Some of the judges in *Esso* also drew on the banker-customer exception to like effect, and another Australian court held that an arbitrator had no power to prevent the government from disclosing material to state agencies provided that doing so was in the public interest.[21]

The confidentiality (or at least potential confidentiality) of arbitration was recognised to extend to subsequent court proceedings in *Department of Economic Policy and Development of the City of Moscow v. Bankers Trust.*[22] The court stated:

The courts when called upon to exercise the supervisory role assigned to them under Arbitration Act 1996 are acting as a branch of the state, not as a mere extension of the consensual arbitral process. Nevertheless, they are acting in the public interest to facilitate the fairness and well-being of a consensual method of dispute resolution, and both the rule committee and the courts can still take into account the parties' expectations regarding privacy and confidentiality when agreeing to arbitrate.

The court distinguished between matters requiring permission to appeal, such as appeals on points of law under §69 where the public

---

[17] *Id.* at 1050.

[18] [1995] 1 EGLR 102.

[19] LCIA §30.1; ICC §28.2; WIPO §75, and: UNCITRAL §32.5.

[20] Op. cit.

[21] Commonwealth of Australia v. Cockatoo Dockyard Pty Ltd, [1995] 36 NSWLR 662.

[22] [2004] 4 All ER 746.

interest outweighs the parties' desire for continuing privacy, and other arbitration claims where the starting point is reversed. The particular issue in *Bankers Trust* was the publication of the judgment. The Court of Appeal upheld the judge's decision not to permit publication but did allow a summary. The general rule remains that the arbitral proceedings are themselves private but where appeals to the national courts are concerned, there is a necessary (but limited) relaxation of that principle.

French case law also recognises the confidentiality of arbitration. The most often cited example is *Aita v. Ojjeh*[23] wherein the very bringing of a challenge to the court was held to violate the confidentiality. Similarly, the New Zealand Arbitration Act 1996 (§14) expressly incorporates a wide confidentiality provision.

Although there are differing views on the confidentiality of arbitration, most institutional rules that address it likewise respect the confidentiality,[24] even the Australian decision recognises the inherent confidentiality of all documents produced under compulsion within the arbitration. Nevertheless, it remains a wise precaution to agree an express confidentiality provision, especially for documents produced. This should be done either in the terms of reference or the first procedural order. Some institutional rules specifically provide for this, for example, Article 3(12) of the IBA Rules provides that all documents produced pursuant to the IBA Rules are confidential to the Arbitral Tribunal and the parties and that they are to be used only in connection with the arbitration.

Whether or not the confidentiality is expressed or implied, it remains a fact of life that policing confidentiality is extremely difficult. Any threatened or actual breach of the confidentiality is best countered promptly with an application for an injunction to restrain the threatened breach (or any further breach) and an allied claim for damages. An extreme example, especially if a breach by the Arbitral Tribunal itself, may merit irregularity in the award itself.

---

[23] Cour d'appel, Paris, 18 February 1986, 1986 REV. ARB. 583.

[24] LCIA §30.1 (". . . the parties undertake . . . to keep confidential . . . all materials in the proceedings . . ."); Swiss Rules §43.1 (". . . the parties undertake . . . to keep confidential . . . all materials submitted by another party . . ."); WIPO§74(a) (" . . . any documentary or other evidence . . . shall be treated as confidential . . .") but the ICC Rules and UNCITRAL are silent.

CHAPTER 21
ENFORCEMENT OF DISCOVERY BY ASSISTANCE FROM NATIONAL COURTS

The possibility that the Arbitral Tribunal might draw an unspecified inference may be little comfort in the face of (at least a perception of) a wholesale disregard by one party of the Arbitral Tribunal's procedural order on discovery.

If a party is unhappy with the other party's (non)compliance with orders on discovery, the first step for an aggrieved party is to apply back to the Arbitral Tribunal for a further order. It is unlikely that a party will have given no discovery whatsoever; rather, the argument is more likely to be over the limited extent of the discovery. A simple refusal to give any discovery is unlikely to justify immediate recourse to the national courts by the aggrieved party. Instead, an order for the discovery of specific documents should be sought from the Tribunal. At some stage, it may be appropriate for the Arbitral Tribunal to make a peremptory order for discovery. A peremptory order is one with a defined time period for compliance and is final in its terms—although it need not be final in the sense that an award is final, rather it is a final opportunity for a party to comply. It is when that fails to elicit the required documents that the aggrieved party—or possibly the Arbitral Tribunal—needs to look elsewhere.

National courts of the seat of the arbitration often act in aid of arbitrations. Article 27 of the UNCITRAL Model Law provides:

> The arbitral tribunal or a party with the approval of the arbitral tribunal may request from a competent court of this State assistance in taking evidence. The court may execute this request within its competence and according to its rules on taking evidence.

National laws make specific provision, for example, §42 of the Arbitration Act 1996 permits the English court to make an order requiring a party to comply with a peremptory order of the Arbitral Tribunal. The parties can, however, contract out of the right to seek court enforcement. The jurisdiction under §42 can only be exercised where the court is satisfied that the applicant has exhausted "any available arbitral process" in respect of the failure to comply. Although it could be argued

111

that the drawing of adverse inferences is an "available arbitral process", that is not a correct understanding of the section. §41(7) gives statutory backing to the power to draw adverse inferences, and if that were a sufficient "available arbitral process," it would remove much of the purpose of §42. On the contrary, the drawing of adverse inferences is not a "process" rather it is a power for non-compliance.

In some cases, it may be preferable to request the Arbitral Tribunal make a final interim award on discovery in order to aid enforcement, especially overseas. That may, however, be unnecessary. It is clear that whatever terminology, the Arbitral Tribunal may use to describe its decision, the courts will look at the substance of the decision rather than the label used. The Paris Court of Appeal's decision in *Braspetro Oil Services v. The Management and Implementation Authority of the Great Man-Made River Project*[1] makes it clear that

> The qualification of [a decision as an] award does not depend on the terms used by the arbitrators . . . This reasoned decision—by which the arbitrators considered the contradictory theories of the parties . . . and solved, in a final manner, the dispute . . . and thereby ending the dispute submitted to them—appears to be an exercise of its jurisdictional power . . . notwithstanding its qualification as an "order" . . . the decision . . . is thus indeed an award.

The French decision was plainly correct and the decision was plainly a final award. The application of similar reasoning has applied the same logic to orders for the production of documents, albeit that the production was the substantive relied sought and not merely procedural. The decision of the U.S. Court of Appeals for the Seventh Circuit in *Publicis Communications and Publicis SA v. True North Communications Inc*[2] concerned an unreasoned "order" to disclose certain documents. The Court held that the essential finality for recognition or enforcement was present, and held:

> Although Publicis suggests that our ruling will cause the international arbitration earth to quake and mountains crumble, resolving this case actually requires determining only whether

---

[1] Paris Cour d'Appel 1/7/99, *reproduced in* 14(9) INT'L. ARB. REP. at Sec. D. (1999).

[2] 206 F.3d 725, 728 - 9 (7th Cir. 2000).

this particular order by this particular arbitration tribunal regarding these [documents] was final. The tribunal's order resolved the dispute, or was supposed to, at any rate. . . . A ruling on a discreet, time sensitive issue may well be final and ripe for confirmation even though other claims remain to be addressed by arbitrators.

Although these decisions may give some comfort, the better course is not to seek to enforce procedural orders directly and, rather, to seek the assistance of national courts. That being said, national courts are generally reluctant to interfere with the party autonomy. As the court stated in *Anangel Peace Compania Naviera SA v. Bacchus International Commerce Corporation:*[3]

. . . although arbitrators have an overriding duty to act fairly as between the parties in all matters before them regarding the conduct of proceedings, basically they are the masters of their own procedure.

The court will act in aid of the reference but not usurp the functions of the Arbitral Tribunal therefore not substitute its own view for that of the arbitrators but will assist in enforcing the findings of the Arbitral Tribunal.

---

[3] [1981] 1 Lloyd's Rep 452, 453-4.

CHAPTER 22
DATA PROTECTION AND DISCOVERY

Data protection and discovery are not happy bedfellows; discovery is the disclosure of data under compulsion whereas data protection is intended to prevent such disclosure. The underlying legal principles of both are often in conflict in the context of commercial arbitration in the U.S. and in the Member States of the European Union. In this regard, neither the disclosure nor discovery rules of the U.S. and European courts have been harmonised with data protection laws. This often places in a dilemma companies that are doing business in the U.S., especially European companies doing business in the U.S. or that have their parent company, a subsidiary, or an affiliate in the U.S. because they are forced to either comply with compulsory discovery/ disclosure obligations or protect their employee's and customer's data.) The problem is not so acute for discovery given by U.S. companies as the U.S. does not have comprehensive data protection legislation. Although a signatory to the 1981 OECD Guidelines, the U.S. has not implemented them domestically. Instead, a sectoral approach, with a mix of legislation, regulation and self-regulation, is utilised. The introduction of European Directive 95/46/EC could have therefore restricted the ability of U.S. organisations to engage in transactions with their European counterparts, for it prohibited the transfer of personal data to non EU states that do not meet the "adequacy" standard for the protection of privacy.

As a result of this, the U.S. Department of Commerce developed the "safe harbour" system in consultation with the European Commission. This offers a method by which U.S. organisation can comply with the Directive. The EU approved "safe harbour" in July 2000. Organisations that sign up to the scheme are certified as offering "adequate" protection under the terms of the Directive, thus enabling transactions between those organisations and European organisations to proceed smoothly and within the law.

The U.S. Department of Commerce Safe Harbour website provides:

The decision by U.S. organizations to enter the safe harbor is entirely voluntary. Organizations that decide to participate in the safe harbor must comply with the safe harbor's requirements and publicly declare that they do so. To be assured of safe harbor benefits, an organization needs to self certify annually to the

Department of Commerce in writing that it agrees to adhere to the safe harbor's requirements, which includes elements such as notice, choice, access, and enforcement. It must also state in its published privacy policy statement that it adheres to the safe harbor. The Department of Commerce will maintain a list of all organizations that file self certification letters and make both the list and the self certification letters publicly available. To qualify for the safe harbor, an organization can (1) join a self-regulatory privacy program that adheres to the safe harbor's requirements; or (2) develop its own self regulatory privacy policy that conforms to the safe harbor.

Organisations seeking to adhere to the safe harbour requirements must comply with seven safe harbour principles: Notice, choice, onward transfer, access, security, data integrity, and enforcement.[1] Enforcement of safe harbour is carried out primarily by the private sector. Private sector self regulation and enforcement is backed up as required by government enforcement of the federal and state unfair and deceptive statutes. This ensures that safe harbour is backed by the force of law.

Recent amendments to U.S. pre-trial discovery procedures require the responding party to search for and produce electronically stored information (ESI) regardless of where that information is stored within the corporate information technology infrastructure. Often, ESI stored within with a facility located in, for example, an EU Member State may be subject to discovery in the U.S.

Under European Data Protection Directive 95/46/EC, "personal data" is any information relating to an identified or identifiable natural person; "processing" of personal data includes the disclosure of personal data by transfer to a third party. Responsive electronic files and e-mails (including electronic files attached to e-mails) may contain personal data. An example would be responsive e-mails that contain personal data relating to the responding party's customers. The Directive further restricts the transfer to any non-EU state that does not afford the same privacy protections as an EU Member State. In this regard, the United States is expressly recognised as a country that does not afford such protections.

---

[1] *See* Safe Harbor website, available at http://www.export.gov/safeHarbor/.

Unfortunately, the laws and regulations surrounding when and how data can be transferred to the United States remain a web of confusion with no necessarily clear answers. There are, however, certain best practices that should be followed when transferring "personal data" to the United States for the purposes of discovery.

First, personal data may generally be transferred if the data subject—e.g., the customer—has given its unambiguous prior consent. It is, however, uncommon to ask for the consent to a disclosure for discovery purposes in advance.

Second, data transfer may also be permitted if the legitimate interests of the responding party prevail. This "balancing of interests" necessarily leaves the responding party with the uncertainty whether the national data protection authorities, if becoming aware of the data transfer, will actually find that the responding party's legitimate interest in defending its rights in an international commercial arbitration outweighs the conflicting interests of the data subjects.

Third, even if the personal data can be transferred in principle, a transfer is justified under Article 26(2)(d) Data Protection Directive only if "the transfer is necessary or legally required ... for the establishment, exercise or defence of legal claims." Interestingly, however, the "Article 29 Working Party," an advisory board composed of the national data protection authorities of each EU Member State, claims in its "Working document on a common interpretation of Article 26(1) of Directive 95/46/EC" of 25 November 2005 that the exception of Article 26(2)(d) "can only be applied if the rules governing . . . this type of international situation have been complied with, notably as they derive from the provisions of the Hague Conventions of 18 March 1970 ('Taking of Evidence' Convention) . . ." As a consequence, the transfer of electronic files and e-mails to the United States in compliance with the Hague Convention would become particularly burdensome in most Member States. Moreover, Member States like Germany have declared that they will not execute Letters of Request under the Hague Convention that were "issued for the purpose of obtaining pre-trial discovery of documents as known in Common Law countries."

Fourth, transfer could also take place under the guise of a "safe harbour" or "binding corporate contract." Corporations that have implemented privacy policies consistent with the Data Protection Directive are permitted, in exchange, to transfer the data to the United States.

Finally, it is within an Arbitral Tribunal's discretion to order discovery even if the responding party is forced to infringe European data protection law although the Tribunal should be slow to order the infringement of this, or indeed any, law. When ordered, this places the company in a difficult position of having to violate the EU Directive or face potential sanctions before the Arbitral Tribunal.

In order to address the conflicting obligations regarding discovery and data protection, the parties can take several practical steps. Generally speaking, whereas U.S. companies are likely to have implemented strict data retention policies that require the erasure of backup data once they are no longer required, their European affiliates might still take a rather more lax approach. For companies with a transatlantic business focus, it is therefore worth developing uniform, worldwide data retention policies that limit the amount of unnecessarily stored data.

Strategically speaking, the data protection laws of the EU Member States also offer various opportunities to avoid, limit, or delay the discovery of unfavourable data stored in Europe. Some U.S. courts are alert to objections against discovery requests if the requested party would be in violation of EU data protection laws. In *Volkswagen v. Valdez*,[2] the Texas Supreme Court reversed a decision that required Volkswagen to produce its corporate phone book as, in order to do so, Volkswagen would be in violation of German data protection law.

The responding party should also make sure that a protective order is included in any order for disclosure that contains language that allows the redaction of non-responsive personal data in electronic documents of European origin that are otherwise responsive. The dissemination of responsive personal data by the requesting party should be explicitly limited, if not prohibited, under the protective order. A specimen order is at appendix 20.

Finally, if companies with operations in the United States, would be well advised to secure a "safe harbour" or "binding corporate contract" status that would allow the transfer of data to the United States consistent with the EU data protection laws.

---

[2] 909 S.W.2d 900 (Tex. 1995).

CHAPTER 23
FOREIGN LANGUAGES AND TRANSLATIONS

The very nature of the international aspects of international arbitration results in documents often being in more than one language. It is convenient to refer to languages other than the language of the arbitration as "foreign" in the same manner that laws other than those of the seat of the arbitration are "foreign." Many practitioners and parties in international arbitration are conversant in more than one language but there will inevitably be differing standards of linguistic skill and, hence, differing understandings of a document. For this reason it is invariably sensible to have foreign language documents translated into a common language (invariably the language of the arbitration). If a party wants an additional translation into the mother tongue of the party, it can do so at its own expense.

As translation is not a science, there is inevitably the potential to have disputes as to the accuracy of a translation, especially in respect to translations of technical documents, those written in colloquial terms, or those that use terms of art. Arbitral Tribunals are aware of the potential for such disputes to take undue prominence. A pragmatic solution is that the parties agree on a translator and/or that the Arbitral Tribunal seek its own translation as required, especially if the expertise of the Tribunal does not extend to resolving disputed translations.

Appendix 21 is a sample order on how an Arbitral Tribunal might deal with documents in foreign languages.

CHAPTER 24
DOCUMENTS FOR IMPEACHMENT

Rule 26 of the Federal Rules of Civil Procedure permits a party to withhold documents to be used solely for impeachment. This is a peculiar feature of U.S. discovery and is not replicated in, for example, English discovery. The prevailing view is that it has no place in international commercial arbitration.

Arbitration should be conducted in an efficient and economical manner with the parties treated with equality and being entitled to know the evidence that other parties intend to rely upon. The concept of documentary ambush is repugnant to these ideals. Certainly, the English courts have recognised this. In 1988, it was thought permissible to retain documents for impeachment purposes,[1] however, this practice changed in 1994[2] in favour of the "cards on the table" approach in favour of requiring discovery even where there was reason to believe that the evidence would be adjusted to take account of the impeachment evidence.

None of the institutional rules permit withholding of impeachment documents and, on the contrary, the rules invariably have the reference expressly or impliedly to "all" or "any" documents either relied upon or relevant. This "cards-on-the-table" approach is also consistent with Preamble 4 to the IBA Rules: "The taking of evidence shall be conducted on the principle that each Party shall be entitled to know, reasonably in advance of any Evidentiary Hearing, the evidence on which the other Parties rely." It is difficult to see how withholding documents for impeachment accords with that principle.

In the event that a party suspects that another party is withholding impeachment documents, it would be wise to flush this out with a request to produce any documents intended to be relied upon for impeachment purposes. The requested party must either discover them or withhold them (if the Arbitral Tribunal permits), but the argument as to whether the Arbitral Tribunal should permit withholding may indicate the nature of the documents intended to be used.

---

[1] McGuiness v. Kellogg [1988] 1 WLR 913.

[2] Khan v. Armaguard [1994] 1 WLR 1204.

A pragmatic solution is to order that documents that have not been disclosed cannot be relied upon without the consent of the Arbitral Tribunal. The probative value of the document and the impeachment can then be assessed, as can the cynicism of the withholding. Equally, if raised, the Arbitral Tribunal can make a specific direction in an early procedural order.

Merely to reflect the U.S. practice of withholding documents for impeachment (rather than condoning the practice), the sample order at Appendix 12 provides for the non-discovery and withholding of impeachment documents. That provision does not appear in Appendices 13 and 14.

CHAPTER 25
CONTINUING DUTY OF DISCOVERY

In common law jurisdictions discovery is widely recognised as a "continuing obligation." The same would apply in civil law jurisdictions: if a document that came to light post-discovery is perceived to be relevant and a party wanted to rely upon it, it would and should be discovered albeit late (subject always to the right of the Arbitral Tribunal to exclude late evidence).

Article 3(10) of the IBA Rules recognises this concept that something relevant may come to light after the original round of discovery but equally seeks to prevent abuse by permitting additional disclosure after documents produced by another party, witness statements, expert reports or the submissions of another party only within a defined time period.

In practical terms the Arbitral Tribunal is likely to permit discovery even at a late stage in the proceedings, provided it is not unfair to one of the parties. This fairness test will usually be answered by whether the recipient of the discovery has sufficient time to deal with the documents discovered late, not only in terms of time to consider them but also to address the issues raised by the documents. If sufficient time is available the fact that the documents were late by reference to a procedural order or institutional rule is likely to be overlooked. The probative value outweighs the procedural breach. If insufficient time is available the receiving party may be forced to seek an adjournment of the evidentiary hearing. Usually, unless there are powerful reasons to the contrary, the Arbitral Tribunal is likely to give a short adjournment to allow for the material to be considered. It is only in the most extreme cases that the new documents are likely to be excluded completely. It is, however, well recognised that busy arbitrators cannot re-convene in the same way as the judges of national courts. They have other international commitments and many have busy practices outside arbitration whereas judges are usually full-time and can, to some extent, manage the court diary. If late discovery led to a request for a lengthy adjournment because a party could not properly consider and address the documents, the Arbitral Tribunal would be faced with the difficult decision of balancing the evils of a further delay in justice as against the inherent unfairness of not admitting all the evidence that a party wishes to rely upon. It is likely that the Arbitral Tribunal's decision will depend upon the particular facts of the dispute in question.

CHAPTER 26
ELECTRONIC DOCUMENTS

It is well recognised that the vast majority of documents are now held electronically rather than in paper form. Electronic documents include emails, word processing files, databases web pages, and text or sms messages. The tendency to copy many recipients to an email message, for example, considerably increases the volume of electronic documents and the ability to store them relatively cheaply and easily without physical storage space results in many more documents being kept than might have been the case with paper copies. In equivalent paper storage the volumes are nearly beyond comprehension.[1] The use of electronic communication distinguishes it from paper documents. Much electronic communication is a substitute for face-to-face meetings or telephone calls. It can often be very informal and hence of quite different "look-and-feel" to paper documents. Finally, there is permanence to electronic communication that does not exist in face-to-face meetings or telephone calls. The issues are not, however, new. The English High Court recognised that electronic documents would be within the scope of discovery in 1975.[2] The Federal Rules of Civil Procedure have included electronic documents since 1993.

The location of paper documents is relatively easy. There will typically be a master file and whilst individuals working on a team may have "shadow files" nearly all the paper will be in the main project file(s). In contrast, electronic data can be more widespread. The ability to forward and copy creates many different storage locations: A sends an email to B copied to C and D. C forwards his copy to E who in turn forwards it to F who replies to A and so the chain can continue. If the original message is retained in the body of the email, the traffic will be apparent but some organisations (anxious to maintain their environmental credentials—lest it has to be printed out) omit the text of

---

[1] The most basic measurement of computer data is a "byte." A byte is made up of 8 bits. A bit is a binary digit: "0" or "1." A byte typically represents a number or letter. 1,024 bytes equal a "kilobyte;" 1,048,576 bytes equal a "megabyte" (something like 500 typewritten pages); 1,073,741,824 bytes equal a "gigabyte" (something like 500,000 typewritten pages) and 1,099,511,627,776 bytes equal a "terabyte" (something like 500 billion typewritten pages). A CD-ROM with 650 MB capacity could hold 325,000 typewritten pages and a modern laptop with 200GB capacity 100 million pages. In considering e-disclosure these volumes of data should be kept in mind.

[2] Grant v. Southwestern and County Properties Ltd [1975] Ch 185.

an email being replied to. In a complex exchange, this can cause issues of tying together a chain of emails. Moreover, it creates a wide circle of custodians: people who hold data and those who do hold data may do so in many different ways. An email could be initially stored on a PC, laptop, or blackberry (or all three) and, thereafter, be backed-up on servers and storage tapes, often off-site.

The proliferation of emails and their storage gives them a degree of permanency. If the A sends an email to B, copied to C and himself, A may delete it from his inbox but it will remain in his sent items, if he deletes it from there it will remain on the memory of the computer unless and until overwritten and even then computer forensic specialists can retrieve the information either from the PC itself by using special tools or from back-up tapes. Even if it is truly deleted by A, both B and C will have copies. To this extent, the final eradication of data is rare—it will, in all probability, reside somewhere in some form.

This permanence is to be contrasted with the ability to change documents. Most obviously, word processed documents can be edited and the text changed. Some IT systems have routine automatic deletion to free up server space and back-up tapes are kept only for relatively short periods after which they too are overwritten.

These and other issues present unique problems for dealing with e-documents and taking a snapshot of a computer system or preventing an automatic deletion policy being (further) implemented may be impractical.

The attitude of the courts in respect to the fundamental difference between paper and electronic documents was illustrated in *Byers v. Illinois State Police*:[3]

> Computer files, including e-mails, are discoverable . . . However, the court is not persuaded by the plaintiffs' attempt to equate traditional paper-based discovery with the discovery of e-mail files . . . Chief among these differences is the sheer volume of electronic information. E-mails have replaced other forms of communication besides just paper-based communication. Many informal messages that were previously relayed by telephone or at the water cooler are now sent by e-mail. Additionally,

---

[3] 53 Fed. R. Serve. 3d 740 (N. D. Ill. 2002). This was cited with approval in the English case of Digicel v. Cable & Wireless [2008] EWHC 2522 (Ch).

computers have the ability to capture several copies (or drafts) of the same e-mail, thus multiplying the volume of documents. All of these e-mails must be scanned for both relevance and privilege. Also, unlike paper-based discovery, archived e-mails typically lack a coherent filing system. Moreover, data archival systems commonly store information on magnetic tapes which have become obsolete. Thus, parties incur additional costs in translating the data from the tapes into useable form.

In both the U.S. and England, the definition of "documents" in the national courts clearly encompasses electronic documents. For example, Rule 34(a) of the Federal Rules of Civil Procedure 2007 acknowledges that "document" extends to information in electronic format.

The English Civil Procedure Rules provides a broad definition of "document," including "anything in which information of any description is recorded." The Practice Direction that supplements the definition continues:

This extends to electronic documents, including e-mail and other electronic communications, word processed documents and databases. In addition to documents that are readily accessible from computer systems and other electronic devices and media, the definition covers those documents that are stored on servers and back-up systems and electronic documents that have been "deleted". It also extends to additional information stored and associated with electronic documents known as metadata.

Article 1 of the IBA Rules defines a document as "a writing of any kind, whether recorded on paper, electronic means ... or any other mechanical or electronic means of storing or recording information." This wide definition is likely to encompass most, if not all, of the records that fall within the above-mentioned definition in the English Civil Procedure Rules.

Accordingly, it could not be clearer that when giving discovery; electronic discovery will play a large part and it will be sensible either for the parties to reach agreement as to the extent of e-discovery or to seek an early ruling from the Arbitral Tribunal.

Before embarking on a more detailed review of some aspects of nuances of e-disclosure, an acknowledgement of the considerable work in this area undertaken by the Sedona conference needs to be made.

The Sedona Principles and Glossary are invaluable to a better understanding of the issues.[4]

Practice will inevitably vary with experience of e-disclosure. The US system has been codified in the Federal Rules of Civil Procedure 2007. It directs that the topic be addressed early in the case. Specifically, parties must disclose the electronic documents they have and where they are stored,[5] and they must confer and discuss how to deal with electronic documents and their preservation.[6] Similar provisions are to be found in the English rules of procedure albeit expressed in different language. The Practice Direction to Part 31 of the Civil Procedure has a new paragraph 2A that re-emphasises the wide definition of document and has a "meet and confer" type provision[7] and that the parties should cooperate as to the format of production.

The Advisory Committee Notes to the Federal Rules of Civil Procedure 2007 encourage the parties to address the form of any production of electronic documents. Electronic documents can be printed and reproduced in paper or supplied electronically. If the latter it can be produced in native format (being the manner in which it was originally stored) or it a "PDF"[8] or "TIFF"[9] image. Both have advantages. Native format generally carries with it metadata. This is, in essence, information about information. It can provide a great deal of information about a document. As the guide to U.S. federal judges describes it:

> Metadata, which most computer users will never see, provide information about an electronic file, such as the date it was

---

[4] The documents are available at http://www.thesedonaconference.org.

[5] Rule 26(a)(1)(B).

[6] Rule 26(f)(3): if documents are destroyed there may be sanctions for doing so although Rule 37(f) creates a relief against sanctions where destruction is a "result of the routine, good-faith operation of an electronic information system." The key issues are likely to be when the duty to preserve arose (which could, of course, be well before a reference is commenced) and the extent of that duty (which will in turn depend on what is known of the dispute, who the relevant custodians might be and what data might be relevant). The Sedona Principles acknowledge that a perfect system of preservation may be impossible. Reasonable, good faith efforts should be sufficient in the vast majority of cases.

[7] The parties should discuss issues of preserving and searching for electronic data before the first case management conference.

[8] Portable Document Format.

[9] Tagged Image File Format.

created, its author, when and by whom it was edited, what edits were made, and in the case of an email, the history of its transmission.[10]

For this reason, a producing party will often be reticent to produce in native format. Production in PDF or TIFF is generally accepted. It gives the advantage of being susceptible to Bates Numbering[11] and it may have some metadata attached to the file. It will not permit the image to be manipulated.

The Guidance to Arbitrators published by the ICDR concerning Exchanges of Information permits the producing party to produce electronic documents in the form "most convenient and economical for it . . . unless there is a compelling need for access to the documents in a different form".

In the U.S. Federal Rules of Civil Procedure, the (sensible) distinction is drawn between "reasonably accessible" and "not reasonably accessible" documents. The primary obligation is to produce from reasonably accessible documents. A party does not have to produce from documents that are not "reasonably accessible because of undue burden or cost."[12] The undue burden or cost can be "trumped" by "good cause" but then that can be subject to conditions the most usual of which is that the requesting rather than the producing party bear the cost of production.[13] It is another instance of balancing need and cost and there can be no definitive answer that it will always be appropriate to act in one way or another.[14]

---

[10] Managing Discovery of Electronic Information: A Pocket Guide for Judges (2007), available at http://www.uscourts.gov/rules/eldscpkt.pdf.

[11] Bates Numbering is a system of numbering or coding documents as they are scanned.

[12] Rule 26(b)(2)(B).

[13] Although doing so does not relieve the producing party from considering the material for relevance and privilege which may well be a considerable burden in itself.

[14] For examples of courts on both sides of the Atlantic grappling with these issues, *see, e.g.,* the U.S. court case Bullis v. Nichols, 2005 WL 1838634 (W.D. Wash. Aug. 1, 2005)(in which the court refused to order the production of email on the basis that it would entail the production of 166,000 emails); and the English case, Marlton v. Tectronix UK Holdings [2003] EWHC 383 (in which the court held that what might be reasonable in one case might not be in another).

The leading case in this area in the U.S. is *Zubulake* v. *UBS Warburg*.[15] *Zubulake* identified five categories of data accessibility and, hence, the burden of production.[16] The Sedona principles likewise distinguish between accessible and inaccessible data. In assessing the balance between need and cost, the Advisory Committee Notes on the Federal Rules lists seven helpful factors to bear in mind:

(1) The specificity of the discovery request;

(2) The quantity of information available from other more readily accessible sources;

(3) The failure to produce relevant information that seems likely to have existed but is no longer available either at all or on readily accessible sources;

(4) The likelihood of finding relevant material that cannot be obtained from other readily accessible sources;

(5) The perceived importance and usefulness of the information sought;

(6) The importance of the issues at stake in the litigation, and;

(7) The parties' resources.

These are sensible guidelines and, suitably adapted, should be adopted by arbitral tribunals facing these issues. Again the English Civil Procedure Rules have a balancing exercise in assessing what is a reasonable search. The non-exhaustive list of matters that may be relevant as to the extent of a reasonable search are:[17]

---

[15] The various rounds of the litigation being reported at 217 F.R.D. 309 (S.D.N.Y. 2003), 229 F.R.D. 422 (S.D.N.Y. 2004), 220 F.R.D. 212 (S.D.N.Y. 2003) 216 F.R.D. 280 (S.D.N.Y. 2003).

[16] Those categories include: (1) active, online data accessed on a day-to-day basis; (2) "near-line" data stored on optical or magnetic disks capable of being accessed automatically or by computerised means; (3) "offline storage archives" such as those included in category (2) above but where manual intervention is required to access the data; (4) "back-up tapes" which, because they mirror the computer structure, are unlikely to be organised for ease of searching, and; (5) "erased, fragmented or damaged data" that can only be retrieved by significant processing.

[17] CPR 31 PD 2A.4.

(a) The number of documents involved.

(b) The nature and complexity of the proceedings.

(c) The ease and expense of retrieval of any particular document. This includes:

    (i) The accessibility of electronic documents or data including e-mail communications on computer systems, servers, back-up systems and other electronic devices or media that may contain such documents taking into account alterations or developments in hardware or software systems used by the disclosing party and/or available to enable access to such documents.

    (ii) The location of relevant electronic documents, data, computer systems, servers, back-up systems and other electronic devices or media that may contain such documents.

    (iii) The likelihood of locating relevant data.

    (iv) The cost of recovering any electronic documents.

    (v) The cost of disclosing and providing inspection of any relevant electronic documents.

    (vi) The likelihood that electronic documents will be materially altered in the course of recovery, disclosure or inspection.

(d) The significance of any document which is likely to be located during the search.

The enormous bulk of the electronic material that is likely to be disclosed and the limitations of the human eye—especially that of the weary paralegal late at night—to pick up every privileged document results in a significant risk that a privileged item may slip through undetected. In consequence the U.S. Federal Rules of Civil Procedure has special rules[18] to claw-back privileged material that has been inadvertently disclosed in the process of e-discovery

At a practical level, the vast bulk of data that may require to be considered can be significantly reduced by running the population

---

[18] Rule 26(b)(5)(B).

131

through a filter of "keyword searches"[19] and de-duplication.[20] With the huge volumes of data now stored as email, it is often an unreasonably onerous task to manually review each document. In consequence, the discovery review is commonly limited by keyword searches. This filters out those documents <u>not</u> having one or more of the keywords present by allowing, through the filter, those that have one or more of the keywords. This can be an invaluable aid to a sensible, cost-effective, and proportionate approach to discovery. However, running keyword searches over a large database can still be expensive and consequently it is advisable to agree on keyword lists as much as possible, or at least be able to demonstrate that a fair and reasonable approach has been taken to performing the search. It is also important to consider, and if necessary to agree, on whether the search will extend to metadata and/or deleted items (or other categories of non-active data), since these sources of information can often be extremely revealing. *Digicel v. Cable & Wireless*[21] is an example of the court grappling with keyword searches.

If there are serious issues but the burden and cost appear high, the arbitral tribunal may wish to consider a partial disclosure. An example of this is illustrated in *Zubulake v. UBS Warburg*,[22] a case involving an issue over the restoration of seventy-seven back-up tapes. The court ordered a sample of five tapes to be restored to assess the evidential value of the material and the cost of doing so. Similarly, in *Flexsys Americas LP v. Kumho Tire USA Inc,*[23] the court was faced with the issue of whether the plaintiff should produce documents relating to one custodian or from every employee. The court ordered production from ten custodians of the defendant's choice. In *Digicel v. Cable &*

---

[19] Keyword searches are expressly recognised in the Practice Direction to the English Civil Procedure Rules Part 31 (paragraph 2.A.5): "It may be reasonable to search some or all of the parties' electronic storage systems. In some circumstances, it may be reasonable to search for electronic documents by means of keyword searches (agreed as far as possible between the parties) even where a full review of each and every document would be unreasonable. There may be other forms of electronic search that may be appropriate in particular circumstances."

[20] Some studies show that effective filtering techniques by custodian, time and date, file size, keywords and de-duplication can reduce the number of documents to be reviewed by up to 75%.

[21] [2008] EWHC 2522 (Ch).

[22] 216 F.R.D. 280 (S.D.N.Y. 2003).

[23] 1:05-CV-156, 2006 WL 3526794 (N.D. Ohio Dec. 6, 2006).

Wireless,[24] the court ordered the restoration of back-up tapes sufficient to search the email accounts of seven individuals and, because of the difficulty of identifying the accounts, the parties were directed to "meet and confer" and, thereafter, the lawyer for the party responsible for the restoration was to report progress every 10 days or so to the other lawyer.

The IBA Rules—applied with varying degrees of flexibility and rigidity—should be sufficient to deal with most applications and issues that an arbitral tribunal is called upon to determine relating to e-disclosure. They have stood the test of time as a benchmark for "paper" disclosure and can be sufficiently applied to electronic documents albeit that they do not specifically address electronic documents beyond including electronic documents within the definition of "document."

The starting point of the application of the IBA Rules to e-disclosure is to recognise that they seek to manage the tensions between common and civil law jurisdictions. As has already been mentioned, the IBA Rules include within the definition of document electronic documents.[25] Article 3 provides for Requests to Produce[26] and there is no reason why such a Request cannot be in respect of electronic documents. A disputed Request to Produce is resolved by, among other things, the application of the Article 9.2 criteria.[27] These criteria include an "unreasonable burden to produce"[28] and "considerations of fairness or equality of the Parties that the Arbitral Tribunal determines to be compelling."[29] This gives the arbitral tribunal a wide discretion such that the tribunal can, and no doubt would, consider similar matters to those in the Federal Rules of Civil Procedure and the Civil Procedure Rules. Furthermore, there seems no reason why, having had regard to the Article 9.2 criteria (and as necessary the Federal Rules of Civil Procedure and the Civil Procedure Rules guidance), the arbitral tribunal could not, for example, direct keyword searches and otherwise restrict the scope of the discovery of

---

[24] *Supra*, n.21.

[25] Article 1 defines "document" as including writing stored by electronic means. The use of "writing" does not fit well with images or audio files, still less metadata. A wider definition of electronically-stored information might be preferable but unless and until there is any amendment to the IBA Rules, it is doubtful that this will cause any real difficulties as arbitral tribunals will, as ever, take a robust common sense approach.

[26] Article 3.2.

[27] Article 3.6.

[28] Article 9.2(c).

[29] Article 9.2(g).

electronic data and hence reduce the time and cost of the production of such data. Similarly, the form of production is a matter the tribunal could deal with under wide procedural powers afforded to tribunals—e.g., Article 15 of the ICC Rules.

It has already been suggested earlier in this work that at the Preliminary Meeting parties should agree on how to address issues of electronic data. Arbitral tribunals will certainly encourage or even, where appropriate, direct parties to "meet and confer" over these issues.

Equally, issues of the burden of costs associated with electronic data can sometimes be dealt with under existing procedural tools. Costs capping (limiting the recoverable costs a party or the parties) and costs orders[30] can be made in some jurisdictions.

Finally, the obligation to preserve does not fit well with the IBA Rules. Article 9.4 enables adverse inferences to be drawn but that does not address the basic obligation to preserve. Articles 3.7 and 7 of the IBA Rules might be used to require production of, for example, a copy of the hard drive of a computer so as to ensure its continued existence. Alternatively, interim or conservatory measures—e.g., Article 23 of the ICC Rules—might be used to preserve data. The possibility of the tribunal making any such order would no doubt prompt sensible accommodations to be reached by the parties themselves. Generally, sanctions are likely to be a matter of near last resort; tribunals are likely to regard the "stick" of sanctions as a failure to encourage the parties by sufficient "carrot" to resolve such issues themselves.

In summary, whilst the IBA Rules do not specifically address the many issues that have arisen in electronic data discovery and have fallen behind the advances in the civil procedures in the domestic courts of the U.S. and England, they remain a framework that can be sufficiently adapted to cover most, if not all, situations. The over-codification of the IBA Rules or other procedural rules is not to be welcomed. Tribunals, educated as to the nuances and unique features of electronic data, can continue to do justice between the parties with existing tools.

Appendix 22 is a sample order an Arbitral Tribunal might make especially if electronic issues were perceived as a likely issue.

---

[30] Institutional rules may permit the making of costs orders at any stage e.g. ICC §31.2 & Stockholm §44 but others permit only costs orders in the award c.f. LCIA §28.3, SIAC §31 & AAA §31.

CHAPTER 27
LEGAL PROFESSIONAL PRIVILEGE: WHO AND WHAT IS COVERED?

International commercial arbitration has its own unique set of problems and this is nowhere more true than in relation to the legal advice privilege. International arbitration will often involve parties, witnesses, and documents from potentially a number of different countries, each having its own system of law. The same dispute may feature in related proceedings before the courts in a number of countries or arbitral tribunals with seats in different countries. This can give rise to complex problems as to the admissibility of evidence—on a jurisdiction-by-jurisdiction basis—of materials that may be susceptible to a claim to privilege in some countries but not in others. It is, therefore, critical to be aware of which communications will be protected by privilege.

A. Introduction to Privilege

Legal professional privilege (or attorney-client privilege and the work-product doctrine in the U.S.) is a rule that entitles a party, during the course of legal proceedings, to withhold from its opponent and from the court, evidence in whatever form, that is within the scope of the privilege.

Legal professional privilege itself is divided into two branches— "legal advice privilege" (broadly equivalent to attorney-client privilege) and "litigation privilege" (broadly equivalent to work-product doctrine). Broadly, the legal advice privilege covers confidential communications between a lawyer and his client made for the purpose of giving or receiving legal advice. On the other hand, the litigation privilege covers confidential communications made between a lawyer and a client or a third party for the dominant[1] purpose (or perhaps more simply "made in the relevant legal context"[2]) of being used in connection with actual or pending litigation. It can readily be seen that advice sought in connection with litigation may be covered by both advice privilege and litigation privilege.

---

[1] Waugh v. British Railways Board [1980] AC 521.

[2] Three Rivers District Council v. Governor and Company of the Bank of England (No. 6) [2005] 1 AC 610.

Although a privileged communication can be withheld from opponents and from the court in proceedings before English courts, or before arbitral tribunals where English law is applied, it does not follow that it will be accorded the same treatment in proceedings before a foreign court or a tribunal applying foreign law. Of course, there may well be similar, if not identical, rules applicable in the foreign court, particularly in Commonwealth and other countries whose legal system is common law based. However, wherever legal advice is given in circumstances where it might be relevant to potential proceedings before a foreign court, the client would be well advised to seek the guidance of a lawyer in the appropriate jurisdiction as to how that court will approach questions of legal professional privilege.

The approach of an Arbitral Tribunal applying English law is that all communications falling within the scope of legal professional privilege will be protected irrespective of how a foreign court would treat them. Whilst litigation privilege has been recognised for many centuries, legal advice privilege is relatively modern and was first recognised by Lord Brougham in *Greenough v. Gaskell*.[3] Lord Brougham described legal advice privilege as resting on principles founded on " . . . a regard to the interest of justice which cannot be upheld and to the administration of justice which cannot go on without the aid of men skilled in jurisprudence, in the practice of the court and in those matters which form the subject of all judicial proceedings. If the privilege did not exist at all everyone would be thrown upon his own resources: deprived of all professional assistance a man would not venture to consult any skilful person or would only dare to tell his counsel half his case." This general principle of privilege is extremely widely recognised there can be no legal system in the civilised world jurisdiction that does not recognise and enforce it.

The latest and most definitive English view has come from the House of Lords in *Three Rivers District Council v. Governor and Company of the Bank of England (No. 6).*[4] It is clear from this decision that the modern approach to privilege still rests on matters of principle such that attorney-client communications are treated differently from other confidential communications, for example, doctor-patient or priest-penitent communications. In these other areas, there is a balance to be

---

[3] (1833) 1 My & K 98, 103.

[4] [2005] 1 AC 610.

struck between the public and private interest in preserving confidences and the administration of justice requiring disclosure of confidential material. But in relation to lawyer and client, no such balancing act applies, since the policy decision is that privilege should provide confidentiality.

The extent of the legal advice privilege was considered in *Balabel v. Air India.*[5] Taylor LJ said that: "Legal advice is not confined to telling the client the law; it must include advice as to what should prudently and sensibly be done in the relevant legal context" and "to extend privilege without limit to all solicitor and client communications upon matters within the ordinary business of a solicitor and referable to that relationship [would be] too wide." This passage, approved by the House of Lords in *Three Rivers*, makes it clear that not all communications between solicitor and client are subject to legal advice privilege. The U.S. also recognises that not all advice from a lawyer is legal advice and that legal advice is an essential element of the attorney-client privilege.[6]

Lord Scott of Foscote explained how judges would approach marginal cases when deciding whether or not a communication attracted legal advice privilege. He said:

> The judge called upon to make the decision should ask whether the advice relates to the rights, liabilities, obligations or remedies of the client either under private law or under public law. If it does not, then, in my opinion, legal advice privilege would not apply. If it does so relate then, in my opinion, the judge should ask himself whether the communication falls within the policy underlying the justification for legal advice privilege in our law. Is the occasion on which the communication takes place and is the purpose for which it takes place such as to make it reasonable to expect the privilege to apply? The criteria must, in my opinion, be an objective one.[7]

The English approach to the legal advice privilege is recognised in many other common law jurisdictions. In *Upjohn Co v. United States,*[8]

---

[5] [1988] Ch 317, 330 – 1.

[6] United States v. United Shoe Mach. Corp., 89 F. Supp. 357, 359 (D. Mass. 1950).

[7] [2005] 1 AC 610, 651.

[8] 449 U.S. 383, 389 (1981).

Justice Rehnquist in the Supreme Court said that the purpose of legal professional privilege was "to encourage full and frank communication between attorneys and their clients and thereby promote broader public interests in the observance of law and administration of justice." He further stated that "[t]he privilege recognises that sound legal advice or advocacy serves public ends and that such advice or advocacy depends upon the lawyer's being fully informed by the client." Similar doctrines exist in Canada.[9]

In leading cases in Australia and New Zealand, the justification for a rule affording particular protection to confidential communications between lawyers and clients has been expressed on a broader policy basis than merely to ensure candour. In *Baker v. Campbell,*[10] a decision of the High Court of Australia, Murphy J said that "The client's legal privilege is essential for the orderly and dignified conduct of individual affairs in a social atmosphere which is being poisoned by official and unofficial eavesdropping and other invasions of privacy" and Wilson J said "In fostering the confidential relationship in which legal advice is given and received, common law is serving the ends of justice because it is facilitating the orderly arrangement of the client's affairs as a member of the community."

The Guidance to Arbitrators published by the ICDR concerning Exchanges of Information states that:

> The tribunal should respect applicable rules of privilege or professional ethics and other legal impediments. When the parties, their counsel or their documents would be subject under applicable law to different rules, the tribunal should to the extent possible apply the same rule to both sides, giving preference to the rule that provides the highest level of protection.

This may be a laudable approach but any Arbitral Tribunal should appreciate that it places equality of treatment over the strict legal approach to privilege that may well vary from country to country and party to party.

---

[9] Jones v. Smith [1999] 1 SCR 455.

[10] (1983) 153 CLR 52.

B. Qualification of the Lawyer

English law has long made it clear that the privilege is only available to communications with a lawyer who is properly qualified. As early as 1792, Buller J said in *Wilson v. Rastall,*[11] that "[t]he privilege is confined to the cases of Counsel, solicitor and attorney . . . I take the distinction to be now well settled, but the privilege extends to those three enumerated cases at all times, but that it is confined to these cases only." Similarly, Lord Brougham in *Greenough v. Gaskall* referred to "men skilled in jurisprudence" and to "professional assistance."[12] More recently, in *New Victoria Hospital v. Ryan,*[13] Tucker J said:

But there is a more fundamental reason for not affording privilege to these documents. That is because, in our opinion, the privilege should be strictly confined to legal advisors such as solicitors and Counsel, who are professionally qualified, who are members of professional bodies, who are subject to the rules and etiquette of their professions, and who owe a duty to the court. This is a clearly defined and easily identifiable qualification for the attachment of privilege. To extend the privilege to unqualified advisors such as personnel consultants is in our opinion unnecessary and undesirable."

The requirement of professional status was echoed by the Court of Appeal in the Australian case of *Vance v. Air Marshall McCormack in his capacity as Chief of Air Force*[14] in which the court found:

Admission to practice of itself carries with it an obligation to conform to the powers of the court to remove or suspend a legal practitioner for conduct that the court considers justifies such determination . . . The person whose name is on the roll of barristers, solicitors . . . is entitled to practise as a barrister and solicitor in any Territory unless suspended or disentitled by court order. The court has power to order that any person on the roll not be entitled to practise if that person is guilty of misconduct.

---

[11] (1792) 4 Durn & E 753.

[12] (1833) 1 My & K at 103.

[13] [1993] ICR 201, 203-4.

[14] [2004] ACTSC 78.

The person remains bound to uphold the standards of conduct and to observe the duties undertaken upon admission to the roll of practitioners. The holding of a practising certificate reinforces that regime and makes it more immediately applicable but the underlying obligations subsist, even if a current practising certificate is not held.

It is thus clear that it is the admission to a professional body with a right to practice as a professional within a system of discipline and ethics is the hallmark of the lawyer who may invoke the privilege with regard to communications. Communications with other persons who give legal advice and/or are named as legal advisers, but who do not fall within the control of a professional body, are highly unlikely to be protected by privilege.

If necessary, the court can embark on an enquiry to ascertain whether such disciplinary and ethical strictures exist and bind the foreign lawyer. As Crispin J said in *Kennedy v. Wallace*:[15]

> If an advisor is a lawyer admitted to practise in the foreign country, as was agreed here, it seems to me unnecessary to require evidence about legal and ethical practices and controls by foreign courts . . . The position may be different if the circumstances otherwise raise questions as to the position of the lawyer. There may be a question whether the advisor is a lawyer at all, properly understood.

It is clear, therefore, that where there is an undisputed admission to practice as a professional in a foreign jurisdiction, the court will generally accept, without further enquiry, that the appropriate system of discipline and ethics applies. However, where questions are raised or the advisor is not a professional admitted in the relevant jurisdiction to practice, the court may need to undertake a factual enquiry to assess the true position.

In the U.S., it appears that similar principles are applied. In *United States v. Kovel*,[16] it was held that the privilege attaches to communications with a non-lawyer provided they were made with a view

---

[15] [2004] FCAFC 337.

[16] 296 F.2d 918 (2nd Cir. 1961).

to legally advise. This would apply to non-lawyer employees of the lawyer (in *Kovel* it was an accountant) including clerks as well as anyone engaged at the behest of the lawyer such as an interpreter or doctor.

There are limited statutory exceptions in England that permit other professions to claim privilege, for example, trade mark agents and patent attorneys under sections 280 and 284 of the Copyright, Designs and Patents Act 1998. These statutory provisions set out the limited exceptions to the general principle that, for the purposes of a privilege to arise, the communication must be with a qualified lawyer. For example, it is clear that beyond the statutory concessions, patent attorneys have no privilege.[17]

However, it does not matter whether the lawyer is qualified in England or some other foreign jurisdiction. As was held in *Re Duncan*,[18] "The basis of the privilege is just as apt to cover foreign legal advisors as English lawyers, provided only that the relationship of lawyer and client subsists between them." In reaching this conclusion, the court drew upon *Lawrence v. Campbell*[19] in which it was said "A question has been raised as to whether the privilege in the present case is an English or a Scots privilege; but sitting in an English court, I can only apply the English rule as to privilege, but I think that the English rule as to privilege applies to a Scots solicitor and law agent practicing in London, and therefore the letters in question are privileged from production". Similarly, in *Bunbury v. Bunbury*[20] it was held that a case prepared for submission to a lawyer in Holland for his opinion was privileged.

Aldous J came to the same conclusion in the English case *International Business Machines and others v. Phoenix International Computers Limited*[21] when he said, "The nationality of the foreign lawyer is as irrelevant as his address for this purpose." The same appears to be the case in the U.S.[22]

---

[17] Wilden Pump Engineering Co v. Fusfield [1985] FSR 159.

[18] [1968] P 306, 311.

[19] (1859) 4 Drew 485, 491.

[20] (1839) 2 Beav 173.

[21] [1995] FSR 184, 199.

[22] In re Rivastigmine Patent Litigation, 237 F.R.D. 69, 74 (S.D.N.Y. 2006). The U.S. privilege law applies "if a communication with a foreign patent agent involves a U.S. patent application" but foreign privilege law applies if the communication involves a foreign patent application. *See also* In re Philip Servs. Corp Sec. Litigation, 2005 U.S. Dist LEXIS 22998 (S.D.N.Y. Oct. 7, 2005) and Renfield Corp v. E Remy Martin, 98 F.R.D. 442, 444 (D. Del. 1982).

In the U.S., each state has different rules on attorney-client privilege. Rule 501 of the Federal Rules of Evidence provides that the federal court will apply federal law if the claim is based on federal law, and state law if the claim is based on state law. Federal courts will apply the law of the state in which the document is "domiciled", which will normally result in the document being domiciled in the state to which it has the most significant relationship or the state that has the greatest interest in the document in issue. This will usually result in the applicable state law being either the law of the state where the communication took place or where the attorney-client relationship was centred. Both tests may render the same result.

Similarly, civil law jurisdictions tend to require a professional qualification before the privilege can be invoked.

C. In-House Lawyers

It will not matter whether the lawyer is employed in public or private practice, or is employed by a government or commercial organisation. As Lord Denning MR said in *Alfred Crompton Amusement Machines Limited v. Customs and Excise Commissioners (No. 2)*:[23]

> The law relating to discovery was developed by the Chancery Courts in the first half of the nineteenth century. At that time nearly all legal advisors were in independent practice on their own account. Nowadays it is very different. Many barristers and solicitors are employed as legal advisors, the whole time, by a single employer. Sometimes the employer is a great commercial concern. At other times, it is a government department or a local authority . . . In every case these legal advisors do legal work for their employer and for no one else. They are paid, not by fees for each piece of work but by a fixed annual salary. They are, no doubt, servants or agents of the employer . . . They are regarded by the law as in every respect in the same position as those who practice on their own account. The only difference is that they act for one client only, and not for several clients. They must uphold the same standards of honour and of etiquette. They are subject to the same duties to their client and to the court.

---

[23] [1972] 2 QB 102.

They must respect the same confidences. They and their clients have the same privileges.

The same principle applies in the U.S. In *United States v. United Shoe Machinery Corp,*[24] the court said that there were not " . . . sufficient differences to distinguish [house counsel and outside counsel] for purposes of the attorney-client privilege."

In-house lawyers are, however, treated differently in most civil law jurisdictions. They are generally not permitted to join the national bar association.[25] Knowledge held by in-house lawyers in these jurisdictions is more generally treated as a business secret rather than legally privileged information, so is protected but under a different regime. For example, in *Louis Vuitton Malletier v. Dooney & Bourke Inc,*[26] the U.S. District Court held that communications with a French in-house counsel were not privileged as there was no expectation of confidentiality. Care may need to be taken when legal advice is sought from such lawyers. It is clear that ultimately whether a successful privilege can be invoked may be a matter of chance. For example, the English in-house lawyer can be quite satisfied that his advice is privileged in a domestic environment but it would not be so privileged in a competition investigation by the European Commission.[27] That itself may be no particular cause for concern—but if, say, French law, itself not recognising the privilege of an in-house lawyer, was the same as English in disregarding the national law under which the advice may have been given and direct that in French proceedings the advice of the English in-house lawyer was not privileged in any proceedings where French law applied, the potential effect could be enormous and reach far outside competition investigations. The only safe route may be the use of external counsel in appropriate cases and the choice of the seat of the arbitration may have far reaching consequences.

---

[24] 68 F. Supp. at 360.

[25] *E.g.* Belgium, Greece, Italy, France, Lithuania, Latvia, the Czech Republic, Hungary, Sweden and Austria. This group (and Luxemburg and Finland) does not extend privilege to employed lawyers. However, the United Kingdom, Denmark, Ireland, Portugal, Spain, Germany and the Netherlands permit bar or law society membership (some subject to conditions).

[26] 2006 U.S. Dist LEXIS 87096 (S.D.N.Y. Nov. 30, 2006).

[27] Australian Mining and Smelting Europe Ltd v. Commission for the European Communities (155/79) [1983] QB 878 (ECJ) and Akzo Nobel Chemicals Ltd v. Commission for the European Communities [2008] Bus LR 348.

D. Legal Advice Required

It is equally important to recognise that the privilege will not attach to the communications of an in-house lawyer, just as a lawyer in private practice, who is not giving advice in the "relevant legal context". Taylor LJ commented in *Balabel v. Air India* that the privilege did not apply to an in-house lawyer's communications when he was performing a wholly executive function. Similarly, Lord Denning said in *Alfred Crompton*:

> It does sometimes happen that such a legal advisor does work for his employer in another capacity, perhaps of an executive nature. Their communications in that capacity would not be the subject of legal professional privilege. So the legal advisor must be scrupulous to make that distinction. Being a servant or agent too, he may be under more pressure from his client. So he must be careful to resist it. He must be as independent in the doing of right as any other legal advisor.[28]

The Court of Appeal of Australia in *Vance* made a similar comment:

> It seems to us that, where client legal privilege is claimed over documents produced by an in-house lawyer ... the question is whether the document would meet the statutory test of being a confidential document, that is to say, was it prepared in such circumstances that the person who prepared it was under an expressed or implied obligation not to disclose its contents, whether or not the obligation arises under law . . . Where the lawyer is employed real questions as to the nature of their role and duty may arise.[29]

The concept of legal rather than business advice is fairly universally recognised and certainly applies in England, the U.S., most common law jurisdictions, and some civil law jurisdictions such as Switzerland.

E. Waiver

It is a precondition to privilege that the documents in question are confidential. If confidentiality is lost, by, for example, publication in the

---

[28] [1972] 2 QB, at 129.

[29] [2005] ACTCA 35, at para. 24.

public domain, then privilege is lost. There can, however, be limited disclosure without waiving privilege.[30]

Sometimes privilege in a document is waived for a specific purpose, for example, a witness might have had a statement taken by both parties but was called to give evidence only by one. The other party will have its lawyers' notes of the interview and these would be privileged. If the witness said something contrary to the statement given to the other party it could produce the notes of the interview and suggest to the witness that the account given, as evidenced by the notes, was the true account of events. Once privilege is waived as to either part of a document or part of a file that partial waiver may waive the entirety of the document or file. As the court said in *Great Atlantic Insurance v. Home Insurance*:

> Once it is decided that the memorandum deals with only one subject matter, it seems to me that it might be or appear dangerous or misleading to allow the plaintiffs to disclose part of the memorandum and to assert privilege over the remainder. In the present case the suspicions . . . which have not unnaturally been aroused by the disclosure of part of the memorandum can only be justified or allayed by disclosing the whole.[31]

The party waiving privilege cannot "cherry pick"[32] what it wants to disclose. Any waiver is to be judged objectively and not subjectively.[33] Where a privileged document is disclosed and inspected by mistake the position is surprisingly complex. In the U.S. courts have come to different conclusions as to whether inadvertent disclosure constitutes a waiver. Compare *In re Sealed Case*,[34] where the privilege was held to have been waived by inadvertent disclosure, with *Aramony v. United Way of America*[35], where privilege was held not to have been waived. In England the position for litigation, or at least the principles, are clearly

---

[30] B v. Auckland District Law Society [2003] 2 AC 736, 761.

[31] [1981] 1 WLR 529, 536

[32] A phrase used in R v. Secretary of State for Transport Ex. p Factortame Ltd [1997] 9 Admin LR 591, 598 and *see also* Dunlop Slazenger International Ltd v. Joe Bloggs [2003] EWCA Civ 901, CA.

[33] *See* Great Atlantic, *supra*, and the Australian case Mann v. Carnell [1999] 201 CLR 1, 13.

[34] 877 F.2d 976 (D.C Cir. 1989).

[35] 969 F. Supp. 226, 235 (S.D.N.Y. 1997).

set out in *Al Fayed v. Commissioner of Police for the Metropolis* and these would give considerable guidance to a Tribunal considering such issues:

1) A party giving inspection of documents must decide before doing so what privileged documents he wishes to allow the other party to see and what he does not.

2) Although the privilege is that of the client and not the solicitor, a party clothes his solicitor with ostensible authority (if not implied or express authority) to waive privilege in respect of relevant documents.

3) A solicitor considering documents made available by the other party to litigation owes no duty of care to that party and is in general entitled to assume that any privilege which might otherwise have been claimed for such documents has been waived.

4) In these circumstances, where a party has given inspection of documents, including privileged documents which he has allowed the other party to inspect by mistake, it will in general be too late for him to claim privilege in order to attempt to correct the mistake by obtaining injunctive relief.

5) However, the court has jurisdiction to intervene to prevent the use of documents made available for inspection by mistake where justice requires, as for example in the case of inspection procured by fraud.

6) In the absence of fraud, all will depend upon the circumstances, but the court may grant an injunction if the documents have been made available for inspection as a result of an obvious mistake.

7) A mistake is likely to be held to be obvious and an injunction granted where the documents are received by a solicitor and:

   a) the solicitor appreciates that a mistake has been made before making some use of the documents; or

   b) it would be obvious to a reasonable solicitor in his position that a mistake has been made;

   c) and, in either case, there are no other circumstances which would make it unjust or inequitable to grant relief.

8) Where a solicitor gives detailed consideration to the question whether the documents have been made available for inspection by mistake and honestly concludes that they have not, that fact will be a relevant (and in many cases an important) pointer to the conclusion that it would not be obvious to the reasonable solicitor that a mistake had been made, but is not conclusive; the decision remains a matter for the court.

9) In both the cases identified in 7) a) and b) above there are many circumstances in which it may nevertheless be held to be inequitable or unjust to grant relief, but all will depend upon the particular circumstances.

10) Since the court is exercising an equitable jurisdiction, there are no rigid rules.[36]

F. Self-Incrimination

The privilege against self-incrimination may be invoked during civil proceedings, including arbitration, whenever there is a reasonable risk of possible future criminal prosecution. Although differing slightly in terms, the basic concept of such a privilege is recognised in both European civil law regimes and common law based systems. In the Commonwealth countries, the privilege is a common law or statutory defined principle, whilst in the U.S. it is enshrined in the constitution as the Fifth Amendment.

The risk of self-incrimination must be real and appreciable and not a mere remote possibility.[37] *Hoffman v. United States*[38] held that a witness response will be considered incriminatory when it furnishes a "link in the chain of evidence needed to prosecute" and, in *Emspak v. United States*,[39] the court referred to building on a "seemingly harmless answer" that might lead to a link to a crime.

The risk of prosecution must generally be within the national jurisdiction itself. In *Murphy v. Waterfront Commission*,[40] however, the

---

[36] [2002] EWCA Civ 780.

[37] R v. Boyes ,(1861) 121 ER 730.

[38] 341 U.S. 479 (1951).

[39] 349 U.S. 190 (1955).

[40] 378 U.S. 52 (1964).

Supreme Court held that the Fifth Amendment privilege had no internal jurisdictional limitation within the U.S. The privilege protected both the state witness at the federal level and a federal witness at the state level. This gave rise to claims to justify an extra-territorial reach but this was resolved by the Supreme Court in *United States v. Balsys*[41] which held that a witness could not invoke the Fifth Amendment with regard to a prosecution outside the U.S. This appears to be a universal view for those jurisdictions that have had to consider the point—the risk of prosecution must be within the jurisdiction.

The privilege distinguishes between "independent" and "compelled" evidence. The former is not susceptible to the privilege but the latter is. This has been recognised in England by *C plc v. P*[42] and *Re Westinghouse Uranium Contract*[43] where the House of Lords said " . . . the tendency to expose to a penalty would be increased if the documents in question were to be validated . . . by sworn evidence, as opposed to being, as they are now, pieces of paper found in a file." In *United States v. Hubbell*,[44] the Supreme Court referred to "the settled proposition that a person may be required to produce specific documents even though they contain incriminating assertions of fact or belief because the creation of those documents was not 'compelled' within the meaning of the [Fifth Amendment] privilege;" however, the Court went on to state that:

On the other hand, we have also made it clear that the act of producing documents in response to a subpoena may have a compelled testimonial aspect. We have held that "the act of production" itself may implicitly communicate "statements of fact". By "producing documents in compliance with a subpoena, the witness would admit that the papers existed, were in his possession or control, and were authentic" . . . The "compelled testimony" that is relevant in this case is not to be found in the contents of the documents produced in response to the subpoena. It is, rather, the testimony inherent in the act of producing the documents ... It was unquestionably necessary for respondent to make extensive use of "the contents of his own mind" in

---

[41] 524 U.S. 666 (1998).

[42] [2007] EWCA Civ 493.

[43] [1978] AC 547, 612.

[44] 530 U.S. 27, 35 (2000).

identifying the hundreds of documents responsive to the requests in the subpoena.[45]

Differing views exist in Australia[46] and Canada.[47]

The European view of whether the privilege is consistent with the Article 6 of the European Convention on Human Rights (the guarantee of a fair hearing) is demonstrated in *Saunders v. United Kingdom*[48] in which the European Court of Human Rights held that the privilege "does not extend to the use . . . of material which may be obtained from the accused through the use of compulsory powers but which has an existence independent of the will of the suspect . . . ." In other words, the ECHR has also recognised that the privilege does not extend to existing independent evidence.

Discovery remains a production under compulsion in proceedings before national courts. The position in arbitration is less clear in light of the consensual and voluntary nature of the process.[49] Accordingly, it is unclear whether the privilege can be invoked in arbitration. In many cases, it would seem inappropriate to invoke the privilege as it is not produced under compulsion in the same manner as proceedings before national courts but particularly strict rules or procedures may produce a contrary result.

Another facet of the rule against self-incrimination is the civil law notion that a party cannot be made to testify against his self-interest. This notion has the effect that civil law regimes do not generally consider that internal documents—e.g., internal communications between employees or officers of a party, not including a lawyer—have to be disclosed. One of the changes from the 1983 to 1999 IBA Rules was the removal of an exclusively external definition of the extent of discovery. The current position now permits any discovery—i.e., it includes internal documents—subject to the limits in Article 9(4).

---

[45] *Id.* at 36, 40, 43.

[46] Environment Protection Authority v. Caltex Refining Co Pty, (1992-3) 178 CLR 477.

[47] Thompson Newspapers v. Canada, (1990) 67 DLR (4th) 161.

[48] (1997) 23 EHRR 313, at para. 69.

[49] *See* Dolling Baker v. Merrett [1990] 1 WLR 1205.

G. Without Prejudice Privilege

It is now well-established that written or oral communications made as part of negotiations genuinely aimed at, but not resulting in, settlement of a dispute are not generally admissible in evidence in litigation (or arbitration) between the parties over that dispute. Those communications are described as "privileged." The underlying philosophy is that parties should be encouraged to settle their disputes without recourse to national courts or arbitration as appropriate. They should not be discouraged from doing so by the fear that whatever they might say could be used against them subsequently in a tribunal thereafter constituted to adjudicate the dispute.

The use of the words "without prejudice" may indicate whether the privilege attaches to the communications in question but it is not necessarily determinative of the issue.

The basis for the "without prejudice" rule is said to be part contract and part public policy. The contractual element arises from a notional implied agreement between the parties that what is said in negotiations cannot be used before the appropriate tribunal. The public policy element is also founded on encouraging parties to settle but not only prevents the usage of the communication before the appropriate tribunal but also prevents a party from having to produce the communication to another.

As between the parties to any negotiation, the position is quite clear. The communications are not admissible as evidence but nevertheless should be discovered (in contrast to other types of privilege). The right to discovery does not necessarily depend upon the admissibility of documents in evidence.[50] It follows that a note of a without prejudice conversation is properly discoverable.[51] There are sound policy reasons for discovery of without prejudice communications notwithstanding they are not admissible in evidence not least so that the management of the parties (which may be different at the time of the arbitration than at the time of the negotiation) and their counsel know the negotiations that have occurred and are on a level playing field for any submissions on costs and so as to be better informed on ongoing settlement attempts.

One key issue is whether the parties are in dispute or at least a sufficient dispute to trigger the privilege. The public policy

---

[50] O'Rourke v. Darbishire [1920] AC 581.

[51] Parry v. News Group Newspapers [1990] New LJ 1719.

considerations apply equally to communications before the arbitration has commenced to those during the currency of the arbitration. As Lord Mance said in *Bradford & Bingley plc v. Rashid*:[52]

> The existence of a dispute and of an attempt to compromise it are at the heart of the rule whereby evidence may be excluded . . . The rule does not of course depend upon disputants already being engaged in litigation. But there must as a matter of law be a real dispute capable of settlement in the sense of compromise . . . .

It follows that arbitration does not have to be proximity in time to the eventual arbitration provided there is proximity of the subject matter. The question is whether the parties did, or might reasonably, have contemplated arbitration if they did not agree.[53]

Greater issues arise on communications made for the purpose of settlement with other parties. For example, there may be a claim against three defendants and the claimant settles with two. Is the remaining defendant entitled to discovery of the settlement communications with the two that have settled? The leading English case is *Rush & Tompkins v. Greater London Council*[54] in which the House of Lords held that public policy protected negotiations from being disclosed to third parties:

> In multi-party litigation, it is not an infrequent experience that one party takes an unreasonably intransigent attitude that makes it extremely difficult to settle with him. . . . it would I think, place a serious fetter on negotiations between other parties if they knew that everything that passed between them would ultimately have to be revealed to the one obdurate litigant.[55]

But what if the communication is with a non-party? It could be the case that if one party to arbitration were unsuccessful, it would seek an indemnity from a non-party with whom it discusses the case and the strategy to adopt. Equally, a subsidiary may report or communicate with its holding company. Insofar as such communications take place with a

---

[52] [2006] 1 WLR 2066, 2091.

[53] Framlington v. Barnetson [2007] EWHC Civ 502.

[54] [1989] AC 1280, 1305.

[55] The same principle applies in Australia: Field v. Commissioner for Railways for NSW (1957) 99 CLR 285, 291.

view to better enabling a party to conduct the claim more effectively, or to better advise on it, they are likely to be privileged (legal advice or litigation privilege). Insofar as they attempt to settle they would be covered by the without prejudice privilege for the reasons given above.

Of course whether a document should be discovered at all will depend on the nature of the order made for discovery. If the order does encompass "without prejudice privilege" documents, it may be appropriate for a detailed statement of the privilege claimed so that the Arbitral Tribunal can rule on whether the privilege is properly claimed. This is unlikely to be relevant for litigation privilege (only the date such privilege first arose is likely to be relevant) but it may helpfully be set out in detail for without prejudice privilege (and also for legal advice privilege).

A possible variation or extension to the "without prejudice privilege" is the mediation privilege. The ill-formed concept is feeling its way in many jurisdictions. The Uniform Mediation Act has been enacted in a number of U.S. states.[56] The Act has clear provisions in §4 providing for privilege against discovery and the inadmissibility and non-discoverability of mediation documents. There are limited exceptions to the basic rule in §§5 and 6 but these would not surprise most practitioners.

The concept of a special mediation privilege was rejected in *Brown v. Rice and Patel*[57] in which the judge held that mediation is merely assisted negotiation and that the same rules on the admissibility of "without prejudice" evidence apply. This accepts that such evidence can be admissible to determine whether a concluded settlement was reached. This is an exception to the general rule. The other most likely reason that parties may wish to refer to evidence involving mediation is to address the question of costs. Generally, an Arbitral Tribunal should not investigate why mediation did not produce a settlement[58] or why mediation was refused.[59]

---

[56] District of Columbia, Illinois, Iowa, Nebraska, New Jersey, Ohio, South Dakota, Utah, Vermont and Washington.

[57] [2007] EWHC 625.

[58] Halsey v. Milton Keynes General NHS Trust [2004] 1 WLR 3002.

[59] Reed Executive PLC v. Reed Business Information [2004] EWCA Civ 887.

CHAPTER 28
NON-PARTY DISCOVERY

It will sometimes be the case that the documents in the hands of the parties may not tell the whole story and one or other party seeks documents belonging to another entity, which is not a party to the arbitration. Arbitration derives from an agreement between parties to submit disputes to the decision of arbitrators. By the very nature of seeking discovery from non-parties, they are not parties to the agreement to arbitrate and the authority to compel them to produce documents must derive from outside the arbitration agreement.

The difficulty in securing documentary evidence from reluctant overseas witnesses is well known in international arbitrations. The 1970 Hague Convention is not directly applicable to arbitrations but might be invoked indirectly as discussed below. Parties that wish to obtain evidence located overseas must invoke the judicial procedures available in the national courts—a process that can be expensive and time-consuming. The need to have some remedy is recognised by the IBA Rules that provide in Article 3(8) that a party may ask the Arbitral Tribunal to take whatever steps are available to obtain the documents sought. A similar provision exists as Article 4(10), whereby a party may ask the Arbitral Tribunal to take whatever steps are available to obtain the testimony of any witness. Additionally, in accordance with Article 4(11), the Arbitral Tribunal can order a party to provide or use its best endeavours to provide, a witness for testimony. However, instances of a Tribunal itself taking steps to obtain documents are rare.

The most accommodating jurisdiction for non-party discovery is, perhaps unsurprisingly, the U.S. Pursuant to 28 U.S.C. §1782, a court may grant discovery if: i) the target of the discovery "resides or is found" within the district; ii) the requesting party is a foreign or international tribunal or an "interested person" in the foreign proceeding, and; iii) the discovery is requested "for use in a proceeding in a foreign or international tribunal." It can thus be seen that the Tribunal itself, whilst capable of making the application, need not do so as any party is competent to make the application itself. Indeed, it seems almost inconceivable that the Tribunal would make the application in these circumstances.

Although both the U.S. Courts of Appeals for the Second and Fifth Circuits[1] held in 1999 that the statute did not extend to include arbitral tribunals, that position was doubted after the decision of the Supreme Court in *Intel Corp. v. Advanced Micro Devices Inc*[2] in 2004. *Intel* held that a federal district court could provide assistance to a complainant in European Commission competition proceedings. *Intel* also held that notwithstanding that §1782 does not require that the proceeding in a foreign tribunal actually had to be underway. It was sufficient that it be within "reasonable contemplation."

The District Court of New Jersey in *In re Oxus Gold PLC*[3] decided similarly. *Oxus Gold* distinguished rather than overtly disagreed with the previous cases from the Second and Fifth Circuits on the ground that it concerned a bilateral investment treaty signed by sovereign States. More recently, the position for commercial arbitration has been clarified by the decision of the Atlanta Federal Court in *In re Roz Trading Ltd.*[4] The court granted a motion seeking discovery in aid of a foreign commercial arbitration tribunal in Austria. The Atlanta court held that:

[a]lthough the Supreme Court in Intel did not address the precise issue of whether private arbitral panels are "tribunals" within the meaning of the statute, it provided sufficient guidance for this court to determine that arbitral panels convened by the [International Arbitration Centre of the Austrian Federal Economic Chamber] are "tribunals" within the statute's scope.

The Supreme Court in *Intel* noted a change in the legislative language from "in any judicial proceeding pending in any court in a foreign country" to "in a proceeding in a foreign or international tribunal" and held that "'tribunal' . . . includes . . . arbitral tribunals . . . as well as conventional . . . courts."[5] Although an appeal against *Roz Trading* was dismissed, it was on the basis that it was not a final and

---

[1] *See* Nat'l Broad. Co. Inc v. Bear Stearns & Co Inc., 165 F.3d 184 (2d Cir. 1999) (which held that §1782 covered governmental or intergovernmental arbitral tribunals, conventional courts, and state-sponsored adjudicatory bodies) and Rep. of Kazakhstan v. Beidermann Int'l, 168 F.3d 880 (5th Cir. 1999), respectively.

[2] 542 U.S. 241 (2004).

[3] 2006 WL 2927615 (D.N.J. Oct 11, 2006).

[4] 469 F. Supp. 2d 1221, 1224 (N.D.Ga. 2006).

[5] 542 U.S. at 248-49.

binding decision because it envisaged further proceedings on the scope of the production. Any substantive appeal has to await the substantive decisions on the extent of discovery. In any event, we can expect an ongoing attempt to use §1782 in aid of foreign arbitrations.[6]

§1782 remains a discretionary weapon as the Supreme Court made clear in *Intel*. It *"authorizes, but does not require, discovery assistance . . ."*.[7] The court, in exercising the discretion, can grant relief conditional upon a reciprocal exchange of information and the foreign tribunal can place conditions on its acceptance to maintain parity between the parties.[8]

If §1782 is for any reason unavailable, there are certain U.S. states that have enacted either the Uniform Interstate and International Procedural Act or the Uniform Foreign Deposition Act. Pennsylvania has enacted the former and New York the latter. As a result, both states have granted motions in aid of foreign international arbitrations.[9] Equally, Rule 27 of the Federal Rules of Civil Procedure has also been used to obtain evidence.[10] Additionally, the United States Federal Arbitration Act 1925, §7 provides that the Tribunal may summon a person before them and produce material documents. A non-party ordered to produce documents will have been able to argue before the Tribunal whether that is appropriate and, it would appear, is also able to have that exercise of discretion reviewed by the state courts.[11]

---

[6] Several successful attempts have been made. *See* In re Hallmark Cap. Corp., 534 F. Supp. 2d 951, 958 (D. Minn. 2007) (discovery in aid of an Israeli arbitration); In re Babcock Borsig AG, 2008 WL 4748208 (D. Mass. Oct. 30, 2008) (discovery in aid of an ICC with a seat in Dusseldorf) and Comision Ejecutiva Hidroelectrica del Rio Lempa v. Nejapa Power Co LLC, 2008 WL 4809035 (D. Del. Oct. 14. 2008), but the Third Circuit has recently followed the Fifth Circuit, holding that private tribunals were not within §1782: Comision Ejecutiva Hidroelectrica del Rio Lempa v. El Paso Corp., 2008 WL 5070119 (S.D. Tex. Nov. 20, 2008).

[7] Intel, *supra* n.5, at 266.

[8] Euromepa SA v. R. Esmerian *Inc*, 51 F. 3d 1095, cited with approval in *Intel*.

[9] Quijada v. Unifruiti, 12 Pa. D. & C. 4th 225 (1991) and Hendler & Murray v. Lambert, 511 N.Y.S. 2d 941 (N.Y. App. Div. 1987), respectively.

[10] Deiulemar Compagnia di Navigacione SpA MV v. Allegra v. Pacific Eternity SA, Golden Union Shipping, 198 F.3d 473 (9th Cir. 1999).

[11] Matter of Daniel L. Berglund v. Arthroscopic Laser Surgery Ctr of San Diego, LP (July 18, 2008; DJDAR 10967).

Opting to obtain documents at the final evidentiary hearing runs the risk that, if the content of the documents is not known, the documents could prove to be adverse, sufficiently complex, voluminous or equivocal and proper use cannot be made of them. In the same way that inter discovery between the parties is often only useful if it is provided significantly before the evidentiary hearing, documents from third parties is likewise only of full value if obtained before, rather than at, the evidentiary hearing. §7 has been successfully used for obtaining pre-hearing discovery in the Fourth and Eighth Circuits but only if there is a "special need or hardship"[12] (Fourth Circuit) or if the non-party is "intricately related to the parties involved in the arbitration"[13] (Eighth Circuit). The Third Circuit appears to permit document production if a witness is compelled to attend and produce the documents as a "hearing" is not limited to final evidentiary hearings but can cover a variety of preliminary hearings[14] and this approach seems to be shared by the Second Circuit.[15] Thus the precise situation of the arbitral seat within the U.S. may be determinative of non-party discovery. A still further layer of complexity derives from state law, if the parties have agreed (they will rarely do so), that that shall govern the arbitration.[16]

There is nothing, so far as an English court is concerned, necessarily improper in commencing proceedings in another jurisdiction solely for the purposes of garnering evidence for use in English proceedings. In *South Carolina Insurance v. Assurantie Maatschappij "de Zeven Provincien"*[17] the House of Lords held that it was for a party to gather evidence as it saw fit provided it was lawful in the country where the gathering was attempted. Those courts—in this case, the U.S. courts—would be the ones to decide whether to allow the proceedings. This is consistent with the Supreme Court in *Intel* rejecting the notion that

---

[12] Comsat Corp v. Nat'l Sci. Found., 190 F.3d 269, 271 (4th Cir. 1999).

[13] In re Sec. Life Ins Co of Am., 228 F.3d 865 870-1 (8th Cir. 2000).

[14] Hay Group Inc v. EBS Acquisition Corp, 360 F 3d 404, 407-411 (3rd Cir. 2004).

[15] Life Receivables Trust v. Syndicate 102 at Lloyds of London, 549 F. 3d 210 (2d Cir. Nov. 25 2008).

[16] For example, Florida Stat. §684.15: "The arbitral tribunal may issue subpoenas or other demands for the attendance of witnesses or for the production of books, records, documents, and other evidence, may administer oaths, may order depositions to be taken or other discovery obtained, without regard to the place where the witness or other evidence is located . . ."

[17] [1987] A.C. 24.

§1782 required that, documents should only be discovered, if the foreign jurisdiction would be able to order the production of them:

> A foreign nation may limit discovery within its domain for reasons peculiar to its own legal practices, culture, or traditions—reasons that do not necessarily signal objection to aid from United States federal courts . . . When the foreign tribunal would readily accept relevant information discovered in the United States, application of a foreign-discoverability rule would be senseless.[18]

However, if the foreign proceedings are considered to have been issued oppressively, the English courts will prevent such undue pressure. For example, in *Omega Holdings v. Kozeny*,[19] the English court issued an injunction restraining U.S. proceedings which sought to depose witnesses in circumstances in which the same witnesses were due to tender witness statements and attend for cross-examination in the English proceedings. The English court held that such depositions would allow double cross-examination and create unnecessary duplication and that it would be unconscionable to allow the depositions to continue.

The position of aid given under English law is less clear. The statute that might be thought to be the logical starting point — the Evidence (Proceedings in Other Jurisdictions) Act 1975—refers, in §1, to requests "by or on behalf of a court or tribunal . . . exercising jurisdiction . . . outside the United Kingdom." The English court in *Commerce and Industry Co of Canada v. Certain Underwriters at Lloyds of London*[20] held that these words did not extend to private tribunals, so it appears that the legislation does not apply to normal international commercial arbitration.[21] In any event, any request made under the Evidence Act 1975 has to be made by the Arbitral Tribunal itself, rather than the parties and many Tribunals would not wish to become involved especially given the costs regime that exists in England where the loser pays.

---

[18] 542 U.S. at 244.

[19] [2002] C.L.R. 132.

[20] [2002] 1 WLR 1323.

[21] It may be possible for a party to foreign litigation (i.e. outside the UK) to obtain documents generated in an arbitration with its seat in the UK under this Act: Rio Tinto Zinc Corporation v. Westinghouse Electric Corporation [1978] AC 547, 633.

Nevertheless, in this case, the court decided that jurisdiction does exist under the Arbitration Act 1996. §44 provides for the court to have the same powers in relation to arbitral proceedings as it does for proceedings before a court in England in relation to a number of listed items. There is no reference to discovery but there is a reference to the "taking of the evidence of witnesses . . . ." An application under §44 should be made by one of the parties and not by the arbitral tribunal (see §44(4)) and, indeed, it can only be made with the agreement of all other parties or the permission of the Tribunal.

The powers of the court under §44 are not limited to arbitrations pending in England[22] as §2(3) expressly extends the ambit of §44 to arbitrations with a seat outside of the England but preserves a discretion such that the court need not exercise the powers if it considers it inappropriate to do so. §2(3) marked a change from the previous statute and the common law that prevented English courts acting in aid of an arbitration with a seat outside England. Furthermore, it is clear from §44(5) that the court will only act if the Tribunal is unable to do so and the *lex arbitri* is unable to assist in granting the same relief.

Applications under these provisions have been attempted in England. On the facts, in *Commerce and Industry* itself the court declined to assist the New York tribunal. It did so on two grounds. First, on the ground that the procedure under the curial law of having depositions as a pre-condition to giving oral evidence differed too far from English procedure. The examination that the Tribunal sought from the English court was akin to a pre-trial deposition but the witnesses would still have to attend to give oral evidence for that evidence to be admitted in the arbitration. The court held that the examination appeared to be merely aimed at finding out whether evidence existed to support a case. That kind of fishing exercise was alien to English procedure and hence the court was not willing to sanction it. Second, there was insufficient material to show that the witnesses would have an important bearing on the issues that the Tribunal had to decide.

It is clear, therefore, that the English courts have jurisdiction to aid foreign tribunals and clearly better evidence could be marshalled on another application so as to have better prospects of success. The more difficult issue will be where the relevant procedures under the curial law, or at least the procedure adopted by the Tribunal, differ from those of

---

[22] Strictly, England, Wales, and Northern Ireland.

England. With careful planning there seems no reason in principle why, if the examination would stand as the substantive evidence, the jurisdiction under §44 could not be used effectively.

Subsequently, an attempt was made in *BNP Paribas v. Deloitte & Touche*[23] to use §43 of the Arbitration Act 1996 to seek an order that a non-party give disclosure. BNP was in arbitration with Avis concerning the price it paid for a group of companies. BNP alleged that Avis had falsely represented the value of the companies. By way of defence, Avis relied on the fact that Deloitte had audited the accounts. BNP sought, with the support of the Arbitral Tribunal, discovery of what amounted to a very wide description of Deloitte's working papers for the relevant accounts. §43 permits a court to aid an arbitration by securing the attendance of witnesses and such witnesses can be required to produce documents. However, English jurisprudence is clear that whilst a witness can be compelled to produce specific documents (albeit compendiously described) he cannot be compelled to produce a class of documents. In *BNP* the court held the request was, in effect, for a class of documents and it refused the application. Careful consideration, therefore, needs to be given to the question of what documents are being sought from the non-party.

Although the applicants failed in both *Commerce and Industry* and *BNP*, the applicant in *The Tasman Spirit*[24] had more success and secured an order under both §43 and §44 against a non-party for the inspection and copying of specified documents and the attendance of a witness with documents at the evidentiary hearing. Again the court stressed the need for specific identification of the documents but it is clear that a narrow and focussed approach can succeed. However, success comes at a price; English courts will expect an applicant to meet the third party's costs of both the application and compliance with it.

The narrow and focussed requirement to document requests against non-parties in England derives from the "mere witness" rule. The "mere witness" rule provides that discovery cannot be obtained from a person against whom there is no independent cause of action and who could be subpoenaed to attend the trial. Nevertheless, there is an intermediate category of bystander without whose "action ... the [wrongdoing] could never have been committed." In these circumstances, the English courts

---

[23] [2004] 1 Lloyds Rep 233.

[24] [2005] 1 Lloyds Rep 525.

permit a wider discovery—indeed "full information" under the rule in *Norwich Pharmacal v. Commissioners of Customs and Excise.*[25] This permits pieces of the jigsaw (indeed the final piece) to be obtained to complete the cause of action. This could be used against a bank through which money was laundered, government departments who might have import records (as was the case in *Norwich Pharmacal*) or could be used to discover the identity of a corporate mole. The key feature is the relationship between the non-party against whom discovery is sought and the wrongdoer. Thus, newspapers that innocently published incorrect details on a proposed takeover had a sufficient relationship with those who wished to manipulate the market in the shares by disseminating the incorrect document, for discovery to be given against them.[26] As the decision in *Norwich Pharmacal* relied on a somewhat obscure decision of the Massachusetts Supreme Court in *Post v. Toledo Cincinnati and St Louis Railroad Co*[27] so it would appear similar jurisdiction exists in the U.S. Equally, it is available in Jersey[28] and the availability of such jurisdiction in the off-shore financial centres can be vital to gather evidence of wrongdoing where the proceeds are sheltered off-shore.

An Arbitral Tribunal seated in Switzerland may approach a competent national court to assist in compelling a witness to give testimony under the Swiss Private International Law Act 1987 Article 184(2). The Swiss Act makes no reference to the production of documents but it seems that used in conjunction with the Hague Convention—permitting a party to request documents from a witness— the Swiss court, pursuant to a request from the Arbitral Tribunal, could issue a letter of request to a foreign court to subpoena a witness and produce documents if the foreign court could do so for its internal proceedings using Article 10 of the Convention. Furthermore, Article 51 of the Federal Act on the Federal Civil Procedure Rules 1976 provides that third parties are obliged to provide the court with documents they possess.

---

[25] [1974] AC 133.

[26] Interbrew SA v. Financial Times [2002] 1 Lloyds Rep 542.

[27] 11 N. E. 540 (Mass. 1887).

[28] Macdoel v. Federal Republic of Brazil [2007] JCA 069.

CHAPTER 29
BUNDLES

All of the work that goes into discovery may be wasted if the relevant material cannot be presented carefully and logically to the Arbitral Tribunal. It is suggested that discovery should not normally be presented to the Arbitral Tribunal at the time it is produced. By doing so, a party runs the risk that the Tribunal, being overcome with an enormous quantity of material, cannot sensibly consider it all, much of which might subsequently be found irrelevant. Very considerable cost might be incurred without benefit to the parties. It is preferable for the parties to exchange material and decide what ought to be presented to the Arbitral Tribunal as a "common bundle" suitably before any evidentiary hearing. Clearly in cases of very modest amounts of material, simultaneous transmission to the Arbitral Tribunal might be efficient but the practice of annexing significant documents to the memorials, pleadings, or statements of case will give the Arbitral Tribunal an insight into the key documents and their relevance to the issues in dispute.

Considerable skill goes into the agreement of "common bundles" and the organisation, pagination, and production of bundles—especially those that avoid duplication. An Arbitral Tribunal functions far more effectively—and perhaps can only function properly—if members of the Arbitral Tribunal, counsel, and witnesses all have good common bundles. Colour-coding (to show the origin of a document as being from one of the parties), Bates numbering—i.e., with a prefix or suffix to identify the party that disclosed the document—and similar methods of identification can be important in document-heavy arbitrations. Core bundles containing the key documents can also be useful.

Lest there be any confusion over the status of "common bundles", it can be appropriate for the Arbitral Tribunal to make clear the status that the bundle has in terms of whether the documents are merely accepted as accurate copies or whether there is any wider understanding of their meaning, admissibility and the weight that should be attributed to them. Under strict rules of evidence, it may be necessary to prove that letters and other communications were sent. The preferable route is to assume everything is a proper copy of what it purports to be and which was sent and received in the usual course of the type of communication unless otherwise shown. Appendix 23 is a sample order that an Arbitral Tribunal might make to avoid ambiguity and issues on the consequences of "agreed" bundles.

CHAPTER 30
WITNESS STATEMENTS

Most Arbitral Tribunals will be motivated to ensure that the oral stages of the reference and, in particular, the evidentiary hearings are as limited as possible. Typically much more than two weeks is unusual. In order to achieve this, there has to be economy in dealing with each witness. This is usually achieved by each witness making a statement—and occasionally, in addition, a statement in reply—and examination-in-chief or direct examination being limited to confirming name and address, position and status and confirmation that the statement is true. In some instances, somewhere between a few and thirty minutes will also be spent in either bringing out key issues or examining a witness on the evidence of the opposing party.[1] Similarly, cross-examination is usually relatively brief—no more than a couple of hours. This is either expressly or impliedly on the basis that, contrary to some rules in national courts, if the positive case is not put to the opposing witnesses in cross-examination the evidence of that witness is treated as admitted.

The IBA Rules on the Taking of Evidence in International Commercial Arbitration (1999) has detailed rules for such statements.[2]

Witness statements are invariably drafted by counsel from instructions from the witness and that is widely accepted, indeed, the IBA Rules make this clear as do the LCIA Rules. Equally, it is permissible to assist witnesses to testify with confidence; indeed, there are a number of commercial organisations that train witnesses to testify. They do so using specimen facts rather than the facts of any particular case. The same procedure can be used to assist witnesses in effectively recalling key facts. What is generally regarded as impermissible is to coach a witness as to what to say and how to say it. Clearly counsel who planned with a witness to mislead the Arbitral Tribunal would not serve the interests of his client but would also risk severe sanctions.

The most persuasive witness evidence is that tested under cross-examination and notwithstanding able cross-examination, holds up well.

---

[1] This will be along the lines of "You have seen what Mr A, the managing director of B, says in paragraph C of his statement – do you agree with that? And if not, why not?"

[2] There is also much good practice in the International Institute for Conflict Prevention and Resolution's Protocol on Disclosure of Documents and Presentation of Witnesses in Commercial Arbitration available to download at www.cpradr.org.

Equally, evidence that is corroborated, ideally by contemporaneous documentary evidence, or by another witness, is better then uncorroborated evidence. With this in mind, the careful drafting of witness statements having full regard to the documents disclosed is an important function of counsel. If there is a corroborating document, refer to it in the witness statement.

Whilst the IBA Rules stipulate what must be included in the statement —e.g., formalities such as name and address, relationship with any of the parties, background, qualifications and experience, an affirmation of truth and signature and date—there is little guide as to how statements should be drafted. The IBA Rules provide for:

> . . . a full and detailed description of the facts, and the source of the witness's information as to those facts, sufficient to serve as that witness's evidence in the matter in dispute . . . .

Good practice dictates the following guidelines for drafting witness statements:

- The statement should have the heading of the reference as for the written pleadings.

- The name and address of the witness should be given. It is quite permissible to use the business address of the witness where he is giving evidence in the capacity as an officer or employee of a company including a party. If a witness has, for example, retired and does not wish to give his home address a practical solution is to say "*of London, England and for the purposes of this reference care of [address of counsel for the party calling that witness]*." At some stage, the Arbitral Tribunal may have to be invited to rule on whether the address should be disclosed. Provided some reasonable grounds are made out—e.g., fear of reprisal— the Tribunal is likely to accept a non-specific address.

- The statement should be drafted in the first person singular: "*I am the managing director of the claimant . . .*" "*On [date] I met Mr B of the respondent and we discussed . . .*".

- Documents should be referred to where they support the evidence being given. Usually the documents should be bundled and either attached or served separately but with the statement. The bundle should have page numbers so that the witness can refer at the beginning to the bundle: *"Served with this statement is a bundle of documents that I refer to and marked "A". References to pages are to pages of this bundle."* In the main text of the statement, the witness might refer to the bundle in this way: *"On [date] I met Mr B of the respondent and we discussed . . . my note of that meeting is at pages [x] to [y]."*

- The status of the witness should be given and his relationship to any party. Where relevant, his experience and qualifications should be given: *"I am the managing director of the Claimant and have held that position since [date]. Prior to that, I was the finance director and held that position since [date]. In [year], I graduated from [name] university with a degree in [subject] and I qualified as a chartered accountant in [year]. I worked in private practice for [name of accountancy firm] for [x] years before moving to industry. My full c.v. is at pages [x] to [y]."*

- The statement(s) should prove those facts that have been pleaded in the written pleadings and it is helpful (at least internally) for counsel to mark-up a copy of the written pleadings with which witness can prove the facts relied upon. If there is an omission it is better to spot it when preparing the statements than when challenged by the Arbitral Tribunal.

- The evidence should distinguish between evidence from the witness' own knowledge and which derive from information and belief and, if the latter, the source of the information or the basis for the belief should be given. Generally, it is permissible for everything to be assumed to be from the witness' own knowledge unless the contrary is said and indeed this may the proper inference from the words used but it is common practice to use a paragraph declaring that: *"The contents of this my statement are within my own knowledge save where I indicate that they are either matters where my information is derived from another source when I indicate the source of the information or are matters I believe to be true when I give the basis for my belief."*

- If it is apparent from the pleadings (or witness statement that can be responded to by a statement in reply) that an event is denied, additional detail may lend credibility to the witness' account: *"On [date] I met Mr B of the respondent and we discussed . . . I note that it is denied that we met on that day. I recall the meeting clearly as it had been raining heavily that day and my*

165

shoes were very wet and Mr B and I joked about the weather. Mr B was good enough to lend me an umbrella for my return journey. A meteorological report for [place] on [date] is at page X and my letter to Mr B returning the umbrella and the waybill for the return of the umbrella to Mr B is at pages Y and Z."

- The statement generally should be in chronological order but if there are various issues, it can be effective to deal with each issue in turn and, within each section, to deal with matters chronologically.

- It is quite acceptable to explain why a witness would not have done what is alleged even though it is not a fact as such: *"The Respondent contends that I agreed that it could deliver the kitchen [product] late. Not only is it common sense that I would not have done so but I have fitted out many hotels and am very aware that a properly functioning kitchen is essential to the successful opening of an hotel. If the Respondent did not deliver the kitchen [product] on the contractual date and instead delivered on the later date it contends I agreed, it would have been impossible to open on the date we had publicised and for which we had taken substantial bookings. Being aware of those matters I simply would not have agreed to the later date. In any event the late delivery of the kitchen [product] did cause the late opening that is the subject of this claim."*

- There is no need to include legal arguments or law unless it helps the narrative in which case it should be referred to only in passing and usually on the basis of advice: *"The refusal to deliver the kitchen [product] was, I am advised, a repudiatory breach of contract that was accepted by my letter of [date]."* The advice itself should not be produced or referred to in any greater detail. An exception to this rule is where foreign law is sought to be proven – although proof of foreign law is regarded in some jurisdictions as a question of fact, it should not be grouped with factual statements as it is proved by legal opinion.

A. Summoning Reluctant Witnesses

The provision of witness statements is voluntary and a party will call those witnesses it has available to it and who are favourable to its case. Some witnesses are reluctant to attend and there are various mechanisms to ensure attendance. The typical witness who is summonsed merely requires some form of compulsion to excuse himself from his current employment, to circumvent some perceived confidentiality, and avoid having to take the time off as holiday. For this sort of witness, it may be possible to have a sensible dialogue with the new employer and come to some satisfactory arrangement that enables the witness to attend. For those that need something more, the Tribunal may be persuaded to write and ask for assistance but for most cases the assistance of national courts may be required.

CHAPTER 31
EXPENSES OF WITNESSES

A party is, of course, perfectly at liberty to meet the expenses of a witness in attending an evidentiary hearing. This will normally include travel and accommodation costs. A party can also properly compensate a witness for time devoted to the reference either at a normal hourly or daily rate. Provided there is no element of bounty in this, it is perfectly acceptable under most laws.

As the American Bar Association Model Rules of Professional Conduct puts it, a lawyer should not "counsel or assist a witness to testify falsely, or offer an inducement to a witness that is prohibited by law."[1] The accompanying Guidance provides that:

> [I]t is not improper to pay a witness's expenses . . . on terms permitted by law. The common law rule in most jurisdictions is that it is improper to pay an occurrence witness any fee for testifying . . . .

An "occurrence" witness is simply another manner of describing a witness of fact. The Guidance might appear, at first reading, to outlaw any payment of a fee as opposed to expenses but this is not the case. The American Bar Association Standing Committee on Ethics and Professional Responsibility has issued a formal opinion[2] which states: ". . . compensating a witness for loss of time which he could have devoted to other pursuits does not constitute payment of an 'expense' incurred by the witness. Nor, on the other hand, does compensating a witness for his loss of time amount to paying him a 'fee for testifying.'" The Committee noted that the Model Rules of Professional Conduct replaced a Model Code which expressly provided that "a lawyer may . . . acquiesce in the payment of . . . reasonable compensation to a witness for his loss of time in attending and testifying . . ." and continued that "there is nothing in the history of Rule 3.4(b) to indicate that the drafters of the model Rules intended to negate this concept . . . ." The Committee further noted that certain statutes expressly permitted the payment to lay witnesses for

---

[1] Rule 3.4(b).

[2] ABA Formal Opinion 96-402.

"the reasonable value of time lost in attendance at any such trial, hearing or proceeding."[3]

This ability extends to a reasonable amount of time spent preparing to testify including time spent in reviewing and researching material. As a matter of good practice, it should always be made clear that the fee is not for the substance or efficacy of the evidence but to compensate for lost time.

There will, however, always be limits on what is proper. In *Golden Door Jewelry Creations v. Lloyds Underwriters Non-Marine Association,*[4] the court held the insurer's attorneys had violated Rule 3.4(b) by acquiescing in the payment of two witnesses of fact. For the original information, one was paid U.S. $100,000, the other U.S. $25,000; for depositions, one was paid U.S. $95,000, the other U.S. $25,000; for living expenses, one was paid U.S. $65,000, the other U.S. $22,000, and; for appearing as a witness at a criminal trial, one was paid U.S. $72,000.

In terms of assessing what is reasonable, the New York State Bar Association Committee on Professional Ethics has said:

> We must attempt to draw the line between compensation that enhances the truth seeking process by easing the burden of testifying witnesses, and compensation that serves to hinder the truth seeking process because it tends to 'influence' witnesses to 'remember' things in a way favourable to the side paying him.

The California State Bar has contributed that: "Possible objective bases upon which to determine reasonable compensation might include the witness' rate of pay if currently employed, what the witness last earned if currently unemployed, or what others might earn for comparable activity"[5] and the State Bar of Arizona has pithily summed matters up: "a fee may appear unreasonable if the fee is so high that the witness is 'better off' than she would have been if she spent the time otherwise earning an income rather than testifying or preparing to testify."[6]

---

[3] 18 U.S.C. §201(j).

[4] 865 F. Supp. 1516 (1994).

[5] California State Bar Standing Committee on Professional Responsibility and Conduct, Formal Opinion 1997 – 149.

[6] State Bar of Arizona Committee on the Rules of Professional Conduct, Formal Opinion 1997-07.

In England the Solicitors Code of Conduct paragraph 11.07 provides:

You must not make, or offer to make, payments to a witness dependent upon the nature of the evidence given or upon the outcome of the case.

The Guidance to the rule provides that "There is no objection to your paying reasonable expenses to witnesses and reasonable compensation for loss of time attending court."

All of this guidance appears pragmatic. Plainly problems arise where either the evidence is bought whether by paying a fee or paying expenses that are unrelated to and exceed actual cost or by paying on the result of the evidence. Either is wrong and not only would the amounts so paid not be recoverable as costs if that party were successful and entitled to costs, the weight to be attached to the witnesses evidence would be seriously affected by the fact of such payment and the Arbitral Tribunal could properly reject the evidence in its entirety if it felt that the payment so undermined the evidence as to make it of no credibility. If counsel were conscious of the payment, there could also be professional sanctions.

CHAPTER 32
EXPERT EVIDENCE

Many references may raise issues that either cannot sensibly be resolved without expert testimony or which the determination of which are greatly assisted by expert testimony. In consequence, and in addition to documentary evidence and witness statements, it is common practice to adduce the evidence of experts. Expectations as to the manner in which experts are selected, appointed, and give evidence can, however, vary greatly.

To many the notion of expert evidence in arbitration is an anathema as the arbitral tribunal are appointed for their expertise. This is indeed often the case for trade arbitrations with disputes on, say, quality. The preponderance of lawyers as arbitrators necessitates that technical evidence is given by experts. This results in expert evidence on, among others, engineering, science, trade practice, foreign law and accounting. The issues upon which expert evidence is adduced are therefore not on whether something occurred but why or how it occurred or on the consequences of a breach of contract, such as the damages naturally arising flowing from the breach. The common feature is that the evidence is of opinion.[1] Necessarily, there can be a range of opinion typically with a narrower range within which reasonable professionals could quite properly differ. This makes the function of the Arbitral Tribunal all the more difficult.

Historically, it was often said that expert evidence is precluded on the ultimate issue but that rule is now abolished in most common law countries.[2] Provided an Arbitral Tribunal does not abrogate its responsibility and effectively delegate the decision-making process to the expert, it is quite proper to adduce expert evidence and, if two or more experts opine on the same issue, it is the function of the Arbitral Tribunal, using its own expertise or experience as necessary, to prefer the opinions of one expert over another.

Expertise has been used as a tool to the determination of disputes since at least the 14th century. One of the earliest references to the use of

---

[1] There are limited exceptions discussed later in this chapter.

[2] In England, see §§3(1) and 3(3) of the Civil Evidence Act 1972; Molnlycke AB v. Proctor & Gamble [1994] RPC 49, at 113; and Routestone Limited v. Minories Finance Limited [1997] BCC 180, at 188H.

expert assistance is in *Buckley v. Rice Thomas*[3] when it was said: "If matters arise in our law which concern other sciences or faculties we commonly apply for the aid of that science or faculty which it concerns, which is an honourable and commendable thing in our law." This was done by juries having special skill or experience—the oral evidence of factual witnesses was not commonplace until the 17th century and oral evidence from experts followed about a century later.[4]

Plainly, an expert must have the required degree of expertise. As was elegantly explained in *R v. Robb*,[5] a party cannot "fairly [be] asked to meet evidence of opinion given by a quack, a charlatan or an enthusiastic amateur." Whether the proposed expert has the required degree of expertise is a matter for the Arbitral Tribunal and there is little general guidance. Rule 702 of the American Federal Rules of Evidence terms an expert "a witness qualified as an expert by knowledge, skill experience, training or education." The laws of New South Wales provide: "a person [who] has specialised knowledge based on the person's training, study and experience"[6] and English law refers to "knowledge or experience".[7] In practice, an Arbitral Tribunal is unlikely to face the questioned expertise of a proffered expert but it may occur.

A. Directions

Clearly, the potential for expert evidence should be raised at an early stage and certainly at the first procedural hearing.[8] The Arbitral Tribunal can then decide whether to permit expert evidence and what directions are required. A sample order permitting expert evidence is at Appendix 24. The parties will probably have a good idea of the issues upon which the Tribunal would be assisted by expert evidence but a frank dialogue will narrow the issues and ensure that the parties have the same expectations of the precise issues and extent of expert evidence. For example, there may

---

[3] (1554) 1 Plowd 118.

[4] Carte v. Boehm (1766) 3 Burr. 1905 and Folkes v. Chadd (1782) 3 Doug 157.

[5] (1991) 93 Cr.App.Rep 161, 166.

[6] §79 Evidence Act 1995.

[7] §4(1) Civil Evidence Act 1972.

[8] This and many of the other points discussed in this chapter are also considered good practice in the International Institute for Conflict Prevention and Resolution's Protocol on Disclosure of Documents and Presentation of Witnesses in Commercial Arbitration available to download at www.cpradr.org.

be an issue over the structure of a bridge. One party might appoint a surveyor and another an engineer. This can significantly affect the smooth-running of the reference and may necessitate an adjournment.

It will be rare that the Tribunal will permit more than one expert in a specified discipline. More than one discipline may be required resulting in more than two experts assisting the Tribunal.

B. Independence and Impartiality

Plainly, it is essential that an expert is independent and impartial. Some institutional rules expressly provide for this.[9] Some national laws support this—e.g., German law. German arbitration law permits a party to challenge a tribunal appointed expert on the grounds of justifiable doubts as to independence or impartiality on the same basis that an arbitrator could be challenged. Any challenge is likely to be either when a report is served or when the expert is called to give evidence. However, it is clear, at least in England, that the fact of a close personal friendship or professional acquaintance does not, of itself, prohibit an expert from giving evidence.[10] Clearly, however, it may go to the weight that an Arbitral Tribunal puts on that evidence. Equally, again at least in England, an employee can, in theory, give expert evidence but again the weight attributed to the evidence may be (considerably) less.[11]

C. Remuneration

It will be extremely rare for an expert to be paid on a contingency or conditional basis and, in the unlikely event that he is so remunerated, it is highly likely that a Tribunal would consider that sufficiently affected his independence so as to render his evidence inadmissible.[12]

---

[9] LCIA and ICDR.

[10] Liverpool Roman Catholic Archdiocesan Trustees v. Goldberg Times 9 March 2001. The subsequent decision of the trial judge to exclude the evidence reported at [2001] 1 WLR 2337 was disapproved by the Court of Appeal in R (Factortame Limited) v. Transport Secretary (No. 8) [2003] QB 381.

[11] Field v. Leeds City Council (2000) 32 HLR 619.

[12] In exceptional circumstances, accountants providing support services to the main expert were permitted to work under a contingency: R (Factortame Limited) v. Transport Secretary (No. 8) [2003] QB 381, at 410/411.

D. Duties of the Expert

The expert must clearly assist the Tribunal to the best of his ability and tell the truth. In the English case of The Ikarian Reefer,[13] Cresswell J set out the duties of an expert to the court.[14] Although not binding in international commercial arbitration, the guidelines are of good general application and have been widely accepted in many jurisdictions:

I will refer to some of the duties and responsibilities of experts in civil cases because I consider that a misunderstanding on the part of certain expert witnesses . . . as to their duties and responsibilities contributed to the length of the trial . . .

1. Expert evidence presented to the Court should be and should be seen to be the independent product of the expert uninfluenced as to form or content by the exigencies of litigation . . .

2. An expert witness should provide independent assistance to the Court by way of objective unbiased opinion in relation to matters within his expertise . . . An expert witness in the High Court should never assume the role of advocate.

3. An expert witness should state the facts or assumptions on which his opinion is based. He should not omit to consider material facts which detract from his concluded opinion . . . .

4. An expert witness should make it clear when a particular question or issue falls outside his expertise.

5. If an expert's opinion is not properly researched because he considers that insufficient data is available then this must be stated with an indication that the opinion is no more than a provisional one . . . .

6. If after exchange of reports, an expert witness changes his view on a material matter . . . such change of view should be communicated . . . to the other side without delay and when appropriate to the Court.

---

[13] National Justice Compania Naviera SA v. Prudential Assurance Co Ltd [1993] 2 Lloyd's Rep 68, at 81.

[14] The judge was overturned on appeal, but nothing casts any doubt on these guidelines.

7. Where expert evidence refers to photographs, plans, calculations . . . survey reports or other similar documents there must be provided to the opposite party at the same time as the exchange of reports . . . .

E. Challenges

If a challenge to the expert is raised at the time of the report, the Arbitral Tribunal should seek to resolve the issue promptly for, if the Tribunal were to rule an "expert" not to have the required expertise or otherwise be inadmissible, due process dictates that the party have a fair opportunity to find a replacement. If raised at the evidentiary hearing, it is probably preferable to hear the evidence and determine what, if any, weight to attach to it.

As stated above, expert evidence is generally a matter of opinion but not all opinion is expert evidence. For example, the evidence of a witness as to the speed of a car is in the absence of some internal measuring device (the speedometer) or some external measuring device (a speed camera), is usually an opinion based on facts, for example the time taken to move a distance or experience of seeing other cars move along the road.

Such evidence whilst strictly a matter of opinion is properly regarded as a matter of fact.[15] This is given statutory force in England by §3(2) Civil Evidence Act 1972. Such opinion evidence would make, for example, the value of a popular car capable of being established without expert evidence.[16]

Similarly, there is a doctrine of "judicial notice" that mandates judges to take note of what is common knowledge. For example, in *F & K Jabbour v. Custodian of Israeli Absentee Property*[17] the court considered various United Nations documents to establish the dates of hostilities between Israel and various Arab states. Such matters are eminently sensible and such practice should be followed by Arbitral Tribunals.

---

[15] *See, for example*, "Evidence of Opinion and Expert Evidence," Law Reform Committee, 17th Report, Cmnd 4489 (October 1970).

[16] Bandegani v. Norwich Union Fire Insurance Society (unreported 20 May 1999).

[17] [1954] 1 WLR 139, at 143.

F. Tribunal Expertise

Members of the Arbitral Tribunal are often selected because of their own specialist knowledge and this may or may not preclude the need for expert evidence.[18] If the members of the Arbitral Tribunal are competent to do so they may determine issues that would otherwise be the subject of expert evidence. Particular care, however, should be taken where, in a three-arbitrator Tribunal, one party appointed member has the expertise, as issues of due process may arise and where it can be shown that expert evidence was necessary to properly canvass an issue, an Award may be set aside if expert evidence was refused.[19] Where expert evidence is adduced, it is quite proper for an Arbitral Tribunal to reject it and rely on its own skill and experience,[20] indeed, it is quite proper for them to employ such knowledge in reaching a decision. However, the Arbitral Tribunal should not adopt a theory of its own without putting it to the parties for comment for while they are:

> entitled to use their knowledge and experience to fill gaps in the evidence about matters which will be obvious to them but which might be obscure to a layman . . . they ought to draw to the attention of the witnesses the experience which seems to them to suggest that the evidence given is wrong, and ought not to prefer their own knowledge or experience without giving the witness an opportunity to deal with it.[21]

The main benefit of expertise on the Arbitral Tribunal should be to enable it to understand and weigh the merits of the expert evidence adduced by the parties and not to supply it themselves.[22]

Occasionally, the subject matter of a dispute may be highly technical and experts can be called not so much as to give an opinion on the "how" or "why" but as an aid to understanding the issue[23] or the meaning of a

---

[18] Mediterranean and Eastern Export v. Fortress Fabrics [1948] 2 All ER 186.

[19] Johnstone v. Cheape (1817) 5 Dow. 247.

[20] Fox v. Wellfair [1981] 2 Lloyd's Rep 514.

[21] Dugdale v. Kraft Foods [1976] 1 WLR 1288, at 1294-1295.

[22] Top Shop Estates v. C Danino [1985] 1 EGLR 9, at 11.

[23] See, e.g., Kirin - Amgen Inc v. Hoechst Marion Roussel Limited [2004] UKHL 46 (wherein the judges in the House of Lords hearing the appeal were given a series of seminars on DNA technology).

term in a contract[24] that may have a technical meaning and, in doing so, an Arbitral Tribunal can determine whether to ascribe a technical or everyday meaning to a word.

G. Power to Adduce Expert Evidence

The power to direct and receive expert evidence usually derives from the institutional rules incorporated in the arbitration agreement. For example, the ICC Rules refer to both "The Arbitral Tribunal may decide to hear witnesses, experts appointed by the parties or any other person . . ."[25] and to "The Arbitral Tribunal, having consulted the parties, may appoint . . . experts, define their terms of reference and receive their reports. At the request of a party, the parties shall be given the opportunity to question at a hearing any such expert . . . ."[26] Article 20 of the LCIA Rules, Article 25 of the UNCITRAL Rules, and Rule 31 of the AAA Rules refer to witnesses the parties may call but it clearly covers both factual and expert witnesses.[27] Article 21 of the LCIA Rules and Article 27 of the UNCITRAL Rules provide for experts reporting to the Tribunal in a similar manner to the ICC Rules.

H. Who Calls the Expert?

As can be seen above, either the parties may call their own experts or the Tribunal may do so. If the parties are content to have the Tribunal appoint a single expert, that will generally be the cheaper option as the total cost will be for one expert rather than one per party or group of parties—e.g., all respondents with a common interest may be restricted to a single expert—and the time taken at the evidentiary hearing will be less and, hence, at less cost. The Tribunal calling a single expert will be more familiar to lawyers from civil jurisdictions as it is commonly used by courts from civil jurisdictions.

---

[24] Dashwood v. Magniac [1891] 3 Ch 306.

[25] Article 20(3).

[26] Article 20(4).

[27] *See, e.g.,* Article 20.2 of the LCIA Rules – "... whether witness of fact or expert witness."

I. IBA Rules

Article 6 of the IBA Rules sets out a comprehensive code for the Tribunal for the calling of a tribunal appointed expert. The Article provides for the Tribunal to select and appoint the expert. There is no guidance as to how the tribunal might select and appoint but the UNCITRAL Notes of Organising Arbitral Proceedings suggests that the Tribunal might present the parties with a list of names, invite comments, or discuss the "profile" of the expert with the parties. An expert so appointed must have the same independence as if appointed by the parties. The expert can request documents and his report and the documents relied upon should be made available to the parties. The giving of evidence is provided for, as is the parties right to question the expert.

J. Concern over Opinion of Tribunal Appointed Expert

The problem arises when the Tribunal appoints its own expert and one party is sufficiently aggrieved by the opinions expressed by that expert that it wishes to obtain its own report to challenge the expert appointed by the Tribunal. In turn, the other party may wish to rely on the Tribunal appointed expert or even obtain its own report to challenge the report to be obtained by the other party. If the Arbitral Tribunal is minded to rely only on the Tribunal appointed expert, it may result in the bizarre scenario of counsel questioning or cross-examining the Tribunal appointed expert with the assistance of a further expert who may be present at the evidentiary hearing and be plainly disagreeing with the Tribunal appointed expert, but only be able to express his views through questions to the Tribunal appointed expert. It will be evident through this process that the party-appointed expert disagrees with the Tribunal appointed expert.

The resolution of this tussle of what experts to hear will be a matter for the Arbitral Tribunal versed with all the facts but the guidance of the English Court of Appeal in *Daniels v. Walker*[28] may be of considerable assistance:

In a substantial case such as this, the correct approach is to regard the instruction of an expert jointly by the parties as the first step in obtaining expert evidence on a particular issue.

---

[28] [2000] 1 WLR 1382.

It is to be hoped that in the majority of cases it will not only be the first step but the last step. If, having obtained a joint expert's report, a party, for reasons which are not fanciful, wishes to obtain further information before making a decision as to whether or not there is a particular part (or indeed the whole) of the expert's report which he or she may wish to challenge, then they should, subject to the discretion of the court, be permitted to obtain that evidence.

In the majority of cases, the sensible approach will not be to ask the court straight away to allow the dissatisfied party to call a second expert. In many cases it would be wrong to make a decision until one is in a position to consider the position in the round. You cannot make generalisations, but in a case where there is a modest sum involved a court may take a more rigorous approach. It may be said in a case where there is a modest amount involved that it would be disproportionate to obtain a second report in any circumstances. At most what should be allowed is merely to put a question to the expert who has already prepared a report.

. . . In a case where there is a substantial sum involved, one starts, as I have indicated, from the position that, wherever possible, a joint report is obtained. If there is disagreement on that report, then there would be an issue as to whether to ask questions or whether to get your own expert's report. If questions do not resolve the matter and a party, or both parties, obtain their own expert's reports, then that will result in a decision having to be reached as to what evidence should be called. That decision should not be taken until there has been a meeting between the experts involved. It may be that agreement could then be reached; it may be that agreement is reached as a result of asking the appropriate questions. It is only as a last resort that you accept that it is necessary for oral evidence to be given by the experts before the court. The expense of cross examination of expert witnesses at the hearing, even in a substantial case, can be very expensive.

The great advantage of adopting the course of instructing a joint expert at the outset is that in the majority of cases it will have the effect of narrowing the issues. The fact that additional experts may have to be involved is regrettable, but in the majority of cases the expert issues will already have been reduced. Even if you have the unfortunate result that there are three different views as to the right outcome on a particular issue, the expense which will be incurred as result of that is justified by the prospects of it being avoided in the majority of cases.

It is unlikely that an Arbitral Tribunal would appoint its own expert after the parties had instructed their own experts. Whilst acknowledging that it can be difficult to separate the opinions of respected experts on matters that are outside the realm or experience of the members of the Arbitral Tribunal, it is the function of the Arbitral Tribunal to make decisions on the evidence and to appoint its own expert to determine which of two competing views to prefer smacks of an abdication of responsibility. The Arbitral Tribunal should, if at all possible, prefer the views of one expert over the other but if absolutely impossible the instruction of an additional expert may an option.[29]

The instruction of party-appointed experts is not provided for in terms of procedure by most institutional rules but there are many good practices that can be borrowed from national court procedures.

K. Form of the Expert Evidence

Experts' evidence should be submitted in the form of a report. These can be submitted at the same time as the statements of witnesses of fact but it is often preferable for them to follow a suitable interval afterwards, for the factual evidence can often have a bearing on opinion evidence.

It is conventional that experts include a certificate stating that the report is prepared to assist the Arbitral Tribunal and is true. Such certificates or declarations have grown in length in recent years as counsel have demanded greater confirmations and the absence of some form of conventional wording gives the potential to be criticised. A sample form of declaration is at Appendix 25. It is usual, in light of the declaration to this effect and the professional standing of the expert, that the expert is not required to take the oath.

---

[29] Another option may be that the relevant party has not discharged the burden of proof.

Directions can be made for experts to be questioned in writing but this is only usual where there is a single expert. Where there is more than one expert, it is usual for the experts to meet and discuss issues between them with a view to narrowing issues and agreeing on specific items. The aspect of the discussions that the Tribunal is most likely to find of assistance is why the experts have differing views. A report of what the experts can and cannot agree is then drawn up and presented. The items that cannot be agreed can, in appropriate cases, be scheduled with the issue, the rival contentions, and the determination of the Arbitral Tribunal[30] being in separate columns.

L. Concurrent or Sequential Exchange

The general rule is that experts' reports are exchanged simultaneously with other reports from experts of the same discipline. It does not follow that reports from experts of different disciplines need exchange reports at the same time—indeed, it may be positively advantageous for reports to be staggered or sequential. For example, if a structure, say a bridge, were said to be unsound requiring remedial work and the undertaking of the remedial work would cause loss by lost revenues over the period of closure, it might well be logical for the forensic accountants opining on loss to follow the reports on the engineers who would opine on the nature and extent of the remedial work and, hence, the period the bridge may need to be closed for.

In other cases, it may be near impossible for a simultaneous exchange of reports for experts of the same discipline as one party has information key to the provision of a report. For example, one party may allege that the other has overcharged. The pleaded case may refer to the departure from an agreed or reasonable charging structure with the precise amount to be established by expert evidence. In these circumstances it may be difficult or impossible for the expert for the respondent to the allegation to opine on anything useful until the particulars are provided in the report of the expert instructed by the complainant. In such circumstances, sequential exchange may be appropriate.

---

[30] This is done in a similar manner to a Redfern or Scott schedule. *See* Chapter 18 above.

M. Meeting of Experts

Experts can have diametrically opposed views, in part, due to the differing instructions and different material upon which the opinion is sought. When the experts have the opportunity to consider the other expert's report, there may be a considerable narrowing of views. A meeting of experts will often result in much common ground and, in any event, the issues between the experts can be narrowed considerably. Experts can assist the Tribunal by meeting and preparing a report of what they have and have not agreed upon. This can save both time and cost and should be an invariable stage in the presentation of expert evidence.

The meeting can only be of benefit if the experts can talk freely and record areas of agreement and disagreement. It is not the function of the meeting to seek to adjudicate upon or compromise the dispute. It will normally be appropriate for the meeting to be "without prejudice" but the report to be "open."

N. Experts and Evidentiary Hearings

The most usual approach to expert evidence is for the experts to be heard after that party's factual witnesses so, in the ordinary course of events, the claimant would call its factual evidence and then its expert evidence to be followed by the respondent calling its factual evidence and then its expert evidence. This is the classic approach but presents the Arbitral Tribunal with a significant gap between the two experts. This makes it more difficult to compare the rival contentions. Consequently, it is often preferable to have all the factual witnesses heard and then the experts. This also has the advantage of the claimant's expert hearing the factual evidence of the respondent's witnesses should this affect his opinion and the two experts being heard back-to-back.

The more innovative approach is for so-called "expert conferencing" or "hot-tubbing." This involves both experts effectively giving evidence to the Arbitral Tribunal at the same time. The experts are asked to give their opinions on one issue at a time and effectively discuss their reasons before the Arbitral Tribunal. This can have several advantages, not least that one expert might not otherwise be questioned on something raised with the other. It does, however, call for careful handling to ensure that both experts have the opportunity to state his view and that the more powerful or forceful personality does not prevail.

CHAPTER 33
EVIDENTIARY HEARINGS AND ADVOCACY IN INTERNATIONAL COMMERCIAL ARBITRATION

The culmination of all of the preparatory work will be the evidentiary hearing. There will normally only be one albeit, however, if the issues are complex, this may be split into issues of, say, liability and quantum or simply split into specific periods.

Finding a convenient date to all members of the Arbitral Tribunal, counsel and the parties will often prove problematic and it will be necessary to fix an evidentiary hearing well in advance. This may limit the length of hearing that can be fixed necessitating fixing blocks of time and having to use those blocks in the most efficient way. This can be done by a bifurcation of liability and quantum; having the factual witnesses in one block and any experts in a different block; having one party's case and then the other(s) or deciding specific issues in different blocks.

The venue of the evidentiary hearing will be fixed ultimately by the Arbitral Tribunal but usually a consensus emerges from counsel to the parties and the Tribunal. This will usually be at a specialist venue such as the International Dispute Resolution Centre in London or at a hotel or similar venue with rooms for hire. One room is required for the hearing itself and each of the parties will require a retiring room as will the Arbitral Tribunal. Normal secretarial support is invariably helpful or at least the ability to telephone, photocopy, type and print. The major institutions will also assist in the organisation of a venue and support as required. The rooms will have to be paid for at normal commercial rates.

Additionally, it is usual to have a transcript of the proceedings and these are invaluable to enable accurate referencing back to the evidence. The transcript is taken by a stenographer who will require regular breaks (every 1 -1½ hours or so) and facilities are usually available for this to be produced as a transcript within hours or the conclusion of the proceedings for each day. If witnesses wish to give evidence in a language foreign to the language of the reference arrangements will also have to be made for translation. Translation can be either consecutive or simultaneous. Consecutive translation involves the question being put, translated, answered and translated again. This can make the proceedings very slow although the end product is usually more accurate as the translator has more time to translate accurately and the witness may be able to identify errors in the translation. Simultaneous translation involves the translator in a sound-proof booth and the wearing of headphones by those who wish to listen to the translation. If there is a considerable amount of material a team of translators will work together in shifts. Simultaneous translation is considerably quicker but suffers from being less accurate. Ultimately it will be a matter for the Arbitral Tribunal and in all but the most complex cases perhaps involving highly technical evidence or cases of serious allegations, perhaps of fraud or dishonesty, where the precise answer may be particularly important, it is likely the Tribunal will prefer simultaneous translation.

The provision of transcript and translation facilities invariably adds significantly to the cost.

At an early stage of the reference the evidentiary hearing is likely to be set. The advantage of setting a date early is to ensure the availability of the members of the Arbitral Tribunal, counsel, the parties and witnesses. The time set aside for the evidentiary hearing may come as a surprise to some. Even the most complex hearings that might have taken many weeks or months in a national court will be usually given no more than 2 weeks and even this is seen as lengthy. One week or even a few days is more normal. The common law lawyer used to lengthy trials may view this with a mix of horror and concern, but this is due to the common law tradition of a jury who, once empanelled, had to complete the case and the reading aloud of many documents necessitated as historically members of a jury might well not have been literate.

To accommodate the material the Arbitral Tribunal will often sit for longer days than would a court, perhaps 9.00/9.30 – 5.00/5.30 although breaks are usually taken mid-morning and mid-afternoon as well as the midday break. The Tribunal will also place greater reliance on documents including pleadings, written openings (usually agreed to be limited to a stated length) and the evidentiary documents. Furthermore, the more relaxed attitude regarding evidence permits evidence to be admitted without the need for matters that are not agreed to be formally challenged.

Before the evidentiary hearing is convened it will usually be of great assistance to have a pre-hearing conference. That conference can plan precisely how the hearing is to proceed and may timetable the hearing. Experienced counsel will be able to agree much of this between themselves and this will invariably be ratified by the Arbitral Tribunal. Doing so enables witnesses to appear at the correct time saving time cost and inconvenience.

At the evidentiary hearing itself counsel usually make brief opening statements with the claimant going first followed by the respondent. These openings supplement written openings and are usually strictly timetabled. Counsel can and should assume the Arbitral Tribunal are familiar with the pleadings and issues and the oral opening is intended to highlight specific issues. The use of PowerPoint presentations is becoming increasingly prevalent and can be an extremely powerful tool. Illustrating the issues perhaps with photographs that may not strictly relevant to the issues but which might show the subject matter of the dispute (for example, the bridge that is said to be defective or the port at which a vessel was loaded and pictures of the vessel itself) may enable the Arbitral Tribunal to better understand the main issues. Similarly a graphic illustration of the movement of funds in a complex accounting issue may assist far more than a series of bank statements. Such presentations may prove to be controversial if they purport to show a non-agreed summary of the events. As they will usually be designed to have an impact these presentations are rarely made jointly or otherwise agreed. The inevitable protestation from the opponent is usually worth the impact that the presentation will have and the Arbitral Tribunal will usually allow it on the basis of it not being agreed.

The claimant will then call its witnesses in turn and they will be cross-examined and, as necessary, re-examined.[1] The Arbitral Tribunal may have its own questions but will usually raise those after the parties have examined the witness. The original examination is usually little more than verifying name, address, status and position and verifying the truth of the written statement(s) served earlier in the proceedings. Occasionally there may be a few introductory questions to settle the witness, highlight the absolute essence of the evidence of the witness or to address something raised in the statements of other witnesses that has not been otherwise been addressed. This should take 10 – 15 minutes at the most. This practice is not universal but is now extremely popular. Some cultures and some arbitrators will prefer traditional "evidence in chief" or "direct" that involves a witness giving his evidence live and without having served a statement. It is suggested that this approach is inefficient and witness statements and limited evidence in chief is preferable.

Cross-examination is usually relatively brief and usually does not extend more than an hour or so—indeed a half day is considered (very) lengthy. This means that counsel will have to move quickly to the real

---

[1] This is the order of witness testimony provided for in the IBA Rules §8.2.

issues and not engage in point scoring and the cross-examination will have to be carefully prepared. This is the more so where the Arbitral Tribunal is comprised of lawyers from civil law jurisdictions where cross-examination (as known to lawyers from a common law education) is regarded, at best, as embarrassing and unproductive and may be perceived as bullying or humiliating. Nevertheless, if there are plain issues of credibility and especially in allegations of fraud or dishonesty it may be necessary to cross-examine extensively and by reference to contemporaneous documents. If resistance or a lack of comprehension to cross-examination is evident within the Arbitral Tribunal counsel may be well advised to explain both the purpose and the culture behind the process that is to be embarked upon. As evidence in chief is often very limited the evidence in cross-examination may be the only time that a witness has the opportunity to make an impression on the Arbitral Tribunal. It will also be the main opportunity the Tribunal has to assess the veracity of witnesses by assessing demeanour and the way a witnesses carries himself. If evidence in chief is given orally rather than by statement counsel will not have the opportunity to prepare cross-examination and hence there may be delay in the proceedings and a less concise approach.

Re-examination in chief or re-direct is usually restricted to matters that have been raised in cross-examination and here there is a difference between re-examination and cross-examination. The latter is generally not restricted to the matters raised in evidence in chief and can address anything relevant to the issues in the proceedings.

It is generally accepted that witnesses can be present whilst other witnesses are giving evidence. Only an arbitrator from a very traditional civil law background might insist on witnesses not being present whilst giving evidence.

Some arbitrators like to use "confrontation testimony" (also called hot-tubbing) when two or more witnesses on the same issue are questioned simultaneously. This can be messy and unless the issue is a clearly defined and discrete point the questioning can be incoherent. Advocates of this approach see it as enabling the Arbitral Tribunal to see who is in agreement and where they differ and whether testimony is supported by documents. The writer considers it will be rare for this process to work well for factual issues but it can and has been used successfully for expert testimony. Arbitrators from continental Europe may[2] view witnesses as either party representatives or independent third party witnesses. The weight given to the latter by such arbitrators considerably exceeds that given to the former. The party representative witnesses may give evidence from their seat adjacent to their lawyer and not sworn whereas the latter give evidence from the witness box and are sworn.

The available time for a hearing can be split between the parties and this can usually be agreed between the parties and counsel.

Closing speeches are often given but equally often written closing submissions are used instead. This permits accurate cross-referencing to the transcript and other documents. Again it is normal for these closing submissions to be agreed to be limited to a specific length.

The style of advocacy is very much a matter for individual counsel and the facts of the particular case, however, it is abundantly clear that the community of arbitrators prefer the cooperative, consultative and courteous approach. Counsel would be well advised to operate in good faith and be seen to do so; be transparent; well-organised; prompt; be seen to agree on non-disputed or non-important issues; minimise procedural bickering and be concise. Counsel ought to be thoroughly prepared and be seen to be; be sensitive to different cultural sensitivities and of witnesses and the Tribunal.

---

[2] In accordance with practice in local courts.

CHAPTER 34
PRECEDENT

It might be thought that this would be a short chapter both starting and concluding that there was no doctrine of precedent. Certainly, there is no formal doctrine of precedent with one arbitral tribunal obliged to follow decisions of other tribunals. This has sound underpinnings. The privacy and confidentiality of the arbitral process does not make ready access to previous decisions and the basis upon which those decisions were made, accessible. Furthermore, the benefit of international commercial arbitration is to assemble a tribunal from different jurisdictions for the very reason that they will bring with them expertise and wisdom based, in part, on their own backgrounds and experiences. Nevertheless, some decisions are widely reported and it is well known that there are regular seminars and symposia where views are exchanged and respected arbitrators discuss cases that they are involved with albeit on *Chatham House* rules. This leads to a commonality of approach or a distillation of good practice all of which has much to commend it.

In national courts, there are obligations to follow earlier cases. In common law jurisdictions, the doctrine of precedent is well-established and there is an intellectual comfort in relying upon tried and tested solutions. In civil law countries, the doctrine is less well-established. In Switzerland, the persuasive effect of earlier decisions depends upon the detail to which the prior court considered the issue, whether the decision is published, how the judgement is expressed, and the status of the judicial body that has previously applied it. In Spain, there must be two prior decisions with the same line of reasoning for a decision to be binding, and in Mexico, there must be five prior decisions. Rigid adherence to precedent can cause injustice and both the House of Lords in England and the Supreme Court in the U.S. can overturn their own previous decisions.

Neither the International Court of Justice nor the World Trade Organization Appellate Body have a formal doctrine of precedent but certainly in the ICJ there is heavy reliance on previous decisions; effectively a practice of recognising precedent that is not formally recognised.

In practical terms, much of the reliance on precedent are not matters for the substantive award and usually concern matters, for example, on jurisdiction, objections to jurisdiction, powers to award provisional or interim measures, party autonomy, and governing laws. In investment law, though, it seems there is increasing reliance on prior awards in respect to substantive issues. The explanation for why precedent has little bearing on the substantive award is that in commercial international arbitration the issues turn on a bespoke contract and the particular facts that surround it. These issues tend to be fact specific contributing little to precedent and, in any event, are rarely published.

CHAPTER 35
DAMAGES[1]

The primary purpose of the vast majority of arbitrations is to recover compensation for a breach of contract. The procedural wars are but a means to an ultimate end of how much is to be paid. Contracts are concerned with the mutual passing of benefits – generally, money is paid for goods or services. The basic rule is that if one party defaults on its obligation, the loss is the value of the benefit that the other party has been deprived of by that breach. In doing so, the law[2] does not enquire into whether the bargain struck in making the contract was a good or a bad bargain. It is for that reason that the value deprived of under the contract is important.

The guiding principle of damages for a breach of contract is "that sum of money which will put the party who has been injured, or who has suffered, in the same position as he would have been in if he had not sustained the wrong for which he is now getting his compensation or reparation."[3]

In a typical sale of goods case, the breach can be either a non-performance—e.g., a failure to deliver at all—a delayed performance, or a defective performance. Take a contract to purchase a truck. If there is non-performance by the transferor (the seller), the basic loss is the difference between the market price of a replacement truck and the contract price. In defective rather than non-performance—e.g., late delivery—the basic loss is the difference between market value at the date of due delivery and the market value at actual delivery. In the case of a defective product, the basic loss is the market value as represented or as it should have been and the actual market value.

In addition to the basic loss, there may be consequential losses. For example, the truck may have been intended to be profit-earning. A failure to perform or a late or defective performance may all result in lost

---

[1] For those interested in further reading on this subject there is an interesting ICC publication "Evaluation of Damages in International Arbitration" (2006) which is effectively a collection of essays on the subject.

[2] The issue of damages will usually be determined by the substantive law of the contract.

[3] Livingstone v. Raywards Coal Co (1880) 5 App Cas 25, 39.

profits either by using the truck itself or by selling it. In general terms, such losses are recoverable.[4]

Breach of contract by the transferee (the buyer), will generally be the failure to pay the contract price. Generally, these cases are restricted to non-performance although late and defective performance can arise. The basic loss is the opposite of the basic loss arising from the transferor's breach; it is the contract price less the market value.

It is important to have these basic principles in mind when considering the more esoteric issues that arise in the field of damages.

Common law jurisdictions tend to view the proof of loss (the certainty of the figure) as a matter to be alleged with particularity and strictly proved. In contrast, civil law jurisdictions tend to view damages as an exercise in assessing a lump sum that most accurately reflects the general loss. The approach in international commercial arbitration tends to favour the common law approach and require detailed evidence to prove loss. This is often done by experts who give their own assessment of the loss. There is effectively an industry of claims consultants and forensic accountants and others who make their livings writing reports and giving evidence on such matters. Such evidence is invaluable for the Tribunal for that presents an objective assessment of the loss. It must not be overlooked that the loss must be that of the claimant—a claimant cannot recover losses for other companies even if they are associated or within the same group: *Peterson Farms Inc. v. C&M Farming Ltd*[5] where the court criticised the arbitral tribunal for rejecting a challenge to awarding compensation based on the loss suffered by the group of companies.

One matter often overlooked is the link between the breach of contract and the loss. The breach must cause the loss. This is the doctrine of causation. Causation is often abbreviated to the "but for" test: but for the breach would the loss have been suffered? This is, however, to oversimplify matters. The modern common law approach is to consider first the scope of the duty. This stems from the landmark speech of Lord Hoffmann in *Banque Bruxelles Lambert v. Eagle Star.*[6] As Lord Hoffmann said: "The real question in this case is the kind of loss in respect of which the duty is owed." He gave the example, repeatedly

---

[4] Subject to the rules of remoteness and forseeability.

[5] [2004] 1 Lloyd's Rep 603.

[6] [1997] AC 191—the case is often known as SAAMCO.

analysed by jurists, of a mountaineer who would not have gone mountaineering had be been properly advised by his doctor of a weak knee. An injury sustained in an avalanche was not the sort of accident that the doctor was asked to advise about and, hence, the loss was not within the duty owed. Conversely, an accident attributable to the knee giving way high on the mountain that he would not have been on but for the doctor's advice is within the scope of the duty. Similarly, auditors that failed to alert a company that it was insolvent did not cause the further losses that the company said it would not have incurred but for the fact that it remained ignorant of its insolvent state. The auditors did not cause the losses; at best they provided the opportunity for them to be incurred.[7]

If another event intervenes, it is the reasonable anticipation that dictates whether the chain of causation is broken.[8]

Closely linked to causation is the doctrine of foreseeability. The concepts of foreseeability stem from the landmark case of *Hadley v. Baxendale*.[9] The rule in *Hadley v. Baxendale* is said to have two limbs. The aggrieved party can recover, under the first limb, those damages "as may fairly and reasonably be considered either arising naturally . . . or such as may reasonable be supposed to have been in the contemplation of both parties, at the time they made the contract, as a probable result of the breach of it." This has been said to be imputed knowledge; everyone as a reasonable person is taken to know the ordinary consequences of a breach of contract. The second limb covers the situation in which "special circumstances . . . known to both parties" and in that event the damages arising in light of those special circumstances would be recoverable. This has been called actual knowledge. Alternatively, the losses have been called direct and indirect.

Thus, that damage that is considered by the law to be foreseeable and, hence, recoverable depends on knowledge: in effect, there is only one limb to *Hadley v. Baxendale* and it depends on knowledge.[10] The degree of probability that is required is: "'not unlikely' . . . denoting a

---

[7] Galoo v. Bright Grahame Murray [1994] 1 WLR 1360, CA.

[8] Monarch SS v. Karlshamns Oljefabriker [1949] AC 196.

[9] (1854) 9 Ex 341.

[10] Victoria Laundry v. Newman [1949] 2 KB 528, CA.

degree of probability considerably less than an even chance but nevertheless not very unusual and easily foreseeable."[11]

A practical application of these rules can be seen from a case concerning a hotel employing new mini-bars. The new mini-bars were defective and the hotel claimed the return of the rentals, the cost of removal, and lost profits. All three types of loss were held to be direct or under the first limb of *Hadley v. Baxendale*[12] as the very purpose of the replacement mini-bars was to increase revenue and profit deriving from them. It followed that the parties knew that if they failed to perform, the rentals paid would be wasted, they would have to be removed, and profits might be diminished. A similar result was found in *Jackson v. Royal Bank of Scotland.*[13] The bank's account holder imported goods from Thailand for its customer. In error, the bank sent the shipping details to its account holder's customer. Discovering the profit made by the bank's account holder, the customer went direct to the supplier in Thailand. The House of Lords stressed that knowledge had to be assessed at the date of the contract not at the date of the breach. Once it was established that the bank could (at the date of the contract) foresee that disclosing the details of the supplier to the ultimate customer might result in the customer going direct to the supplier the loss of profit from repeat business for the importer was a type of loss that was not unlikely to result from the breach, and the loss was, in principle, recoverable. The remaining exercise was one of quantification. This increasingly complex area of law has had a further recent wrinkle in *The Achilleas*,[14] where the House of Lords held that the foreseeability was both objective in the ordinary sense and objective in the sense of what the parties must have had in mind; the common intention of reasonable parties. If the parties did not intend to hold the party that breaches the contract responsible for a type of loss, it was not foreseeable. Thus, if, in accordance with the practice of ship charterers, a particular type of loss would not be recoverable, a loss of that type would not be recoverable on the facts of a given case.

These principles of foreseeability are found in civil law jurisdictions. For example, Articles 1150 and 1151 of the French Civil Code provide

---

[11] Czarnikow v. Koufos [1969] 1 AC 350.

[12] Hotel Services v. Hilton Hotels [2001] 1 All ER (Comm) 750.

[13] [2005] 2 All ER 271.

[14] [2008] 3 WLR 345.

that a party is only responsible for those things which were foreseen or which ought to have been foreseen and are the immediate and direct result of the breach.

A. Obligation to Mitigate Damages

Many jurists refer to the obligation to mitigate as a duty to mitigate. Such a term is not used here as there is no duty, as such, owed to the party breaching the contract. The obligation to mitigate is such that damages that are unreasonably incurred (and those that have not been reasonably avoided) are not recoverable.

The obligation on the victim of the broken contract is to act reasonably to minimise the loss.

In the U.S., the Uniform Commercial Code, adopted in most states, provides that the seller may resell goods not taken by the buyer and that the buyer may purchase substitute goods in the case of the seller's breach. If such actions are taken in good faith and in a commercially reasonable manner or without delay, the difference between the two prices and incidental costs can be recovered by the aggrieved party (UCC §2-706; §2-712). In contrast to English law, the American system assesses damages as a consequence of the mitigation, whereas English law fixes damages at the time of breach and then introduces the concept of mitigation. These are, however, merely different routes to the same result.

Civil law jurisdictions tend to approach matters from a different standpoint. The primary remedy in, for example, German law is specific performance rather than damages and there is little room for mitigation. Absent exceptional circumstances—e.g., perishable goods —there is no obligation to buy replacement goods in the market. Rather, the German approach as reflected by BGB Art. 254, is to see mitigation as an element of contributory negligence. In the first paragraph of Art. 254, the liability and scope of damages depend on the relative contribution to the loss. The second paragraph provides that the same principles apply when the aggrieved party neglects to prevent or mitigate the loss. Ultimately, whichever system is applied the same result is often achieved by the application of the variety of tools including causation and contributory fault.

The UN Convention on Contract for the International Sale of Goods 1980 (the Vienna Convention) has been widely adopted[15] and provides in Art. 77 that:

> A party who relies on a breach of contract must take such measures as are reasonable in the circumstances to mitigate the loss, including loss of profit, resulting from the breach. If he fails to take such measures, the party in breach may claim a reduction in the damages in the amount by which the loss should have been mitigated.

Most jurisdictions would see this either directly as an obligation to mitigate or as a function of a number of combined principles.

Similarly the UNIDROIT Principles of International Commercial Contracts 2004 provide to much the same effect in Art. 7.4.8.

B. Contributory Fault

It is outside the scope of this work to consider the detailed rules of contributory fault. They may serve to further reduce damages. Equally, a set-off may reduce damages. A true set-off (transactional set-off) amounts to a defence and hence reduces any claim. An independent set-off reduces a claim but it is correct to make an award on the claim and on the counterclaim and allow the parties to net one against the other.

C. Quantifying the Loss

Loss can often be quantified as either a capital loss or as lost profits. If a company breaks a contract the loss will typically be the lost profits to the end of the contract period. As the capital loss amounts to no more than the capitalised value of the stream of profits, most assessments of damage focus on the loss of profits.

In assessing lost profits, one of the more common approaches is the "discounted cash flow" or "DCF" model. The DCF approach is to consider the cash flows of a business (or part of it) into the future and to express their value in today's money by discounting their absolute value to reflect the time value of money. The approach produces a "present value" for the future cash flows. The discount rate should also reflect the

---

[15] With the notable exception of the UK and Japan.

risk associated with the particular cash flows. The financial consequences of the breach can be measured by comparing the cash flows "but for the breach" with the actual cash flows after the breach.

It is both an advantage and a disadvantage of the DCF model is that it does not depend on historic financial performance. It enables the Arbitral Tribunal to award compensation based on losses that would be suffered in the future but it suffers from the disadvantage of involving a projection into the future, permitting widely differing results depending on the assumptions made. As at least some of the relevant period will have expired by trial the Arbitral Tribunal can use that knowledge of what actually happened to assess the damages. This, to many, heretical view has been endorsed by the House of Lords in England recently in *Golden Strait Corp v. Nippon Yusen Kubishika Kaisha.*[16] The House held that considerations of certainty and finality had to yield to the greater importance of achieving an accurate assessment of the damages based on the loss actually incurred. The issue depended on the principles of the law of contract. It was a well-established principle that damages should compensate the victim of a breach of contract for the loss of his contractual bargain. In so far as it was possible the party suffering the breach was, in respect of damages, to be placed in the position it would have been in had the contract been performed. The classic rule of assessment at date of breach generally achieved that result but it was for the courts or arbitrators to find a solution in any case that most fairly compensated the party suffering loss. If a contract for performance over a period had come to an end by reason of a repudiatory breach but might, had it remained on foot, have terminated early on the occurrence of a particular event, the chance of that happening had to be taken into account in an assessment of damages payable for the breach. Similarly, if the lost profits in the year(s) following breach are known, they can be used in the assessment of damages.

This should address some concerns based on projections but inevitably some will remain. Additional issues arise on the discount rates especially as different countries will have different rates of inflation, costs of borrowing, and market volatility in shares. A fair and reasonable discount rate can be difficult to fix and although it may be tempting for a Tribunal to find that the data is too uncertain to enable the Tribunal to arrive at any particular figure with confidence and hence find the case not proven, that is, it is suggested, a matter of last resort. The Arbitral

---

[16] [2007] 2 AC 353.

Tribunal will have competing evidence and the primary duty is to determine the most reliable evidence even if it amounts to buffet style findings—i.e., taking pieces of evidence from different witnesses and from different parties to arrive at the damages for the final award. The risk of uncertainty should not fall on the victim of the breach of contract. As the court said in *Kyocera v. Prudential-Bache*:[17]

> Evidence to establish [lost] profits must not be uncertain or speculative. This rule does not apply to uncertainty or speculation as to the <u>amount</u> of the profits which would have been derived, but to uncertainty and speculation as to whether the loss of profits was the <u>result</u> of the [breach] and whether any such profits would have been derived at all."

The same result is derived from Article 42 of the Swiss Code of Obligations to the effect that a loss that is not ascertainable by calculation is determined by the judge at his discretion having regard to the ordinary course of events and measures taken by the injured party.

Furthermore, the DCF model may be considered inappropriate where the business is a start-up and has never made any profits. This derives from the fact that future profits are less certain if there are no historic profits to provide a benchmark—the converse is the case and the DCF model is best suited to when cash flows can be estimated with reasonable precision.

The limitations of the discounting element of the DCF model have given rise to the use of the weighted average cost of capital ("WACC"). WACC has long been used as a means of assessing the rate of return required on investments and has been developed into the regulatory sphere in setting caps on capital returns in regulated businesses and has also been applied in calculations of loss. The WACC is the average cost of capital invested in a company, weighted by the relative proportions of debt and equity for that company. The typical information required for a WACC calculation is:

- The prospective annual income stream lost;

- The nature of the business that was going to generate that income stream;

---

[17] 299 F.3d 769,790 (9th Cir. 2002).

- The country in which that income stream was going to be generated;
- The cost of debt for that company; and
- The cost of equity of that company.

The main advantage is that by providing a company specific discount rate it applies a more scientific approach to loss than the DCF method. Essentially it considers the rate of return of investment in the specific company rather than a more generic rate of return. The discount rate in the DCF model might be chosen because of the sector the party suffering the loss operates in or to reflect interest rates. WACC identifies the variety of specific factors affecting one company and, because no two companies are identical, each will have a slightly different WACC. WACC is applied at a compounded rate so that the more remote (in time) the losses are, the greater the discounting effect of the WACC. Equally, as the "shopping list" above indicates, the WACC can take into account political instability in a country and many other factors.

Sophisticated though WACC is, it should not be applied without thought and invariably will be a calculation undertaken by a forensic accountant. As has already been mentioned, where there is certainty, there is no need to speculate. A WACC calculation will normally assess damages at the date of breach and, conventionally, interest would be added but the problem with imprudent application of WACC is that you may find that you have allowed for a risk that has not occurred. Take as an example a major infrastructure project in a politically unstable country with a breach of contract in year 1. The matter is referred to arbitration and the award made in year 3. A WACC calculation would factor in the risk of a coup and nationalisation of the infrastructure project. By year 3, however, when the award is rendered, it is known that there has been no coup. It is illogical to factor it in. It follows that, as a matter of logic, WACC should either not be applied at all to matters that are historic at the date of the award, or, if it is to be applied should factor out those discounting factors for matters that are known by the time of the award (that might leave in a discount for the actions of third parties whose conduct in a hypothetical scenario will not be known).

D. Reasonable Performance, Chances and Abuse of Right

It is well established that "if the contract could have been performed by the performance of the alternative least beneficial to the plaintiff, the measure of damages would be regulated by the loss occasioned by non-performance of that alternative."[18] The simple reason for this is that a defendant is not liable in damages for not doing that which he is not bound to do. There are many instances of the application of this principle but it is not universally applied for the strict application can cause injustice.

Take the case where a franchisee was obliged to purchase a given number of garments per year and terminated the contract early. Is the franchisee entitled to say, on the application of the *Deverill v. Burnell* principle that it would have purchased all of the garments as socks (the cheapest garment) or can the innocent franchisor insist on suits (the most expensive garment)? The answer lies in the contract breaker being held to a reasonable method of performance.[19]

If there is a warranty that reasonable care has been used in making an estimate and a price fixed on the basis of that estimate, the damages for an inaccurate estimate are the difference in price agreed on the actual estimate and a properly prepared estimate. That was the position in *Lion Nathan Ltd v. CC Bottlers Ltd.*[20] The parties agreed on the sale of a business on a multiple of earnings. The earnings were estimated and proved inaccurate. The court had to consider what a reasonable estimate would have been and, absent contrary evidence, the reasonable estimate was taken to be the actual result.

In some arbitrations, there is applied a principle of "abuse of right". This effectively limits an aggrieved party from recovering all of the losses on the basis that to do so would be "unfair"; to impose damages of the potential magnitude sought would be ruinous to the contract breaker. The alternative ground to justify the imposition of an abuse of right is that the aggrieved party has not spent the money on the investment that would have led to the gain. To a common law lawyer, whilst those sentiments might be understandable, it results in a something that cannot be rationally supported. There are other routes to do justice to the facts of any such issue. The typical situation where abuse of right has been deployed is where there is a long-term contract and the contract is broken relatively early on. Examples could include the exploitation of suspected

---

[18] Deverill v. Burnell, LR 8 CP 475, 481.

[19] *See, e.g.,* Abrahams v. Herbert Reiach [1922] 1 KB 477 applied in Paula Lee v. Zehil [1983] 2 All ER 390.

[20] [1996] 1 WLR 1438.

oil reserves in distinct phases of exploration, drilling, extraction, and sale. If the contract is terminated during exploration, it is not known whether sufficient reserves would have been found for economic drilling, still less the outcome of the subsequent stages and where the costs of the subsequent stages might not have been even assessed. The prospecting company has, at the time of breach, not spent the money on drilling and the like.

The answer seems to be a more rigorous approach to the loss of a chance which has established jurisprudence at least in some jurisdictions. The application of these established principles[21] can eliminate so-called losses.[22]

If lost opportunity is mere speculative possibility, it does not result in an award of substantial damages as the chance is so low as to be irrelevant. As there are so many variables and each must come to fruition the chances of each step in the chain must be considered. However, cumulative percentages are not aggregated but rather applied to the amount after the first discount.[23] The application of the chances of events occurring in this way can substantially reduce damages.

It is to be noted that events that have occurred can be used to assess damages[24] and, if they depend on actions that the other party could or might have taken, again the reasonable performance of those actions can be taken into account[25] on the assumption that the contract breaker would have performed the contract in a manner most favourable to it. Finally, the use of a sensible WACC calculation can bring reality to otherwise wholly speculative figures. These tools used alone or in combination are sufficient to do justice to the situation of apparent abuse of right rather than the more nebulous concept of abuse of right.[26]

---

[21] *See, e.g.,* Ratcliffe v. Evans (1892) 2 QB 524.

[22] *See* North Sea Energy Holdings v. Petroleum Authority of Thailand [1999] 1 Lloyd's Rep 483 (wherein it was held that there was no real chance of a third party producing oil to be sold and, therefore, no basis for damages).

[23] If the discount for the uncertainty of proving liability is 35% and for causation is 20% the aggregate discount is not 55% but 48% (100% - 35% = 65%. 65% -20% = 52% [or a 48% discount]). *See* Harrison v. Bloom Camillin (No. 2) [2000] Lloyd's Rep PN 404.

[24] Golden Strait Corp v. Nippon Yusen Kubishika Kaisha (op. cit.).

[25] Abrahams v. Herbert Reiach [1922] 1 KB 477.

[26] An abuse of right necessarily accepts the right of the aggrieved party (presumably to damages) but finds that it would be wrong to award the full figure for the loss.

E. Punitive and Exemplary Damages

Punitive or exemplary damages are rare in international commercial arbitration. They are sums not founded on strict compensatory principles; rather they are used to mark conduct of which the tribunal wishes to mark its disapproval. The usual justification is to punish and deter. The second aim is lessened in arbitration as part of the aim of deterrence is to publicise the award of punitive damages so as to deter others. As the Award in arbitration is a private document that is not published, that aim can be defeated although with the increasing trend towards publishing either awards or summaries the publicity is often achieved.

Many jurisdictions simply do not recognise the jurisdiction to award exemplary damages. France, Germany, and Switzerland award damages on the basis of restoring the aggrieved party to the position had the breach not occurred and, although certain non-pecuniary claims are allowed, these are not considered punitive in nature. Similarly, Japan, Korea, and Taiwan do not permit punitive awards.

In England, punitive loss has historically been restricted to claims in tort,[27] but the law might yet recognise exemplary damages for breach of contract, although, it remains a little unclear. It would have to fall into the realm of conduct calculated to result in profit that would exceed the compensation payable. A Canadian court awarded exemplary damages in *Royal Bank of Canada v. Got*.[28]

The most widespread use of punitive damages is in the United States. The view as to whether arbitrators have the power to award punitive damages varies from state to state. Some states take the view that punitive damages may only be awarded if expressly authorised by the contract and others that there is power unless expressly excluded. This latter view is premised on the principle of respect for party autonomy. A yet third view is that punitive damages is a social issue and only permitted by an instrument of the state.[29] The *Garrity* court held that "Punitive damages is a sanction reserved to the State, a public policy of such magnitude as to call for judicial intervention to deter its

---

[27] Rookes v. Barnard [1964] 1 AC 1129.

[28] 178 DLR (4th) 385 (2000) and *see* Hill v. Church of Scientology of Toronto (1995) 126 DLR (4th) 129.

[29] This is known as the Garrity rule from Garrity v. Lyle Stuart Inc., 353 N.E. 2d 793 (N.Y. 1976).

contravention. In any event, the Federal Arbitration Act has been held to authorise punitive damages in interstate and foreign commerce by the Supreme Court in *Mastrobuono v. Shearson Lehman Hutton Inc.*[30] *Mastrobuono* held that the parties may expressly include or exclude the right to punitive damages but if the parties leave it unclear, the right to make such an award will be assumed.

Although rare, there have been a number of cases where punitive damages have been awarded by arbitral tribunals.[31] Several civil law countries also prohibit arbitrators from awarding punitive damages even if the substantive law is that of a different country. For example, the Swedish Arbitration Act expressly prohibits an arbitrator from awarding penalties or fines. The same would appear to apply to Germany and Switzerland.

Care should be taken in making any award for punitive damages as doing so may render enforcement more difficult, even in New York Convention countries, where an award of punitive damages may be challenged on the basis of violating public policy in the enforcing countries.

F. Nominal Damages

If a breach of contract is established but no substantive damages flow from the breach, it may be appropriate to award nominal damages. It is recognition that legal rights have been infringed. The main purpose nowadays is to give a foundation for costs. The aggrieved party will be a "winner" and may seek costs. The point is less relied upon now as the real winner in such a case will not be the parties but their lawyers and, in many instances, unless proving an infringement of legal rights is important, the aggrieved party will in most senses be regarded as having lost. If only nominal damages are recovered, the Arbitral Tribunal will have to consider carefully when there is a victory in the real sense of the word or whether the aggrieved party has simply failed to make out a case for substantive loss.

---

[30] 514 U.S. 52; *see also* Baravati v. Josephthal, Lyon & Ross Inc., 28 F.3d 704, 710 (7th Cir. 1994) (wherein the court held that "In arbitrations governed by [the Federal Arbitration Act], arbitrators are authorized to award punitive damages unless the parties have withdrawn that power.")

[31] Octonia Trading v. Stinnes Interoil (Society of Maritime Arbitrators No 2424 / 1987); Triumph Tankers v. Kerr McGee (Society of Maritime Arbitrators No 2642 / 1990) and Sawtelle v. Waddell & Reed, 754 N.Y.S.2d 264 (N.Y. App. Div. 2003).

G. Liquidated Damages

The parties may, in their contract, stipulate that the effect of the breach shall be the payment of an agreed sum in compensation. In common law countries, these sums are known as liquidated damages or lump sum damages. In civil jurisdictions, similar provisions exist and are often translated as a "penalty."

In common law jurisdictions, such clauses are enforceable provided they are a genuine pre-estimate of loss. It does not matter whether the actual loss is significantly less, provided that the estimate when the contract was made was fair and proper. Often liquidated damages cover a specific breach such as delay and, in those circumstances, a party can claim unliquidated damages in addition for other breaches. If the tribunal finds that the liquidated damages are not a genuine pre-estimate of loss, it is, typically, a penalty and unenforceable at law. The aggrieved party remains entitled to recover such losses as it can prove.

In civil law jurisdictions, the same ability to pre-determine damages is recognised, for example, in Article 1226 of the French Civil Code, although, it vests the judge with a wide jurisdiction to increase or reduce the rate of damage if it is patently excessive or ridiculously low (Article 1152).

H. Moral Damages

There are at least two ICSID cases in which moral damages have been awarded.[32] Moral damages are awarded in addition to pure economic loss in some jurisdictions. In one case, the government had violated its obligation to afford investors fair and equitable treatment. It may be that malicious treatment is required so as to make the liability fault based. An arbitral tribunal minded to award moral damages may have in mind that proof of loss of reputation (and similar "losses") is difficult or impossible to establish. An award should be more than symbolic; it should be proportionate and fairly reflect the loss.

Moral damages will remain rare and conduct justifying any award should be clear and unusual.

---

[32] SARL Benvenuti and Bonfant v. People's Republic of the Congo (ICSID Case No. ARB/77/2) and Desert Line Projects LLC v. The Republic of Yemen (ICSID Case No. ARB/05/17).

I. Disgorgement of Profits

An aggrieved party may have difficulty in proving any loss that it has suffered but may be able to point to profits earned by the wrongdoer by reason of its wrongful act. Damages can be awarded on the basis of a share (or indeed all) of the profit earned by the wrongdoer if justice requires that the aggrieved party is to be compensated. The scope of these sorts of damages has increased recently in England.

An illustration of this principle is *Attorney-General v. Blake.*[33] Blake had worked for the British government as a spy. He was bound by law to keep his career a secret. In breach of that obligation, he wrote his memoirs. The government could not prove any loss – its reputation could not be measured and the evidence of the damages to its spy network too sensitive to reveal. The principle of awarding damages either as an account of profits or a disgorgement of profits reflects the justice of the situation. Blake was ordered to pay over his entire profit from his publishing. Other cases reflect the cost that the wrongdoer ought to have paid for permission to act in what would otherwise be a wrongful way quantified either as a reasonable royalty or as a proportion of the gain.

J. Costs

The expense of management and staff time can be recovered in certain cases. If the time is spent investigating and correcting the wrong costs may be allowed as damages (rather than as costs).[34]

K. Burden of Proof

The general principle of "he who alleges must prove" applies equally to claims for damages. That does not, however, always mean that the Claimant must prove everything as was illustrated in *Sony Computer Entertainment Ltd v. Cinram Logistics Ltd.*[35] An owner who loses its goods due the fault of another is, in principle, entitled to the value of those goods—not the cost. If the party at fault wishes to allege that the

---

[33] [2001] 1 AC 268; and for similar principles *see* City of New Orleans v. Fireman's Charitable Assoc., 43 La. Ann. 447, 9 So. 486 (1891).

[34] *See, for example,* R+V Versicherung AG v. Riak Insurance and Reinsurance Solutions [2006] EWHC 42 and 1075.

[35] [2008] EWCA Civ 955.

sales were not lost as there were replacement orders, it had the burden of proving that.

L. Currency of the Award

Obligations to pay may be in different currencies to reflect the trading done around the world. The primary contractual obligation will be to pay in the original currency; therefore, if an invoice is raised in dollars the obligation to pay will be in dollars. To pay in any other currency risks shifting the exchange rate risk to the recipient. If there is to be payment in any other currency, it should be that at the date of payment, so that the recipient can exchange it back to the original currency and (subject to exchange costs) be left with the right amount.[36] As the House of Lords said in *Miliangos v. George Frank*:[37]

> Any conversion date earlier than the date of payment would, in my opinion, be open to the same objection as the breach date, namely that it would necessarily leave a considerable interval of time between the conversion date and the date of payment. During that interval currency fluctuations might cause the sterling award to vary appreciably from the sum in foreign currency to which the creditor was entitled. In my opinion it would not be justifiable to disturb the existing rule of taking the breach date, merely to substitute for it some other date rather nearer the date of payment but still more or less distant from it. If the date of raising an action in this country were taken for conversion, a period of a year or more might easily elapse, allowing for appeals, before payment was made. The date of judgment would be better but there seems no reason why one should stop short of the last practicable date, which seems to be the date when the court authorises enforcement of the judgment.

And the court said in *Federal Commerce and Navigation Co v. Tradax Export*:[38]

---

[36] Schorsch Meier v. Henin [1975] QB 416.

[37] [1976] AC 443, 502.

[38] [1977] QB 324, 342.

Once it is recognised that judgement can be given in a foreign currency, justice requires that it should be given in every case where the currency of the contract is a foreign currency: otherwise one side or the other will suffer unfairly by the fluctuations of the exchange.

M. The Burden of Taxation

Where the recipient of damages would be taxable on that receipt, the award should be grossed up to take account of that incidence of tax.[39] The same principle applies to compensation for damages to fixed assets and to loss of profits.[40] The point is obvious: it is inequitable to make an award of damages only for those damages to be reduced in real value by being taxed. As the court said in *Diamond v. Campbell Jones*:[41]

Such a profit in the hands of the plaintiff would undoubtedly have attracted income tax . . . . On the other hand, it appears to me that any damages recovered . . . are liable to attract tax as part of the profits or gains of his business . . . I must, I think, award him a gross sum in damages equal to the gross amount of the profit which he would be likely to have made had there been no breach of contract.

Furthermore, the logic of a trading receipt applies whatever the source of that receipt: conventional trading, insurance proceeds, or damages. As the court stated in *Green v. Gliksten*:[42]

To my mind the book value of the timber in the company's books has nothing at all to do with the amount of the loss or with the amount which has been recovered in respect of the loss. The amount recovered is a gain of the company in the course of its business no less than the sale price of the timber would have been, if the timber had been sold in the course of ordinary sales during the continuance of the company's business; and in

---

[39] Green v. Gliksten 14 TC 364 and Raja's Commercial College v. Singh [1977] AC 312.

[40] R v. British Columbia Fir & Cedar Lumber Co [1932] AC 441.

[41] [1961] Ch 22.

[42] [1929] A.C. 381, 384.

estimating the balance of the profits or gains which the company has to bring into account for the purposes of income tax, the amount of the excess of the sum recovered over the book value of the timber in the company's books has to be brought into account just as fully and completely as if there had been a sale in the ordinary course of business at that price.

Whether damages are taxable are a matter for the taxation affairs of the recipient in whichever jurisdiction it has its centre of operations. Naturally, it may be difficult to assess precisely what tax would be payable especially before the amount is ascertained and it may be dependent on what reliefs and marginal tax rates apply. The leading English case on the incidence of tax on damages is *British Transport Commission v. Gourley* where the House of Lords held that it would be unfortunate if its decision:[43]

> . . . were to involve an elaborate assessment of tax liability . . .
> An estimate will be none the worse if it is formed on broad lines,
> even though it may be described as rough and ready. It is
> impossible to assess with mathematical accuracy what reduction
> should be made by reason of the tax position.

This "rough and ready approach" is endorsed in a number of other cases.[44] If the tax rates change, the rate applicable when the tax is to be paid—the date of the award will be the nearest practical date—is the correct rate for this ensures that the receiving party is properly compensated and neither over nor under compensated. The rate applicable at the date of loss may create either an undue burden on the paying party and overcompensate the receiving party or give the paying party a benefit and leave the receiving party with less net recovery than it should have.

N. Interest

Moratory interest is interest awarded regardless of fault. In contrast, compensatory interest aims to restore the aggrieved party to the position it would have been in had the primary relief been granted immediately.

---

[43] [1956] AC 185, 203.

[44] Denny v. Gooda Walker 1996 STC 299 and John v. James 1986 STC 352.

Some jurisdictions (mostly civil) preserve this distinction and some require proof of bad faith[45] or resistance to payment.[46] Common law jurisdictions tend to regard interest as a procedural matter and not a matter of substantive law. Japanese law regards interest as substantive right and, if there is no provision for interest in the contract, no award is made. Much the same position applies under Russian law.

Saudi Arabia has not adopted regulations governing interest in commercial matters. As a consequence, and unlike other Middle Eastern countries that have distinguished between commercial and other civil cases, Saudi Arabia has a prohibition on usury in accordance with the general principles of Shari'a law. Any award that might need to be enforced in Saudi Arabia needs to take this into account as an award that includes interest could be annulled.

Other Middle Eastern countries that have made the distinction between commercial and other civil claims include Kuwait, which by Art. 102 of the Kuwaiti Commercial Code, fixes interest at 7%. Art. 81 of the Law of Commerce in Bahrain is to the same effect. Iran prohibits interest but has an exception in the case of transactions between Iranian nationals and foreigners whose laws permit the payment of interest. Egypt and Iraq have moved away from strict Shari'a and permit interest.

In Europe and the U.S., an award of interest is common place. Asian countries such as China, Taiwan, India, and Korea generally allow interest where there is default in the payment of money. Interest is no more than the price of money (if borrowed) or the opportunity cost of money (if not borrowed). Rates at which interest should be awarded on damages are no different from any other contractual term. The parties will often have stipulated a rate of interest for the late payment of invoices under the contract. The question then arises whether for awards of damages the same rate should apply. Although awards of interest are matters of discretion for the Arbitral Tribunal, it seems right in principle that if the parties have agreed the price of money, that rate should be applied to any award of damages. Of course, there may be good reason why the rate of interest on late paid invoices is higher than might be the case for damages. The parties might know that the product being sold was financed under especially expensive borrowing facilities and that

---

[45] *See, e.g. ,*Art 1153 al. 4 of the French Civil Code.

[46] Lebanese Civil Code Art. 265.

interest on damages might not need to be compensated at the same rate. It is suggested, however, that in normal circumstances a contractual rate apply to any award of interest on damages.

Interest is normally awarded on the entire amount awarded but care should be taken not to overcompensate claimant by awarding interest on the entire amount from the date of breach. For example, interest on lost profits might run from the relevant year of loss rather from the date of breach. Equally, interest should, in principle, not be awarded on tax. The tax is not a loss to the claimant and the claimant will simply be obliged to account to the tax authorities upon receipt. Unless there is a liability to the tax authorities for interest, it should generally not be awarded.

The further issue is whether interest should be awarded on a simple or compound basis. Again, if the point is dealt with elsewhere in the contract, the same principle might be applied to the award of damages. If the issue is not covered elsewhere then, as ever, it is a matter of discretion for the Arbitral Tribunal. The point was recently considered in *Sempra Metals Ltd v. Inland Revenue Commissioners.*[47] The court held that the time had come to recognise that money had a value: the court had a common law jurisdiction to award interest, simple and compound, as damages on claims for the non-payment of debts as well as on other claims for breach of contract and in tort. An Arbitral Tribunal is entitled to take into account the prevailing commercial practice of borrowing and investing on a compound basis.

If no rate is mentioned in the contract, a margin over bank base rates is probably the right starting point. The base rates should be taken as those prevailing in the country where the aggrieved party has its main banking arrangements. The margin may depend on whether the aggrieved party is a net borrower or depositor. A net borrower might be better compensated by say a margin over base rates equivalent to the rate a comparable company would be expected to pay and likewise a net depositor the rate a similar company might command on its deposits. A rate of 1 or, perhaps, 2% over bank base rate might be appropriate.

Finally, it is appropriate to consider whether any and if so what interest should be awarded post-award. In principle, it would seem logical that nearly every award should carry interest post-award down to

---

[47] [2007] 3 WLR 354.

payment. It is difficult to conceive of circumstances that would make it appropriate to not award such interest. It is incumbent on the parties to seek such an award and for the arbitral tribunal to make an award in those terms. Failure to do so can create difficulties. For example, any judgment entered so as to enforce the award can usually only be in the terms of the award. For example, §66(2) of the 1996 Arbitration Act states " . . . *judgment may be entered in terms of the award.*" If the award does not deal with post-award interest, there is nothing an enforcing court can do.[48] If an award does not provide for post-award interest and payment is not made promptly, it may be appropriate to enter judgment in the terms of the award; for judgments may, depending on the jurisdiction, carry interest—e.g., in England under the Judgments Act 1838 judgments carry interest at the rate of 8% on a simple (non-compounded) basis.

---

[48] Walker v. Rowe, [2000] 1 Lloyd's Rep 116.

CHAPTER 36
COSTS IN INTERNATIONAL ARBITRATION

There can be little doubt that international commercial arbitration is expensive. A survey by PricewaterhouseCoopers in 2006 found that whilst 52% of respondents had spent U.S. $100,000 – U.S. $500,000 in their most recent international arbitration, 12% had spent in excess of U.S. $5 million. Similarly, 65% of respondents viewed international arbitration as more expensive than transnational litigation, 23% as about the same, and only 12% as cheaper.

These findings are not surprising. Unlike judges (who are salaried by the state), arbitrators require their fees and expenses to be paid, and these can be substantial. For example, if it is an ICC arbitration where fees are assessed on an *ad valorem* basis—a U.S. $50 million dispute would carry fees for the arbitrators in the range of U.S. $48,750 – U.S. $222,600 per arbitrator. The fee is fixed by the ICC Court taking into consideration the diligence of and time spent by the Arbitral Tribunal, the rapidity of the decision making and complexity of the subject matter. Moreover, there are the fees of the institution itself. Again, a U.S. $50 million dispute under the ICC commands a fee of U.S. $70,800. As an alternative to a fixed fee for the institution, there may be the fees and expenses of a secretary or registrar. In an LCIA arbitration, the time of the registrar is charged at U.K. £200 per hour. Finally, the nature of the constitution of the Arbitral Tribunal is such that any Tribunal will not have facilities to hold hearings. Rooms have to be hired for meetings and hearings, as well as stenographers, creating a layer of cost not found in litigation where the courts are generally provided free by the state.

Those from the U.S. and some civil law regimes may not be as familiar with, or at least have direct experience of, the concept of losing party paying the winning party's costs beyond disbursements or "out-of-pocket" expenses and sometimes a modest fixed cost. The general rule in the U.S. is "that a successful litigant is not permitted to recover his attorney's fees as damages or as reimbursable costs."[1]

---

[1] Grace v. Ludwig, 484 F.2d 1262, 1267 (2d Cir. 1973); the rule is subject to exceptions, including where the contract provides for cost-shifting; where a statute expressly provides and under the court's inherent powers, for example, as sanctions for misconduct.

This "no-costs" rule is predicated on a free access to the courts and penal costs sanctions would inhibit that access. The logic for free access does not apply to a consensual submission to arbitration. The parties have chosen to have their dispute determined by an Arbitral Tribunal and there is no reason why that Tribunal ought not to be in a position to award costs. This is the more so as the parties to international contracts that provide for arbitration would not typically have their recourse to a remedy inhibited by reason of the cost.

Those from common law jurisdictions will have varying experiences of costs orders. The common law courts had no inherent jurisdiction to award costs but the courts of equity had such a power as part of their inherent jurisdiction to award costs as part of the right to give the judgment as an honest man would.[2] That jurisdiction extended "not only to the circumstances under which costs were awarded, but apparently as to the measure and fullness of the costs."[3] Common law countries vary in approach to costs. Some have tariffs that apply absent exceptional circumstances, others allow reasonable costs but the result of the application of that rule can result in recoveries between, say, 30% and 80% of the actual costs expended from country to country. This is the effect of the party and party, standard or normal costs order. Fuller recoveries are reserved for exceptional cases, usually of misconduct—the so-called indemnity costs order although it rarely amounts to a full indemnity.

The authority of arbitrators to award costs has been recognised since at least 1870 when in *Mordue v. Palmer*[4] Lord Mellish said: " . . . when there is a reference [by the common law courts] the arbitrator cannot give any other than costs between party and party. But it is otherwise with Courts of Equity . . . the court gives the arbitrator to award costs as between solicitor and client if he shall think fit." Although this was principally a discussion on the scale or amount of costs, it illustrates the existence of an established jurisdiction.

The logic of allowing costs to be recovered is simple. Invariably the arbitration is concerned with an alleged breach of contract.

---

[2] Lord Hardwicke in The Bailiffs and Burgesses of the Corporation of Burford v. Lenthall (1743) 26 ER 731.

[3] (1888) 39 Ch Div 133; Andrews v. Barnes. The English rule of costs following the event is observed in Australia, Canada, Hong Kong, New Zealand, Singapore, Ireland, and many other commonwealth countries.

[4] (1870) 6 LR Ch App 22.

The underlying principle for damages for a breach of contract is to put the innocent party into the position it would have been in had the contract been properly performed. Had it been properly performed, there would have been no breach, no dispute, no arbitration, and no costs incurred. It is thus consistent with the remedies available for breach of contract to award costs and on a strict application of the logic a full indemnity for costs. Awards of costs also discourage outrageous, fanciful, or unreasonable claims or defences.

The "loser pays" or costs following the event, although not awarded in the U.S., does not mean that awards with such a provision are not enforced by the U.S. courts. Several cases illustrate that the principle does not offend against public policy.[5]

It is for all these reasons that the choice of the constitution of the Arbitral Tribunal (both the party-appointed member(s) and the chairman) can be very important to the parties. Those seeking strong or even punitive costs orders may seek a common law lawyer with an "aggressive" or U.K. background. Those not wanting strong or punitive costs experience may seek a lawyer from a civil law jurisdiction, a U.S. lawyer, or even a non-lawyer.

Costs will be an important issue in the reference. The 12% of respondents to the PricewaterhouseCoopers survey who had spent in excess of U.S. $5 million might be faced with total legal costs exceeding or even considerably exceeding U.S. $10 million. Whilst those sums might be modest in the context of what was in dispute in the references giving rise to those costs, in absolute terms they are significant. The dispute as to who should pay those costs rightly merits careful assessment as the amount in issue would justify a reference all of its own.

---

[5] *See, e.g.*, Hashim v. Hashim, 213 F.3d 1169, 1172 (9th Cir. 2000).

CHAPTER 37
COSTS CAPPING

The English Arbitration Act 1996 contains a specific provision enabling the Arbitral Tribunal to limit recoverable costs. §65 of the Act provides that, unless the parties otherwise agree, the Arbitral Tribunal may prospectively limit the recoverable costs either of the arbitration or any part of the arbitral process. It is important to appreciate that this does not prevent a party from spending a disproportionate amount of costs; the section merely limits the amount that can be recovered.

Any such order can be made or varied at any stage but it is important that it is made sufficiently in advance of the costs being incurred that the limit can be taken into account. For example, at an advanced stage of the proceedings, a party cannot seek an order limiting the costs of the arbitration as a significant part of those costs would have been incurred.

A sample form of words is set out in Appendix 26.

The Arbitral Tribunal may well be assisted if any application for a cap is supported by a schedule of the costs anticipated to be incurred for the arbitration or the particular part of the arbitral process. If a party is conducting its case on the basis of a conditional or contingency fee arrangement with its lawyers, that fact needs to be made known to the Arbitral Tribunal so as to ensure that any cap is made in the knowledge of that fact and the potential for uplift—although it would be inappropriate to reveal the precise terms.[1]

The exercise of cost capping before the English courts has no equivalent statutory basis to the provisions of §65 of the Act. Nevertheless, the courts have an undoubted jurisdiction to cap costs in the same way as under the Act. It does so under its general case management powers. Such powers are likely to be very similar to the general powers bestowed on the Arbitral Tribunal by virtue of most institutional rules. For example, Article 15 (1) of the ICC Rules provides: "The proceedings before the Arbitral Tribunal shall be governed by these Rules and, where these Rules are silent, by any rules which the parties or, failing them, the Arbitral Tribunal may settle on . . . ." It follows that an Arbitral Tribunal will, as do English courts, have inherent jurisdiction to cap costs if deemed appropriate.

---

[1] To do so would indicate the confidence that the lawyer had in the case.

Alternatively, the Arbitral Tribunal may have express costs powers, for example, under Article 31 (2) of the ICC Rules: "Decisions on costs . . . may be taken by the Arbitral Tribunal at any time during the proceedings." An order to cap the costs would seem to be within the scope of both the Article 15 and Article 31 jurisdictions even if there were no statutory provision applicable.

Whether any jurisdiction that may exist should be exercised is, of course, another matter. It is trite that an international commercial arbitration should result in a fair resolution without undue delay or cost[2] and it can be argued that if that is the case there is no need to cap the costs that a party can recover (as opposed to can incur). In any event, the costs should ordinarily be proportionate to the matter in dispute. Assessment after the event may too late—the costs have been incurred and the party and its lawyers have incurred those costs believing them to be recoverable if successful or at least having no reason to believe them irrecoverable. It does not assist in budgeting or planning. Costs-capping is not a straitjacket but a budget that can be revised if good reason is shown.

Arbitral Tribunals may well consider it a proper exercise of discretion to limit not the costs that can be incurred—indeed without express power it will have no power to do so—but those that can be recovered. After all, a party should be entitled, in accordance with party autonomy to decide how it wishes to conduct a claim or defence. If it chooses to engage no lawyers, premier lawyers, or more modest lawyers that is a matter for that party. Equally, how it chooses to run the claim or defence may impact on the cost. That is not to say that a losing party should have to pay for the extravagance of the winning party. The Arbitral Tribunal can reduce the costs at the time of assessment by disallowing costs that it considers unreasonable but the losing party may have no idea whether and if so to what extent that discretion might be exercised. The costs may be held as a weapon over the potentially losing party forcing it to settle earlier and at a higher figure than it would have done had it known that its liability for costs was capped or limited. For these reasons, the proper exercise of the discretion to cap costs at an early stage can be a very effective and, most importantly, a fair strategy.

---

[2] This is set out in § 1 of the English Arbitration Act 1996.

An illustration of the power being used is *R (on the application of the Campaign for Nuclear Disarmament) v. Prime Minister*[3] where CND sought a declaration that UN Resolution 1441 did not mandate the use the force in Iraq. CND sought, and obtained, an order that limited its potential exposure to costs to U.K. £25,000 on the basis that it had limited resources and without the protection sought it could not mount the challenge.

---

[3] [2002] EWHC 2712.

CHAPTER 38
SECURITY FOR COSTS

The cost of pursuing or defending international commercial arbitration can be high. As the proceedings progress, a party will have to fund its own lawyers as well as the Arbitral Tribunal or at least pay potentially substantial deposits against those costs, as well as the administrative costs of any applicable institution.

At a simplistic level, a party accused of wrongdoing can claim to be "innocent until proven guilty." Why should the innocent have to expend considerable money in defending themselves against the unmeritorious claims of the impecunious and be at serious risk of never recovering those costs? To address this potential for injustice, the remedy of security for costs was crafted. Accordingly, it will be the respondent who typically makes an application against a claimant. The rare occasions that a claimant makes an application against a respondent will be where the respondent claims, by counterclaim, and the claimant is in the position of respondent. If a claimant is concerned that a respondent will be unable to meet a costs liability either, it should consider whether it is worthwhile pursuing that respondent at all or consider an injunction to prevent the respondent from dissipating assets to avoid the enforcement of an award against its assets.

The first question to consider is whether there is the potential for a substantive costs order if the innocent party is indeed successful. If not, perhaps because the arbitration agreement, the rules governing the arbitration, or the applicable law provide that each party will bear its own costs irrespective of the outcome, there is, generally, no potential to seek security as the security has to be against a legitimate expectation of recovering costs in the future.

Even if there is the potential for a substantive costs order, applications for security are relatively unusual although there is an increasing trend. Nevertheless, the exercise of jurisdiction will be relatively rare. In *Coppee Lavalin SA NV v. Ken-Ren Chemicals & Fertilisers,*[1] the English House of Lords made an award of security in support of an ICC arbitration relying not so much on the fact that the party was insolvent but that it was being funded by a third party and that justice required the funder, if it wanted the fruits of the reference, to bare

---

[1] [1995] 1 AC 38.

the risk of failure.[2] There are two factors that make applications unusual. First, issues over whether there is any jurisdiction to grant security and, second, the reluctance of the Arbitral Tribunal to exercise such jurisdiction as it may have.

English procedure, no doubt heavily influenced by the ability and willingness to make substantive costs orders, is the most progressive jurisdiction for security for costs. §38(3) Arbitration Act 1996 expressly authorises an Arbitral Tribunal to make orders for security for costs. The discretion is unfettered subject only to it not being used on the sole ground that the claimant is overseas. To this extent the jurisdiction is narrower than English court procedure that expressly allows the fact that the party is overseas to be taken into account. Conversely, the jurisdiction is unfettered in any other way and, hence, broader than the court jurisdiction. The concept of not awarding security simply because the claimant is overseas addresses the inherent issue in international arbitration that parties are most likely to be from different jurisdictions and, to allow security on that ground alone, would have made England an unattractive seat for arbitration.

Reflecting the English practice, the Rules of the LCIA reflect the ability to require security to be given. This is by a rule that expressly addresses the jurisdiction in similar terms to §38(3): Article 25.2 of the LCIA Rules. Similar provisions are found in Article 11.1 of the Arbitration Rules of the Hong Kong International Arbitration Center, Article 28.2(e) of the Australian Centre for International Commercial Arbitration Rules and Article 24(m) of the Singapore International Arbitration Centre Rules. Article 23(1) of the ICC Rules—giving power to grant interim measures—has been used to give security but orders remain relatively uncommon.[3] Article 30 of the ICC Rules is sometimes used as an argument against security on the basis that substantial deposits have to be put up against the costs of the ICC and the Arbitral Tribunal. Whilst this may guard against frivolous claims, it does nothing for the costs of the successful respondent.

---

[2] After much international criticism of the decision, the ability of the court to act in this way has been removed by the Arbitration Act 1996, but the jurisdiction of the Tribunal to do so remains.

[3] The current UNCITRAL Rules do not provide expressly for security for costs but it appears that the forthcoming amendments to the Rules will, it seems, include an express provision. *See* Report of Working Part II (Arbitration and Conciliation) UNCITRAL 47th Sess. at UN Doc A/CN.9/641 (2007).

Although the jurisdiction is unfettered it is highly likely that an Arbitral Tribunal will only then exercise the jurisdiction in circumstances where there are not sufficient available assets to meet any likely costs order. As the English court said in *Azov Shipping v. Baltic Shipping (No.2)*:[4]

> . . . cases will be rare in which a court or indeed an arbitrator would think it right to order security for costs if an applicant for relief had sufficient assets to meet any order for costs and if those assets are available for satisfaction of any such order for costs . . . if it does not have such assets or if such assets are not readily available to satisfy any court order, I would be inclined to make an order for security.

Thus, provided there were sufficient readily available and realisable assets in a country that would enforce an award under the New York Convention, it is unlikely that security would be granted. It follows that the evidence in support of such an application ought to focus on the claimant's assets and their availability to meet any award. Issues such as the extent to which assets are encumbered by mortgages, are readily saleable or otherwise liquid and the location of the assets are all important considerations. A successful application will have credible and reasonable evidence of the inability of the claimant to pay the costs of the successful respondent. This is often given by the respondent having the publicly available accounts of the claimant analysed by an accountant. The Arbitral Tribunal may also appoint an independent expert to provide evidence on these matters.

It is generally not appropriate to address the underlying merits of the claim or the defence; a security application is not the occasion for the Arbitral Tribunal to form a provisional view on the merits unless it can clearly and quickly be demonstrated that there is a high degree of probability of success or failure.[5]

The classic criteria for assessing whether a company should provide security were set out in *Sir Lindsay Parkinson & Co Ltd v. Triplan*.[6]

---

[4] [1999] 2 Lloyds Rep 39.

[5] *Porzelack v. Porzelack* [1987] 1 All ER 1074 and *Keary Developments Ltd v. Tarmac Construction Ltd* [1995] 3 All ER 534, at 540.

[6] [1973] QB 609.

In that case, the court set out the circumstances that might be taken into account in deciding whether to exercise the discretion:

- Whether the claim is bona fide and not a sham;
- Whether the claim has reasonably good prospects of success (in the sense that good prospects are essential for the jurisdiction to be available—as above high probability of success militates further in favour of granting security and high probability of failure against);
- Whether there is admission of money due or an open offer to pay;[7]
- Whether the application is being used oppressively—e.g., so as to stifle a genuine claim;
- Whether the claimant's want of means has been brought about by the conduct of the respondents—e.g., in not paying invoices;
- Whether the application is made late.

If a claimant has legal expenses insurance that would be available to pay the costs of a successful respondent that can be properly taken into account in deciding whether to grant security and if so on what terms: *Al-Koronky v. Time Life Entertainment Group Ltd.*[8]

Equally, the Arbitral Tribunal needs to be vigilant where there is a claim and counterclaim. Where the claim and counterclaim raise the same issues, it might be that the issues are going to be litigated in any event and ordering security may not be just or treat the claimant equally with the respondent. In such case, there is no reason why security cannot be ordered against a respondent in respect of the costs of a counterclaim.

Once the questions of jurisdiction and discretion are satisfied the Arbitral Tribunal must consider how much security is appropriate to order under the circumstances. The amount of any security is within the discretion of the Arbitral Tribunal, which will fix such sum as it deems just, taking into account all of the circumstances. In some cases, the amount of security may be limited to the extra burden or risk involved in seeking to enforce an award for costs subsequently obtained. This might be appropriate where

---

[7] The Tribunal is not permitted to look at without prejudice offers or without prejudice "admissions:" *Simaan Contracting Co v. Pilkington Glass Ltd (No. 2)* [1988] 2 WLR 761.

[8] [2006] EWCA Civ 1123.

there are clearly sufficient assets available to meet any award but the assets are in a different jurisdiction. In other cases, the amount of security may relate to the total costs likely to be incurred in opposing the claim, but it is rare to do so on a full indemnity basis as any subsequent award is unlikely to have that result and all the more so when the prospect of doing so is discounted by the chances of settlement. However, the practice of an arbitrary deduction is wrong and should not be followed.[9]

If security is sought at an early stage, as it should be, the Arbitral Tribunal will fix the amount having regard to the costs already incurred and estimates of the future costs. As the estimates can prove to be wrong, the Arbitral Tribunal can award security down to a particular stage and then review matters or grant security to be provided in tranches—again, with the potential to review. Any review is not of the principles but merely of the amount. This is something the Arbitral Tribunal may consider is dealt with by the Chairman alone. Sample orders for security are in Appendix 27.

In fixing the amount of security, the Arbitral Tribunal must take into account the amount that the claimant (as respondent to the application) is likely to be able to raise. The Arbitral Tribunal should not normally make the continuation of the reference dependant on a condition that cannot be fulfilled as that is unlikely to be a just result. This makes for an interesting tactical decision by claimants; do they seek to persuade the Arbitral Tribunal of their substance and wealth so as to prevent any security from being ordered—or, perhaps, just the additional cost of enforcement—because, if they fail, they cannot thereafter claim, when it comes to consider the amount, that they cannot afford to pay. Conversely, if a claimant seeks to argue that it is impecunious and no security should be ordered as to do so would not be just, if the Arbitral Tribunal does accept the impecunious position, it may award security at a figure that genuinely troubles the claimant.

If the claimant is a nominal claimant effectively pursuing the claim for the benefit of another, it should not be permitted to use its impecunious position to avoid giving security if the real beneficiary of the claim is of substance. As the Arbitral Tribunal would have no jurisdiction over real beneficiary, the appropriate order is to award security against the nominal claimant so as to force the real beneficiary to provide the security.

---

[9] Procon (Great Britain) Ltd v. Provincial Building Co Ltd [1984] 1 WLR 557.

The Arbitral Tribunal, whilst having to consider the evidence at the time of the application, can take into account what is expected to happen in the future.[10]

Traditionally, courts and tribunals in other European jurisdictions have been more reluctant than English courts and tribunals to grant security. There has, however, been a shift towards granting security. This is illustrated by, for example, the revised German arbitration statute which expressly confers the power to grant security.[11] In Switzerland Article 183(1) of the Private International Law Act 1987 confers upon an Arbitral Tribunal the power to grant provisional or interim measures, and has been used occasionally to order security—usually where the claimant is insolvent. Similarly, in France, Articles 808-9 and 827-73 of the New French Code of Civil Procedure, which confers concurrent jurisdiction upon an Arbitral Tribunal and the national courts to grant provisional or interim measures, has also been used to similar effect.

When, and if, it comes to enforce a final award on the merits, the mechanism for doing so will generally be to register the award in the country where the assets are located so as to use the available mechanisms of the local enforcement. Such proceedings are intended to be effectively of an administrative nature rather than a decision on the merits. The award creditor will be the claimant in those court proceedings and the award debtor the defendant. Technically, an award debtor might be able to seek security from the award creditor as claimant but it is plain that the courts should be very reluctant to do so even if the award itself is challenged (and even on the basis that the award was obtained by fraud). It is counter-intuitive to do so and exceptional circumstances would be required to order security.[12]

Finally, it should be mentioned that certain International Conventions exclude the right to grant security. It is outside the scope of this work to consider these Conventions but any practitioner in the fields of carriage of goods or passengers by road or rail or nuclear energy or damage should consider applicable Conventions as should those involving certain countries that have articles directed to security. These include the former Czechoslovakia and Yugoslavia, Hungary, Iraq, Israel, and Turkey.

---

[10] Re Unisoft Group (No. 2) [1993] BCLC 532.

[11] German Code of Civil Procedure (1998) §1041(1).

[12] Gater Assets v. Nak Naftogaz Ukrainiy [2007] 2 Lloyd's Rep 588.

CHAPTER 39
COSTS ORDERS

Whenever called upon to make any decision or award, an Arbitral Tribunal should make an order for costs. Failure to make any order may be an abdication of responsibility and leave the parties in a state of uncertainty. That is not to say that one of the parties must be found to be at fault and made to pay costs. It is quite acceptable to defer a decision on the costs until the end. Deferring the decision or making costs dependant on some future event such as success is entirely proper and, often, the only way that interim costs orders can be made.

Part of the final award should deal with the deferred costs orders as well as the costs liability for the substantive issues. Orders that have been made for "Costs in the Reference" will be dealt with automatically by a decision on the costs of the reference. Costs that have been reserved ought to be specifically considered and either made costs of the reference or made specific orders. If nothing is said costs reserved would fall in with the costs of the reference.

The range of costs orders is large. Some of the more popular orders that might be made with the effect of the term set against them are in Appendix 28.

The Arbitral Tribunal has a wide and unfettered jurisdiction on costs and can craft a costs order to do justice to the particular situation. Those in the appendix are the more usual examples

A. The Applicable Rules for Costs

The key features of all of the Rules are that all require advances or deposits from the parties and all provide for joint and several liability of the parties for the expenses of the Arbitral Tribunal and the institution. They each provide in different ways for the costs of the parties and deserve careful consideration when issues of costs come to be considered.

CHAPTER 40
DISCONTINUANCE AND COSTS

When a claimant commences an arbitration, it causes the respondent to incur costs in defending itself. If the claimant later chooses to terminate the proceedings, the respondent is, on the face of it, entitled to its costs of defending itself through to date of the discontinuance. Its "innocence" (or at least its legal rights as it asserted them) has not been validly called into question.

The general rule governing the costs on discontinuance is that a claimant who discontinues is liable for the costs which the respondent incurred on or before the date of discontinuance.

A claimant who discontinues is, in effect, conceding that it has lost or cannot win. The basic rule has a logical foundation. It reflects the innocence of the respondent. The rule does, however, permit the respondent to apply to have costs assessed on an indemnity (or more generous) basis.[1]

Of more importance is the potential for a claimant to avoid all or part of the costs that would otherwise follow from discontinuance. The courts have on numerous occasions relieved the claimant from the ordinary costs burden.[2]

Examples of the exercise of this discretion to relieve the claimant of the burden to pay costs can be found in *Barretts & Baird (Wholesale) Limited v. Institution of Professional Civil Servants*[3] in which an interlocutory injunction preventing a strike effectively resolved the action and the court, on discontinuance, made no order as to costs up to the conclusion of interlocutory proceedings. In *Britannia Life v. Smith,*[4] similarly the court made no order. The last and perhaps definitive word on the subject came in *RTZ Pension v. ARC.*[5] The court reviewed the

---

[1] Atlantic Bar & Grill v. Post House Hotels Limited [2000] C. P. Rep 32.

[2] For those interested in the scholarly review of the 19th Century cases and, in particular, whether or not there is jurisdiction, as opposed to a discretion, to order a defendant to pay the costs of an arbitration discontinued by the claimant, *see* Richard Roberts Holdings Limited v. Douglas Smith Stimson Partnership (1988) 22 Con LR 60.

[3] [1987] 1 FTLR 121.

[4] [1985] CLY 3968.

[5] [1999] 1 All ER 532.

authorities and approached matters on the basis that where discontinuance incurs in circumstances "tantamount to defeat," the normal costs consequences should follow. The court contemplated that there could be cases in which a defendant should pay the costs of the claimant, in whole or in part, if the defendant had "perversely encouraged a plaintiff into action by concealing the existence of a defence although reasonably invited prior to proceedings to make disclosure" or some "misconduct of the defence in the sense of some act or omission, or course of conduct which is unreasonable or improper for the purposes of [the wasted costs jurisdiction]". No order as to costs might be appropriate if that was "fair and just in all the circumstances." Particular examples considered by the court were "some limited aspects or issues of the defendant's conduct or whether proceedings had become of only 'academic interest'." Nevertheless, the principle circumstance to be borne in mind was that the claimant had "abandoned all the pleaded issues without argument or adjudication and must therefore prima facie be regarded as having lost the day on all of them."

Further examples are *Everton v. WPBSA*[6] and *Jass v. Blackburn.*[7] In *Everton,* the court sanctioned discontinuance with no order of costs due to the bankruptcy of the defendant. In doing so, it accepted that there were circumstances in which the defendant might be deprived of costs and that these included those in which the claimant has "obtained an advantage from suing the defendant" and "when the claim had become academic by some act on the part of the defendant or some independent party."

In *Jass,* the court refused to deprive a defendant of his prima facie costs entitlement notwithstanding that there had been a clearly misleading answer to a very material question. Here too there had been a bankruptcy but not of the particular defendant against whom discontinuance was sought; rather, the spouse of that defendant (the main defendant to the action) had become bankrupt. Nevertheless, allegations of fraud and dishonesty had been made against the particular defendant and the court found that she was entitled to defend those serious allegations and as the claimant had given up the chance to prove these allegations, it had to accept the costs consequences.

---

[6] 2001 WL 1479768.

[7] [2003] EWHC 2963.

In *Walker v. Walker,*[8] the action concerned a claim by a liquidator for misfeasance against the directors of a company. In the course of the proceedings, the liquidator sought to discontinue on the basis that the costs that he was incurring, the assets of the respondents, and the likely recoveries, resulted in the claim not being commercially viable. The judge, at first instance, reached his decision as follows:

> Taking into account what is fair and just, I take into account the following matters: whether the application by the defendant can be safely equated with defeat or acknowledgment of defeat, whether the proceedings had in someway become academic, whether the claimant has obtained some legitimate benefit from the proceedings which it might not otherwise have obtained, what the economic value of the claim is, what the potential benefits of the claim might be, what the strength of the claim on a very prima facie basis is, not so as to conduct a mini trial but simply to see whether there was a reasonable basis for the claim and a continuing reasonable basis for the claim.

The Court of Appeal criticized this reasoning as follows:

> In making that list of the matters which he took into account, the judge made no reference to the relevance of any change (or not) in circumstances between the date when the proceedings were started and the date when the application to discontinue was made or the decision to discontinue was taken. In other words he left out of account any consideration as to why a claim which was started on the basis of certain expectations should be discontinued without an order for costs against the claimant in circumstances where the expectations have not, in fact, changed—even though they may have been re-evaluated.

The Court of Appeal found that the claim had always been "commercially worthless" and, as nothing had changed, there was no basis to depart from the general rule that the discontinuing claimant should pay the costs of his claim on discontinuance to the defendant.

---

[8] [2005] EWCA Civ 247.

The reasoning in *Walker* was applied in *BRG Resources plc v. Rastogi.*[9] The court summarised the state of the law thus:

- It is no part of the function of the court on an application to discontinue to attempt to reach a decision on the whether or not the claim will succeed . . .

- The burden is upon the party who seeks to persuade the court that some other consequence should follow than that the claimant should bear the defendant's costs on discontinuance and the task of the court is to consider whether there is some good reason to depart from the normal order . . .

- The test to be applied is not the simple one of looking at the action as it is and seeing what is the fair and just thing to do at the moment in time . . .

- Justice will normally lead to the conclusion that a defendant who defends himself at substantial expense against a claimant who changes his mind in the middle of the action for no good reason other than that he has re-evaluated the factors which have remained unchanged should be compensated in costs . . . and

- It is not the law that a claimant will only be required to pay the defendant's costs on discontinuance if he is in effect surrendering and acknowledging defeat.

On the facts, the court found the defendant's "totally unreasonable and unjustified stance" had been "unnecessarily aggressive" which had been calculated to "increase costs [and] make compromise at any stage the more difficult." In those circumstances, the claimant was permitted to discontinue and had to pay only 60% of the defendant's costs.

Accordingly, whilst the basic rule of a discontinuing claimant paying the defendant's costs remains and is the clear presumption, discretion remains. The claimant may be relieved of that obligation if he can point to misconduct by the respondent, where there has been a substantive victory at an interim stage and where there is no longer any objectively justifiable reason to continue, by reason of a change in circumstances—e.g., the bankruptcy of the defendant.

---

[9] [2005] EWHC 994.

Arbitral Tribunals should, it is suggested, apply such reasoning to any discontinuance of arbitral proceedings by a claimant although the particular facts will need to be carefully considered especially if there is to be a departure from the general rule of awarding the respondent its costs of the reference and reasons for doing so should be given in the award.

The discontinuance of an arbitral reference should not be permitted in every circumstance. A party might tactically discontinue the reference with a view perhaps to challenging or seeking to impugn an existing interim or partial award. It is clear that a discontinuance can be struck out or set aside if it would amount to an abuse of process. In such circumstances, it may be possible to allow a discontinuance on terms or refuse it altogether so as to permit the Arbitral Tribunal to rule on the substantive issue. This will be a rare step but it is submitted the jurisdiction remains. It may be that, for example, discontinuance could be permitted on terms that the party could not seek to challenge the validity of an existing partial or interim award.[10]

---

[10] Sheltam Railway Co v. Mirambo and Primefuels [2008] EWHC 829.

CHAPTER 41
COSTS OF APPLICATIONS

An Arbitral Tribunal will normally hold one or more preliminary meetings or hearings to deal with administrative and procedural matters.

The normal order at procedural hearings will be "Costs in the Reference." The costs incurred in preparation for, and attendance at, procedural hearings are invariably necessary for the proper conduct of the reference. There will be no winner or loser in making directions for the future conduct of the Reference. As such, the ultimate winner should recover those costs from the ultimate loser.

In other applications—e.g., where one party seeks additional time or some other indulgence from the Arbitral Tribunal—it may be that there is a clear "winner" or "loser." The party seeking the indulgence should pay the costs of the party from whom the indulgence is sought and indeed those of the Arbitral Tribunal. In those circumstances "Costs in any event" awarded in favour of the "winner" will be appropriate.

In more complex applications, whilst there may be a "winner" and a "loser," it may be unclear whether the application was justified. For example, if there is a contested application for discovery, the real issue between the parties may be whether documents are relevant. It may be that the Arbitral Tribunal concludes that the documents might well be relevant and decides to order a party to give additional disclosure but cannot be sure whether the documents will be genuinely relevant to the issues as they emerge at the evidentiary hearing and the Arbitral Tribunal sees the documents. In those circumstances, it may be appropriate to order "Costs reserved". A considered view can then be made to see if the documents are relied upon and are material to the Tribunal's decision.

Equally, it may be that one party has failed to cooperate and, irrespective of any final decision, should not be able to recover its own costs of the application, or that a party appears to have won but the Arbitral Tribunal is not persuaded it should make a "Costs in any event" order. The cooperative party or near "winner" might then be entitled to its—i.e., [Claimant's] or [Respondent's]—"costs in the reference" so that, if it ultimately won the reference, it would recover its costs. The main purpose of such orders is to disentitle one party from recovering its costs whatever the final outcome in terms of costs; thus if an order in an application is made as "Claimant's costs in the reference" and the Claimant goes on and wins the reference and obtains an award that the

Respondent pay the costs of the reference then the costs of that application fall in with the costs of the reference to be paid. If, however, the Respondent were to have won and obtained an award for the costs of the reference neither party would be entitled to recover the costs of that application—even the overall winner of the reference, here the Respondent, would be disentitled to the costs of the application as the Tribunal will have recorded some disapproval of its conduct in relation to the reference.

CHAPTER 42
COSTS OF THE REFERENCE

An Arbitral Tribunal will derive its powers on costs from the applicable national law and the procedural rules. Cases decided under national laws as applied by the courts may have little or no relevance. Nevertheless, the Tribunal must not take into account factors that should not be taken into account, fail to take into account factors that should have been taken into account, nor reach a decision based on an error of law or reach a costs decision which was one which no reasonable Tribunal could have reached. With that in mind the following commentary may assist.

The general rule is that the "loser" or unsuccessful party will be ordered to pay the "winner's" or successful party's costs. This general rule is enshrined in arbitration laws—e.g., §61(2) Arbitration Act 1996 which states ". . . the tribunal shall award costs on the general principle that costs should follow the event . . . "; UNCITRAL Article 40(1) which states: " . . . the costs of the arbitration shall in principle be borne by the unsuccessful party . . . ," or; LCIA Rules Article 28.4 which states: " . . . the Arbitral Tribunal shall make its orders on both arbitration and legal costs on the general principle that costs should reflect the parties relative success and failure . . . ." These are, of course, all subject to party autonomy and the parties are perfectly at liberty to agree otherwise subject to the prevailing national law, for example, §60 Arbitration Act 1996 (where applicable). §60 provides that any agreement that a party will pay all or any part of the costs in any event is valid only if made after the dispute has arisen. This has a lot to commend it—disputes may take any form and to pre-agree a result on costs may be appropriate for the perceived likely dispute but may not fit the unexpected dispute.

In some arbitrations, the substantive result will be a clear "winner" and "loser," a clearly successful party, and a clearly unsuccessful party, or an event that the costs should follow. If the issue is whether A should pay B, a stated sum of money or the effect of certain words in a contract—an "all-or-nothing" case—the result in terms of "winner" and "loser" is relatively easily expressed.

Clearly, at another extreme, there will be arbitrations with multiple issues and many contested issues of fact and law where each of the parties can each take comfort in some success. The task of assessing what costs order does justice to the substantive Award is then more complex.

In re *Elgindata Ltd (No. 2),*[1] the court set out the basic principles as follows:

(i) Costs are in the discretion of the court. (ii) They should follow the event, except where it appears to the court that in the circumstances of the case some other order should be made. (iii) The general rule does not cease to apply simply because the successful party raises issues or makes allegations on which he fails, but where that has caused a significant increase in the length or cost of the proceedings he may be deprived of the whole or part of his costs. (iv) Where the successful party raises issues or makes allegations improperly or unreasonably, the court may not only deprive him of his costs but may order him to pay the whole or a part of the unsuccessful party's costs.

The first task of the Arbitral Tribunal in considering costs is whether to apply the general rule of determining the "winner" and having costs follow the event or whether to make some different order. If the general rule is departed from, brief reasons should be given. The potential to disallow some costs acts as an incentive to moderate claims and defences and for responsible behaviour.

Normally, a departure from the general rule will be where a party has succeeded on only some of the allegations it has made especially where those allegations can be viewed as an issue where distinct costs or time has been spent. The third rule from *Re Elgindata* no longer represents the law in English courts. In those circumstances, it might very well be appropriate to award the "winner" the costs of the issues upon which it was successful but deprive it of those costs related to the issue upon which it was unsuccessful. Either no order for costs can be made on that issue, or the losing party (the successful party on the issue) might be entitled to its costs related to that issue.

This issue based approach is best summarised by the concise comment in *Monsanto Technology v. Cargill International:*[2]

Have you won, have you lost a suitably circumscribed issue, so that you should be deprived of your costs [of that issue], and is

---

[1] [1992] 1 W.L.R. 1207.

[2] [2008] F.S.R. 16.

this an exceptional case such as to lead to an adverse costs order on an issue in favour of the overall loser?

The assessment of costs on issues is possible but complicated and any degree of definition of issues will leave generic costs and the problem of how they should be apportioned. To avoid the problems associated with assessing costs by issue, the Arbitral Tribunal may find it helpful to arrive at a final percentage figure. Thus, if party A were successful on issues X and Y, but failed on issue Z and had incurred its costs in the proportions 60:30:10, the Arbitral Tribunal could simply award 90% of the costs disallowing the 10% incurred on issue Z.

If the Arbitral Tribunal wanted not merely to deprive A of its costs of issue Z but to award those costs to party B on the basis that it was unreasonable to raise and pursue issue Z, the Arbitral Tribunal can do so but will need additional information on, at least, the total amount of costs and the proportions applicable to specific issues in order to do so. If B had spent 50% more costs than A and had incurred them in the proportions 55:25:20 the Arbitral Tribunal might firstly disallow A from recovering its costs of issue Z and permit it to recover only 90% and then net off the costs B spent on issue Z by taking B's 20% of its costs but as they were 50% more than A's costs equating to 30% of A's costs resulting in permitting A to recover 60% of its costs. Although this might be rough-justice it is considerably easier than making issue based costs orders.

Although the Arbitral Tribunal will no doubt continue to refer to the parties as claimant and respondent, it is often easier when discussing some of the issues in this paper to refer to the party paying the costs as the "paying party" and the party to whom the costs are paid as the "receiving party."

A. Multiple Respondents

A claimant might pursue two respondents and succeed against only one. In the ordinary course of things, the successful respondent is entitled to its costs. The real issue is when the claimant reasonably pursued both respondents due to unclear facts as to which of the two was liable. This might arise in a case in which the respondents are two companies in the same group or the respondents are connected in some other way. In those circumstances, it might well be clear that the unsuccessful respondent should ultimately pay not only the costs of the claimant but also those of the successful respondent.

The issue then becomes whether those costs should be paid directly from the unsuccessful respondent to the successful respondent—i.e., a *Sanderson*[3] order—or whether, it is appropriate to order the claimant to pay the successful respondent with the right to recover the amount paid from the unsuccessful respondent—i.e., a *Bullock*[4] order. Where the claimant is of doubtful solvency, a *Sanderson* order does justice to the situation.[5]

B. Standard and Indemnity Costs

The normal consequence of an order for costs is that they are assessed on what is sometimes called a "standard" basis. Alone it is a fairly unhelpful or at least uncertain concept. It is only when it can be compared to the other basis, the indemnity basis, that it can be properly understood. The concepts of standard and indemnity costs are borrowed from the English courts. Here standard costs must be costs reasonably incurred, of a reasonable amount and proportionate and doubt is resolved in favour of the paying party. In contrast, indemnity costs need not be proportionate and the doubt is resolved in favour of the receiving party but again they must be reasonably incurred and of a reasonable amount. Indemnity costs should not be confused with an indemnity for the costs actually incurred. There is some superficial logic in the proposition that the party found to be in the wrong has caused the innocent party to bring the reference, incur costs and obtain an award. If this is regarded as a consequence of the breach of contract, then it can be argued that a full indemnity should be granted. In the same way, that an innocent party has limitations on the damages it can recover; likewise, should it have a limit on the costs that it can recover. An innocent party must act reasonably to mitigate its loss; it can have damages restricted by the concept of an abuse of right and the wrongdoer is only liable for those losses that are foreseeable and not too remote. The wrongdoer can foresee that the innocent party will incur costs but not that it would incur unreasonable costs. In this context an award of reasonable costs reasonably incurred does justice between the parties.

---

[3] Sanderson v. Blyth Theatre Co [1903] 2 KB 533.

[4] Bullock v. London General Omnibus Co [1907] 1 KB 264.

[5] For a discussion of principles on which the exercise might be exercised *see* Mayer v. Harte [1960] 2 All ER 840.

Proportionality, whether expressly incorporated by a definition of "standard" costs or simply as a just pathway consequence of reasonable costs, is likely to feature in the assessment of costs. Plainly, if a party spent disproportionate costs, they are likely to be unreasonable. Arbitral Tribunals might consider proportionality first in the round, considering the amounts in dispute, the number of issues, and the complexity of those issues—essentially, asking themselves whether spending $X was a reasonable and proportionate thing to do in this case. If the answer is "yes", that is probably the end of the proportionality issue and the Arbitral Tribunal can simply consider whether particular aspects of the claimed costs were reasonably incurred and of a reasonable amount. If the answer is "no", then the Arbitral Tribunal must consider what would have been spent had the claim or the defence been conducted proportionality. That figure will effectively cap the liability of the paying party if costs are on a standard basis.

Indemnity costs are awarded when the facts or the conduct takes the matter away from the normal case (in so far as there is ever a normal case). An award of costs on an indemnity basis is not penal, it does not enable a party to recover more costs than he has incurred. On the contrary, the practical effect is simply to minimise the shortfall between what a party has spent and what it recovers. In doing so, such an award of costs more closely reflects the contractual principle of putting the wronged party in the same position as if the contract had been properly performed—i.e., the wronged party would not have had to spend money in prosecuting the claim and defending itself from allegations that ultimately failed. Nor does an award of indemnity costs entitle the receiving party to recover costs unreasonably incurred or of an unreasonable amount. A paying party is accordingly protected from any perceived harsh consequences of such an order.

An award of indemnity costs will be made usually where the conduct of the paying party was unreasonable:[6]

> . . . [20] an award of costs on an indemnity basis is not intended to be penal and [. . .] regard must be had to what in the circumstances is fair and reasonable . . . [28] If costs are awarded on an indemnity basis, in many cases there will be some implicit expression of disapproval of the way in which the litigation has

---

[6] Phoenix Finance v. Federation International de l'Automobile [2002] EWHC 1242 (Ch) and Reid Minty v. Taylor [2002] 1 WLR 2800.

been conducted, but I do not think that this will necessarily be so in every case.

This latter point was also made in *McPhilemy v. Times Newspapers*[7] when the court held there was no stigma attaching to an award of indemnity costs. The judge had been wrong to refuse indemnity costs on the basis that it implied disapproval of the defendant's conduct.

Typical conduct justifying an award of indemnity costs is an allegation of malingering or some other serious allegation of fraud.[8]

If a commercial party embarks on, or brings on itself and pursues, large scale arbitration in a calculated way, that may be deserving of indemnity costs, as was the case in *Amoco v. BAO*.[9] In that case, the claimant sought to avoid a contract that was viewed as unprofitable by putting pressure on the defendant to renegotiate and, when that failed, terminating the contract. As the judge said:

> There is in my judgment a sound basis for concluding that Amoco conducted itself throughout the relevant events on the basis that its commercial interests took precedence over the rights and wrongs of the situation and that it was prepared to risk the outcome of litigation should BAO resist the pressures upon it and take on the challenge. BAO did take it on. It was then met with a constantly changing case as Amoco sought unsuccessfully to find a basis on which it could justify what it had done. If a party embarks on or brings upon itself and pursues litigation of the magnitude of this litigation in such circumstances and suffers a resounding defeat, involving the rejection of much of the evidence adduced in support of its case, in my judgment that provides a proper basis on which it is appropriate to award costs on an indemnity basis. Judged by the same standards I think BAO should now recover the costs it has incurred in consequence unless of course Amoco can show that they were unreasonable.

---

[7] [2001] 4 All ER 861.

[8] Cooper v. P&O Stena Line [1999] 1 Lloyds Rep 734.

[9] Amoco v. BAO [2002] BLR 135.

It might be unreasonable to refuse an offer to settle and this has brought about a practice of claimants offering to settle at, say, 95% of the claimed figure. Respondents might well say that is not really negotiating and represents a mere tactical device. The courts have considered this approach in *Huck v. Robson*[10] and found it perfectly legitimate. Whilst an offer to settle for 99.9% would be tactical and of no effect, a 5% discount was sufficiently material to be taken into account in determining the costs order to be made. On the facts, the majority of the court ordered the defendant to pay the claimant's costs on an indemnity basis.

This analysis is often immaterial for an Arbitral Tribunal that may move directly from findings on the merits to both making a costs order and assessing the amounts. Only in large cases will the Arbitral Tribunal make an order for costs and then proceed, as a separate exercise, to assess the amounts. More often, the process will be truncated to a single exercise. In the exercise of that jurisdiction, the Tribunal will reach a figure that it is considered should be paid. The assessment should proceed by assessing all of the factors in play and coming to a conclusion. In summary that will involve an assessment of (a) whether the successful party has lost on some identifiable part of the case and should be deprived of the costs of that part or issue (or exceptionally should pay the unsuccessful party's costs) (b) whether the costs are proportionate and (c) whether any party has behaved unreasonably so as to increase or decrease the amounts otherwise payable.

C. Conditional and Contingency Fees

In some jurisdictions, notably the U.S., the basis for remuneration of lawyers may not be a function of hourly rates and time spent.[11] It may be a proportion of the recovery or in some other way linked to the value of the claim or the recovery—the so-called "no-win, no-fee." This is unusual in commercial international arbitration but not impossible. If the lawyers are remunerated on this basis, it raises additional problems for the Arbitral Tribunal.

---

[10] [2002] 3 All ER 263.

[11] Although this is the normal way of a lawyer being retained in international commercial arbitration and common in most other litigation other than class actions and personal injury.

The conditional fee[12] can operate at a lower (or no) fee for a loss and a higher fee for success. Regulations can wholly outlaw such arrangements or allow them on terms. In England, for example, conditional fees have been allowed only relatively recently and are subject to a maximum uplift of 100% on what would otherwise have been charged. English solicitors remain unable to undertake work on a contingency fee[13] basis for all contentious proceedings.

If the Tribunal is faced with a costs claim on either a conditional or contingent basis, the first issue is whether the arrangement is lawful. This may be an extremely complicated question with the interaction of, firstly, the proper law of the retainer of the lawyer by the client and whether under that law the arrangement is lawful and, secondly, the *lex arbitri* and whether that permits of payment on that basis.

If the arrangement appears lawful the same principles of recoverability should nevertheless apply. The mere fact that a party has agreed an arrangement to pay either an amount that can only be finally ascertained after the event is not a bar, in principle, to the recovery. It has to be recognised that some element of the cost of a conditional or contingency fee arrangement is to pay for those cases that fail and also for the lawyer being kept out of his money for some time. Necessarily, it is likely that the costs claim on a conditional or contingency is likely to be higher than on a conventional basis. That of itself should not count against the conditional or contingency claim.

The starting point should still be the proportionality and reasonableness of the total fee claim. If the contingency fee passes that test, there is little more that can be said as there are no individual constituents that can be considered as reasonable or otherwise. The fee will be the easier to justify if the opposing party is given notice of the fact that the lawyer is working under a contingency fee albeit without revealing the terms of the fee. The opposing party then has the opportunity to apply to cap the fees and, if it does not take that opportunity, it cannot then complain that the contingency fee operates harshly against him.

---

[12] Here the phrase "conditional fee" will be used to refer to fees that, whilst still based on rates and hours, are conditional on the outcome.

[13] The phrase "contingency fee" will be used to refer to fees that reflect a proportion of the claim or recovery.

The conditional fee has an uplift percentage and that has to be reasonable in light of the risk that is being run. Otherwise, the conditional fee is built from time and rates so the same exercise of assessing the reasonableness can be gone through.

D. Offers to Settle

Before national courts, offers to settle are encouraged as a matter of public policy and to better enable them to do so offers are generally "without prejudice:"

> . . . parties should be encouraged so far as possible to settle their disputes without resort to litigation and should not be discouraged by the knowledge that anything that is said in the course of such negotiations . . . may be used to their prejudice in the course of the proceedings. They should . . . be encouraged to fully and frankly to put their cards on the table.[14]

The policy is that parties to a dispute should be encouraged to compromise and should see courts as a matter of last resort. The policy is also founded on the basis that the courts are organs of the State and, typically, funded by the State. The resources of the courts are precious and should be reserved for those who genuinely cannot resolve differences themselves.

In some national arbitrations, a practice of "sealed offers" has emerged. A sample "sealed offer" is at Appendix 29. As explained in *Tramountana Armadora SA v. Atlantic Shipping Co SA*:[15]

> Offers of settlement of arbitral proceedings can be of three kinds, namely, "without prejudice", "sealed" and "open". A "without prejudice" offer can never be referred to . . . A "sealed offer" is the arbitral equivalent of making a payment into court in settlement[16] . . . Neither the fact, nor the amount, of such a

---

[14] Cutts v. Head [1984] 2 WLR 349.

[15] [1978] 1 Lloyds Rep 391.

[16] Payments into court were an English mechanism of offering to settle. Quite literally the amount offered was paid into the court and the other party, typically the claimant, had 21 days to decide whether to accept. If it did it received the money and an order for costs. Necessarily, the judge determining the case was kept ignorant of the fact and amount of the payment. That regime has now been replaced by a system of written offers.

payment into court can be revealed to the judge trying the case until he has given judgment on all matters other than costs.

Sealed offers are not often used in international arbitration and most offers made with the intention of being referred to when the costs of the reference are to be determined are made without prejudice save as to costs. In either event, they have to be brought to the attention of the Arbitral Tribunal before it decides issues of costs. If the Tribunal renders an award final on all issues save for costs, then it can be addressed on costs in detail and provided with any offers made. If the Tribunal is to decide all issues on the claims and costs at the same time, some mechanism is required to communicate any offer such that the Tribunal does not see it until after making its decision on the merits and when making its decision on costs. The practice of putting offers in sealed envelopes—hence, "sealed offers"—only to be opened when costs are being considered addresses this.

In arbitration, the arrangements are essentially private and the full impact of the public policy is not visited on the arbitration regime. This is the more so when one of the cardinal principles of arbitration is party autonomy and if the parties chose not to settle arguably they should not be penalised for not doing so. Conversely, it is only when offers are considered that the true winner might be discovered.

It is against this background that offers to settle should be considered. Offers naturally enhance the prospects of settlement and are, thus, to be welcomed for it is the other side of the autonomy coin that the parties be permitted to settle on whatever terms they consider appropriate. The real impact of offers is that in light of whatever offers have been made it can be determined whether there is a winner and a loser.

If the claimant claims $100, the respondent offers $70, and the Arbitral Tribunal finds that the respondent is only obliged to pay $60, the respondent can say with some justification that at least after it made its offer to pay $70 it has "won" as, in retrospect the claimant should have taken the offer of $70.

It is this philosophy of winner and loser that has resulted in the practice of split costs orders where there has been an offer that in retrospect the claimant ought to have taken. The usual approach is that, in such a scenario, the claimant is entitled to the $60 that the Arbitral Tribunal found was due and its costs down to a reasonable time after the offer was made, to reflect that it ought to have accepted the offer. The sting is that the respondent is ordinarily entitled to its costs after the notional date when the offer could have been accepted on the grounds that thereafter it was the "winner." It follows that the quantification and timing of offers is crucial.

If a claim is exaggerated (see below) even if an offer is beaten it does not follow that the claimant should have all of its costs. To commence an exaggerated claim, refuse to attempt to settle and narrowly beat an offer can result in receiving costs to the date of the offer but paying costs thereafter as the court would look at the real winner and the conduct of the parties especially the refusal to settle.[17]

To be an effective offer, it should be for the principal amount that it is intended to offer plus interest to the date for acceptance and costs. An offer made inclusive of interest and costs is difficult to assess against an award for an amount that would otherwise attract costs and then trying to assess what the costs would have been at that time.

The Arbitral Tribunal should be kept ignorant of any offers until it has decided all questions other than costs and it should then be informed of such offers as have been made. Even if an offer was non-compliant or was very slightly bettered such offers might be material to the exercise of the overall wide discretion that the Arbitral Tribunal has on costs.

If an award is made on this basis the winner might have a costs liability that exceeds any recovery. Such awards would be enforceable even in jurisdictions not recognising an award of attorney's fees.[18]

E. ADR

The parties may well attempt to resolve their differences and compromise the issues between them while the arbitration reference is pending. The issue arises whether a party should be penalised in costs either for not seeking to resolve differences by alternative dispute resolution or by unreasonably refusing an invitation to participate in ADR or by participating in it unreasonably. The logic of promoting ADR is one of public policy. The national courts of a country are a scarce

---

[17] Painting v. University of Oxford [2005] EWCA Civ 161.

[18] In Blacklink Transport Consultants Pty Ltd v. Von Summer, 856 N.Y.S. 2d 496 (N.Y. Sup Ct. 2008), the court rejected arguments that such an award offended against public policy and due process.

resource and parties should be encouraged to resolve disputes themselves rather than by using the limited and precious resources of the State to determine the dispute. Generally, in international commercial arbitration the focus is not on conserving the State's resources; rather, it is to uphold the principles of party autonomy and freedom of contract. Often, in the context of international disputes where parties have agreed to refer to arbitration, the parties have agreed to assume the burden of costs associated with arbitrating disputes in exchange for the benefit of being able to avoid being subjected to national courts, where they may otherwise be forced to deal with the parochial attitudes of judges, delays, and biases in the process, as well as subjection to a foreign law. Why should a party be penalised in costs for doing what it has agreed to do and indeed in bound to do? The conduct of the parties is inevitably relevant to the issue of costs; a reticent respondent or manipulative claimant can contribute significantly to unnecessary costs If a party has generally behaved unreasonably that should have consequences in terms of costs and unreasonable conduct in the context of seeking to avoid the dispute or compromise the dispute should be no different.

F. Exaggerated Claims

A claimant who pursues an exaggerated and inflated claim must expect to bear the consequences when costs come to be assessed. The general rule is that a claimant who knows or who must be taken to know that its claim is unsustainable, in whole or in part, must expect to be heavily penalised in costs.

In Hooper v. Biddle & Co, a claimant who claimed £3.75m and accepted £38,000 with no interest and with costs to be decided by the court could not be said to have been a significant winner and the court made no order as to costs.[19] In *Jackson v. Ministry of Defence*, an offer of £50,000 had been made and the court allowed the claimant 75% of his costs on the proviso that the reasonableness of specific items could still be challenged if they related to the exaggerated parts of the claim.[20] Finally, in *E Ivor Hughes Education Foundation v. Leach,* a claimant who sought £610,000 and accepted £5,000 and abandoned the remaining

---

[19] Hooper v. Biddle & Co [2006] EWHC 2995.

[20] [2006] EWCA Civ 46.

claim was ordered to pay the costs of the abandoned claim whilst receiving the costs of the modest successful element.[21]

These examples demonstrate the contempt courts have for exaggerated claims. An Arbitral Tribunal, however, should exercise its own discretion on the facts before it however the cases give some guidance.

G. Settlement

It may be that the parties compromise all issues between them other than the costs of the reference and ask the Arbitral Tribunal to decide the incidence of costs. The correct approach, it is suggested, is to make a decision by a final award and conclude matters for the parties. That does not mean, however, that one party has to be ordered to pay the costs of another. It is a perfectly proper exercise of discretion to make a conscious decision to no order as to costs.

In *Boxall v. Waltham Forest Borough Council*,[22] the court indicated a number of factors relevant to the exercise of such discretion. Those relevant to international commercial arbitration are:

- The overriding objective is to do justice between the parties without unnecessary time and cost;

- At each end of the spectrum will be cases where it is obvious, either from the terms of settlement or from the impression formed of the merits that had the issues been fought, who had, or would have, won. The majority of cases will fall in the middle where the position is less clear. How far the Arbitral Tribunal should look at unresolved yet substantial issues will depend on the costs at stake and the conduct of the parties;

- In the absence of good reason to make any other order, the fall-back position is to make no order;

- The Arbitral Tribunal should not discourage the parties from compromising the issues between them by, for example, making concessions at an early stage.

---

[21] [2005] EWHC 1317.

[22] [2000] All ER (D) 2445.

In *Brawley v. Marczynski,*[23] the court clarified that there was no tradition of no order as to costs where a case was settled without judicial intervention.

Conversely, if parties reach a compromise where all issues are resolved including costs that will not affect earlier costs orders. So, for example, if one party was successful on an application for discovery and the Arbitral Tribunal made an order in its favour for the costs of that application, that order would survive a settlement settling the reference on the basis of no order as to costs in a consent award. This can be a trap for the unwary. If you intend to deal with any earlier costs orders, deal with them specifically. This can usually be done by the party in whose favour the order was made agreeing not to enforce or otherwise seek payment of the amounts due under the order. There can be issues in seeking to "overturn" in a final consent award what is otherwise a final award whether termed that or not.

---

[23] [2002] 4 All ER 1060.

CHAPTER 43
COSTS: ASSESSING THE AMOUNTS

Arbitral Tribunals generally assess the amount of costs themselves. Although the members may not have particular expertise in costs (as opposed to the substantive dispute they are asked to determine) this can be balanced by a better understanding of the issues and how they developed before them. Any gaps in the knowledge of the Tribunal and of the appropriate procedure to be adopted (for example what an appropriate hourly rate is) can be met by submissions from the parties. The members of the Tribunal will, however, be in business themselves and will have familiarity with previous cases and their own experiences either as lawyers submitting bills or in paying such bills; hence it is likely that such matters will be wholly outside the experience of the Arbitral Tribunal.

In England under §63 of the Arbitration Act 1996, if the Arbitral Tribunal does not determine the amount of the costs, any party may apply to the court to determine the costs. In practical terms, the court is likely to refer the assessment of the amount to a Costs Judge. The High Court in England has specialist judges (at the Supreme Court Costs Office) whose role it is to assess costs and either an Arbitral Tribunal can make a reference to the court or the parties, if concerned at the delay, can make their own approach.

An award finding that the costs should be "agreed or taxed[1] in default of agreement" is not a reference to the courts. On the contrary it is a neutral phrase indicating that the parties could, in default of agreement, apply to the Arbitral Tribunal to determine the costs.[2]

In determining the amount of the costs, the Arbitral Tribunal is likely to want to follow, expressly or otherwise, the general practice of the English courts. The English courts allow the recovery of costs reasonably incurred of a reasonable amount. The logic for this can be tested by the converse of disallowing costs unreasonably incurred or of an unreasonable amount.

---

[1] "Taxation" was the former name of the process in the English courts of assessing or fixing the amount of the costs. With the modernisation of the terminology in 1999, this was replaced with the concept of "assessment."

[2] M/S Alghanim Industries v. Skandia International Insurance [2001] 2 All ER (Comm) 30.

As has been discussed above, costs can be awarded on a standard basis or an indemnity basis. When assessing the amount the significance of whether the amount payable is assessed on a standard or on an indemnity basis comes into play. Essentially, if costs are assessed on a standard basis it reverses the presumption or burden of proof—the paying party has to establish that costs should not be payable and equally the concept of proportionality does not apply if costs are assessed on the indemnity basis. On a standard basis, doubts are resolved in favour of the paying party and on an indemnity basis in favour of the receiving party. For example, if the Arbitral Tribunal concluded that a particular document ought to take two to three hours to draft, on an indemnity basis it should allow three hours and on a standard basis, two hours.

Most claims for costs will be a function of one or more hourly rates (for the different personnel working on the case) and a number of hours spent by each of them. "The initial estimate of the reasonable attorney's fee is properly calculated by multiplying the number of hours reasonably expended on the litigation times a reasonable hourly rate."[3]

An assessment of costs before the English courts is a detailed procedure. There is a detailed bill specifying precisely what work has been done and what time has been spent where. The bill is supported by vouchers for all of the disbursements and the lawyer's file so that the court can see precisely the work actually done. As has been mentioned above, the English courts have specialist judges whose sole job is to assess recoverable costs. They may conduct hearings lasting days or weeks.

Such procedures are unlikely to be welcomed by an Arbitral Tribunal. A rough assessment of the costs is preferable. Undoubtedly, the Arbitral Tribunal will require some information to make an assessment and a schedule of the time spent and applicable hourly rates is likely to be helpful together with some detail of the disbursements paid. This will give the Arbitral Tribunal information on the costs actually spent by the successful party and hence the absolute maximum that could be awarded.[4]

---

[3] Blum v. Stenson, 465 U.S. 886, 888 (1984).

[4] There is a principle, known as the "indemnity principle," which provides that a party cannot recover more than it is liable to pay its own lawyers thus limiting the recovery to that amount. The exception is clearly where a party has incurred direct costs either by paying disbursements itself of incurred internal costs in pursuing or defending the claim.

The arbitral tribunal will have a wide discretion, for example, in a Singaporean case the court refused to set aside an award of costs of S\$2.8m said to be (a) contrary to public policy as being disproportionate and (b) in breach of natural justice as being allegedly on the basis of an international arbitration practice as to which no evidence was adduced.[5]

By the time it has come to the stage of assessing the amount, the Tribunal will have determined whether it wishes to award costs on less than a 100% basis perhaps because the generally successful party failed on specific issues or otherwise should not recover full costs. Assuming it is told, for example, that the costs incurred by the successful party were \$1,200,000 (based on 2000 hours at \$600ph) and the Tribunal determines that 25% of the costs were incurred on an issue which the successful party failed to establish, and those costs should be disallowed. The Arbitral Tribunal might thereby, for example, reduce the \$1,200,000 by 25% to give \$900,000. This would be the costs actually incurred on the allowable aspects of the claim. The Arbitral Tribunal might then find that some costs are likely to have been incurred unreasonably—an impression of the general conduct might indicate this—or be of an unreasonable amount—e.g., the rates at \$600ph might be too high—and disallow a further 15% for the combined effect of these aspects of unreasonableness to give \$765,000 and it might round this to \$750,000. This apparently crude approach is likely to give a reasonably fair result and save considerable time (and, hence, costs) in arguing over the detail.

The underlying premise for most awards is that they will be reasoned. This applies equally to the costs of the reference although there are a considerable number of awards that do not state the reasons for the decision on costs or on the amount awarded. The amounts involved can be substantial in their own right. Although the process of reasoning might be a little rough and ready the parties are entitled to and the Arbitral Tribunal is obliged to state reasons for the award on costs. To simply say that party A must pay party B \$X in respect of costs, is inadequate. Some reasons for the award must be stated if the award itself is reasoned. Furthermore, the award could be challenged on the basis of a failure to state the reasons in many jurisdictions and most institutional rules require it—e.g., ICC Article 25(2): "An award shall state the reasons upon which it is based."

---

[5] VV v. VW [2008] 2 SLR 929.

Data on prevailing hourly rates may be within the knowledge of the members of the Arbitral Tribunal. If not, there are plenty of published surveys. Perhaps the most well-known in the U.S. is Laffey Matrix;[6] in the U.K., the Guide to the Summary Assessment of Costs gives a wealth of information with Appendix 2 to the Guide providing guideline rates,[7] and the Legal 500 provides an overview of the costs in most jurisdictions.[8]

Rates in the U.K. may seem high in comparison with the U.S., but U.S. lawyers tend to be more aggressive with time recording than their U.K. counterparts resulting in more hours being recorded. This can offset any rate differential.

---

[6] Available on line at www.laffeymatrix.com.

[7] Available on line at http://www.hmcourts-service.gov.uk/publications/guidance/scco/appendix_2.htm.

[8] Available on line at www33.legal500.com.

CHAPTER 44
THE AWARD

The Award is the culmination of a great deal of work both by the arbitrators and by the parties and their counsel.

Before the Award can be drafted, the arbitrators have to decide upon the issues in the reference which may vary considerably in number. If the terms of reference have been drafted with care and precision, or if a list of issues has been drawn up, the issues that fall for determination may simply be reflected by a process of working through those existing documents.

The Arbitral Tribunal will make its decisions carefully and in light of the evidence both factual and expert, by applying the applicable law and the submissions that have been made, all of which will have been canvassed either at a hearing or in memorials or briefs of some kind. Those decisions, together with the reasons for them, are set out in the Award, which may be declaratory—i.e., a statement by the tribunal that a certain state of affairs does or should exist—but is more commonly mandatory, that is to say a direction that one or the other party do certain things, usually pay money in respect of the substantive issues decided and usually also pay money in respect of the costs of the reference.

An international arbitration, even one concerning relatively small issues, is a considerable intellectual and financial exercise. It is also likely to cost a considerable amount of money. The Award is not merely the final product; it is the instrument through which the objectives of the arbitration, the proper determination of the Tribunal as between the parties, are to be given effect. The importance of the Award is self-evident. Necessarily, it must be fit for purpose; it must be enforceable.

In general, that does not require an Award to be made in some particular form or style (although it does perhaps call for a good standard of presentation). As the court said in *Bremer Handelsgesellschaft mbH v. Westzucker GmbH (No. 2); Westzucker GmbH v. Bunge GmbH:*[1]

> No particular form of award is required . . . all that is necessary is that the arbitrators should set out what, on their view of the evidence, did or did not happen, and should explain succinctly why, in the light of what happened, they have reached their decision and what that decision is.

---

[1] (1981) Lloyd's Rep. 130.

The ICC Rules, in Article 27, provide for scrutiny of the draft Award:

> Before signing any Award, the Arbitral Tribunal shall submit it in draft form to the Court. The Court may lay down modifications as to the form of the Award and, without affecting the Arbitral Tribunal's liberty of decision, may also draw its attention to points of substance. No Award shall be rendered by the Arbitral Tribunal until it has been approved by the Court as to its form.

As the wording makes clear the scrutiny is as to form the intention being both to uphold the standards of the ICC and to ensure an enhanced prospect of success in enforcement—should that prove necessary.

A. Binding in Honour

Very rarely parties may have agreed that an Award be binding in honour only, and in consequence the parties will have agreed not to have recourse to enforcement. Care should be taken in such cases to distinguish between i) an agreement that provides itself not to be legally binding and is said to be binding in honour only and ii) an agreement that is binding but to be interpreted honourably. There is some debate as to whether the first type is arbitrable at all. As the agreement could not be enforced in such a jurisdiction, public policy might be a ground to deny recognition and execution. The second type, however, an agreement pointing to the use of extra-legal standards in its interpretation, has been accepted, for example, in England in *Home Insurance Co., and St. Paul Fire and Marine Insurance Co. v. Administration Asiguricor De Stat.*[2] There an arbitration clause was in the following terms: "The award of the Arbitrators . . . shall be final and binding upon all parties without appeal. This Treaty shall be interpreted as an honourable engagement rather than as a legal obligation and the award shall be made with a view of effecting the general purpose of this treaty rather than in accordance with a literal interpretation of its language . . . ." That Court did not accept arguments that the language bound the parties in honour only and not in law. The Court decided that the Arbitral Tribunal were only relieved from strict rules of interpretation.

---

[2] [1983] 2 Lloyd's Rep. 647.

To examine the enforceability of awards one needs to analyse the requirements of relevant jurisdictions. In that context, it is at least arguable that the New York Convention of 1958 is so widely espoused, throughout the World, as to form a sound basis for the analysis of Arbitral Awards, whether or not the country in which enforcement is sought is a signatory to the Convention. That is not to say that an Award that satisfies the NYC criteria necessarily will satisfy the authorities in any other country. The opposite is probably correct; an Award which does not meet the NYC criteria will not satisfy the authorities of a non-signatory even if there is some direct treaty. The basic necessities of a practical Award are considered in the light of the NYC. An Arbitral Award is a document having direct legal force for the parties to the reference. If, in the event, a party does not comply with it voluntarily, then it will have to be enforced.

For that purpose, it must be clear what is the legal standing of the document, who the parties are, what they are required to do, what is the legal basis for that requirement and why that legal basis applies to the matter.

B. Legal Standing

It is trite to say that an arbitral award is made in the context of an arbitration, but that is the source of its standing. The authority of the award is the authority of the Arbitral Tribunal and that authority is the authority granted by the parties in their arbitration agreement and whatever appointment mechanism that agreement creates (or adopts). The award should state that there was an arbitration agreement. In most jurisdictions the arbitration agreement must be evidenced in writing. To satisfy the New York Convention, it must be in writing. The award should identify the agreement, whether it was a separate agreement, or part of some other agreement. If the agreement provided for conditions precedent to arbitration, the award should state how they were met or whether they were waived by agreement of the parties. The fact of an arbitration hearing and of any other material procedural steps should be recorded if they are relevant to the decision and its enforcement. One must bear in mind the necessity of demonstrating that the tribunal was properly constituted and that each party was given an adequate opportunity to state his case. Therefore, decisions on material objections generally should be recorded, if only to demonstrate that they were correctly made.

C. Parties

In some jurisdictions, for an order of the Court to have effect against a corporate body, it may require some formalities, such as the identification of that body by name, registered address, and company reference number. There is a danger, in arbitral hearings, that the precise identity of one or other party will become obscured, particularly when various subsidiary companies or government agencies have been involved together. In the rare event that they are not the parties to the original arbitration agreement, the award must set out the legal basis of any substitution.

D. Requirements

The section presenting the Tribunal's final directions to the parties, the dispositive section of the award, usually comes at its conclusion and is best separated from the remainder by some clear form of words which makes it clear that what follows is what the binding decision of the tribunal is. In one sense, the dispositive section is the only true award, the remainder being its justification. That is why some English awards open the dispositive section with words such as "*. . . and I hereby award and direct as follows . . . ..*" Each direction in the award must be specific, unambiguous and capable of performance by the party against whom it is directed. They should not be conditional save in exceptional circumstances where the possibility of a conditional element in the award has been canvassed and agreed by the parties. A tribunal should avoid any direction, for example, that some thing be done "to the satisfaction of the Tribunal (or of the Tribunal's expert)" for two reasons: one that such an arrangement places the Tribunal (or the expert) in an invidious position which is no longer one of making a judgement between parties; the other that the subjective implication makes the award itself impracticable of enforcement.

E. Reasons

Most awards will be reasoned—indeed §52(4) of the English Arbitration Act 1996 and the ICC and many other Rules provides that awards shall contain reasons—and this should equally apply to the decision on costs. There is no automatic sanction for failing to give reasons rather an aggrieved party can either apply to the Arbitral

Tribunal for reasons or apply to the court where the remedy will usually be to remit the matter back to the Arbitral Tribunal for reasons. It usually difficult to envisage a situation where the absence of reasons necessitated setting aside the award however in the Australian case *Oil Basins Ltd v. BHP Billiton Ltd*[3] the court set aside an award for inadequate reasoning and a failure to deal with relevant evidence. The court held that a retired judge was required to give a higher standard of reasoning in making an award.

F. Legal Basis

This is the analysis of law and fact that founds the award. The best view as to content is that it should be confined to such findings of fact as are necessary, without detailed reasoning leading to those findings of fact. That is because, in most jurisdictions, findings of fact are not appealable and so the discussion which precedes such findings is of little value to the Court. Similarly, such details are not helpful to the Court from whom execution is sought. Nevertheless, where complex technical or factual issues are involved (especially where there are allegations of fraud or other dishonesty), the parties inevitably want and carefully consider a complete set of reasons. In some circumstances, that more complete set of reasons may be provided as an annexe with a clear statement that they do not form part of the award. Care has to be taken, however, that the parties are content about this approach, because the mere declaration that the additional reasons are separate may not mean, of itself, that they are not admissible as evidence if some dispute arises as to the Award.

Needless to say the decision should be a fair and balanced view of the evidence and findings should derive from the evidence adduced and must not, for example, rely on private knowledge of one or more of the arbitrators.

G. Form

Having said that no particular form is required, it may be as well to offer first a frame work and then a checklist of features which may be present in a typical award. There is little jurisprudential basis for this, but it may be helpful. It is fairly natural for individuals to adopt a visual style

---

[3] [2007] VSCA 255, [54] – [60].

close to that of the national court practice with which they are familiar. What follows is to a limited extent English, and may be more formal than is always necessary. The so-called recitals, for example, are only provided to make the award stand on its own and to facilitate enforcement.

What follows is divided into three parts:

- The recitals: the creation of the Tribunal and the preparation of the reference;[4]

- The reasons:[5] the circumstances of the dispute, the evidence adduced and accepted and the decisions of the Tribunal;[6]

- The disposition: the Tribunal's directions which give effect to the award.[7]

As ever it must be borne in mind that the Award has three main purposes. First, to tell the parties what they must do. Second, to explain why the decision has been made and third, that of consideration by an enforcing body or a Court of Appeal, this demands, not formality, but sufficient information to enable the award to stand on its own.

A sample award is at Appendix 30.

H. Partial Awards

The Arbitral Tribunal may issue one or more awards that do not dispose of the entirety of the reference before them. The debate may be whether a decision is an award in the true sense or an order irrespective of what the decision is termed. It may be a decision on an application for interim or provisional relief in the sense that it is a non-final decision.

---

[4] The claims and defences advanced by the parties; the applicable arbitration rules and governing laws and the major phases of the reference (including the submission of memorials and briefs) and the evidentiary hearing and witnesses (including experts).

[5] Under some systems (usually domestic) an award must be unreasoned unless the parties agree otherwise but a reasoned award is the accepted "norm" in international arbitration and some rules expressly require a reasoned award—e.g., ICC Rules Art 25.2.

[6] The award should be clear and unequivocal so as to avoid issues of interpretation and requests for clarification. This is especially so where the relief granted is declaratory or mandatory rather than simply in money terms for an award for the payment of a specific sum ought not to be capable of dispute as to the terms.

[7] This should include the place and date of the award.

On the other hand, there may be decisions that are decisive and determinative of a particular issue or issues. Such awards are sometimes described as "interim" awards but "partial" is probably a better descriptor. Most institutional rules permit such awards.[8] Even if the governing rules permit such awards the Arbitral Tribunal and counsel should ensure that the laws of the seat of the arbitration do not require one final award (and, for counsel, equally that the country of any prospective enforcement does not require one award).

The classic situation of such partial awards is the bifurcation of liability and quantum but equally jurisdiction challenges (whether arbitral jurisdiction or whether a party is bound by the arbitration agreement) are apt for such awards.

Once a final award is issued the Arbitral Tribunal will be *functus officio* and cannot revisit the issues decided in that award. Care should be taken that any new evidence on a subsequent issue (for example at a full evidentiary hearing on the merits) is not likely to impact on the decision made and reflected in the partial award.

I. Dissents

Most institutional rules provide for the potential of a majority decision.[9] Lawyers from civil law jurisdictions may find a dissent an unusual event. A dissent does not affect the enforceability of the award. The decision for the troubled member of the Arbitral Tribunal is whether to formally dissent or whether to express concerns in the body of the award.[10] If a formal dissent is contemplated it is preferable for the decision of the majority and the dissent to be drafted simultaneously so that each can take into the account the reasoning of the other. This enables the common ground to be identified and perhaps for the points of divergence to be narrowed or eliminated.

If the two party-appointed arbitrators take a diverging view, the chairman may take a middle line resulting in 3 different views. In that event some institutional rules provide for the chairman alone to make the

---

[8] ICC Rules Art 23; ICDR Rules Art 21; LCIA Rules Art 25; UNCITRAL Rules Art 26.

[9] ICC Rules Art 8; ICDR Rules Art 5; LCIA Rules Art 5.4; UNCITRAL Rules Art 5.

[10] For example, "Mr X would not have found that [event] occurred and would have been inclined to find that [different event] occurred but does not dissent from the findings of the majority and the relief granted."

decision.[11] Every effort should be made to avoid an award that is "buffet" style with different members subscribing to different aspects of the final award.

J. Awards by Consent

The parties may reach agreement and request the Arbitral Tribunal to issue an award by consent. Issues may arise as to whether the parties can be compelled to submit to a consent award; some institutional rules contemplate the withdrawal of the claim and a simple termination of the reference.[12]

Simply from a standpoint of certainty, an award by consent is probably the right route for the conclusion of most references on this basis. A sample award on this basis is at Appendix 31.

K. Conditional Awards

Although conceptually possible awards conditional upon some agreement by one or more of the parties (for example, not to enforce pending the conclusion of the reference) are best avoided. The relevant rules may not permit a conditional award in any event.

L. Correction of the Award

Most institutional awards permit modest correction of the award.[13] This will usually permit correction or clarification of typographical, computational or similar errors and not wholesale modification or revision. The jurisdiction is not there to permit parties to reargue points already put and determined nor to permit the Tribunal to have second thoughts. When the Tribunal has made its decision it is *functus officio* and without specific entitlement under rules or national law has no power to alter its decision. The ICC Bulletin "Correction and Interpretation of Arbitral Awards Under the ICC Rules of Arbitration"[14] is illustrative of the restrictive nature of the power to correct:

---

[11] ICC Rules Art 25.1; LCIA Rules Art 26.3.

[12] ICDR Rules Art 29.1; LCIA Rules Art 26.8; UNCITRAL Rules 34.1 (compare ICC Rules Art 34.1).

[13] ICC Rules Art 29; LCIA Rules Art 27; ICDR Rules Art 30; UNCITRAL Rules Art 36.

[14] ICC Ct Bulletin Vol 13, No. 1 (2002) 61.

One of the main fears of the drafters of the 1998 Rules regarding Article 28 was that losing parties would resort to it automatically, in an attempt to appeal the tribunal's decision on the merits. In addition to prolonging ICC proceedings, this would undermine the finality of ICC awards, which is generally considered an attractive feature of ICC arbitration. Besides, this was not the intended purpose of Article 29, which was rather to allow tribunals to express more clearly the substantive findings set forth in an award, not to change findings or make new findings.[15]

Tribunals may find some assistance from cases arising from the English Administration of Justice Act 1982 in the context of correcting errors in wills. In *Wordingham v. Royal Exchange Trust Co. Ltd. and Another*[16] the Court sought to define "clerical error" and held that "Clerical error" in s.20 (1)(a)Administration of Justice Act 1982 meant an error made while recording the intended words of the testator rather than an error made in carrying the testator's intentions into effect:

> In the first supplement to Theobald on Wills, 14th ed. (1982), the editor introduces the provisions of section 20(1)(a) under the heading of "requirements for rectification." Halfway through paragraph G he says:

> "The expression 'clerical error' points to the nature of the error, not to the person who made it. It appears to cover the situation where the material words were inserted in, or omitted from, the will owing to an error on the part of the testator, the draftsman or the engrosser, who did not advert to the significance and effect of the words inserted or omitted."

> In support of that passage is cited In re Morris [1971] P 62 . In that case Latey J. approved a passage in Mortimer on Probate, Law & Practice, 2nd ed. (1927), p. 80:

---

[15] *See* the Bulletin also at p.64 "Article 29 was not meant to empower tribunals to change the substance of their awards" and at p. 71 "Article 29 ... has functioned well, offering a clear procedure for repairing small errors."

[16] [1992] Ch. 412.

"Where the mind of the draftsman has never really been applied to the words in a particular clause, and the words are introduced into the will per *in curiam*, without advertence to their significance and effect, by a mere clerical error on the part of the draftsman or engrosser, the testator is not bound by the mistake unless the introduction of such words was directly brought to his notice."

That passage must equally apply where the error is one of omission and not inclusion.

There is further support for the passage in the supplement to Theobald on Wills in certain obiter comments of Nicholls J. in In re Williams, decd. [1985] 1 WLR 905. That was a case which was dealt with under section 21 of the Act of 1982 but Nicholls J. dealt briefly with section 20 by saying, at pp. 911-912:

"In passing, I note that there is no claim for rectification in the present case. It was suggested in the course of argument that section 20 could not apply to a home-made will such as the one before me, because 'clerical error' in section 20(1)(a) suggests a clerk. I do not accept this. A testator writing out or typing his own will can make a clerical error just as much as someone else writing out or typing a will for him."

My attention was drawn to an Australian case, Reg. v. Commissioner of Patents, Ex parte Martin (1953) 89 C.L.R. 381. That was a case where the court was construing a section of certain legislation dealing with patents which provided:

"The commissioner may on the request in writing accompanied by the prescribed fee correct any clerical error in the Register of Patents or in any proceedings under this Act . . ."

In that case the applicant had applied for the registration of a patent inadvertently declaring in his application that he was the actual inventor of the invention concerned whereas in fact he was the assignee. The decision was a majority decision with Williams A.C.J. dissenting but on grounds which are irrelevant to this case. In his dissenting judgment Williams A.C.J. said, at p. 395:

"A clerical error, I would think, occurs where a person either of his own volition or under the instructions of another intends to write something and by inadvertence either omits to write it or writes something different."

In the leading judgment of the majority Fullagar J. said, at p. 406:

"But the characteristic of a clerical error is not that it is in itself trivial or unimportant, but that it arises in the mechanical process of writing or transcribing. There is no evidence that the mistake so arose in the present case, and it is very difficult to see how it could have so arisen. The mistake, however innocently made, consists in a simple mis-statement of fact, and that is the whole of the matter."

Williams A.C.J. cited the English case, In re Sharp's Patent, Ex parte Wordsworth (1840) 3 Beav. 245, to assist him in construing the words "clerical error." In that case Lord Langdale M.R. said in the penultimate paragraph of his judgment, at p. 254:

"And in every case which has occurred, it has plainly been intended to do no more than to amend mere slips or clerical errors made by the parties, or the agents of the parties, who intending to make an accurate enrolment, have, by mere inadvertence, made an enrolment which was not what it purported to be, a true statement of that which the party intended at the time . . ."

It does not seem to me that there is any conflict between the definitions of "clerical error" contained in the judgments of Williams A.C.J. and that of Fullagar J. although it was submitted to me that there was such conflict.

It seems to me that the words "clerical error" used in section 20(1)(a) of the Act of 1982 are to be construed as meaning an error made in the process of recording the intended words of the testator in the drafting or transcription of his will. That meaning is to be contrasted with an error made in carrying his intentions into effect by the drafter's choice of words and with a mistaken choice of words because of a failure to understand the testator's intentions, a circumstance covered by subsection (b).

Making such a correction may also impact on the costs award and that very situation arose in *Gannet Shipping Ltd v. Eastrade Commodities Inc.*[17] That concerned §57(3) Arbitration Act 1996 which provides: "*The tribunal may on its own initiative or on the application of a party (a) correct an award so as to remove any clerical mistake or error arising from an accidental slip or omission . . . .*" Similar provisions are found in most institutional rules. The arbitrator made an award that included an amount for a greater amount than the parties had agreed was the correct figure. A costs award was also made on the perceived ground that the success had been larger than it really had been. On an application to remit the award for reconsideration, the court found that the mistake as to the amount was a "slip" because it was wrong and it was "accidental" as there had been no intention to use the wrong figure. The costs error which had been predicated on the accidental slip "arose from" the accidental slip and hence that too could be corrected.

---

[17] [2002] 1 All ER (Comm) 297.

APPENDIX 1
LAWS OF THE ARBITRATION

Lex Arbitri – the law governing the arbitral proceedings – usually the law of the country of the place or "seat" of the arbitration – essentially the same as the *lex fori*

Lex Causae – the law governing the cause or question to be determined, it can be more specifically referred to as:

lex domicilii – law of domicile

lex patriae – law of nationality

lex locus contractus – law of country where contract is made

lex loci solutionis – law of country where contract is to be performed

lex loci deliciti – law of country where a tort is committed

lex situs – law of the country where the thing is situated

lex loci actus – law of the country where a legal act takes place

lex monetae – law of the country in whose currency a debt or other obligation is expressed

Lex Fori – the domestic law of the forum

Applicable Law – see Substantive Law

Curial Law – the law governing the conduct of the specific reference

Governing Law – see Substantive Law

Substantive Law – the law governing the substantive issues in dispute

Proper Law of the Contract - see Substantive Law

APPENDIX 2
SAMPLE FORMAL PARTS OF AWARD ON NON-COMPLIANCE WITH CONDITION PRECEDENT

[set out usual introductory parts]

[set out provisions and non-compliance]

The Tribunal therefore formally declares and awards:

A. that it has no jurisdiction over the matters referred to it by reason of the failure to comply with the condition precedent to any such jurisdiction;

B. [that the claims against the Respondent are dismissed without prejudice to the right to make a further request for arbitration after compliance with the condition precedent];

C. [that the claims are stayed pending compliance with the condition precedent];

D. [that the Claimant shall pay the Respondent's costs of the arbitration [to date] [on an indemnity basis] such costs to be assessed by the Tribunal in default of agreement];

E. [all other decisions, [including the assessment of costs,] are reserved for a further award(s)].

APPENDIX 3
SAMPLE REQUEST FOR ARBITRATION

IN THE MATTER OF AN ARBITRATION UNDER THE RULES OF
THE INTERNATIONAL CHAMBER OF COMMERCE
BETWEEN:

A

Claimant

v.

B

Respondent

REQUEST FOR ARBITRATION

A. Introduction

1. By this Request for Arbitration (the Request) A requests arbitration of its dispute with the Respondent, B.

2. The parties have agreed that disputes between them shall be resolved by arbitration under the Rules of Arbitration (the Rules) of the International Chamber of Commerce (ICC).

3. The dispute arises out of an agreement dated [date] executed by A and B (the Agreement). A copy of the Agreement is annexed.

4. The purpose of the Request is to comply with Article 4 of the Rules and set out a general summary of the matters in dispute. For the avoidance of doubt A reserves the right to raise any and all further claims arising out of or in connection with the disputed matters described in this Request or otherwise arising between the parties under the Agreement. Further A reserves the right to produce such further documents, evidence of fact, expert opinion or legal arguments as may be necessary to present its case or rebut any case that may be put forward by the Respondent.

B. The Parties and Their Representation

5. The Claimant A, is a company organized under the laws of ... (company registration number ...) which operates as a ... A's principal place of business is located at:

6. A is represented in this arbitration by [name] whose address for correspondence and the service of all notices and other documents in connection with this arbitration is as follows:

7. The Respondent B, is a company organized under the laws of ... (company registration number ...) which operates as a ... B's registered office is at:

8. B is, so far as A is aware, represented by:

C. The Agreement to Arbitrate and Governing Law

9. Clause [X] of the Agreement contains the parties' agreement to arbitrate and provides:

   [set out arbitration clause]

10. Clause [Y] of the Agreement provides [set out clause dealing with governing law]

11. Accordingly, there shall be three arbitrators, the seat is London and the language and governing law are English.

D. A's Nomination of an Arbitrator

12. A nominates D for confirmation by the Secretary General or the ICC Court as its party-appointed arbitrator. A calls upon the Respondent to nominate an arbitrator for confirmation and thereafter calls upon the ICC Court to appoint a Chairman unless the parties should agree that they or their nominated arbitrators should first attempt to agree a Chairman, in which event the ICC will be notified.

13. D's contact details are as follows:

14. So far as A is aware, D is independent of the parties.

E. Summary of Claim

15. [set out summary claim]

F. Relief Claimed

16. A seeks an award (including all and any necessary interim, partial or provisional awards; declarations; accounts and enquiries and the dismissal of all and any claims of the Respondent) as follows:

[set out relief claimed]

[signed and dated]

A's Counsel

APPENDIX 4
SAMPLE ANSWER TO REQUEST

IN THE MATTER OF AN ARBITRATION UNDER THE RULES OF
THE INTERNATIONAL CHAMBER OF COMMERCE
BETWEEN:

A

Claimant

v.

B

Respondent

ANSWER TO REQUEST FOR ARBITRATION

A. Introduction

1. In this Answer B sets out its defence to the claims advanced by A in the Request and sets-off and counterclaims as appearing below.

2. The purpose of this Answer is to comply with Article 5 of the ICC Rules and set out a general summary of the matters in dispute. For the avoidance of doubt B reserves the right to raise any and all further claims arising out of or in connection with the disputed matters described in this Answer or otherwise arising between the parties under the Agreement as defined in the Request. Further B reserves the right to produce such further documents, evidence of fact, expert opinion or legal arguments as may be necessary to present its case or rebut any case that may be put forward by the Claimant.

B. The Respondent and Its Representation

3. B, is a company organized under the laws of … (company registration number …) which operates as a … B's registered office is at:

4. B is represented by:

C. The Agreement to Arbitrate and Governing Law

5. B concurs on the place of the arbitration, the applicable rules of laws and the language of the arbitration as stated by A. *[or as the case may be]*

D. B's Nomination of an Arbitrator

6. B concurs that there should be 3 arbitrators and B nominates E for confirmation by the Secretary General or the ICC Court as its party-appointed arbitrator. B calls upon the ICC Court to appoint a Chairman unless the parties should agree that they or their nominated arbitrators should first attempt to agree a Chairman, in which event the ICC will be notified.

7. E's contact details are as follows:

8. So far as B is aware, E is independent of the parties.

E. A's Claims in the Request

9. B comments as to the nature and circumstances of the dispute as follows:

10. B identifies below each of the heads of claim in the Request and summarises B's position to each of them as follows:

F. B's Set-Off and Counterclaim

11. B will set-off so much of its counterclaim appearing below as may be necessary in diminution or extinction of A's claims.

12. [set out summary claim]

G. Relief Claimed

13. B seeks an award (including all and any necessary interim, partial or provisional awards; declarations and accounts and enquiries) as follows:
    - the dismissal of all and any claims of the Claimant
    - [set out additional relief claimed]

    [signed and dated]

    B's Counsel

APPENDIX 5
SAMPLE JOINT LETTER TO POTENTIAL CHAIRMAN FROM COUNSEL TO PARTIES

Dear [name]

[Name of Arbitration Reference]

We write to enquire whether you would be willing and able to accept a nomination to act as Chairman of a panel of three arbitrators in the above ICC arbitration.

The proceedings relate to .....

In order to ensure that there is no conflict of interest in your acting as Chairman, we set out below some additional information concerning the parties:

1) A is a company incorporated in ..., with company registration number ... , with its registered office at ....

2) B is a company incorporated in ... with company registration number..., with its registered office at ...

A is represented by ... and B is represented by ... The contact details of these firms appear below:

The dispute resolution provision in the agreement provides for any arbitration proceedings to be conducted in accordance with the Rules of Arbitration of the International Chamber of Commerce. The dispute resolution provision further provides that there shall be three arbitrators, the venue of the proceedings shall be ... and the language of the proceedings is to be ... The agreement is governed by ... law.

The party nominated arbitrators are:

By A: Mr C of ....

By B: Mr D of ....

If we can assist further in any way please do not hesitate to contact us.

Yours faithfully

[signed]   [signed]
A's counsel   B's counsel

Copy for information:
Mr C and Mr D

APPENDIX 6
SAMPLE AGENDA FOR FIRST MEETING

A v. B

Preliminary Meeting Agenda for [date and time] at [venue]

1   Welcome from Chairman

2   Introduction of attendees – both representatives of parties[1] and counsel

3   Confirmation that arbitration pursuant to arbitration clause in agreement dated [date] between [parties]

4   Confirmation that [name] institutional rules apply OR if none whether any should apply

5   Seat of arbitration [ability to have hearings at another venue]; language to be [state]

6   Confirmation that no change of name of any party; any changes to be notified

7   Address for service / communication confirmed; any changes to be notified

8   Any issues as to appointment of Tribunal

9   Any issues as to jurisdiction of Tribunal

10 Whether appropriate to take any disputed jurisdiction as preliminary issue or any other preliminary issue

11 Procedure for reference:[2] timetable for

---

[1] The Tribunal invites appropriate senior representatives of the parties to attend the preliminary meeting. The Tribunal does not expect any resolution of issues at the meeting, since its purpose is procedural rather than substantive. Nevertheless, the Tribunal considers that attendance of senior representatives enables a better understanding by those representatives of the issues, time and cost of the process which may itself promote settlement.

[2] The Tribunal invites the parties through their respective counsel to confer (and meet as necessary) to seek to agree a procedure that they consider meets the needs of the disputes referred to the Tribunal. Any agreement is subject to the agreement of the Tribunal. All timescales should be carefully considered and the Tribunal invites the parties to place a reasonable timeframe on procedural steps so that applications for extensions are kept to a minimum.

11.1   pleadings
11.2   list of issues[3]
11.3   discovery
11.4   statements of witnesses
11.5   experts' reports
11.6   pre-hearing briefs
11.7   oral / evidentiary hearing[4]
11.8   post-hearing briefs

12   Expectations as to behaviours
12.1   confidentiality[5]
12.2   serving documents[6]

---

[3] The Tribunal is likely to be assisted by the compilation of a list of issues identifying the issues on the face of the pleadings. Any disputed application—e.g., for discovery—should be by reference to that list. The list will further determine the issues that ought to be addressed in witness statements and experts' reports, and will dictate those issues that the Tribunal should determine in its Award. The list can be amended as necessary with the consent of all parties and the Tribunal.

[4] The List of Issues may result in certain issues being decided in advance of others. The Tribunal will not consider there should be absolute bar on deciding issues sequentially.

[5] The UNCITRAL Notes on Organizing Arbitral Proceedings provide a useful checklist of what might be considered confidential: "The material or information that is to be kept confidential (e.g. pieces of evidence, written and oral arguments, the fact that the arbitration is taking place, identity of the arbitrators, content of the award); measures for maintaining confidentiality of such information and hearings; whether any special procedures should be employed for maintaining the confidentiality of information transmitted by electronic means (e.g., because communication equipment is shared by several users, or because electronic mail over public networks is considered not sufficiently protected against unauthorized access); circumstances in which confidential information may be disclosed in part or in whole (e.g., in the context of disclosures of information in the public domain, or if required by law or a regulatory body)." (paragraph 32). The Tribunal will consider any specific request for express confidentiality but pending any such specific direction the Tribunal will expect the parties to observe the confidentiality in such matters.

[6] Again the UNCITRAL Notes are helpful: "Among various possible patterns of routing, one example is that a party transmits the appropriate number of copies to the arbitral tribunal, or to the arbitral institution, if one is involved, which then forwards them as appropriate. Another example is that a party is to send copies simultaneously to the arbitrators and the other party or parties. Documents and other written communications directed by the arbitral tribunal or the presiding arbitrator to one or more parties may also follow a determined pattern, such as through the arbitral institution or by direct transmission. For some communications, in particular those on organizational matters (e.g. dates for hearings), more direct routes of communication may be agreed, even if, for example, the arbitral institution acts as an intermediary for documents such as the statements of claim and defence, evidence or written arguments." (paragraph 34).

12.3   retention of documents[7]

12.4   meet and confer regarding documents especially electronic data[8]

12.5   pleadings[9]

12.6   discovery[10]

The Tribunal will consider any specific request but would expect documents, especially pleadings and statements and the like, to be sent simultaneously to the Tribunal and the other party. The Tribunal would normally expect correspondence to be sent to each member of the Tribunal and simultaneously sent to the other parties.

[7] The parties are expected to retain all material documents and not to destroy anything that may be material to the issues the Tribunal have to determine. This may involve suspending the effect of document destruction policies, especially those relating to computer records. Failure to comply may result in an adverse inference being drawn by the Tribunal.

[8] If the parties expect electronic data (e-discovery or e-disclosure) to be material in the reference they are expected to meet and confer to consider what agreements can be reached as to:

(1)   what data is stored where;

(2)   whether any data is stored in a medium that is not readily accessible;

(3)   whether disclosure can be limited by reference to custodian, keyword searches and otherwise; and

(4)   the format in which any production is given in. If the parties are unable to agree recourse should be had to the Tribunal at the earliest opportunity.

[9] Parties may prepare pleadings as they see fit; however the Tribunal indicates that it will be assisted if the parties could adhere to the following principles:

(1)   material facts are to be asserted and in general it will not be appropriate to plead evidence in any detail;

(2)   key documents (such as contracts, formal notices and the like) may be annexed to pleadings but not evidential documents unless likely to be determinative of a key issue;

(3)   propositions of law may be asserted but legal argument should be avoided unless likely to be determinative of a key issue;

(4)   pleadings should be concise statements from which the Tribunal can readily ascertain the issues between the parties; and

(5)   the parties should consider the benefit of responsive pleadings with each document incorporated with the preceding one.

[10] Discovery is a process designed to ensure that the parties each have access to all material documents and it operates to compel parties to produce to each other documents that are material to the issues to be determined, whether they help or hinder the party that has possession of them. In order to give discovery the parties will have to search for documents to be disclosed. The search may include searching computers and other sources of storage of electronic media. If there are disputes over the extent of discovery

12.7 witness statements[11]
12.8 experts[12]
12.9 evidentiary hearing[13]
12.10 submission of unscheduled briefs and other documents[14]

13 Arrangements for evidentiary hearing, including:

13.1 transcript
13.2 translations of written documents
13.3 interpretation of oral testimony
13.4 other special requirements

14 Award[15]

15 Communications with Tribunal always to be copied to other side and overtly endorsed to that effect

16 Further / next meeting(s) / conference(s)

17 Any other business

18 Close of proceedings

---

the Tribunal will expect the parties to confer and seek to agree a suitable protocol. If disputes persist the Tribunal will expect the parties to bring such dispute to the attention of the Tribunal as soon as possible so as to limit the impact of any delayed compliance.

[11] The Tribunal will expect statements to be the words of the witness and, although it is proper for counsel to assist in the drafting of a statement, it should remain the evidence of the witness and not what counsel might want a witness to say. The Tribunal will expect the witness to verify the truth of the statement on oath or affirm that it is true.

[12] Experts will be expected to acknowledge a primary duty to assist the Tribunal rather then the party on whose behalf they are retained. Experts should meet and seek to narrow issues between them and identify in a suitable manner those issues upon which they agree and those where they do not, and should expect that the Tribunal may require their evidence to be given by witness conferencing.

[13] The Tribunal anticipates that witnesses will be examined by the party calling them and then cross-examined on their statements, including by reference to any document on the record. The Tribunal accepts that it is appropriate for witnesses to be prepared for giving evidence by an explanation of the process, the key issues the Tribunal is asked to determine and the key documents on the record but they should not be coached in what to say or how to respond to questions. Mock cross-examination on the facts of this case is likely to be regarded as a breach of this behaviour.

[14] The Tribunal will retain the right to refuse to admit to the record any brief or submission that has not been directed to be filed and served.

[15] The Tribunal will [use its best endeavours to] deliver its Award no later than [date].

APPENDIX 7
SAMPLE TERMS OF REFERENCE

IN THE MATTER OF AN ARBITRATION UNDER THE RULES OF THE INTERNATIONAL CHAMBER OF COMMERCE

		CASE No.
	A	
		Claimant
	v.	
	B	
		Respondent

TERMS OF REFERENCE

(Issued pursuant to Article 18 of the Rules of Arbitration of the International Chamber of Commerce)

The Arbitral Tribunal:	C (Chairman)
	D
	E

TABLE OF CONTENTS (if necessary)

A. Full Names and Descriptions of the Parties

1. A (A) is a company organized under the laws of … (company registration number …) which operates as a … A's principal place of business is located at:

2. A is represented by …

3. B (B), is a company organized under the laws of … (company registration number …) which operates as a … B's registered office is at:

4. B is represented by:

B. Addresses of the Parties for Notification Purposes

5. The addresses of the parties, to which notifications and communications may validly be made, are as follows:

   For A: ...

   For B: ...

C. Overview of Proceedings

6. This arbitration concerns an agreement entered into by A and B on [date] (the Agreement). As provided for in Clause [X] of the Agreement, the arbitration is to be conducted in accordance with the ICC Rules. Clause [X] reads as follows: [set out arbitration clause]

7. Clause [X] of the Agreement provides that it is governed and shall be construed in accordance with the laws of ...

8. The arbitration no. ... was commenced by A by the filing of its Request for Arbitration dated ... (the Request). The named respondent is B.

9. B submitted its Answer to the Request on ... (the Answer).

10. A submitted a Reply to the Answer on ... (the Reply).

D. Summary of the Parties' Respective Positions

11. A summary of the parties' respective claims and defences is made below for the purpose of satisfying the requirements of Article 18(1)(c) of the Rules of Arbitration of the International Court of Arbitration of the International Chamber of Commerce (the ICC Rules). This summary is not to be understood as foreclosing the making of arguments or the introduction of evidence or facts not expressly referred to herein. Subject to the ICC Rules and applicable rules of procedure applicable, the Arbitral Tribunal (the Tribunal) shall have the power, on application by either party, to allow amendments to the pleadings on such terms, if any, as the Tribunal may deem appropriate.

12. [set out summary of the position of A]

13. [set out summary of the position of B]

E. Issues to Be Determined

14. The issues to be determined by the Tribunal are those arising from the submissions, statements, applications and pleadings of the parties and include any question of fact or law that the Tribunal may deem necessary to decide in order to determine such issues within the limits of Article 19 of the ICC Rules.

F. Full Names, Descriptions and Addresses of the Arbitrators

15. The Chairman of the Tribunal, confirmed by the [Secretary General of the] ICC International Court of Arbitration pursuant to Article 9(2) of the ICC Rules on ..., is: [insert name and contact details]

16. The co-arbitrator proposed by A, confirmed by the [Secretary General of the] ICC International Court of Arbitration pursuant to Article 9(2) of the ICC Rules on ..., is: [insert name and contact details]

17. The co-arbitrator proposed by B, confirmed by the [Secretary General of the] ICC International Court of Arbitration pursuant to Article 9(2) of the ICC Rules on ..., is: [insert name and contact details]

G. The Place of the Arbitration

18. Pursuant to Clause [X] of the Agreement, the place of arbitration is [place] where the arbitration shall have its seat.

19. Members of the Tribunal may hold meetings outside of [place] at their discretion. Similarly, any hearings or meetings involving the parties and/or their respective counsel may be held outside of [place] at the discretion of the Tribunal after consultation with the parties.

H. Particulars of the Applicable Procedural Rules, and Other Matters

20. The parties agree that the arbitrators have been properly and validly appointed, and hereby confirm that neither party is aware

of any ground to challenge the appointment of the Tribunal or any of its members.

21. Pursuant to Clause [X] of the Agreement, the language of the arbitral proceedings shall be [X].

22. Documents submitted to the Tribunal in any other language shall be accompanied by a translation into [X]. The parties will make good faith efforts to agree on the translation of such documents. Witnesses may give oral evidence in their mother tongue, provided that arrangements for interpretation to the satisfaction of the Tribunal are made by the party calling the witnesses in question.

23. Subject to any mandatory rules under the laws of England and Wales relating to international arbitration procedure and any relevant provisions of the ICC Rules (in particular Article 15 and Articles 20(1) and 20(2)), the rules of procedure to be followed shall be as determined by the Tribunal in its discretion, after consultation with the parties. In determining such rules, the parties have agreed that the *IBA Rules on the Taking of Evidence in International Arbitration (1999)* shall serve as guidelines for the Tribunal.

24. The Tribunal may hold one or more preparatory conferences to consider such matters as it considers expedient to deal with by way of such conferences.

25. Interlocutory applications shall be made in writing:

    25.1. Requests for the fixing of time limits or for extensions of time shall be determined by the Chairman of the Tribunal alone, after such consultation with the other members of the Tribunal and the parties as he considers appropriate;

    25.2. Interim or interlocutory applications, other than requests for the fixing of time limits or for extensions of time, may be determined, at the discretion of the Tribunal, by the Chairman in consultation with the other members of the Tribunal or by the full Tribunal. The holding of a hearing prior to the determination of such interlocutory application is within the discretion of the Tribunal.

26. The Tribunal may, in its discretion, decide to make one or more interim or partial awards after consultation with the parties.

27. All awards shall be in writing and shall state the reasons upon which they are based.

28. The parties, counsel and the members of the Tribunal shall notify all parties, all signatories of the present Terms of Reference and the Secretariat of any change of name, description, address, telephone or fax number. In the absence of any such notification, communications sent in accordance with these Terms of Reference shall be valid.

29. Copies of any communication from a party to the Tribunal shall be sent to the other party and to the Secretariat. Submissions to the Tribunal shall be made by fax and/or email, with a hard copy to follow by mail or courier. Ordinary correspondence may be submitted by fax and/or email alone.

30. Neither party shall object to any reasonable extension of time which the Tribunal may ask the International Court of Arbitration to grant in relation to the time-limit within which the Tribunal must render the Final Award.

31. The Tribunal shall not act as *amiable compositeur*.

32. These Terms of Reference pursuant to Article 18 of the ICC Rules of Arbitration applicable to this arbitration have been drawn up in [X] copies and have been agreed and duly signed and executed as follows:

[signed by the arbitrators and the parties]

APPENDIX 8
SAMPLE LIST OF ISSUES

IN THE MATTER OF AN ARBITRATION UNDER THE RULES OF
THE INTERNATIONAL CHAMBER OF COMMERCE

CASE No.

A

Claimant

– and –

B

Respondent

LIST OF ISSUES

Introduction

In this List of Issues Claimant A is the owner of goods insured by Respondent B. The goods were damaged and the principal issue is whether the policy of insurance should respond to the damage.

This List identifies in broad terms the main issues in the reference. It does not limit the jurisdiction of the Tribunal nor prescribe the correct legal test for any issue and does not restrict submissions on the law. The order of issues does not convey the relative importance of the issues nor bind the Arbitral Tribunal as to the manner in which evidence is to be adduced in relation thereto or indicate the order in which the issues are to be considered and/or determined at any evidential hearing.

Issues

1. Were the Goods packed in bales adequate to withstand the ordinary incidents of the voyage—did the Goods suffer from an inherent vice.

2. Was there heavy rain in Bombay between 11 and 15 July 2007 (and specifically on 12 July).

3. Between 11 and 15 July 2007 were the Goods wetted before loading or whilst in the holds as a result of rain entering the holds.

4. Was there seriously inclement weather on 22 July 2007, was sea water forced into the hold by reason of any such seriously inclement weather and / or sea conditions and were the Goods damaged by any such ingress of water.

5. What was the extent of the damage to the Goods on discharge.

6. Were the Goods rebaled and if so what works were undertaken.

7. What was the purpose of any rebaling and works to the Goods.

8. Were the Goods damaged by an insured peril.

9. If so, is liability excluded by either or both of Clause 4 of the Institute Cargo Clauses or s55 Marine Insurance Act

The following issues are not in dispute:

A. That there was a valid policy of insurance.

B. That the policy incorporated the Institute Cargo Clauses and was otherwise subject to the Marine Insurance Act.

C. The Vessel was loaded with the Goods for a voyage from Bombay to Hamburg.

D. The Vessel left Bombay on 15 July and arrived in Hamburg on 3 August 2007.

E. Some damage to the Goods was apparent when the Goods were discharged.

[signed and dated by the arbitrators and the parties]

APPENDIX 9
SAMPLE LETTER FOR THE APPOINTMENT OF A SECRETARY

From the [Chairman of the Arbitral Tribunal] [sole arbitrator] to the Parties' Representatives / Counsel

"Gentlemen,

The members of the arbitral tribunal have conferred and consider that in the discharge of their duties they would be greatly assisted by the appointment of a secretary to the tribunal. It is apparent that this arbitration will involve considerable documentation and the tribunal would prefer that the appointment is made at an early stage of the proceedings.

The tribunal proposes to appoint ABC of [law firm] of [address] as secretary. ABC is an attorney / solicitor / paralegal qualified in [date]. His/her curriculum vitae is attached. Initial enquiries made of ABC indicate that there is no conflict of interest, and that he/she would be independent and impartial. I have previously worked with ABC in this manner on [number] occasions. Neither of my co-arbitrators has worked with ABC before. ABC is employed by [law firm], of which I am a partner. If the appointment is confirmed ABC will be asked to make a declaration in a like form to that made by the members of the tribunal and the appointment will be conditional upon satisfactory completion of such declaration.

The [institution] Rules make no reference to the appointment of a secretary but the right and power to do so is recognised by [e.g. if an ICC arbitration *a Note issued by the ICC Secretariat in 1995* or if an ICDR arbitration *Canon VI of the Code of Ethics* or if nothing applicable *the international arbitration community*].

The functions of the proposed secretary would be to assist the members of the tribunal by fulfilling such functions as required of him/her by the chairman. These may include:

- providing administrative support in particular by:
    - coordinating the diaries of the members of the tribunal;

- o to the extent necessary handling accounting and financial matters for the tribunal;

- o to the extent necessary obtaining translations of documents or submissions;

- o remaining aware of and managing the correspondence and ensuring it is all dealt with by the tribunal promptly;

- o maintaining a central file or record; and

- o remaining aware of and managing the submissions and evidence adduced by the parties;

- providing research capabilities, in particular by:

  - o identifying from the record all evidence on a certain point;

  - o preparing at the request of the tribunal summaries of submissions or evidence; and

  - o researching at the request of the tribunal specific points of law or practice;

- organising procedural and evidentiary hearings and conference calls;

- attending and taking notes at any hearing or conference call and preparing minutes;

- drafting the procedural section of any order or award and letters of a procedural nature.

It will be no part of the function of the secretary to be part of the deliberations of the tribunal, although he/she may be present when the tribunal deliberate and may identify matters that should be considered. Nor shall it be any part of the function of the secretary to have any part in the decisions of the tribunal or drafting any substantive part of any order, award or letter.

Any communication between the secretary and one of the parties shall be copied to all other parties. The secretary will make a note of any telephone communication with any of the parties but, as such communication is likely to be organisational in nature, a copy will not be circulated unless the content of the communication becomes material.

The secretary will be remunerated at the hourly rate of £/$/€ X. The aggregate remuneration shall be paid [in addition to the fees due to the members of the tribunal as an expense] [from the fees due to the members of the tribunal].

The parties are invited to confer and jointly indicate whether they agree to the appointment of ABC as secretary on the basis set out in this letter and, if not, whether they have any joint alternative proposals that the tribunal might consider. The tribunal, whilst inviting the parties' agreement reserves the right to make such appointment and on such terms as it considers appropriate.

May I please hear from the parties by [date].

Yours etc."

APPENDIX 10
SAMPLE ORDER FOR LIMITING WRITTEN PLEADINGS

1. The Claimant shall submit its [Statement of Claim][1] on or before [date].

2. The Respondent shall submit its [Statement of Defence] [and any Counterclaim] on or before [date].

3. The Claimant shall submits its [Statement of Reply] [and Defence to Counterclaim] on or before [date]

4. [The Respondent shall submit its [Statement of Reply to the Defence to Counterclaim] on or before [date]].

5. Each written pleading should not exceed 25 pages in length without the permission of the Arbitral Tribunal, save that Statements of Reply [whether to the Defence or to the Defence to Counterclaim] should not exceed 10 pages. Each pleading should have reasonable line spacing, margin and font size. If the Arbitral Tribunal gives permission to exceed 25 pages [or 10 pages as the case may be] a brief summary should be given of the entire pleading.

6. [Each written pleading shall incorporate all documents relied upon and the statements of witnesses of fact relied upon.][2]

7. Further particulars or details of a pleading should only be sought and provided if necessary for a party to properly understand the case it has to meet.

8. The parties are encouraged to respond to the previous pleading by setting out their response after each paragraph of the previous pleading in a single document, and the parties should provide their pleadings electronically for this purpose if requested.

---

[1] As in the main text, the terminology for the written pleadings is variable, and whatever terminology is adopted appropriate changes may be incorporated.

[2] For matters that are not "fact-heavy" the composite statement of case that has pleading, documents and witness statements can be efficient in terms of time and cost. The Tribunal might then be able to proceed directly to an evidentiary hearing (subject to the need for any expert evidence).

APPENDIX 11
SAMPLE RESPONSIVE AND AMALGAMATED DEFENCE WITH CLAIM

IN THE MATTER OF AN ARBITRATION UNDER THE RULES OF
THE INTERNATIONAL CHAMBER OF COMMERCE

CASE No.

A

Claimant

– and –

B

Respondent

STATEMENT OF DEFENCE
(INCORPORATING STATEMENT OF CLAIM)

C1. By a policy of marine insurance, reference number XY1001, dated 1 June 2007 ("the Policy") the Defendant agreed to insure 6,000 metric tonnes cotton cloth ("the Goods") against the perils enumerated in the policy, including perils of the sea, for a voyage from Bombay to Hamburg on board the motor vessel "Starcruiser" ("the Vessel") to take place in July 2007.

D1. C1 is admitted.

C2. The Claimant is and was at all material times the owner of the Goods and fully interested in the Policy, a copy of which is attached as Annex A to these Particulars of Claim, to which reference will be made for its full terms, meaning and effect.

D2. C2 is admitted.

C3. The Policy incorporated the Institute Cargo Clauses (A) (a copy of which is attached as Annex B). Clause 1 provides: "This insurance covers all risks of loss of or damage to the subject-matter insured except as provided in Clauses 4, 5, 6 and 7 below ..."

D3. C3 is admitted.

C4. Further, Clause 16 of the Institute Cargo Clauses (A) provides:

"It is the duty of the Assured and their servants and agents in respect of loss recoverable hereunder

16.1 to take such measures as may be reasonable for the purpose of averting or minimising such loss, and

16.2 to ensure that all rights against carriers, bailees or other third parties are properly preserved and exercised and the Underwriters will, in addition to any loss recoverable hereunder, reimburse the Assured for any charges properly and reasonably incurred in pursuance of these duties."

D4. C4 is admitted. Further,

(a) Coverage under the Policy was subject to the General Exclusion Clause 4 of the Institute Cargo Clauses (A) which provided that,

"4. In no case shall this insurance cover ....

"4.3 loss damage or expense caused by insufficiency or unsuitability of packing or preparation of the subject matter insured (for the purpose of this Clause 4.3 "packing" shall be deemed to include storage in a container or liftvan but only when such stowage is carried out prior to attachment of this insurance or by the Assured or their servants.)

4.4 loss damage or expense caused by inherent vice or nature of the subject matter insured...."

(b) Further, section 55(2)(c) of the Marine Insurance Act 1906 provides,

"55. Included and excluded losses

(1) Subject to the provisions of this Act, and unless the policy otherwise provides, the insurer is liable for any loss proximately caused by a peril insured against, but, subject as aforesaid, he is not liable for any loss which is not proximately caused by a peril insured against.

(2) In particular –

....

(c) Unless the policy otherwise provides, the insurer is not liable for ordinary wear and tear, ordinary leakage and breakage, inherent vice or nature of the subject-matter insured, or for any loss proximately caused by rats or vermin, or for any injury to machinery not proximately caused by maritime perils."

C5. The Goods were shipped on board the Vessel at Bombay on or about 15 July 2007 and packed in bales of 400 bags each.

D5. C5 is admitted. There had been heavy rain at the port in Bombay between 11 and 15 July 2007.

C6. On or about 8 August 2007, the Vessel arrived at Hamburg where the Goods were discharged. During the course of the voyage and/or discharge, a number of bales in which the Goods were packed, broke and a large quantity of the Goods became loose in the Vessel's holds and in lighters.

D6. C6 is admitted to the extent that the Vessel arrived in Hamburg on 3 August 2007 and that the Goods were found to have suffered some damage and the packaging had failed causing Goods to spill.

C7. Further, on discharge, it was discovered that 1,000 bales of the Goods stowed in No.s 1 and 2 holds had been damaged by wetting. These damaged goods had a market value of US$50,000 as particularised in Annex C to the Claim.

D7. No admissions are made as to C7.

C8. The damage of the Goods occurred during the currency of the policy by reason of a peril or perils insured against, namely perils of the seas.

PARTICULARS

(a) On 22 July 2007, the Vessel encountered extremely heavy weather with storm force winds of up to force 12 on the Beaufort Scale and high, rough and pounding seas.

(b) The damaged cargo was situated in and beneath the hatch coamings and ventilator openings and was damaged by the inflow of sea water forced into the holds by the heavy weather.

(c) Further or alternatively, rainwater entered the holds when the Vessel was berthed at Bombay during loading on 12 July 2007.

D8. C8 is denied:

(a) No admissions are made as to the weather conditions there referred to.

(b) The Goods were shipped on board wetted by rain before loading.

C9. The Claimants arranged for the Goods which were not damaged to be rebaled and thereby incurred expense, amounting to US$100,000 in respect of the cost of such rebaling and of the additional handling and landing charges incurred by reason of the condition of the Goods, together with additional storage costs, particulars of which are set out in Annex C to these Particulars of Claim.

D9. No admissions are made to the expenses referred to in C9.

C10. Accordingly, the Claimant is entitled to recover

(a) the sum of US$50,000 being the value of those of the Goods damaged by wetting in transit as a result of a peril insured against;

(b) the further sum of US$100,000, pursuant to clause 16 of the Institute of Cargo Clauses (A), being the expenditure incurred by them in taking steps to safeguard and/or preserve the Goods insured and to avoid what would otherwise have been loss or damage within the terms of the policy for which the Defendant would have had to indemnify them.

D10. C10 is denied:

(a) Damage by wetting was caused by exposure of the Goods to rain prior to loading;

(b) Further, the Goods were packed in bales which were defective and inadequate to withstand the ordinary incidents of the insured voyage in that the bale straps (being made of paper) were too weak to keep the bales and their contents secure, during ordinary and necessary handling and carriage.

(c) Accordingly,

    (i) It is denied that any loss or damage to the Goods was suffered by the Claimant as a result of any insured peril. The Goods as shipped were suffering from inherent vice.

    (ii) If (which is not admitted) the Claimant incurred expenditure in respect of the rebaling and/or additional handling and landing charges, and/or additional storage costs referred to in Annex C to the Particulars of Claim, the same was due to inherent vice of the cargo and/or the insufficiency or unsuitability/inadequacy of its packing and the Defendant is not liable to the Claimant as alleged or at all by virtue of s.55(2)(c) of the Marine Insurance Act 1906 and/or the exclusion of liability under clauses 4.3 and 4.4 of the Institute Cargo Clauses (A).

    (iii) Further or alternatively, these expenses were not incurred by the Claimant in order to avert any loss or damage to or in and about the safeguard or preservation of the Goods. The expenses were incurred in order to discharge the Goods or to discharge the same more easily and from the Vessel. Accordingly, such expenditure was not incurred for the purpose of averting or minimising the loss and does not fall within Clause 16 (Minimising Losses) of the Institute Cargo Clauses (A).

C11. Wrongfully and in breach of contract the Defendant has failed and/or refused to pay the sum of US$100,000 and the sum of US$50,000 or any part thereof.

D11. It is admitted that the Defendant has refused to pay the sums demanded by the Claimant as alleged in C11 but it is denied that it was in breach of contract in doing so.

C12. As at the date of this statement of case, the sterling equivalent of US$150,000 is £75,000 calculated at an exchange rate of £1 = $2.

D12. C12 is admitted.

C13. The Claimant claims interest at the rate of 1% above Bank of England base rate on all sums found to be due pursuant to section 49 Arbitration Act 1996.

AND the Claimant claims:

(1) Under paragraph 8, US$100,000 alternatively damages.

(2) Under paragraph 11, US$50,000 alternatively damages.

(3) Interest on (1) and (2) above.

D13. In the premises, the Defendant denies liability as alleged or at all.

[signed and dated]

APPENDIX 12
SAMPLE LETTER OF APPLICATION TO TRIBUNAL FOR VARIOUS ORDERS (INCLUDING DISCOVERY)

Sirs,

Claimant v Respondent

Please accept this letter as an application on behalf of [Claimant] [Respondent] for an order in the following terms:

- That the Tribunal determine as a preliminary issue in advance of all other issues the following issue: [whether on the proper construction of the agreement dated [date] between the parties the Tribunal has jurisdiction to determine the claim in paragraph [x] of the Claimant's Brief] [whether the claims in paragraphs [x – z] were commenced within the appropriate limitation period] [what the proper law of the agreement dated [date] between the parties is]

- That the [Respondent] do state whether it has in its possession, custody or control the documents or classes of documents listed in the schedule to this application and, if so, to disclose the same to the [Claimant] by list and provide copies on request or make out a valid reason for non-disclosure.

- That the Respondent having failed to [serve its Memorial / give disclosure / offer for exchange its witness statements etc] in compliance with paragraph [x] of the procedural order for directions dated [date] the Respondent be ordered to do so no later than 4pm CET on [date] and that in default [set out sanction sought].

- That the parties do have permission to adduce expert evidence limited to one expert each on the question of [issue] and that the reports of the experts be served by 4pm CET on [date]; that the experts meet and confer to narrow the differences between them by [date] and that the experts produce a joint statement identifying those matters upon which they are able and not able to agree by 4pm CET on [date].

- etc.

and for such further or other relief by order, direction or award as may appear necessary to give full effect to the application.

The grounds upon which this application is made are as follows:

- [as to the preliminary issue] that a final interim award on the issue may be determinative of the issues of a substantial part of the issues referred to the Tribunal for determination and will give rise to a substantial saving in time and cost.

- [as to disclosure] that the documents are relevant and material to the issues in the case and to the outcome for the reasons set out in column 3 to the schedule to this application; that each such document is not in the possession, custody or control of the [Claimant] and that the [Claimant] believes such documents or classes of documents are in the possession, custody or control of the [Respondent] for the reasons given in column 4 of the schedule attached to this application.

- [as to failure to comply with earlier order] that the [Respondent] has failed to comply with the Tribunal's order dated [date].

- [as to expert evidence] that by paragraph [x] of the [Claimant's Brief] it contends that [the design of the bridge is and was defective] and by paragraph [x] of the [Respondent's Brief] it [denies defective design] and as the same is reflected in paragraph [x] of the List of Issues and that in consequence there is an issue between the parties as to [whether the design is defective] and the same is properly determined by the Tribunal in light of expert opinion evidence.

- etc.

The evidence in support of this application is set out in the attached witness statement of [name] dated [date].

The [Claimant] will invite you to make an order at the conclusion of your deliberations that the [Respondent] do forthwith pay the [Claimants] costs of this application in a fixed sum. The Claimant will file and serve a schedule of costs within [x] days of filing its evidence in reply.

We invite you to:

a. direct that the [Respondent] file any evidence in response no later than 4pm CET on [date];

b. direct that the [Claimant] file any evidence in reply no later than 4pm CET on [date];

c. determine this application [with] [without] a hearing. [Our time estimate for the hearing is [x] hours.]

We remain available to assist the Tribunal in any further way it may consider of assistance.

Yours etc.

Schedule to Disclosure Application

Item	Description of Document or Class	Relevance and Materiality	Reason for Believing that Held by Respondent	Respondents Comments on Relevance and Materiality[1]	Respondents Comments on Whether Held	Tribunal's Decision
1	Notes of meeting on [date] between A and B and all subsequent documents recording what transpired at such meeting	Paragraph [x] of the List of Issues / paragraphs [x] of the Claimant's Brief as denied by paragraph [x] of the Respondent's Brief shows that the parties disagree as to the events of this meeting where, the Claimant contends, it was agreed that [agreement]	B was seen by A to be making notes at the meeting and his evidence will be to that effect; it is commercial custom to take notes of important meetings; B would have reported to his colleagues on the outcome of the meeting. Respondent's documents [x, y and z] are notes of meetings taken by B and circulated internally within Respondent showing a pattern of behaviour to do so.	Respondent accepts that if such document existed it would be material. The Respondent's searches have not revealed the existence of any note or subsequent communication.	Respondent has searched B's hard copy files relating to the agreements with Claimant and the hard copy files of C and D (B's colleagues working with him on such matters) and has undertaken an electronic search using the words and phrases attached marked R1 (which list was agreed by the Claimant) against B's Outlook email system covering the week prior to the meeting to 2 months after the meeting.	
2	Etc	Etc	Etc	Etc	Etc	

---

[1] The Respondent's columns would not be completed at the time of the application but are shown completed by the Respondent by way of illustration.

APPENDIX 13
SAMPLE ORDER FOR FULL DISCOVERY

1. Each party shall give by 4pm on (date) discovery to every other party.

2. Discovery shall be given of those documents that:

   a. are in the control of that party, and

   b. may be used or relied upon and that are relevant to the claims or defences of any party or are relevant to matters otherwise in issue.

3. Discovery shall be given by listing each document or category or class of documents

4. The list shall identify documents in a convenient order and manner, shall assert any claims to privilege by reference to any category or class of documents, shall state what has become of any documents that a party did have but no longer has control of and shall be signed by or on behalf of the party as complete and correct.

5. Document shall include any medium in which information of any description is recorded.

6. Control shall include physical possession, right to possession, right to inspect or make copies.

7. Relevancy shall include documents that may not be admissible as evidence if the discovery may lead to the discovery of admissible evidence.

8. Discovery shall include documents that are relevant to the claims or defences of any party, notwithstanding that discovery may be adverse to the interests of the party giving that discovery.

9. Discovery shall be given of internal documents.

10. Discovery need not be given of documents to be used solely for impeachment.

11. Discovery need not be given of numerous copies of the same document unless they have been modified or altered so as to make them separate documents.

12. All discovered documents other than those:

    a. in respect of which a claim to privilege has been made or,

    b. where the party giving discovery no longer has control

    may be inspected by any other party by appointment on reasonable notice and that party irrespective of exercising the right to physically inspect may require copies to be provided. Copies shall be provided in a manner agreed between the parties.

13. Subject to 10 above, documents not discovered cannot be relied upon without the permission of the Arbitral Tribunal.

14. Without prejudice to other duties of confidentiality a party to whom a document has been disclosed must keep it confidential and may use the document only for the purposes of the arbitration unless the discovering party agrees.

APPENDIX 14
SAMPLE ORDER FOR REDUCED DISCOVERY

1. Each party shall give by 4pm on (date) discovery to every other party.

2. Discovery shall be given of those documents that:

    a. are in the control of that party, and

    b. are relied upon, support another party's case or adversely affect any party's case and are found after a reasonable search.

3. Discovery shall be given by listing each document or category or class of documents.

4. The list shall identify documents in a convenient order and manner, shall assert any claims to privilege by reference to any category or class of documents, shall state what has become of any documents that a party did have but no longer has control of, state any category or class of documents not searched for and shall be signed by or on behalf of the party as complete and correct.

5. Document shall include any medium in which information of any description is recorded.

6. Control shall include physical possession, right to possession, right to inspect or make copies.

7. Discovery shall include documents that relevant to the claims or defences of any party, notwithstanding that discovery may be adverse to the interests of the party giving that discovery.

8. Discovery shall be given of internal documents.

9. Discovery need not be given of numerous copies of the same document unless they have been modified or altered so as to make them separate documents.

10. All discovered documents other than those:

    a. in respect of which a claim to privilege has been made or,

    b. where the party giving discovery no longer has control

may be inspected by any other party by appointment on reasonable notice and that party, irrespective of exercising the right to physically inspect, may require copies to be provided. Copies shall be provided in a manner agreed between the parties.

11. Documents not discovered cannot be relied upon without the permission of the Arbitral Tribunal.

12. Without prejudice to other duties of confidentiality, a party to whom a document has been disclosed must keep it confidential and may use the document only for the purposes of the arbitration unless the discovering party agrees.

APPENDIX 15
SAMPLE ORDER FOR LIMITED DISCOVERY – ONLY DOCUMENTS RELIED UPON

1. Each party shall give by 4pm on (date) discovery to every other party.

2. Discovery shall be given of those documents relied upon.

3. Discovery shall be given by listing each document or category or class of documents

4. The list shall identify documents in a convenient order and manner, shall assert any claims to privilege by reference to any category or class of documents and shall be signed by or on behalf of the party as complete and correct.

5. Document shall include any medium in which information of any description is recorded.

6. All discovered documents may be inspected by any other party by appointment on reasonable notice and that party, irrespective of exercising the right to physically inspect, may require copies to be provided. Copies shall be provided in a manner agreed between the parties.

7. Documents not discovered cannot be relied upon without the permission of the Arbitral Tribunal.

8. Without prejudice to other duties of confidentiality, a party to whom a document has been disclosed must keep it confidential and may use the document only for the purposes of the arbitration unless the discovering party agrees.

APPENDIX 16
SAMPLE ORDER FOR LIMITING DISCOVERY

1. Each party must use its best endeavours to agree with all other parties on an appropriate method of limiting the extent of discovery; in particular, by seeking to agree to limit the documents discovered in specific categories or classes, whether by reference to a time period, author, recipient, subject matter, location and nature of document, or otherwise.

2. In the absence of agreement between the parties, any party may apply to the Arbitral Tribunal for an order limiting the scope of discovery.

ICC (International Chamber of Commerce)	LCIA (London Court of International Arbitration)	IBA (International Bar Association Rules)	AAA (American Arbitration Association)	UNCITRAL	CIETAC (China Int Economic & Trade Arbitration Commission Rules)	JCAA (Japan Commercial Arbitration Association Rules)
No express provisions regarding disclosure. The Tribunal may determine the time, manner and form in which materials about the identity of the witness and about his / her testimony should be exchanged between the parties and presented to the Tribunal (Art. 20).	Arbitral Tribunal has power to order any party to produce any document or classes of document which the Tribunal deems relevant. (Art. 22.l(e)).	Each party must disclose all documents available to it on which it relies, including public documents and those in the public domain, within the time period ordered by the Tribunal. Any party may apply to the Tribunal for an order that the other party produce documents. Such a Request to Produce must describe the documents in sufficient detail to allow them to be identified, describe how they are relevant and material to the outcome of the case, and confirm that they are not in the possession of the requesting party. (Art. 3)	Tribunal may direct production of documents (Rule 21). For large complex commercial cases the parties may agree on discovery subject to the Tribunal's right to limit or direct in the event that the parties cannot agree. (Rule L4).	No specific rules on discovery. The Tribunal may require the parties to produce documents, exhibits or other evidence at any time before the hearings (Art. 24.3).	The Tribunal has the power to order the parties to produce, within a specified time. The Tribunal may refuse to admit any evidence produced outside such period. Failure to produce any or any sufficient evidence shall have consequences.(Art. 36).	A party may apply to present evidence (Rule 36).

DIS (German Arbitration Institution Rules)	SCC (Stockholm Chamber of Commerce Rules)	WIPO (World Intellectual Property Organization Rules)	ZCC (Zurich Chamber of Commerce Rules)	SIAC (Arbitration Rules of the Singapore International Arbitration Centre)	ICSID (International Centre for Settlement of Investment Disputes)	BCICAC (British Columbia International Commercial Arbitration Centre)	ACICA (Australian Centre for International Commercial Arbitration)
There is no express provision for discovery of documents. However, the Tribunal has the power to order the production of documents in order to establish the facts of the case (Sec 27.1).	No express provision.	The Tribunal may, at any time during the arbitration, at the request of a party or on its own motion, order a party to produce such documents or other evidence as it considers necessary or appropriate (Art. 48(b)).	Each party may call upon the other to disclose specified documents relevant to the dispute. The Tribunal may, in case of refusal or on its own motion, order the presentation of documents (Art. 42).	Statements of Case are accompanied by supporting documents. The Tribunal has power to order a party to produce relevant documents in its possession or control. (Rules 16 and 24)	Statements of Case are accompanied by supporting documents. The Tribunal may call upon the parties to produce documents. (Rules 24 and 34).	Tribunal may require a party to deliver a summary of the documents relied upon and may require a party to produce documents. (Art. 25)	Subject to specific agreement otherwise Tribunal shall have regard to but not be bound to apply the IBA Rules. (Art. 27)

APPENDIX 18
SAMPLE PROCEDURAL ORDER FOR DISCOVERY DISPUTES

1. If any party is dissatisfied with the discovery of any other party it shall first make a reasoned request in writing to that other party and stipulate a reasonable time within which the requested documents are to be provided.

2. The reasoned request must:

   a. Describe the document in sufficient detail to identify it or describe a narrow and specific category or class of documents, limited so far as possible, including by time period, author, recipient, subject matter, location and nature of document,

   b. State the basis upon which it is believed the document or category or class exists,

   c. Describe how the documents requested are relevant and material to the outcome of the case, where possible by reference to specific paragraphs or sections of any existing Request for Arbitration, Answer, Memorial, Statement of Case, Points of Claim or Defence or similar document.

   d. State that the documents requested are not in the control of the requesting party,

   e. State the basis upon which it is believed the document or category or class is in the control of the other party, and

   f. Be presented in tabular form and provided in electronic copy (whether in addition to or instead of paper copy).

3. If the parties are unable to agree upon any further discovery, to compromise the request the party against whom the request was made shall respond within a reasonable time and in tabular form to those requests where the parties have been unable to agree explaining why the discovery sought is resisted.

4. If the parties are still unable to agree, the latest tabular form of the request and response(s) shall be submitted to the Arbitral

Tribunal with a request for a specific direction or procedural order.

5. Upon receipt of a request from any party, the Arbitral Tribunal may determine the request or may in its discretion call for any further submission or comment, convene a meeting or hearing, and otherwise act as it considers necessary to determine the request.

6. Any party is at liberty to request the Arbitral Tribunal to set a time period for compliance with the steps in this part of this Order, but the parties are expected to deal promptly with these directions absent any specific direction of the Arbitral Tribunal.

APPENDIX 19
SAMPLE ORDER STATING CHAIRMAN'S ROLE IN DECIDING DISCOVERY DISPUTES

1. The Chairman alone [shall] [may] determine all applications concerning the fixing of time limits or for extensions of time relating to discovery.

2. All other applications concerning discovery may be determined, at the discretion of the Arbitral Tribunal, by the Chairman alone; otherwise they shall be determined by the full Arbitral Tribunal.

3. In any instance where a matter is being decided by the Chairman alone, he may consult with other members of the Arbitral Tribunal as he considers appropriate. Any decision taken by the Chairman alone shall, if ratified by the other members of the Tribunal, be treated for all purposes as if a decision of the full Tribunal.

4. Applications concerning discovery shall be made in writing and may be determined, at the discretion of the Arbitral Tribunal or by the Chairman alone, as the case may be, on paper.

5. The Arbitral Tribunal or the Chairman alone, as the case may be, may hold a hearing if deemed appropriate.

APPENDIX 20
SAMPLE ORDER FOR DISCLOSURE OF INFORMATION THAT MAY CONTAIN PERSONAL DATA

If the discovery ordered to be given above includes or may include any document that includes or may include any personal data, the party giving disclosure may redact any personal data [whatsoever] [that is not relevant or responsive to the matters in issue].

[Any disclosed document that contains any personal data shall be identified by the party giving disclosure. Any such document so disclosed and inspected shall be restricted to the counsel and experts of the party to whom the document is produced and, for the avoidance of doubt, not to the party itself].

APPENDIX 21
SAMPLE ORDER GOVERNING TREATMENT OF FOREIGN LANGUAGES AND TRANSLATIONS

1. If the parties submit documents that are not in the language of the arbitration arrangements shall be made for translation.

2. The parties should, as soon as practicable, discuss any issues that may arise regarding documents in foreign languages and endeavour to agree upon a method of translation satisfactory to the parties, typically by using a common translator. If the parties are unable to agree they should inform the Arbitral Tribunal as soon as practicable. The Arbitral Tribunal may determine the identity of the translator or may, in its discretion, call for any further submission or comment, convene a meeting or hearing, and otherwise act as it considers necessary to determine the issue.

3. A party shall procure and tender to the other parties a translation of those documents that it intends to rely upon.

4. If the parties agree upon a translator, the Arbitral Tribunal will, save in exceptional circumstances, accept translations undertaken by the agreed translator and without the need for the translator to give evidence.

5. If a party wishes to take issue with the accuracy of any translation it shall do so promptly after the provision of the translation and the parties should endeavour to agree upon a translation. If the parties are unable to agree, they should inform the Arbitral Tribunal as soon as practicable and, if it appears to the Arbitral Tribunal that the accuracy of the translation may have a significant bearing on the case, the Arbitral Tribunal may, after having consulted with the parties, appoint a Tribunal-Appointed translator to report to it in such manner and on such terms as the Arbitral Tribunal may determine.

APPENDIX 22
SAMPLE ORDER GOVERNING TREATMENT OF ELECTRONIC DOCUMENTS

1. Document is defined to include any medium in which information of any description is recorded. This extends to electronic documents, including e-mail and other electronic communications, word-processed documents, and databases. In addition to documents that are readily accessible from computer systems and other electronic devices and media, the definition covers those documents that are stored on servers and back-up systems and electronic documents that have been "deleted." It also extends to additional information stored and associated with electronic documents known as metadata.

2. The parties should, as soon as practicable, discuss any issues that may arise regarding searches for and the preservation and discovery of electronic documents. This may involve the parties providing information about the categories of electronic documents within their control, the computer systems, electronic devices and media on which any relevant documents may be held, the storage systems maintained by the parties, and their document retention policies. It may be reasonable to search for electronic documents on some or all of the parties' electronic storage systems by means of keyword searches, rather than review each and every document and discover the entire contents. The parties should in appropriate cases seek to agree on keyword or other searches as far as possible at an early stage. In the case of difficulty or disagreement, the matter should be referred to the Arbitral Tribunal for directions at the earliest practical date.

3. The parties should co-operate at an early stage as to the format in which electronic documents are to be provided on inspection. In the case of difficulty or disagreement, the matter should be referred to the Arbitral Tribunal for directions at the earliest practical date.

4. The Arbitral Tribunal declares that the existence of electronic documents impacts upon the extent to which it is proportionate

and reasonable to search for and discover those documents. The factors that the Arbitral Tribunal may determine to be relevant in deciding the proportionality and reasonableness of a search for and the discovery of electronic documents include (but are not limited to):

a. The number of the documents,

b. The nature and complexity of the case,

c. The ease and expense of retrieval, and

d. The significance of any document that may be located.

5. [If any document produced in discovery is subject to a claim of privilege, the party making the claim may notify any party that received the document of the claim and the basis for it. After being notified, a party must promptly return or destroy the specified document and any copies it has; must not use or disclose the document; and must take reasonable steps to retrieve the document if the party disclosed it before being notified.]

APPENDIX 23
SAMPLE ORDER GOVERNING TREATMENT OF BUNDLES

1. The parties should agree on a bundle of documents for use at the hearing.

2. The bundle should contain all documents that any of the parties wishes to rely upon in chronological order and numbered on consecutive pages.

3. The Arbitral Tribunal will accept the bundle as accurate copies of the original documents.

4. Nothing in the agreement of a bundle constitutes or indicates any agreement to the meaning, admissibility or evidentiary weight of any document or that a communication was sent or transmitted.

5. The Arbitral Tribunal will assume that all documents in the bundle are agreed as admissible and that a communication was sent on the date it purports to have been sent and was received in the normal course of transmission, unless the contrary is shown.

6. The Arbitral Tribunal may ascribe such meaning and evidentiary weight to a document as may be appropriate, consistent with any other evidence.

APPENDIX 24
SAMPLE ORDER PERMITTING EXPERT EVIDENCE

1. The parties have permission to call the following expert witnesses in respect of the following issues:

   1.1 [one structural engineer each on the issue of the structural integrity of the bridge partially constructed under the contract dated [x] and made between [y] and [z] as more particularly identified in paragraph [aa] of the list of issues] ...

   1.2 [one forensic accountant each on the issue of the loss and damage (if any) arising from the termination of the contract dated [x] and made between [y] and [z] as more particularly identified in paragraph [ab] of the list of issues]...

2. In respect of the expert evidence permitted under the preceding paragraph:

   2.1 Directions for carrying out inspections/taking samples/ conducting experiments/performance of calculations shall be [that the structural engineers shall meet at the bridge on a date to be agreed between the parties but no later than [date] to take such samples and measurements as they consider necessary] ...

   2.2 Experts in the same field to hold discussions to seek to reach agreements on figures and underlying data, agreements on matters of opinion and otherwise narrow issues, by [date] as to the structural engineers and [date] as to the forensic accountants.

   2.3 Experts in the same field to prepare a schedule identifying those matters upon which they are agreed and those matters upon which they cannot agree (explaining the difference between them), such schedule to be prepared by [date] as to the structural engineers and [date] as to the forensic accountants.

   2.4 Experts' reports setting out the substance of the evidence to be given to be exchanged by [date] as to the structural engineers and [date] as to the forensic accountants

2.5 The experts to attend the evidential hearing [fixed for the two-week period commencing [date]] [to be fixed] to be questioned on their reports.

OR

3. A single expert shall be appointed to report to the Arbitral Tribunal on the following issue(s) [as per 1.1 and 1.2 above]....

4. The following directions shall govern the appointment of the single joint expert:

4.1 The parties are to agree on the instructions to the expert(s) by [date].

4.2 In default of agreement by [date], the latest drafts of the proposed instructions are to be submitted to the Arbitral Tribunal, which may either settle the instruction itself, permit separate instructions to be submitted, or make such other direction as may be appropriate (including convening a conference to settle the instructions)

4.3 The expert(s) are to be instructed to report by [date].

4.4 The parties have permission to ask reasonable (in nature and amount) questions in writing of the expert on such report by [date], and the expert is instructed to respond by [date].

4.5 The expert(s) to attend the evidentiary hearing [fixed for the 2-week period commencing [date]] [to be fixed] to be questioned on such report(s).

APPENDIX 25
SAMPLE DECLARATION BY EXPERT

1. I understand that my duty in providing written reports and giving evidence is to help the Tribunal. I confirm that I have complied and will continue to comply with my duty.

2. I confirm that insofar as the facts stated in my report are within my own knowledge, I have made clear which they are and I believe them to be true, and that the opinions I have expressed represent my true and complete professional opinion.

3. I have endeavoured to include in my report those matters of which I have knowledge or of which I have been made aware that might adversely affect the validity of my opinion. I have clearly stated any qualifications to my opinion.

4. I have indicated the sources of all information I have used.

5. I have not without forming an independent view included or excluded anything which has been suggested to me by others (in particular, my instructing lawyers).

6. I will notify those instructing me immediately and confirm in writing if for any reason my existing report requires correction or qualification.

7. I confirm that:

   7.1. Other than as disclosed in this report, I do not have any conflict of interest of any kind in acting in this matter;

   7.2. I do not consider that any interest which I have disclosed affects my suitability to act as an expert witness on any issue on which I have to give evidence;

   7.3. I will notify my instructing lawyers immediately if, between the date of this report and the date of the hearing of my evidence, there is any change in circumstances which affect my declarations at paragraphs 7.1 and 7.2 above.

8. I understand that:

   8.1. my report, subject to any corrections before swearing as to its correctness, will form the evidence to be given under oath or affirmation; and

   8.2. I may be cross-examined on my report by a cross-examiner assisted by an expert and/or by the Tribunal.

9. I confirm that I have not entered into any arrangement where the amount or payment of my fees is in any way dependent on the outcome of the case.

APPENDIX 26
CHECKLIST OF KEY COMPONENTS OF AN AWARD

Below is a non-exhaustive checklist which may also serve as a framework for an award:

Front or Cover page – not always needed on a brief award but a helpful guide to a number of incidental matters

Case Number
>123456/2008
>and in the matter of an Arbitration

Case Title   [under the Rules of the ICC International Court of Arbitration] between
>ABC Co. Inc (United States of America)
>Claimant

>and

>DEF SA (France)
>Respondent

>Identify that it is an arbitration — mention rules only if rules were adopted.

>Short formal identification of the Parties. Usually appropriate to refer to country under whose laws the party subsists or is incorporated.

Award Title [FIRST/SECOND/THIRD....]
>[INTERIM][FINAL][PROVISIONAL][PARTIAL]
>AWARD
>[on a preliminary application] [reserved as to costs]

>Describe the award as accurately and succinctly as possible

Title Date   [date]

>Care needs to be taken to be sure that the title date is in line with the date of making the award. Some arbitrators do not date the title at all.

Arbitral Tribunal
>JKL Chairman
>MNO
>PQR

>Not always needed on a title page but helpful to the enforcing Court if it has to appreciate the background of the matter.

Locus   London

>Asserts the locus of the reference. Should correspond with other references to the locus and may not be necessary in the title at all

Counsel   Representing Claimant
>STU
>Representing Respondent
>VWX

>Not always needed on a title page but may be helpful to the enforcing Court if it has to recall a submission by counsel who that counsel represents.

Main text

The first page of the award will normally commence with a repetition of some, but not all of the information presented on the Cover Sheet. Generally, the other information will be seen in the so-called recitals.

Note that it is not essential to commence the text with recitals in the suggested, or indeed any form, or at all. Narrative reasoned awards are very common and may well suffice. In most jurisdictions there is no set format for an award. These suggestions are advanced as one way of ensuring that an enforcing court will have sufficient information for its decision.

Table of Contents Not essential but useful to allow the reader to navigate quickly through the Award.

Introduction

Agreement   Set out the agreement under which the arbitration arises, its date and parties.

Contact Details	Give contact details for each party. Identify any relevant change of name of status, registered address, company number and jurisdiction under whose laws the entity exists.
Arbitration clause	Recite the arbitration clause in the agreement
Arbitral Tribunal	Recite the appointment of the Tribunal as necessary with party-appointed members and chairman. Set out the acceptances of appointment and declarations of independence. If appointments were ratified by the institution say so.
Contact details of Arbitral Tribunal	Set out contact details of the members of the Tribunal.
	It is generally not necessary to identify professional expertise but in some technical references it may be helpful to identify expertise.
History	Brief timeline explaining the commencement of the reference, the request for arbitration and answer before the appointment of the Tribunal.
Procedural History	Set out procedural history subsequent to appointment of Tribunal including procedural orders, timetable and compliance with institutional rules for the progress of the reference. Identify the written submissions the Tribunal received.
Hearings	Set out the evidential hearings that took place.
Representation	Identify counsel (and any material changes) and contact details.
Narrative explanation of Award	Explain that it is interim, provisional, partial or final award. If partial identify the part (say, liability only).

Background

Parties	Set out the business and function of the parties and how they came to enter into the agreement.

The Agreement

Terms

Set out the terms of the agreement.

Variations to the Agreement

Amendments

If the agreement was amended, how and when it was amended and the terms of the agreement after any amending agreement.

History

Events

Set in chronological order the undisputed history of events.

Submissions

Pleadings

Set out the contentions in the pleadings starting with the claim and then the defence. Then deal with any counterclaim.

Issues

Issues

Set out issues to be determined.

Discussion

Findings

Although not the formal part of the award this is the meat of it where the evidence and submissions are discussed and findings made, issue by issue both on the facts and law.

Formal Award

Award

Formal declaratory or mandatory findings are made, interest as necessary is dealt with and costs both of the parties, the Tribunal and the institution.

Signature

The members of the Arbitral Tribunal will each sign. Witnessing is not normally necessary but is common.

Place and date

The place the Award is made (which will be the place of the reference) and the date of the Award are stated.

APPENDIX 27
SAMPLE CONSENT AWARD

IN THE MATTER OF AN ARBITRATION UNDER THE RULES OF
THE INTERNATIONAL CHAMBER OF COMMERCE

CASE No.

A

Claimant

v.

B

Respondent

AGREED AWARD

The Arbitral Tribunal: C (Chairman)

D

E

1. This arbitration concerns an agreement entered into by A and B on [date] (the Agreement). As provided for in Clause [X] of the Agreement, the arbitration was conducted in accordance with the [ICC Rules]. Clause [X] reads as follows: [set out arbitration clause]

2. Clause [X] of the Agreement provides that it is governed and shall be construed in accordance with the laws of ....

3. The arbitration no. ... was commenced by A by the filing of its Request for Arbitration dated ... (the Request). The named respondent was B.

4. B submitted its Answer to the Request on ... (the Answer).

5. A submitted a Reply to the Answer on ... (the Reply).

6. The Chairman of the Tribunal, confirmed by the [Secretary General of the] ICC International Court of Arbitration pursuant to Article 9(2) of the ICC Rules on ..., is: [insert name and contact details]

339

7. The co-arbitrator proposed by A, confirmed by the [Secretary General of the] ICC International Court of Arbitration pursuant to Article 9(2) of the ICC Rules on ..., is: [insert name and contact details]

8. The co-arbitrator proposed by B, confirmed by the [Secretary General of the] ICC International Court of Arbitration pursuant to Article 9(2) of the ICC Rules on ..., is: [insert name and contact details]

9. Pursuant to Clause [X] of the Agreement, the place of arbitration is [place] where the arbitration had its seat.

10. On [date] the parties informed the Tribunal that a settlement had been reached between the parties.

11. In accordance with the parties' request for an Agreed Award the Tribunal awards and directs as follows:

   11.1 that the terms of settlement agreed between the parties and annexed hereto be and the same are made an award to the same effect and status as any other award on the merits; and

   11.2 otherwise this reference is terminated.

[Date]

[Place]

[Signed]

APPENDIX 28
SAMPLE COSTS CAPPING ORDER

The recoverable costs of [the arbitration] [discovery] [the expert(s) in respect of whom permission has been given in paragraph [x] above] shall be limited to £ / $[x],000, subject always to the permission of the Arbitral Tribunal to give permission for such figure to be exceeded at any stage [save that any costs awarded in favour of a party on an interim application shall not count towards the said £ / $[x],000].

APPENDIX 29
TYPES OF COSTS ORDERS

- **"Costs in the Reference:"** used at an interim stage where the intention is that the party in whose favour the Arbitral Tribunal ultimately makes an order for costs is entitled to the costs of that part of the reference to which the order relates.

- **"Costs in any event:"** used at an interim stage where the intention is that the party in whose favour the Arbitral Tribunal makes such an order is entitled to the costs of that part of the reference to which the order relates, irrespective of whatever other order(s) is (are) made in the Reference.

- **"Costs Reserved:"** used when the Arbitral Tribunal wishes to defer to a later date the decision; it is generally understood that if no further order is made the costs are treated as Costs in the Reference (see above).

- **"Claimant's / Respondent's costs in the Reference:"** used to make a provisional decision. The party in whose favour the order is made is entitled to the costs of that part of the reference to which the order relates provided it also has a final costs order of the substantive issues in its favour as well. If the final costs order is made in favour of another party the order effectively becomes "No Order as to Costs."

- **"Costs thrown away:"** little used. Used to address costs that have been incurred but have been wasted. Can be combined with "Costs of and caused by."

- **"Costs of and caused by:"** normally used to address the costs of an amendment to a Memorial or Statement of Case and in those circumstances covers the preparation for and attendance at the application and the consequential amendments to the other Memorials or Statements of Case.

- **"No order as to Costs" or "Each party to pay its own Costs:"** used where each party is to bear its own costs of that part of the proceedings to which the order relates irrespective of any subsequent order.

- **"The Claimant / Respondent shall pay the Respondent's / Claimant's costs of the arbitration:"** used as a final order once the substantive decision has been made.

APPENDIX 30
SAMPLE ORDERS FOR SECURITY FOR COSTS

1A. It is ordered that the Claimant gives security for the Respondent's costs of the claim in the sum of £ / $ / €.

    or

1B. It is ordered that the Claimant gives security for the Respondent's costs of the claim in the sum of £ / $ / € down to the completion of [the memorials] [disclosure and inspection] [witness statements] [expert evidence] with permission to apply for a further sum or sums thereafter.

    or

1C. It is ordered that the Claimant gives security for the Respondent's costs of the claim in the sum of £ / $ / € down to the completion of the memorials; the further sum of £ / $ / € down to the completion of disclosure and inspection; the further sum of £ / $ / € down to the completion of witness statements; the further sum of £ / $ / € down to the completion of expert evidence with permission to apply to both parties to amend such sums.

2. Such security be given by [lodging with the Respondent's counsel such sum, such sum and all accrued interest to be held by the Respondent's counsel to the order of the Arbitral Tribunal] [provision of a bank guarantee in a form and from a bank acceptable to the Claimant's counsel] or in such other manner as may be agreed by the parties, by [date] [the following dates respectively].

3. In default of the security being given as directed, all further proceedings be stayed until such security is given.

APPENDIX 31
SAMPLE "SEALED OFFER"

To: Counsel for Opposing Party

From: Counsel to Offering Party.

Dear Sirs,

[matter reference]

Confidential and Without Prejudice Save as to Costs

We have carefully considered the merits of the respective claims and counterclaims. Taking all these matters into account, our client is prepared to compromise this reference by the payment of $/£/€ [x] plus your client's reasonable costs.

This offer is open for acceptance for a period of 21 days – such period expires at 4pm on [date].

This offer is:

1. without prejudice to the documents, evidence of fact, expert opinion or legal arguments, submissions and briefs as may be necessary to present our client's case or rebut any case that may be put forward by your client;

2. made for purely commercial reasons and should not be construed as an admission or an acceptance of likely failure if this matter were to proceed to a Final Award;

3. confidential in the sense that it should not be communicated:

   3.1. to the Arbitral Tribunal otherwise than in accordance with its terms; or

   3.2. to anyone unconnected with the reference — you may, naturally, communicate it to your client and other advisors and experts but not publish it generally;

4. in the event that it is not accepted, to be referred to the Arbitral Tribunal after it has made its Award on matters of liability and quantum and the Award is final in all respects save as to costs or

after the Arbitral Tribunal has reached its conclusions on such matters, as the case may be. At that stage it may be relied upon in support of an application for an Award of costs on the grounds that your client ought to have accepted this offer and, in consequence, after the date of this offer, it is our client that has been successful or otherwise that it was not reasonable to continue the reference and on such other grounds as may then seem appropriate. In the event that the Arbitral Tribunal bifurcate and wish to receive separate submissions on costs and make a separate Award on costs this letter may be included in the submissions as to costs. In the event that the Arbitral Tribunal wish to receive submissions on costs before it has reached its conclusions on liability and quantum this letter may be included in the submissions to the Arbitral Tribunal as an offer that a party (without identifying which party) has made and which the Arbitral Tribunal are invited to take into account in making its Award on costs. The letter itself will be sealed in an envelope clearly marked that the Tribunal should not open it until it has reached its conclusions on liability and quantum.

5. open for acceptance as stated above. It cannot be accepted thereafter without our consent in writing.

In the event that this offer is accepted and we are unable to agree the amount of your reasonable costs such amount is to be assessed and determined by the Arbitral Tribunal.

Yours etc.

APPENDIX 32
UNCITRAL MODEL LAW ON INTERNATIONAL COMMERCIAL ARBITRATION

Part One
UNCITRAL Model Law on International
Commercial Arbitration

(United Nations documents A/40/17,
annex I and A/61/17, annex I)

**(As adopted by the United Nations Commission on
International Trade Law on 21 June 1985,
and as amended by the United Nations Commission
on International Trade Law on 7 July 2006)**

CHAPTER I. GENERAL PROVISIONS

Article 1. Scope of application[1]

(1) This Law applies to international commercial[2] arbitration, subject to any agreement in force between this State and any other State or States.

(2) The provisions of this Law, except articles 8, 9, 17 H, 17 I, 17 J, 35 and 36, apply only if the place of arbitration is in the territory of this State.

---

[1] Article headings are for reference purposes only and are not to be used for purposes of interpretation.

[2] The term "commercial" should be given a wide interpretation so as to cover matters arising from all relationships of a commercial nature, whether contractual or not. Relationships of a commercial nature include, but are not limited to, the following transactions: any trade transaction for the supply or exchange of goods or services; distribution agreement; commercial representation or agency; factoring; leasing; construction of works; consulting; engineering; licensing; investment; financing; banking; insurance; exploitation agreement or concession; joint venture and other forms of industrial or business cooperation; carriage of goods or passengers by air, sea, rail or road.

(Article 1(2) has been amended by the Commission at its thirty-ninth session, in 2006)

(3) An arbitration is international if:

(a) the parties to an arbitration agreement have, at the time of the conclusion of that agreement, their places of business in different States; or

(b) one of the following places is situated outside the State in which the parties have their places of business:

(i) the place of arbitration if determined in, or pursuant to, the arbitration agreement;

(ii) any place where a substantial part of the obligations of the commercial relationship is to be performed or the place with which the subject-matter of the dispute is most closely connected; or

(c) the parties have expressly agreed that the subject matter of the arbitration agreement relates to more than one country.

(4) For the purposes of paragraph (3) of this article:

(a) if a party has more than one place of business, the place of business is that which has the closest relationship to the arbitration agreement;

(b) if a party does not have a place of business, reference is to be made to his habitual residence.

(5) This Law shall not affect any other law of this State by virtue of which certain disputes may not be submitted to arbitration or may be submitted to arbitration only according to provisions other than those of this Law.

Article 2. Definitions and rules of interpretation

For the purposes of this Law:

(a) "arbitration" means any arbitration whether or not administered by a permanent arbitral institution;

(b) "arbitral tribunal" means a sole arbitrator or a panel of arbitrators;

(c) "court" means a body or organ of the judicial system of a State;

350

(d) where a provision of this Law, except article 28, leaves the parties free to determine a certain issue, such freedom includes the right of the parties to authorize a third party, including an institution, to make that determination;

(e) where a provision of this Law refers to the fact that the parties have agreed or that they may agree or in any other way refers to an agreement of the parties, such agreement includes any arbitration rules referred to in that agreement;

(f) where a provision of this Law, other than in articles 25*(a)* and 32(2) *(a)*, refers to a claim, it also applies to a counter-claim, and where it refers to a defence, it also applies to a defence to such counter-claim.

Article 2 A. International origin and general principles
(As adopted by the Commission at its thirty-ninth session, in 2006)

(1) In the interpretation of this Law, regard is to be had to its international origin and to the need to promote uniformity in its application and the observance of good faith.

(2) Questions concerning matters governed by this Law which are not expressly settled in it are to be settled in conformity with the general principles on which this Law is based.

Article 3. Receipt of written communications

(1) Unless otherwise agreed by the parties:

(a) any written communication is deemed to have been received if it is delivered to the addressee personally or if it is delivered at his place of business, habitual residence or mailing address; if none of these can be found after making a reasonable inquiry, a written communication is deemed to have been received if it is sent to the addressee's last-known place of business, habitual residence or mailing address by registered letter or any other means which provides a record of the attempt to deliver it;

(b) the communication is deemed to have been received on the day it is so delivered.

(2) The provisions of this article do not apply to communications in court proceedings.

Article 4. Waiver of right to object

A party who knows that any provision of this Law from which the parties may derogate or any requirement under the arbitration agreement has not been complied with and yet proceeds with the arbitration without stating his objection to such non-compliance without undue delay or, if a time-limit is provided therefor, within such period of time, shall be deemed to have waived his right to object.

Article 5. Extent of court intervention

In matters governed by this Law, no court shall intervene except where so provided in this Law.

Article 6. Court or other authority for certain functions of arbitration assistance and supervision

The functions referred to in articles 11(3), 11(4), 13(3), 14, 16(3) and 34(2) shall be performed by ... [Each State enacting this model law specifies the court, courts or, where referred to therein, other authority competent to perform these functions.]

CHAPTER II. ARBITRATION AGREEMENT

Option I

Article 7. Definition and form of arbitration agreement (As adopted by the Commission at its thirty-ninth session, in 2006)

(1) "Arbitration agreement" is an agreement by the parties to submit to arbitration all or certain disputes which have arisen or which may arise between them in respect of a defined legal relationship, whether contractual or not. An arbitration agreement may be in the form of an arbitration clause in a contract or in the form of a separate agreement.

(2) The arbitration agreement shall be in writing.

(3) An arbitration agreement is in writing if its content is recorded in any form, whether or not the arbitration agreement or contract has been concluded orally, by conduct, or by other means.

(4) The requirement that an arbitration agreement be in writing is met by an electronic communication if the information contained therein is accessible so as to be useable for subsequent reference; "electronic communication" means any communication that the parties make by means of data messages; "data message" means information generated, sent, received or stored by electronic, magnetic, optical or similar means, including, but not limited to, electronic data interchange (EDI), electronic mail, telegram, telex or telecopy.

(5) Furthermore, an arbitration agreement is in writing if it is contained in an exchange of statements of claim and defence in which the existence of an agreement is alleged by one party and not denied by the other.

(6) The reference in a contract to any document containing an arbitration clause constitutes an arbitration agreement in writing, provided that the reference is such as to make that clause part of the contract.

Option II

Article 7. Definition of arbitration agreement
(As adopted by the Commission at its thirty-ninth session, in 2006)

"Arbitration agreement" is an agreement by the parties to submit to arbitration all or certain disputes which have arisen or which may arise between them in respect of a defined legal relationship, whether contractual or not.

Article 8. Arbitration agreement and substantive claim before court

(1) A court before which an action is brought in a matter which is the subject of an arbitration agreement shall, if a party so requests not later than when submitting his first statement on the substance of the dispute, refer the parties to arbitration unless it finds that the agreement is null and void, inoperative or incapable of being performed.

(2) Where an action referred to in paragraph (1) of this article has been brought, arbitral proceedings may nevertheless be commenced or continued, and an award may be made, while the issue is pending before the court.

Article 9. Arbitration agreement and interim measures by court

It is not incompatible with an arbitration agreement for a party to request, before or during arbitral proceedings, from a court an interim measure of protection and for a court to grant such measure.

CHAPTER III. COMPOSITION OF ARBITRAL TRIBUNAL

Article 10. Number of arbitrators

(1) The parties are free to determine the number of arbitrators.

(2) Failing such determination, the number of arbitrators shall be three.

Article 11. Appointment of arbitrators

(1) No person shall be precluded by reason of his nationality from acting as an arbitrator, unless otherwise agreed by the parties.

(2) The parties are free to agree on a procedure of appointing the arbitrator or arbitrators, subject to the provisions of paragraphs (4) and (5) of this article.

(3) Failing such agreement,

    (a) in an arbitration with three arbitrators, each party shall appoint one arbitrator, and the two arbitrators thus appointed shall appoint the third arbitrator; if a party fails to appoint the arbitrator within thirty days of receipt of a request to do so from the other party, or if the two arbitrators fail to agree on the third arbitrator within thirty days of their appointment, the appointment shall be made, upon request of a party, by the court or other authority specified in article 6;

    (b) in an arbitration with a sole arbitrator, if the parties are unable to agree on the arbitrator, he shall be appointed, upon request of a party, by the court or other authority specified in article 6.

(4) Where, under an appointment procedure agreed upon by the parties,

    (a) a party fails to act as required under such procedure, or

    (b) the parties, or two arbitrators, are unable to reach an agreement expected of them under such procedure, or

(c) a third party, including an institution, fails to perform any function entrusted to it under such procedure, any party may request the court or other authority specified in article 6 to take the necessary measure, unless the agreement on the appointment procedure provides other means for securing the appointment.

(5) A decision on a matter entrusted by paragraph (3) or (4) of this article to the court or other authority specified in article 6 shall be subject to no appeal. The court or other authority, in appointing an arbitrator, shall have due regard to any qualifications required of the arbitrator by the agreement of the parties and to such considerations as are likely to secure the appointment of an independent and impartial arbitrator and, in the case of a sole or third arbitrator, shall take into account as well the advisability of appointing an arbitrator of a nationality other than those of the parties.

Article 12. Grounds for challenge

(1) When a person is approached in connection with his possible appointment as an arbitrator, he shall disclose any circumstances likely to give rise to justifiable doubts as to his impartiality or independence. An arbitrator, from the time of his appointment and throughout the arbitral proceedings, shall without delay disclose any such circumstances to the parties unless they have already been informed of them by him.

(2) An arbitrator may be challenged only if circumstances exist that give rise to justifiable doubts as to his impartiality or independence, or if he does not possess qualifications agreed to by the parties. A party may challenge an arbitrator appointed by him, or in whose appointment he has participated, only for reasons of which he becomes aware after the appointment has been made.

Article 13. Challenge procedure

(1) The parties are free to agree on a procedure for challenging an arbitrator, subject to the provisions of paragraph (3) of this article.

(2) Failing such agreement, a party who intends to challenge an arbitrator shall, within fifteen days after becoming aware of the constitution of the arbitral tribunal or after becoming aware of any circumstance referred to in article 12(2), send a written statement of

the reasons for the challenge to the arbitral tribunal. Unless the challenged arbitrator withdraws from his office or the other party agrees to the challenge, the arbitral tribunal shall decide on the challenge.

(3) If a challenge under any procedure agreed upon by the parties or under the procedure of paragraph (2) of this article is not successful, the challenging party may request, within thirty days after having received notice of the decision rejecting the challenge, the court or other authority specified in article 6 to decide on the challenge, which decision shall be subject to no appeal; while such a request is pending, the arbitral tribunal, including the challenged arbitrator, may continue the arbitral proceedings and make an award.

Article 14. Failure or impossibility to act

(1) If an arbitrator becomes *de jure* or *de facto* unable to perform his functions or for other reasons fails to act without undue delay, his mandate terminates if he withdraws from his office or if the parties agree on the termination. Otherwise, if a controversy remains concerning any of these grounds, any party may request the court or other authority specified in article 6 to decide on the termination of the mandate, which decision shall be subject to no appeal.

(2) If, under this article or article 13(2), an arbitrator withdraws from his office or a party agrees to the termination of the mandate of an arbitrator, this does not imply acceptance of the validity of any ground referred to in this article or article 12(2).

Article 15. Appointment of substitute arbitrator

Where the mandate of an arbitrator terminates under article 13 or 14 or because of his withdrawal from office for any other reason or because of the revocation of his mandate by agreement of the parties or in any other case of termination of his mandate, a substitute arbitrator shall be appointed according to the rules that were applicable to the appointment of the arbitrator being replaced.

CHAPTER IV. JURISDICTION OF ARBITRAL TRIBUNAL

Article 16. Competence of arbitral tribunal to rule on its jurisdiction

(1) The arbitral tribunal may rule on its own jurisdiction, including any objections with respect to the existence or validity of the arbitration agreement. For that purpose, an arbitration clause which forms part of a contract shall be treated as an agreement independent of the other terms of the contract. A decision by the arbitral tribunal that the contract is null and void shall not entail *ipso jure* the invalidity of the arbitration clause.

(2) A plea that the arbitral tribunal does not have jurisdiction shall be raised not later than the submission of the statement of defence. A party is not precluded from raising such a plea by the fact that he has appointed, or participated in the appointment of, an arbitrator. A plea that the arbitral tribunal is exceeding the scope of its authority shall be raised as soon as the matter alleged to be beyond the scope of its authority is raised during the arbitral proceedings. The arbitral tribunal may, in either case, admit a later plea if it considers the delay justified.

(3) The arbitral tribunal may rule on a plea referred to in paragraph (2) of this article either as a preliminary question or in an award on the merits. If the arbitral tribunal rules as a preliminary question that it has jurisdiction, any party may request, within thirty days after having received notice of that ruling, the court specified in article 6 to decide the matter, which decision shall be subject to no appeal; while such a request is pending, the arbitral tribunal may continue the arbitral proceedings and make an award.

CHAPTER IV A. INTERIM MEASURES AND PRELIMINARY ORDERS

(As adopted by the Commission at its thirty-ninth session, in 2006)

Section 1. Interim measures

Article 17. Power of arbitral tribunal to order interim measures

(1) Unless otherwise agreed by the parties, the arbitral tribunal may, at the request of a party, grant interim measures.

(2) An interim measure is any temporary measure, whether in the form of an award or in another form, by which, at any time prior to the

issuance of the award by which the dispute is finally decided, the arbitral tribunal orders a party to:

(a) Maintain or restore the status quo pending determination of the dispute;

(b) Take action that would prevent, or refrain from taking action that is likely to cause, current or imminent harm or prejudice to the arbitral process itself;

(c) Provide a means of preserving assets out of which a subsequent award may be satisfied; or

(d) Preserve evidence that may be relevant and material to the resolution of the dispute.

Article 17 A. Conditions for granting interim measures

(1) The party requesting an interim measure under article 17(2)*(a)*, *(b)* and *(c)* shall satisfy the arbitral tribunal that:

(a) Harm not adequately reparable by an award of damages is likely to result if the measure is not ordered, and such harm substantially outweighs the harm that is likely to result to the party against whom the measure is directed if the measure is granted; and

(b) There is a reasonable possibility that the requesting party will succeed on the merits of the claim. The determination on this possibility shall not affect the discretion of the arbitral tribunal in making any subsequent determination.

(2) With regard to a request for an interim measure under article 17(2)*(d)*, the requirements in paragraphs (1)*(a)* and *(b)* of this article shall apply only to the extent the arbitral tribunal considers appropriate.

Section 2. Preliminary orders

Article 17 B. Applications for preliminary orders and conditions for granting preliminary orders

(1) Unless otherwise agreed by the parties, a party may, without notice to any other party, make a request for an interim measure together with an application for a preliminary order directing a party not to frustrate the purpose of the interim measure requested.

(2) The arbitral tribunal may grant a preliminary order provided it considers that prior disclosure of the request for the interim measure to the party against whom it is directed risks frustrating the purpose of the measure.

(3) The conditions defined under article 17A apply to any preliminary order, provided that the harm to be assessed under article 17A(1)(a), is the harm likely to result from the order being granted or not.

Article 17 C. Specific regime for preliminary orders

(1) Immediately after the arbitral tribunal has made a determination in respect of an application for a preliminary order, the arbitral tribunal shall give notice to all parties of the request for the interim measure, the application for the preliminary order, the preliminary order, if any, and all other communications, including by indicating the content of any oral communication, between any party and the arbitral tribunal in relation thereto.

(2) At the same time, the arbitral tribunal shall give an opportunity to any party against whom a preliminary order is directed to present its case at the earliest practicable time.

(3) The arbitral tribunal shall decide promptly on any objection to the preliminary order.

(4) A preliminary order shall expire after twenty days from the date on which it was issued by the arbitral tribunal. However, the arbitral tribunal may issue an interim measure adopting or modifying the preliminary order, after the party against whom the preliminary order is directed has been given notice and an opportunity to present its case.

(5) A preliminary order shall be binding on the parties but shall not be subject to enforcement by a court. Such a preliminary order does not constitute an award.

Section 3. Provisions applicable to interim measures and preliminary orders

Article 17 D. Modification, suspension, termination

The arbitral tribunal may modify, suspend or terminate an interim measure or a preliminary order it has granted, upon application of any party or, in exceptional circumstances and upon prior notice to the parties, on the arbitral tribunal's own initiative.

Article 17 E. Provision of security

(1) The arbitral tribunal may require the party requesting an interim measure to provide appropriate security in connection with the measure.

(2) The arbitral tribunal shall require the party applying for a preliminary order to provide security in connection with the order unless the arbitral tribunal considers it inappropriate or unnecessary to do so.

Article 17 F. Disclosure

(1) The arbitral tribunal may require any party promptly to disclose any material change in the circumstances on the basis of which the measure was requested or granted.

(2) The party applying for a preliminary order shall disclose to the arbitral tribunal all circumstances that are likely to be relevant to the arbitral tribunal's determination whether to grant or maintain the order, and such obligation shall continue until the party against whom the order has been requested has had an opportunity to present its case. Thereafter, paragraph (1) of this article shall apply.

Article 17 G. Costs and damages

The party requesting an interim measure or applying for a preliminary order shall be liable for any costs and damages caused by the measure or the order to any party if the arbitral tribunal later determines that, in the circumstances, the measure or the order should not have been granted. The arbitral tribunal may award such costs and damages at any point during the proceedings.

Section 4. Recognition and enforcement of interim measures

Article 17 H. Recognition and enforcement

(1) An interim measure issued by an arbitral tribunal shall be recognized as binding and, unless otherwise provided by the arbitral tribunal, enforced upon application to the competent court, irrespective of the country in which it was issued, subject to the provisions of article 17 I.

(2) The party who is seeking or has obtained recognition or enforcement of an interim measure shall promptly inform the court of any termination, suspension or modification of that interim measure.

(3) The court of the State where recognition or enforcement is sought may, if it considers it proper, order the requesting party to provide appropriate security if the arbitral tribunal has not already made a determination with respect to security or where such a decision is necessary to protect the rights of third parties.

Article 17 I. Grounds for refusing recognition or enforcement[3]

(1) Recognition or enforcement of an interim measure may be refused only:

    (a) At the request of the party against whom it is invoked if the court is satisfied that:

        (i) Such refusal is warranted on the grounds set forth in article 36(1)*(a)*(i), (ii), (iii) or (iv); or

        (ii) The arbitral tribunal's decision with respect to the provision of security in connection with the interim measure issued by the arbitral tribunal has not been complied with; or

        (iii) The interim measure has been terminated or suspended by the arbitral tribunal or, where so empowered, by the court of the State in which the arbitration takes place or under the law of which that interim measure was granted; or

    (b) If the court finds that:

        (i) The interim measure is incompatible with the powers conferred upon the court unless the court decides to reformulate the interim measure to the extent necessary to adapt it to its own powers and procedures for the purposes of enforcing that interim measure and without modifying its substance; or

        (ii) Any of the grounds set forth in article 36(1)*(b)*(i) or (ii), apply to the recognition and enforcement of the interim measure.

---

[3] The conditions set forth in article 17 I are intended to limit the number of circumstances in which the court may refuse to enforce an interim measure. It would not be contrary to the level of harmonization sought to be achieved by these model provisions if a State were to adopt fewer circumstances in which enforcement may be refused.

(2) Any determination made by the court on any ground in paragraph (1) of this article shall be effective only for the purposes of the application to recognize and enforce the interim measure. The court where recognition or enforcement is sought shall not, in making that determination, undertake a review of the substance of the interim measure.

Section 5. Court-ordered interim measures

Article 17 J. Court-ordered interim measures

A court shall have the same power of issuing an interim measure in relation to arbitration proceedings, irrespective of whether their place is in the territory of this State, as it has in relation to proceedings in courts. The court shall exercise such power in accordance with its own procedures in consideration of the specific features of international arbitration.

CHAPTER V. CONDUCT OF ARBITRAL PROCEEDINGS

Article 18. Equal treatment of parties

The parties shall be treated with equality and each party shall be given a full opportunity of presenting his case.

Article 19. Determination of rules of procedure

(1) Subject to the provisions of this Law, the parties are free to agree on the procedure to be followed by the arbitral tribunal in conducting the proceedings.

(2) Failing such agreement, the arbitral tribunal may, subject to the provisions of this Law, conduct the arbitration in such manner as it considers appropriate. The power conferred upon the arbitral tribunal includes the power to determine the admissibility, relevance, materiality and weight of any evidence.

Article 20. Place of arbitration

(1) The parties are free to agree on the place of arbitration. Failing such agreement, the place of arbitration shall be determined by the arbitral tribunal having regard to the circumstances of the case, including the convenience of the parties.

(2) Notwithstanding the provisions of paragraph (1) of this article, the arbitral tribunal may, unless otherwise agreed by the parties, meet at any place it considers appropriate for consultation among its members, for hearing witnesses, experts or the parties, or for inspection of goods, other property or documents.

Article 21. Commencement of arbitral proceedings

Unless otherwise agreed by the parties, the arbitral proceedings in respect of a particular dispute commence on the date on which a request for that dispute to be referred to arbitration is received by the respondent.

Article 22. Language

(1) The parties are free to agree on the language or languages to be used in the arbitral proceedings. Failing such agreement, the arbitral tribunal shall determine the language or languages to be used in the proceedings. This agreement or determination, unless otherwise specified therein, shall apply to any written statement by a party, any hearing and any award, decision or other communication by the arbitral tribunal.

(2) The arbitral tribunal may order that any documentary evidence shall be accompanied by a translation into the language or languages agreed upon by the parties or determined by the arbitral tribunal.

Article 23. Statements of claim and defence

(1) Within the period of time agreed by the parties or determined by the arbitral tribunal, the claimant shall state the facts supporting his claim, the points at issue and the relief or remedy sought, and the respondent shall state his defence in respect of these particulars, unless the parties have otherwise agreed as to the required elements of such statements. The parties may submit with their statements all documents they consider to be relevant or may add a reference to the documents or other evidence they will submit.

(2) Unless otherwise agreed by the parties, either party may amend or supplement his claim or defence during the course of the arbitral proceedings, unless the arbitral tribunal considers it inappropriate to allow such amendment having regard to the delay in making it.

Article 24. Hearings and written proceedings

(1) Subject to any contrary agreement by the parties, the arbitral tribunal shall decide whether to hold oral hearings for the presentation of evidence or for oral argument, or whether the proceedings shall be conducted on the basis of documents and other materials. However, unless the parties have agreed that no hearings shall be held, the arbitral tribunal shall hold such hearings at an appropriate stage of the proceedings, if so requested by a party.

(2) The parties shall be given sufficient advance notice of any hearing and of any meeting of the arbitral tribunal for the purposes of inspection of goods, other property or documents.

(3) All statements, documents or other information supplied to the arbitral tribunal by one party shall be communicated to the other party. Also any expert report or evidentiary document on which the arbitral tribunal may rely in making its decision shall be communicated to the parties.

Article 25. Default of a party

Unless otherwise agreed by the parties, if, without showing sufficient cause,

(a) the claimant fails to communicate his statement of claim in accordance with article 23(1), the arbitral tribunal shall terminate the proceedings;

(b) the respondent fails to communicate his statement of defence in accordance with article 23(1), the arbitral tribunal shall continue the proceedings without treating such failure in itself as an admission of the claimant's allegations;

(c) any party fails to appear at a hearing or to produce documentary evidence, the arbitral tribunal may continue the proceedings and make the award on the evidence before it.

Article 26. Expert appointed by arbitral tribunal

(1) Unless otherwise agreed by the parties, the arbitral tribunal

(a) may appoint one or more experts to report to it on specific issues to be determined by the arbitral tribunal;

(b) may require a party to give the expert any relevant information or to produce, or to provide access to, any relevant documents, goods or other property for his inspection.

(2) Unless otherwise agreed by the parties, if a party so requests or if the arbitral tribunal considers it necessary, the expert shall, after delivery of his written or oral report, participate in a hearing where the parties have the opportunity to put questions to him and to present expert witnesses in order to testify on the points at issue.

Article 27. Court assistance in taking evidence

The arbitral tribunal or a party with the approval of the arbitral tribunal may request from a competent court of this State assistance in taking evidence. The court may execute the request within its competence and according to its rules on taking evidence.

CHAPTER VI. MAKING OF AWARD AND TERMINATION OF PROCEEDINGS

Article 28. Rules applicable to substance of dispute

(1) The arbitral tribunal shall decide the dispute in accordance with such rules of law as are chosen by the parties as applicable to the substance of the dispute. Any designation of the law or legal system of a given State shall be construed, unless otherwise expressed, as directly referring to the substantive law of that State and not to its conflict of laws rules.

(2) Failing any designation by the parties, the arbitral tribunal shall apply the law determined by the conflict of laws rules which it considers applicable.

(3) The arbitral tribunal shall decide *ex aequo et bono* or as *amiable compositeur* only if the parties have expressly authorized it to do so.

(4) In all cases, the arbitral tribunal shall decide in accordance with the terms of the contract and shall take into account the usages of the trade applicable to the transaction.

Article 29. Decision-making by panel of arbitrators

In arbitral proceedings with more than one arbitrator, any decision of the arbitral tribunal shall be made, unless otherwise agreed by the parties, by a majority of all its members. However, questions of procedure may be decided by a presiding arbitrator, if so authorized by the parties or all members of the arbitral tribunal.

Article 30. Settlement

(1) If, during arbitral proceedings, the parties settle the dispute, the arbitral tribunal shall terminate the proceedings and, if requested by the parties and not objected to by the arbitral tribunal, record the settlement in the form of an arbitral award on agreed terms.

(2) An award on agreed terms shall be made in accordance with the provisions of article 31 and shall state that it is an award. Such an award has the same status and effect as any other award on the merits of the case.

Article 31. Form and contents of award

(1) The award shall be made in writing and shall be signed by the arbitrator or arbitrators. In arbitral proceedings with more than one arbitrator, the signatures of the majority of all members of the arbitral tribunal shall suffice, provided that the reason for any omitted signature is stated.

(2) The award shall state the reasons upon which it is based, unless the parties have agreed that no reasons are to be given or the award is an award on agreed terms under article 30.

(3) The award shall state its date and the place of arbitration as determined in accordance with article 20(1). The award shall be deemed to have been made at that place.

(4) After the award is made, a copy signed by the arbitrators in accordance with paragraph (1) of this article shall be delivered to each party.

Article 32. Termination of proceedings

(1) The arbitral proceedings are terminated by the final award or by an order of the arbitral tribunal in accordance with paragraph (2) of this article.

(2) The arbitral tribunal shall issue an order for the termination of the arbitral proceedings when:

    (a) the claimant withdraws his claim, unless the respondent objects thereto and the arbitral tribunal recognizes a legitimate interest on his part in obtaining a final settlement of the dispute;

(b) the parties agree on the termination of the proceedings;

(c) the arbitral tribunal finds that the continuation of the proceedings has for any other reason become unnecessary or impossible.

(3) The mandate of the arbitral tribunal terminates with the termination of the arbitral proceedings, subject to the provisions of articles 33 and 34(4).

Article 33. Correction and interpretation of award; additional award

(1) Within thirty days of receipt of the award, unless another period of time has been agreed upon by the parties:

(a) a party, with notice to the other party, may request the arbitral tribunal to correct in the award any errors in computation, any clerical or typographical errors or any errors of similar nature;

(b) if so agreed by the parties, a party, with notice to the other party, may request the arbitral tribunal to give an interpretation of a specific point or part of the award.

If the arbitral tribunal considers the request to be justified, it shall make the correction or give the interpretation within thirty days of receipt of the request. The interpretation shall form part of the award.

(2) The arbitral tribunal may correct any error of the type referred to in paragraph (1)*(a)* of this article on its own initiative within thirty days of the date of the award.

(3) Unless otherwise agreed by the parties, a party, with notice to the other party, may request, within thirty days of receipt of the award, the arbitral tribunal to make an additional award as to claims presented in the arbitral proceedings but omitted from the award. If the arbitral tribunal considers the request to be justified, it shall make the additional award within sixty days.

(4) The arbitral tribunal may extend, if necessary, the period of time within which it shall make a correction, interpretation or an additional award under paragraph (1) or (3) of this article.

(5) The provisions of article 31 shall apply to a correction or interpretation of the award or to an additional award.

CHAPTER VII. RECOURSE AGAINST AWARD

*Article 34. Application for setting aside as exclusive
recourse against arbitral award*

(1) Recourse to a court against an arbitral award may be made only by an application for setting aside in accordance with paragraphs (2) and (3) of this article.

(2) An arbitral award may be set aside by the court specified in article 6 only if:

(a) the party making the application furnishes proof that:

(i) a party to the arbitration agreement referred to in article 7 was under some incapacity; or the said agreement is not valid under the law to which the parties have subjected it or, failing any indication thereon, under the law of this State; or

(ii) the party making the application was not given proper notice of the appointment of an arbitrator or of the arbitral proceedings or was otherwise unable to present his case; or

(iii) the award deals with a dispute not contemplated by or not falling within the terms of the submission to arbitration, or contains decisions on matters beyond the scope of the submission to arbitration, provided that, if the decisions on matters submitted to arbitration can be separated from those not so submitted, only that part of the award which contains decisions on matters not submitted to arbitration may be set aside; or

(iv) the composition of the arbitral tribunal or the arbitral procedure was not in accordance with the agreement of the parties, unless such agreement was in conflict with a provision of this Law from which the parties cannot derogate, or, failing such agreement, was not in accordance with this Law; or

(b) the court finds that:

(i) the subject-matter of the dispute is not capable of settlement by arbitration under the law of this State; or

(ii) the award is in conflict with the public policy of this State.

368

(3) An application for setting aside may not be made after three months have elapsed from the date on which the party making that application had received the award or, if a request had been made under article 33, from the date on which that request had been disposed of by the arbitral tribunal.

(4) The court, when asked to set aside an award, may, where appropriate and so requested by a party, suspend the setting aside proceedings for a period of time determined by it in order to give the arbitral tribunal an opportunity to resume the arbitral proceedings or to take such other action as in the arbitral tribunal's opinion will eliminate the grounds for setting aside.

CHAPTER VIII. RECOGNITION AND ENFORCEMENT OF AWARDS

Article 35. Recognition and enforcement

(1) An arbitral award, irrespective of the country in which it was made, shall be recognized as binding and, upon application in writing to the competent court, shall be enforced subject to the provisions of this article and of article 36.

(2) The party relying on an award or applying for its enforcement shall supply the original award or a copy thereof. If the award is not made in an official language of this State, the court may request the party to supply a translation thereof into such language.[4]

(Article 35(2) has been amended by the Commission at its thirty-ninth session, in 2006)

Article 36. Grounds for refusing recognition or enforcement

(1) Recognition or enforcement of an arbitral award, irrespective of the country in which it was made, may be refused only:

   (a) at the request of the party against whom it is invoked, if that party furnishes to the competent court where recognition or enforcement is sought proof that:

---

[4] The conditions set forth in this paragraph are intended to set maximum standards. It would, thus, not be contrary to the harmonization to be achieved by the model law if a State retained even less onerous conditions.

(i) a party to the arbitration agreement referred to in article 7 was under some incapacity; or the said agreement is not valid under the law to which the parties have subjected it or, failing any indication thereon, under the law of the country where the award was made; or

(ii) the party against whom the award is invoked was not given proper notice of the appointment of an arbitrator or of the arbitral proceedings or was otherwise unable to present his case; or

(iii) the award deals with a dispute not contemplated by or not falling within the terms of the submission to arbitration, or it contains decisions on matters beyond the scope of the submission to arbitration, provided that, if the decisions on matters submitted to arbitration can be separated from those not so submitted, that part of the award which contains decisions on matters submitted to arbitration may be recognized and enforced; or

(iv) the composition of the arbitral tribunal or the arbitral procedure was not in accordance with the agreement of the parties or, failing such agreement, was not in accordance with the law of the country where the arbitration took place; or

(v) the award has not yet become binding on the parties or has been set aside or suspended by a court of the country in which, or under the law of which, that award was made; or

(b) if the court finds that:

(i) the subject-matter of the dispute is not capable of settlement by arbitration under the law of this State; or

(ii) the recognition or enforcement of the award would be contrary to the public policy of this State.

(2) If an application for setting aside or suspension of an award has been made to a court referred to in paragraph (1)*(a)*(v) of this article, the court where recognition or enforcement is sought may, if it considers it proper, adjourn its decision and may also, on the application of the party claiming recognition or enforcement of the award, order the other party to provide appropriate security.

Part Two

Explanatory Note by the UNCITRAL secretariat
on the 1985 Model Law on International Commercial
Arbitration as amended in 2006[1]

1. The UNCITRAL Model Law on International Commercial Arbitration ("the Model Law") was adopted by the United Nations Commission on International Trade Law (UNCITRAL) on 21 June 1985, at the end of the eighteenth session of the Commission. The General Assembly, in its resolution 40/72 of 11 December 1985, recommended "that all States give due consideration to the Model Law on International Commercial Arbitration, in view of the desirability of uniformity of the law of arbitral procedures and the specific needs of international commercial arbitration practice". The Model Law was amended by UNCITRAL on 7 July 2006, at the thirty-ninth session of the Commission (see below, paragraphs 4, 19, 20, 27, 29 and 53). The General Assembly, in its resolution 61/33 of 4 December 2006, recommended "that all States give favourable consideration to the enactment of the revised articles of the UNCITRAL Model Law on International Commercial Arbitration, or the revised UNCITRAL Model Law on International Commercial Arbitration, when they enact or revise their laws (...)".

2. The Model Law constitutes a sound basis for the desired harmonization and improvement of national laws. It covers all stages of the arbitral process from the arbitration agreement to the recognition and enforcement of the arbitral award and reflects a worldwide consensus on the principles and important issues of international arbitration practice. It is acceptable to States of all regions and the different legal or economic systems of the world. Since its adoption by UNCITRAL, the Model Law has come to represent the accepted international legislative standard for a modern arbitration law and a significant number of jurisdictions have enacted arbitration legislation based on the Model Law.

---

[1] This note was prepared by the secretariat of the United Nations Commission on International Trade Law (UNCITRAL) for informational purposes only; it is not an official commentary on the Model Law. A commentary prepared by the Secretariat on an early draft of the Model Law appears in document A/CN.9/264 (reproduced in UNCITRAL Yearbook, vol. XVI — 1985, United Nations publication, Sales No. E.87.V.4).

3. The form of a model law was chosen as the vehicle for harmonization and modernization in view of the flexibility it gives to States in preparing new arbitration laws. Notwithstanding that flexibility, and in order to increase the likelihood of achieving a satisfactory degree of harmonization, States are encouraged to make as few changes as possible when incorporating the Model Law into their legal systems. Efforts to minimize variation from the text adopted by UNCITRAL are also expected to increase the visibility of harmonization, thus enhancing the confidence of foreign parties, as the primary users of international arbitration, in the reliability of arbitration law in the enacting State.

4. The revision of the Model Law adopted in 2006 includes article 2 A, which is designed to facilitate interpretation by reference to internationally accepted principles and is aimed at promoting a uniform understanding of the Model Law. Other substantive amendments to the Model Law relate to the form of the arbitration agreement and to interim measures. The original 1985 version of the provision on the form of the arbitration agreement (article 7) was modelled on the language used in article II (2) of the Convention on the Recognition and Enforcement of Foreign Arbitral Awards (New York, 1958) ("the New York Convention"). The revision of article 7 is intended to address evolving practice in international trade and technological developments. The extensive revision of article 17 on interim measures was considered necessary in light of the fact that such measures are increasingly relied upon in the practice of international commercial arbitration. The revision also includes an enforcement regime for such measures in recognition of the fact that the effectiveness of arbitration frequently depends upon the possibility of enforcing interim measures. The new provisions are contained in a new chapter of the Model Law on interim measures and preliminary orders (chapter IV A).

A. Background to the Model Law

5. The Model Law was developed to address considerable disparities in national laws on arbitration. The need for improvement and harmonization was based on findings that national laws were often particularly inappropriate for international cases.

1. Inadequacy of domestic laws

6. Recurrent inadequacies to be found in outdated national laws include provisions that equate the arbitral process with court litigation and fragmentary provisions that fail to address all relevant substantive law issues. Even most of those laws that appear to be up-to-date and comprehensive were drafted with domestic arbitration primarily, if not exclusively, in mind. While this approach is understandable in view of the fact that even today the bulk of cases governed by arbitration law would be of a purely domestic nature, the unfortunate consequence is that traditional local concepts are imposed on international cases and the needs of modern practice are often not met.

7. The expectations of the parties as expressed in a chosen set of arbitration rules or a "one-off" arbitration agreement may be frustrated, especially by mandatory provisions of applicable law. Unexpected and undesired restrictions found in national laws may prevent the parties, for example, from submitting future disputes to arbitration, from selecting the arbitrator freely, or from having the arbitral proceedings conducted according to agreed rules of procedure and with no more court involvement than appropriate. Frustration may also ensue from non-mandatory provisions that may impose undesired requirements on unwary parties who may not think about the need to provide otherwise when drafting the arbitration agreement. Even the absence of any legislative provision may cause difficulties simply by leaving unanswered some of the many procedural issues relevant in arbitration and not always settled in the arbitration agreement. The Model Law is intended to reduce the risk of such possible frustration, difficulties or surprise.

2. Disparity between national laws

8. Problems stemming from inadequate arbitration laws or from the absence of specific legislation governing arbitration are aggravated by the fact that national laws differ widely. Such differences are a frequent source of concern in international arbitration, where at least one of the parties is, and often both parties are, confronted with foreign and unfamiliar provisions and procedures. Obtaining a full and precise account of the law applicable to the arbitration is, in such circumstances often expensive, impractical or impossible.

9.   Uncertainty about the local law with the inherent risk of frustration may adversely affect the functioning of the arbitral process and also impact on the selection of the place of arbitration. Due to such uncertainty, a party may hesitate or refuse to agree to a place, which for practical reasons would otherwise be appropriate. The range of places of arbitration acceptable to parties is thus widened and the smooth functioning of the arbitral proceedings is enhanced where States adopt the Model Law, which is easily recognizable, meets the specific needs of international commercial arbitration and provides an international standard based on solutions acceptable to parties from different legal systems.

B. Salient features of the Model Law

1. Special procedural regime for international commercial arbitration

10.   The principles and solutions adopted in the Model Law aim at reducing or eliminating the above-mentioned concerns and difficulties. As a response to the inadequacies and disparities of national laws, the Model Law presents a special legal regime tailored to international commercial arbitration, without affecting any relevant treaty in force in the State adopting the Model Law. While the Model Law was designed with international commercial arbitration in mind, it offers a set of basic rules that are not, in and of themselves, unsuitable to any other type of arbitration. States may thus consider extending their enactment of the Model Law to cover also domestic disputes, as a number of enacting States already have.

(a) Substantive and territorial scope of application

11.   Article 1 defines the scope of application of the Model Law by reference to the notion of "international commercial arbitration". The Model Law defines an arbitration as international if "the parties to an arbitration agreement have, at the time of the conclusion of that agreement, their places of business in different States" (article 1 (3)). The vast majority of situations commonly regarded as international will meet this criterion. In addition, article 1 (3) broadens the notion of internationality so that the Model Law also covers cases where the place of arbitration, the place of contract performance, or the place of the subject-matter of the dispute is situated outside the State where the parties have their place of business, or cases where the parties have

expressly agreed that the subject-matter of the arbitration agreement relates to more than one country. Article 1 thus recognizes extensively the freedom of the parties to submit a dispute to the legal regime established pursuant to the Model Law.

12. In respect of the term "commercial", the Model Law provides no strict definition. The footnote to article 1 (1) calls for "a wide interpretation" and offers an illustrative and open-ended list of relationships that might be described as commercial in nature, "whether contractual or not". The purpose of the footnote is to circumvent any technical difficulty that may arise, for example, in determining which transactions should be governed by a specific body of "commercial law" that may exist in some legal systems.

13. Another aspect of applicability is the territorial scope of application. The principle embodied in article 1 (2) is that the Model Law as enacted in a given State applies only if the place of arbitration is in the territory of that State. However, article 1 (2) also contains important exceptions to that principle, to the effect that certain articles apply, irrespective of whether the place of arbitration is in the enacting State or elsewhere (or, as the case may be, even before the place of arbitration is determined). These articles are the following: articles 8 (1) and 9, which deal with the recognition of arbitration agreements, including their compatibility with interim measures ordered by a court, article 17 J on court-ordered interim measures, articles 17 H and 17 I on the recognition and enforcement of interim measures ordered by an arbitral tribunal, and articles 35 and 36 on the recognition and enforcement of arbitral awards.

14. The territorial criterion governing most of the provisions of the Model Law was adopted for the sake of certainty and in view of the following facts. In most legal systems, the place of arbitration is the exclusive criterion for determining the applicability of national law and, where the national law allows parties to choose the procedural law of a State other than that where the arbitration takes place, experience shows that parties rarely make use of that possibility. Incidentally, enactment of the Model Law reduces any need for the parties to choose a "foreign" law, since the Model Law grants the parties wide freedom in shaping the rules of the arbitral proceedings. In addition to designating the law governing the arbitral procedure, the territorial criterion is of considerable practical importance in respect of articles 11, 13, 14, 16, 27 and 34, which entrust State courts at the place of arbitration with

functions of supervision and assistance to arbitration. It should be noted that the territorial criterion legally triggered by the parties' choice regarding the place of arbitration does not limit the arbitral tribunal's ability to meet at any place it considers appropriate for the conduct of the proceedings, as provided by article 20 (2).

(b) Delimitation of court assistance and supervision

15. Recent amendments to arbitration laws reveal a trend in favour of limiting and clearly defining court involvement in international commercial arbitration. This is justified in view of the fact that the parties to an arbitration agreement make a conscious decision to exclude court jurisdiction and prefer the finality and expediency of the arbitral process.

16. In this spirit, the Model Law envisages court involvement in the following instances. A first group comprises issues of appointment, challenge and termination of the mandate of an arbitrator (articles 11, 13 and 14), jurisdiction of the arbitral tribunal (article 16) and setting aside of the arbitral award (article 34). These instances are listed in article 6 as functions that should be entrusted, for the sake of centralization, specialization and efficiency, to a specially designated court or, with respect to articles 11, 13 and 14, possibly to another authority (for example, an arbitral institution or a chamber of commerce). A second group comprises issues of court assistance in taking evidence (article 27), recognition of the arbitration agreement, including its compatibility with court-ordered interim measures (articles 8 and 9), court-ordered interim measures (article 17 J), and recognition and enforcement of interim measures (articles 17 H and 17 I) and of arbitral awards (articles 35 and 36).

17. Beyond the instances in these two groups, "no court shall intervene, in matters governed by this Law". Article 5 thus guarantees that all instances of possible court intervention are found in the piece of legislation enacting the Model Law, except for matters not regulated by it (for example, consolidation of arbitral proceedings, contractual relationship between arbitrators and parties or arbitral institutions, or fixing of costs and fees, including deposits). Protecting the arbitral process from unpredictable or disruptive court interference is essential to parties who choose arbitration (in particular foreign parties).

2. *Arbitration agreement*

18. Chapter II of the Model Law deals with the arbitration agreement, including its recognition by courts.

(a) Definition and form of arbitration agreement

19. The original 1985 version of the provision on the definition and form of arbitration agreement (article 7) closely followed article II (2) of the New York Convention, which requires that an arbitration agreement be in writing. If the parties have agreed to arbitrate, but they entered into the arbitration agreement in a manner that does not meet the form requirement, any party may have grounds to object to the jurisdiction of the arbitral tribunal. It was pointed out by practitioners that, in a number of situations, the drafting of a written document was impossible or impractical. In such cases, where the willingness of the parties to arbitrate was not in question, the validity of the arbitration agreement should be recognized. For that reason, article 7 was amended in 2006 to better conform to international contract practices. In amending article 7, the Commission adopted two options, which reflect two different approaches on the question of definition and form of arbitration agreement. The first approach follows the detailed structure of the original 1985 text. It confirms the validity and effect of a commitment by the parties to submit to arbitration an existing dispute (*"compromis"*) or a future dispute (*"clause compromissoire"*). It follows the New York Convention in requiring the written form of the arbitration agreement but recognizes a record of the "contents" of the agreement "in any form" as equivalent to traditional "writing". The agreement to arbitrate may be entered into in any form (e.g. including orally) as long as the content of the agreement is recorded. This new rule is significant in that it no longer requires signatures of the parties or an exchange of messages between the parties. It modernizes the language referring to the use of electronic commerce by adopting wording inspired from the 1996 UNCITRAL Model Law on Electronic Commerce and the 2005 United Nations Convention on the Use of Electronic Communications in International Contracts. It covers the situation of "an exchange of statements of claim and defence in which the existence of an agreement is alleged by one party and not denied by another". It also states that "the reference in a contract to any document" (for example, general conditions) "containing an arbitration clause constitutes an arbitration agreement in writing provided that the reference is such as to make that clause part of the contract".

It thus clarifies that applicable contract law remains available to determine the level of consent necessary for a party to become bound by an arbitration agreement allegedly made "by reference". The second approach defines the arbitration agreement in a manner that omits any form requirement. No preference was expressed by the Commission in favour of either option I or II, both of which are offered for enacting States to consider, depending on their particular needs, and by reference to the legal context in which the Model Law is enacted, including the general contract law of the enacting State. Both options are intended to preserve the enforceability of arbitration agreements under the New York Convention.

20. In that respect, the Commission also adopted, at its thirty-ninth session in 2006, a "Recommendation regarding the interpretation of article II, paragraph 2, and article VII, paragraph 1, of the Convention on the Recognition and Enforcement of Foreign Arbitral Awards, done in New York, 10 June 1958" (A/61/17, Annex 2).[2] The General Assembly, in its resolution 61/33 of 4 December 2006 noted that "in connection with the modernization of articles of the Model Law, the promotion of a uniform interpretation and application of the Convention on the Recognition and Enforcement of Foreign Arbitral Awards, done in New York, 10 June 1958, is particularly timely". The Recommendation was drafted in recognition of the widening use of electronic commerce and enactments of domestic legislation as well as case law, which are more favourable than the New York Convention in respect of the form requirement governing arbitration agreements, arbitration proceedings, and the enforcement of arbitral awards. The Recommendation encourages States to apply article II (2) of the New York Convention "recognizing that the circumstances described therein are not exhaustive". In addition, the Recommendation encourages States to adopt the revised article 7 of the Model Law. Both options of the revised article 7 establish a more favourable regime for the recognition and enforcement of arbitral awards than that provided under the New York Convention. By virtue of the "more favourable law provision" contained in article VII (1) of the New York Convention, the Recommendation clarifies that "any interested party" should be allowed "to avail itself of rights it may have, under the law or treaties of the country where an arbitration agreement is sought to be relied upon, to seek recognition of the validity of such an arbitration agreement".

---

[2] Reproduced in Part Three hereafter.

(b) Arbitration agreement and the courts

21.   Articles 8 and 9 deal with two important aspects of the complex relationship between the arbitration agreement and the resort to courts. Modelled on article II (3) of the New York Convention, article 8 (1) of the Model Law places any court under an obligation to refer the parties to arbitration if the court is seized with a claim on the same subject-matter unless it finds that the arbitration agreement is null and void, inoperative or incapable of being performed. The referral is dependent on a request, which a party may make not later than when submitting its first statement on the substance of the dispute. This provision, where adopted by a State enacting the Model Law, is by its nature binding only on the courts of that State. However, since article 8 is not limited in scope to agreements providing for arbitration to take place in the enacting State, it promotes the universal recognition and effect of international commercial arbitration agreements.

22.   Article 9 expresses the principle that any interim measures of protection that may be obtained from courts under their procedural law (for example, pre-award attachments) are compatible with an arbitration agreement. That provision is ultimately addressed to the courts of any State, insofar as it establishes the compatibility between interim measures possibly issued by any court and an arbitration agreement, irrespective of the place of arbitration. Wherever a request for interim measures may be made to a court, it may not be relied upon, under the Model Law, as a waiver or an objection against the existence or effect of the arbitration agreement.

3. Composition of arbitral tribunal

23.   Chapter III contains a number of detailed provisions on appointment, challenge, termination of mandate and replacement of an arbitrator. The chapter illustrates the general approach taken by the Model Law in eliminating difficulties that arise from inappropriate or fragmentary laws or rules. First, the approach recognizes the freedom of the parties to determine, by reference to an existing set of arbitration rules or by an ad hoc agreement, the procedure to be followed, subject to the fundamental requirements of fairness and justice. Secondly, where the parties have not exercised their freedom to lay down the rules of procedure or they have failed to cover a particular issue, the Model Law ensures, by providing a

set of suppletive rules, that the arbitration may commence and proceed effectively until the dispute is resolved.

24. Where under any procedure, agreed upon by the parties or based upon the suppletive rules of the Model Law, difficulties arise in the process of appointment, challenge or termination of the mandate of an arbitrator, articles 11, 13 and 14 provide for assistance by courts or other competent authorities designated by the enacting State. In view of the urgency of matters relating to the composition of the arbitral tribunal or its ability to function, and in order to reduce the risk and effect of any dilatory tactics, short time-periods are set and decisions rendered by courts or other authorities on such matters are not appealable.

4. Jurisdiction of arbitral tribunal

(a) Competence to rule on own jurisdiction

25. Article 16 (1) adopts the two important (not yet generally recognized) principles of "*Kompetenz-Kompetenz*" and of separability or autonomy of the arbitration clause. "*Kompetenz-Kompetenz*" means that the arbitral tribunal may independently rule on the question of whether it has jurisdiction, including any objections with respect to the existence or validity of the arbitration agreement, without having to resort to a court. Separability means that an arbitration clause shall be treated as an agreement independent of the other terms of the contract. As a consequence, a decision by the arbitral tribunal that the contract is null and void shall not entail *ipso jure* the invalidity of the arbitration clause. Detailed provisions in paragraph (2) require that any objections relating to the arbitrators' jurisdiction be made at the earliest possible time.

26. The competence of the arbitral tribunal to rule on its own jurisdiction (i.e. on the foundation, content and extent of its mandate and power) is, of course, subject to court control. Where the arbitral tribunal rules as a preliminary question that it has jurisdiction, article 16 (3) allows for immediate court control in order to avoid waste of time and money. However, three procedural safeguards are added to reduce the risk and effect of dilatory tactics: short time-period for resort to court (30 days), court decision not appealable, and discretion of the arbitral tribunal to continue the proceedings and make an award while the matter is pending before the court. In those cases where the arbitral tribunal decides to combine its decision on jurisdiction with an award

on the merits, judicial review on the question of jurisdiction is available in setting aside proceedings under article 34 or in enforcement proceedings under article 36.

(b) Power to order interim measures and preliminary orders

27.   Chapter IV A on interim measures and preliminary orders was adopted by the Commission in 2006. It replaces article 17 of the original 1985 version of the Model Law. Section 1 provides a generic definition of interim measures and sets out the conditions for granting such measures. An important innovation of the revision lies in the establishment (in section 4) of a regime for the recognition and enforcement of interim measures, which was modelled, as appropriate, on the regime for the recognition and enforcement of arbitral awards under articles 35 and 36 of the Model Law.

28.   Section 2 of chapter IV A deals with the application for, and conditions for the granting of, preliminary orders. Preliminary orders provide a means for preserving the status quo until the arbitral tribunal issues an interim measure adopting or modifying the preliminary order. Article 17 B (1) provides that "a party may, without notice to any other party, make a request for an interim measure together with an application for a preliminary order directing a party not to frustrate the purpose of the interim measure requested". Article 17 B (2) permits an arbitral tribunal to grant a preliminary order if "it considers that prior disclosure of the request for the interim measure to the party against whom it is directed risks frustrating the purpose of the measure". Article 17 C contains carefully drafted safeguards for the party against whom the preliminary order is directed, such as prompt notification of the application for the preliminary order and of the preliminary order itself (if any), and an opportunity for that party to present its case "at the earliest practicable time". In any event, a preliminary order has a maximum duration of twenty days and, while binding on the parties, is not subject to court enforcement and does not constitute an award. The term "preliminary order" is used to emphasize its limited nature.

29.   Section 3 sets out rules applicable to both preliminary orders and interim measures.

30. Section 5 includes article 17 J on interim measures ordered by courts in support of arbitration, and provides that "a court shall have the same

power of issuing an interim measure in relation to arbitration proceedings irrespective of whether their place is in the territory of the enacting State, as it has in relation to proceedings in courts". That article has been added in 2006 to put it beyond any doubt that the existence of an arbitration agreement does not infringe on the powers of the competent court to issue interim measures and that the party to such an arbitration agreement is free to approach the court with a request to order interim measures.

5. Conduct of arbitral proceedings

31. Chapter V provides the legal framework for a fair and effective conduct of the arbitral proceedings. Article 18, which sets out fundamental requirements of procedural justice, and article 19 on the rights and powers to determine the rules of procedure, express principles that are central to the Model Law.

(a) Fundamental procedural rights of a party

32. Article 18 embodies the principles that the parties shall be treated with equality and given a full opportunity of presenting their case. A number of provisions illustrate those principles. For example, article 24 (1) provides that, unless the parties have agreed that no oral hearings be held for the presentation of evidence or for oral argument, the arbitral tribunal shall hold such hearings at an appropriate stage of the proceedings, if so requested by a party. It should be noted that article 24 (1) deals only with the general entitlement of a party to oral hearings (as an alternative to proceedings conducted on the basis of documents and other materials) and not with the procedural aspects, such as the length, number or timing of hearings.

33. Another illustration of those principles relates to evidence by an expert appointed by the arbitral tribunal. Article 26 (2) requires the expert, after delivering his or her written or oral report, to participate in a hearing where the parties may put questions to the expert and present expert witnesses to testify on the points at issue, if such a hearing is requested by a party or deemed necessary by the arbitral tribunal. As another provision aimed at ensuring fairness, objectivity and impartiality, article 24 (3) provides that all statements, documents and other information supplied to the arbitral tribunal by one party shall be communicated to the other party, and that any expert report or

evidentiary document on which the arbitral tribunal may rely in making its decision shall be communicated to the parties. In order to enable the parties to be present at any hearing and at any meeting of the arbitral tribunal for inspection purposes, they shall be given sufficient notice in advance (article 24 (2)).

(b) Determination of rules of procedure

34. Article 19 guarantees the parties' freedom to agree on the procedure to be followed by the arbitral tribunal in conducting the proceedings, subject to a few mandatory provisions on procedure, and empowers the arbitral tribunal, failing agreement by the parties, to conduct the arbitration in such a manner as it considers appropriate. The power conferred upon the arbitral tribunal includes the power to determine the admissibility, relevance, materiality and weight of any evidence.

35. Autonomy of the parties in determining the rules of procedure is of special importance in international cases since it allows the parties to select or tailor the rules according to their specific wishes and needs, unimpeded by traditional and possibly conflicting domestic concepts, thus obviating the earlier mentioned risk of frustration or surprise (see above, paras. 7 and 9). The supplementary discretion of the arbitral tribunal is equally important in that it allows the tribunal to tailor the conduct of the proceedings to the specific features of the case without being hindered by any restraint that may stem from traditional local law, including any domestic rule on evidence. Moreover, it provides grounds for displaying initiative in solving any procedural question not regulated in the arbitration agreement or the Model Law.

36. In addition to the general provisions of article 19, other provisions in the Model Law recognize party autonomy and, failing agreement, empower the arbitral tribunal to decide on certain matters. Examples of particular practical importance in international cases are article 20 on the place of arbitration and article 22 on the language to be used in the proceedings.

(c) Default of a party

37. The arbitral proceedings may be continued in the absence of a party, provided that due notice has been given. This applies, in particular, to the failure of the respondent to communicate its statement of defence

(article 25 *(b)*). The arbitral tribunal may also continue the proceedings where a party fails to appear at a hearing or to produce documentary evidence without showing sufficient cause for the failure (article 25 *(c)*). However, if the claimant fails to submit its statement of claim, the arbitral tribunal is obliged to terminate the proceedings (article 25 *(a)*).

38. Provisions that empower the arbitral tribunal to carry out its task even if one of the parties does not participate are of considerable practical importance. As experience shows, it is not uncommon for one of the parties to have little interest in cooperating or expediting matters. Such provisions therefore provide international commercial arbitration its necessary effectiveness, within the limits of fundamental requirements of procedural justice.

6. Making of award and termination of proceedings

(a) Rules applicable to substance of dispute

39. Article 28 deals with the determination of the rules of law governing the substance of the dispute. Under paragraph (1), the arbitral tribunal decides the dispute in accordance with the rules of law chosen by the parties. This provision is significant in two respects. It grants the parties the freedom to choose the applicable substantive law, which is important where the national law does not clearly or fully recognize that right. In addition, by referring to the choice of "rules of law" instead of "law", the Model Law broadens the range of options available to the parties as regards the designation of the law applicable to the substance of the dispute. For example, parties may agree on rules of law that have been elaborated by an international forum but have not yet been incorporated into any national legal system. Parties could also choose directly an instrument such as the United Nations Convention on Contracts for the International Sale of Goods as the body of substantive law governing the arbitration, without having to refer to the national law of any State party to that Convention. The power of the arbitral tribunal, on the other hand, follows more traditional lines. When the parties have not chosen the applicable law, the arbitral tribunal shall apply the law (i.e., the national law) determined by the conflict-of-laws rules that it considers applicable.

40. Article 28 (3) recognizes that the parties may authorize the arbitral tribunal to decide the dispute *ex aequo et bono* or as *amiables compositeur*. This type of arbitration (where the arbitral tribunal may decide the dispute

on the basis of principles it believes to be just, without having to refer to any particular body of law) is currently not known or used in all legal systems. The Model Law does not intend to regulate this area. It simply calls the attention of the parties on the need to provide clarification in the arbitration agreement and specifically to empower the arbitral tribunal. However, paragraph (4) makes it clear that in all cases where the dispute relates to a contract (including arbitration *ex aequo et bono*) the arbitral tribunal must decide in accordance with the terms of the contract and shall take into account the usages of the trade applicable to the transaction.

(b) Making of award and other decisions

41. In its rules on the making of the award (articles 29-31), the Model Law focuses on the situation where the arbitral tribunal consists of more than one arbitrator. In such a situation, any award and other decision shall be made by a majority of the arbitrators, except on questions of procedure, which may be left to a presiding arbitrator. The majority principle applies also to the signing of the award, provided that the reason for any omitted signature is stated.

42. Article 31 (3) provides that the award shall state the place of arbitration and shall be deemed to have been made at that place. The effect of the deeming provision is to emphasize that the final making of the award constitutes a legal act, which in practice does not necessarily coincide with one factual event. For the same reason that the arbitral proceedings need not be carried out at the place designated as the legal "place of arbitration", the making of the award may be completed through deliberations held at various places, by telephone or correspondence. In addition, the award does not have to be signed by the arbitrators physically gathering at the same place.

43. The arbitral award must be in writing and state its date. It must also state the reasons on which it is based, unless the parties have agreed otherwise or the award is "on agreed terms" (i.e., an award that records the terms of an amicable settlement by the parties). It may be added that the Model Law neither requires nor prohibits "dissenting opinions".

7. Recourse against award

44. The disparity found in national laws as regards the types of recourse against an arbitral award available to the parties presents a major

difficulty in harmonizing international arbitration legislation. Some outdated laws on arbitration, by establishing parallel regimes for recourse against arbitral awards or against court decisions, provide various types of recourse, various (and often long) time periods for exercising the recourse, and extensive lists of grounds on which recourse may be based. That situation (of considerable concern to those involved in international commercial arbitration) is greatly improved by the Model Law, which provides uniform grounds upon which (and clear time periods within which) recourse against an arbitral award may be made.

(a) Application for setting aside as exclusive recourse

45. The first measure of improvement is to allow only one type of recourse, to the exclusion of any other recourse regulated in any procedural law of the State in question. Article 34 (1) provides that the sole recourse against an arbitral award is by application for setting aside, which must be made within three months of receipt of the award (article 34 (3)). In regulating "recourse" (i.e., the means through which a party may actively "attack" the award), article 34 does not preclude a party from seeking court control by way of defence in enforcement proceedings (articles 35 and 36). Article 34 is limited to action before a court (i.e., an organ of the judicial system of a State). However, a party is not precluded from appealing to an arbitral tribunal of second instance if the parties have agreed on such a possibility (as is common in certain commodity trades).

(b) Grounds for setting aside

46. As a further measure of improvement, the Model Law lists exhaustively the grounds on which an award may be set aside. This list essentially mirrors that contained in article 36 (1), which is taken from article V of the New York Convention. The grounds provided in article 34 (2) are set out in two categories. Grounds which are to be proven by one party are as follows: lack of capacity of the parties to conclude an arbitration agreement; lack of a valid arbitration agreement; lack of notice of appointment of an arbitrator or of the arbitral proceedings or inability of a party to present its case; the award deals with matters not covered by the submission to arbitration; the composition of the arbitral tribunal or the conduct of arbitral proceedings are contrary to the effective agreement of the parties or, failing such agreement, to the Model Law. Grounds that a court may consider of its own initiative are

as follows: non-arbitrability of the subject-matter of the dispute or violation of public policy (which is to be understood as serious departures from fundamental notions of procedural justice).

47. The approach under which the grounds for setting aside an award under the Model Law parallel the grounds for refusing recognition and enforcement of the award under article V of the New York Convention is reminiscent of the approach taken in the European Convention on International Commercial Arbitration (Geneva, 1961). Under article IX of the latter Convention, the decision of a foreign court to set aside an award for a reason other than the ones listed in article V of the New York Convention does not constitute a ground for refusing enforcement. The Model Law takes this philosophy one step further by directly limiting the reasons for setting aside.

48. Although the grounds for setting aside as set out in article 34 (2) are almost identical to those for refusing recognition or enforcement as set out in article 36 (1), a practical difference should be noted. An application for setting aside under article 34 (2) may only be made to a court in the State where the award was rendered whereas an application for enforcement might be made in a court in any State. For that reason, the grounds relating to public policy and non-arbitrability may vary in substance with the law applied by the court (in the State of setting aside or in the State of enforcement).

8. Recognition and enforcement of awards

49. The eighth and last chapter of the Model Law deals with the recognition and enforcement of awards. Its provisions reflect the significant policy decision that the same rules should apply to arbitral awards whether made in the country of enforcement or abroad, and that those rules should follow closely the New York Convention.

(a) Towards uniform treatment of all awards irrespective of country of origin

50. By treating awards rendered in international commercial arbitration in a uniform manner irrespective of where they were made, the Model Law distinguishes between "international" and "non-international" awards instead of relying on the traditional distinction between "foreign" and "domestic" awards. This new line is based on substantive grounds

rather than territorial borders, which are inappropriate in view of the limited importance of the place of arbitration in international cases. The place of arbitration is often chosen for reasons of convenience of the parties and the dispute may have little or no connection with the State where the arbitration legally takes place. Consequently, the recognition and enforcement of "international" awards, whether "foreign" or "domestic", should be governed by the same provisions.

51. By modelling the recognition and enforcement rules on the relevant provisions of the New York Convention, the Model Law supplements, without conflicting with, the regime of recognition and enforcement created by that successful Convention.

(b) Procedural conditions of recognition and enforcement

52. Under article 35 (1) any arbitral award, irrespective of the country in which it was made, shall be recognized as binding and enforceable, subject to the provisions of article 35 (2) and of article 36 (the latter of which sets forth the grounds on which recognition or enforcement may be refused). Based on the above consideration of the limited importance of the place of arbitration in international cases and the desire of overcoming territorial restrictions, reciprocity is not included as a condition for recognition and enforcement.

53. The Model Law does not lay down procedural details of recognition and enforcement, which are left to national procedural laws and practices. The Model Law merely sets certain conditions for obtaining enforcement under article 35 (2). It was amended in 2006 to liberalize formal requirements and reflect the amendment made to article 7 on the form of the arbitration agreement. Presentation of a copy of the arbitration agreement is no longer required under article 35 (2).

(c) Grounds for refusing recognition or enforcement

54. Although the grounds on which recognition or enforcement may be refused under the Model Law are identical to those listed in article V of the New York Convention, the grounds listed in the Model Law are relevant not only to foreign awards but to all awards rendered in the sphere of application of the piece of legislation enacting the Model Law. Generally, it was deemed desirable to adopt, for the sake of harmony, the same approach and wording as this important Convention. However, the

first ground on the list as contained in the New York Convention (which provides that recognition and enforcement may be refused if "the parties to the arbitration agreement were, under the law applicable to them, under some incapacity") was modified since it was viewed as containing an incomplete and potentially misleading conflict-of-laws rule.

Further information on the Model Law may be obtained from:

UNCITRAL secretariat
Vienna International Centre
P.O. Box 500
1400 Vienna
Austria
Telephone: (+43-1) 26060-4060
Telefax: (+43-1) 26060-5813
Internet: www.uncitral.org
E-mail: uncitral@uncitral.org

Part Three

Recommendation regarding the interpretation of article II, paragraph 2, and article VII, paragraph 1, of the Convention on the Recognition and Enforcement of Foreign Arbitral Awards, done in New York, 10 June 1958, adopted by the United Nations Commission on International Trade Law on 7 July 2006 at its thirty-ninth session

The United Nations Commission on International Trade Law,

Recalling General Assembly resolution 2205 (XXI) of 17 December 1966, which established the United Nations Commission on International Trade Law with the object of promoting the progressive harmonization and unification of the law of international trade by, inter alia, promoting ways and means of ensuring a uniform interpretation and application of international conventions and uniform laws in the field of the law of international trade,

Conscious of the fact that the different legal, social and economic systems of the world, together with different levels of development, are represented in the Commission,

Recalling successive resolutions of the General Assembly reaffirming the mandate of the Commission as the core legal body within the United Nations system in the field of international trade law to coordinate legal activities in this field,

Convinced that the wide adoption of the Convention on the Recognition and Enforcement of Foreign Arbitral Awards, done in New York on 10 June 1958,[1] has been a significant achievement in the promotion of the rule of law, particularly in the field of international trade,

Recalling that the Conference of Plenipotentiaries which prepared and opened the Convention for signature adopted a resolution, which states, inter alia, that the Conference "considers that greater uniformity of

---

[1] United Nations, *Treaty Series*, vol. 330, No. 4739.

national laws on arbitration would further the effectiveness of arbitration in the settlement of private law disputes",

Bearing in mind differing interpretations of the form requirements under the Convention that result in part from differences of expression as between the five equally authentic texts of the Convention,

Taking into account article VII, paragraph 1, of the Convention, a purpose of which is to enable the enforcement of foreign arbitral awards to the greatest extent, in particular by recognizing the right of any interested party to avail itself of law or treaties of the country where the award is sought to be relied upon, including where such law or treaties offer a regime more favourable than the Convention,

Considering the wide use of electronic commerce,

Taking into account international legal instruments, such as the 1985 UNCITRAL Model Law on International Commercial Arbitration,[2] as subsequently revised, particularly with respect to article 7,[3] the UNCITRAL Model Law on Electronic Commerce,[4] the UNCITRAL Model Law on Electronic Signatures[5] and the United Nations Convention on the Use of Electronic Communications in International Contracts,[6]

Taking into account also enactments of domestic legislation, as well as case law, more favourable than the Convention in respect of form requirement governing arbitration agreements, arbitration proceedings and the enforcement of arbitral awards,

Considering that, in interpreting the Convention, regard is to be had to the need to promote recognition and enforcement of arbitral awards,

---

[2] Official Records of the General Assembly, Fortieth Session, Supplement No. 17 (A/40/17), annex I, and United Nations publication, Sales No. E.95.V.18.

[3] Ibid., Sixty-first Session, Supplement No. 17 (A/61/17), annex I.

[4] Ibid., *Fifty-first Session, Supplement No. 17* (A/51/17), annex I, and United Nations publication, Sales No. E.99.V.4, which contains also an additional article 5 bis, adopted in 1998, and the accompanying Guide to Enactment.

[5] Ibid., *Fifty-sixth Session, Supplement No. 17* and corrigendum (A/56/17 and Corr.3), annex II, and United Nations publication, Sales No. E.02.V.8, which contains also the accompanying Guide to Enactment.

[6] General Assembly resolution 60/21, annex.

1. *Recommends* that article II, paragraph 2, of the Convention on the Recognition and Enforcement of Foreign Arbitral Awards, done in New York, 10 June 1958, be applied recognizing that the circumstances described therein are not exhaustive;

2. *Recommends also* that article VII, paragraph 1, of the Convention on the Recognition and Enforcement of Foreign Arbitral Awards, done in New York, 10 June 1958, should be applied to allow any interested party to avail itself of rights it may have, under the law or treaties of the country where an arbitration agreement is sought to be relied upon, to seek recognition of the validity of such an arbitration agreement.

APPENDIX 33
ICC RULES OF ARBITRATION

Introductory Provisions

Article 1

International Court of Arbitration

1. The International Court of Arbitration (the "Court") of the International Chamber of Commerce (the "ICC") is the arbitration body attached to the ICC. The statutes of the Court are set forth in Appendix 1. Members of the Court are appointed by the Council of the ICC. The function of the Court is to provide for the settlement by arbitration of business disputes of an international character in accordance with the Rules of Arbitration of the International Chamber of Commerce (the "Rules"). If so empowered by an arbitration agreement, the Court shall also provide for the settlement by arbitration in accordance with these Rules of business disputes not of an international character.

2. The Court does not itself settle disputes. It has the function of ensuring the application of these Rules. It draws up its own Internal Rules (Appendix II).

3. The Chairman of the Court, or, in the Chairman's absence or otherwise at his request, one of its Vice-Chairman shall have the power to take urgent decisions on behalf of the Court, provided that any such decision is reported to the Court at its next session.

4. As provided for in its Internal Rules, the Court may delegate to one or more committees composed of its members the power to take certain decisions, provided that any such decision is reported to the Court at its next session.

5. The Secretariat of the Court (the "Secretariat") under the direction of its Secretary General (the "Secretary General") shall have its seat at the headquarters of the ICC.

Article 2
Definitions

In these Rules:

(i) "Arbitral Tribunal" includes one or more arbitrators.

(ii) "Claimant" includes one or more claimants and "Respondent" includes one or more respondents.

(iii) "Award" includes, inter alia, an interim, partial or final Award.

Article 3
Written Notifications or Communications; Time Limits

1. All pleadings and other written communications submitted by any party, as well as all documents annexed thereto, shall be supplied in a number of copies sufficient to provide one copy for each party, plus one for each arbitrator, and one for the Secretariat. A copy of any communication from the Arbitral Tribunal to the parties shall be sent to the Secretariat.

2. All notifications or communications from the Secretariat and the Arbitral Tribunal shall be made to the last address of the party or its representative for whom the same are intended, as notified either by the party in question or by the other party. Such notification or communication may be made by delivery against receipt, registered post, courier, facsimile transmission, telex, telegram or any other means of telecommunication that provides a record of the sending thereof.

3. A notification or communication shall be deemed to have been made on the day it was received by the party itself or by its representative, or would have been received if made in accordance with the preceding paragraph.

4. Periods of time specified in, or fixed under the present Rules, shall start to run on the day following the date a notification or communication is deemed to have been made in accordance with the preceding paragraph. When the day next following such date is an official holiday, or a non-business day in the country where the notification or communication is deemed to have been made, the period of time shall commence on the first following business day.

Official holidays and non-business days are included in the calculation of the period of time. If the last day of the relevant period of time granted is an official holiday or a non-business day in the country where the notification or communication is deemed to have been made, the period of time shall expire at the end of the first following business day.

COMMENCING THE ARBITRATION

Article 4

Request for Arbitration

1. A party wishing to have recourse to arbitration under these Rules shall submit its Request for Arbitration (the "Request" to the Secretariat, which shall notify the Claimant and Respondent of the receipt of the Request and the date of such receipt.

2. The date on which the Request is received by the Secretariat shall, for all purposes, be deemed to be the date of the commencement of the arbitral proceedings.

3. The Request shall, inter alia, contain the following information:

   (a) the name in full, description and address of each of the parties;

   (b) a description of the nature and circumstances of the dispute giving rise to the claims;

   (c) a statement of the relief sought, including, to the extent possible, an indication of any amount(s) claimed;

   (d) the relevant agreements and, in particular, the arbitration agreement;

   (e) all relevant particulars concerning the number of arbitrators and their choice in accordance with the provisions of Articles 8, 9 and 10, and any nomination of an arbitrator required thereby; and

   (f) any comments as to the place of arbitration, the applicable rules of law and the language of the arbitration.

4. Together with the Request, the Claimant shall submit the number of copies thereof required by Article 3(i) and shall make the advance payment an administrative expenses required by Appendix III

("Arbitration Costs and Fees") in force on the date the Request is submitted. In the event that the Claimant fails to comply with either of these requirements, the Secretariat may fix a time limit within which the Claimant must comply, failing which the file shall be closed without prejudice to the right of the Claimant to submit the same claims at a later date in another Request.

5. The Secretariat shall send a copy of the Request and the documents annexed thereto to the Respondent for its Answer to the Request once the Secretariat has sufficient copies of the Request and the required advance payment.

6. When a party submits a Request in connection with a legal relationship in respect of which arbitration proceedings between the same parties are already pending under these Rules, the Court may, at the request of a party, decide to include the claims contained in the Request in the pending proceedings provided that the Terms of Reference have not been signed or approved by the Court. Once the Terms of Reference have been signed or approved by the Court, claims may only be included in the pending proceedings subject to the provisions of Article 19.

Article 5

Answer to the Request, Counterclaims

1. Within 30 days from the receipt of the Request from the Secretariat, the Respondent shall file an Answer (the "Answer") which shall, inter alia, contain the following information:

   (a) its name in full, description and address;

   (b) its comments as to the nature and circumstances of the dispute giving rise to the claim(s);

   (c) its response to the relief sought;

   (d) any comments concerning the number of arbitrators and their choice in light of the Claimant's proposals and in accordance with the provisions of Articles 8, 9 and 10, and any nomination of an arbitrator required thereby; and

   (e) any comments as to the place of arbitration, the applicable rules of law and the language of the arbitration.

2. The Secretariat may grant the Respondent an extension of the time for filing the Answer, provided the application for such an extension contains the Respondent's comments concerning the number of arbitrators and their choice, and, where required by Articles 8, 9 and 10, the nomination of an arbitrator. If the Respondent fails to do so, the Court shall proceed in accordance with these Rules.

3. The Answer shall be supplied to the Secretariat in the number of copies specified by Article 3(l).

4. A copy of the Answer and the documents annexed thereto shall be communicated by the Secretariat to the Claimant.

5. Any counterclaims made by the Respondent shall be filed with its Answer and shall provide:

    (a) a description of the nature and circumstances of the dispute giving rise to the counterclaim(s); and

    (b) a statement of the relief sought, including, to the extent possible, an indication of any amount(s) counter-claimed.

6. The Claimant shall file a Reply to any counterclaim within 30 days from the date of receipt of the counterclaims communicated by the Secretariat. The Secretariat may grant the Claimant an extension of time for filing the Reply.

Article 6

Effect of the Arbitration Agreement

1. Where the parties have agreed to submit to arbitration under the Rules, they shall be deemed to have submitted ipso facto to the Rules in effect on the date of commencement of the arbitration proceedings unless they have agreed to submit to the Rules in effect on the date of their arbitration agreement.

2. If the Respondent does not file an Answer, as provided by Article 5, or if any party raises one or more pleas concerning the existence, validity or scope of the arbitration agreement, the Court may decide, without prejudice to the admissibility or merits of the plea or pleas, that the arbitration shall proceed if it is prima facie satisfied that an arbitration agreement under the Rules may exist. In such a case, any decision as to the jurisdiction of the Arbitral Tribunal shall be taken by the Arbitral Tribunal itself. If the Court is not so satisfied, the

parties shall be notified that the arbitration cannot proceed. In such a case, any party retains the right to ask any court having jurisdiction whether or not there is a binding arbitration agreement.

3. If any of the parties refuses or fails to take part in the arbitration or any stage thereof, the arbitration shall proceed notwithstanding such refusal or failure.

4. Unless otherwise agreed, the Arbitral Tribunal shall not cease to have jurisdiction by reason of any claim that the contract is null and void or allegation that it is non-existent provided that the Arbitral Tribunal upholds the validity of the arbitration agreement. The Arbitral Tribunal shall continue to have jurisdiction to determine the respective rights of the parties and to adjudicate their claims and pleas even though the contract itself may be non-existent or null and void.

THE ARBITRAL TRIBUNAL

Article 7

General Provisions

1. Every arbitrator must be and remain independent of the parties involved in the arbitration.

2. Before appointment or confirmation, a prospective arbitrator shall sign a statement of independence and disclose in writing to the Secretariat any facts or circumstances which might be of such a nature as to call into question the arbitrator's independence in the eyes of the parties. The Secretariat shall provide such information to the parties in writing and fix a time limit for any comments from them.

3. An arbitrator shall immediately disclose in writing to the Secretariat and to the parties any facts or circumstances of a similar nature which may arise during the arbitration.

4. The decisions of the Court as to the appointment, confirmation, challenge or replacement of an arbitrator shall be final and the reasons for such decisions shall not be communicated.

5. By accepting to serve, every arbitrator undertakes to carry out his responsibilities in accordance with these Rules.

6. Insofar as the parties have not provided otherwise, the Arbitral Tribunal shall be constituted in accordance with the provisions of Articles 8, 9 and 10.

Article 8
Number of Arbitrators

1. The disputes shall be decided by a sole arbitrator or by three arbitrators.

2. Where the parties have not agreed upon the number of arbitrators, the Court shall appoint a sole arbitrator, save where it appears to the Court that the dispute is such as to warrant the appointment of three arbitrators. In such case, the Claimant shall nominate an arbitrator within a period of 15 days from the receipt of the notification of the decision of the Court, and the Respondent shall nominate an arbitrator within a period of 15 days from the receipt of the notification of the nomination made by the Claimant.

3. Where the parties have agreed that the dispute shall be settled by a sole arbitrator, they may, by agreement, nominate the sole arbitrator for confirmation. If the parties fail to nominate a sole arbitrator within 30 days from the date when the Claimant's Request for Arbitration has been received by the other party, or within such additional time as may be allowed by the Secretariat, the sole arbitrator shall be appointed by the Court.

4. Where the dispute is to be referred to three arbitrators, each party shall nominate in the Request and the Answer, respectively, one arbitrator for confirmation by the Court. If a party fails to nominate an arbitrator, the appointment shall be made by the Court. The third arbitrator, who will act as chairman of the Arbitral Tribunal, shall be appointed by the Court, unless the parties have agreed upon another procedure for such appointment, in which case the nomination will be subject to confirmation pursuant to Article 9. Should such procedure not result in a nomination within the time limit fixed by the parties or the Court, the third arbitrator shall be appointed by the Court.

Article 9

Appointment and Confirmation of the Arbitrators

1. In confirming or appointing arbitrators, the Court shall consider the prospective arbitrator's nationality, residence and other relationships with the countries of which the parties or the other arbitrators are nationals and the prospective arbitrator's availability and ability to conduct the arbitration in accordance with these Rules. The same shall apply where the Secretary General confirms arbitrators pursuant to Article 9(2).

2. The Secretary General may confirm as co-arbitrators, sole arbitrators and chairman of Arbitral Tribunals persons nominated by the parties or pursuant to their particular agreements, provided they have filed a statement of independence without qualification or a qualified statement of independence has not given rise to objections. Such confirmation shall be reported to the Court at its next session. If the Secretary General considers that a co-arbitrator, sole arbitrator or chairman of an Arbitral Tribunal should not be confirmed, the matter shall be submitted to the Court.

3. Where the Court is to appoint a sole arbitrator or the chairman of an Arbitral Tribunal, it shall make the appointment upon a proposal of a National Committee of the ICC that it considers to be appropriate. If the Court does not accept the proposal made, or if the National Committee fails to make the proposal requested within the time limit fixed by the Court, the Court may repeat its request or may request a proposal from another National Committee that it considers to be appropriate.

4. Where the Court considers that the circumstances so demand, it may choose the sole arbitrator or the chairman of the Arbitral Tribunal from a country where there is no National Committee, provided that neither of the parties objects within the time limit fixed by the Court.

5. The sole arbitrator or the chairman of the Arbitral Tribunal shall be of a nationality other than those of the parties. However, in suitable circumstances and provided that neither of the parties objects within the time limit fixed by the Court, the sole arbitrator or the chairman of the Arbitral Tribunal may be chosen from a country of which any of the parties is a national.

6. Where the Court is to appoint an arbitrator on behalf of a party which has failed to nominate one, it shall make the appointment upon a proposal of the National Committee of the country of which that party is a national. If the Court does not accept the proposal made, or if the National Committee fails to make the proposal requested within the time limit fixed by the Court, or if the country of which the said party is a national has no National Committee, the Court shall be at liberty to choose any person whom it regards as suitable. The Secretariat shall inform the National Committee, if one exists, of the country of which such person is a national.

Article 10

Multiple Parties

1. Where there are multiple parties, whether as Claimant or as Respondent, and where the dispute is to be referred to three arbitrators, the multiple Claimants, jointly, and the multiple Respondents, jointly, shall nominate an arbitrator for confirmation pursuant to Article 9.

2. In the absence of such a joint nomination and where all parties are unable to agree to a method for the constitution of the Arbitral Tribunal, the Court may appoint each member of the Arbitral Tribunal and shall designate one of them to act as chairman. In such case, the Court shall be at liberty to choose any person it regards as suitable to act as arbitrator, applying Article 9 when it considers this appropriate.

Article 11

Challenge of Arbitrators

1. A challenge of an arbitrator, whether for an alleged lack of independence or otherwise, shall be made by the submission to the Secretariat of a written statement specifying the facts and circumstances on which the challenge is based.

2. For a challenge to be admissible, it must be sent by a party either within 30 days from receipt by that party of the notification of the appointment or confirmation of the arbitrator, or within 30 days from the date when the party making the challenge was informed of the facts and circumstances on which the challenge is based if such date is subsequent to the receipt of such notification.

3. The Court shall decide on the admissibility, and, at the same time, if necessary, on the merits of a challenge after the Secretariat has afforded an opportunity for the arbitrator concerned, the other party or parties and any other members of the Arbitral Tribunal, to comment in writing within a suitable period of time. Such comments shall be communicated to the parties and to the arbitrators.

Article 12

Replacement of Arbitrators

1. An arbitrator shall be replaced upon his death, upon the acceptance by the Court of the arbitrator's resignation, upon acceptance by the Court of a challenge or upon the request of all the parties.

2. An arbitrator shall also be replaced on the Court's own initiative when it decides that he is prevented de jure or de facto from fulfilling his functions, or that he is not fulfilling his functions in accordance with the Rules or within the prescribed time limits.

3. When, on the basis of information that has come to its attention, the Court considers applying Article 12(2), it shall decide on the matter after the arbitrator concerned, the parties and any other members of the Arbitral Tribunal have had an opportunity to comment in writing within a suitable period of time. Such comments shall be communicated to the parties and to the arbitrators.

4. When an arbitrator is to be replaced, the Court has discretion to decide whether or not to follow the original nominating process. Once reconstituted, and after having invited the parties to comment, the Arbitral Tribunal shall determine if and to what extent prior proceedings shall be repeated before the reconstituted Arbitral Tribunal.

5. Subsequent to the closing of the proceedings, instead of replacing an arbitrator who has died or been removed by the Court pursuant to Articles 12(1) and 12(2), the Court may decide, when it considers it appropriate, that the remaining arbitrators shall continue the arbitration. In making such determination, the Court shall take into account the views of the remaining arbitrators and of the parties and such other matters that it considers appropriate in the circumstances.

THE ARBITRAL PROCEEDINGS

Article 13

Transmission of the File to the Arbitral Tribunal

The Secretariat shall transmit the file to the Arbitral Tribunal as soon as it has been constituted, provided the advance on costs requested by the Secretariat at this stage has been paid.

Article 14

Place of the Arbitration

1. The place of the arbitration shall be fixed by the Court unless agreed upon by the parties.

2. The Arbitral Tribunal may, after consultation with the parties, conduct hearings and meetings at any location it considers appropriate unless otherwise agreed by the parties.

3. The Arbitral Tribunal may deliberate at any location it considers appropriate.

Article 15

Rules Governing the Proceedings

1. The proceedings before the Arbitral Tribunal shall be governed by these Rules, and, where these Rules are silent, by any rules which the parties or, failing them, the Arbitral Tribunal may settle on, whether or not reference is thereby made to the rules of procedure of a national law to be applied to the arbitration.

2. In all cases, the Arbitral Tribunal shall act fairly and impartially and ensure that each party has a reasonable opportunity to present its case.

Article 16

Language of the Arbitration

In the absence of an agreement by the parties, the Arbitral Tribunal shall determine the language or languages of the arbitration, due regard being given to all relevant circumstances, including the language of the contract.

Article 17

Applicable Rules of Law

1. The parties shall be free to agree upon the rules of law to be applied by the Arbitral Tribunal to the merits of the dispute. In the absence of any such agreement, the Arbitral Tribunal shall apply the rules of law which it determines to be appropriate.

2. In all cases the Arbitral Tribunal shall take account of the provisions of the contract and the relevant trade usages.

3. The Arbitral Tribunal shall assume the powers of an amiable compositeur or decide ex aequo et bono only if the parties have agreed to give it such powers.

Article 18

Terms of Reference; Procedural Timetable

1. As soon as it has received the file from the Secretariat, the Arbitral Tribunal shall draw up, on the basis of documents or in the presence of the parties and in the light of their most recent submissions, a document defining its Terms of Reference. This document shall include the following particulars:

   (a) the full names and descriptions of the parties;

   (b) the addresses of the parties to which notifications and communications arising in the course of the arbitration may be made;

   (c) a summary of the parties' respective claims and of the relief sought by each party, with an indication to the extent possible of the amounts claimed or counterclaimed;

   (d) unless the Arbitral Tribunal considers it inappropriate, a list of issues to be determined;

   (e) the full names, descriptions and addresses of the arbitrators;

   (f) the place of the arbitration; and

   (g) particulars of the applicable procedural rules and, if such is the case, reference to the power conferred upon the Arbitral Tribunal to act as amiable compositeur or to decide ex aequo et bono.

2. The Terms of Reference shall be signed by the parties and the Arbitral Tribunal. Within two months of the date on which the file has been transmitted to it, the Arbitral Tribunal shall transmit to the Court the Terms of Reference signed by it and by the parties. The Court may extend this time limit pursuant to a reasoned request from the Arbitral Tribunal or on its own Initiative if it decides it is necessary to do so.

3. If any of the parties refuses to take part in the drawing up of the Terms of Reference or to sign the same, they shall be submitted to the Court for approval. When the Terms of Reference are signed in accordance with Article 18(2) or approved by the Court, the arbitration shall proceed.

4. When drawing up the Terms of Reference, or as soon as possible thereafter, the Arbitral Tribunal, after having consulted the parties, shall establish in a separate document a provisional timetable that it intends to follow for the conduct of the arbitration and shall communicate it to the Court and the parties. Any subsequent modifications of the provisional timetable shall be communicated to the Court and the parties.

Article 19

New Claims

After the Terms of Reference have been signed or approved by the Court, no party shall make new claims or counterclaims which fall outside the limits of the Terms of Reference unless it has been authorized to do so by the Arbitral Tribunal, which shall consider the nature of such new claims or counterclaims, the stage of the arbitration and other relevant circumstances.

Article 20

Establishing the Facts of the Case

1. The Arbitral Tribunal shall proceed within as short a time as possible to establish the facts of the case by all appropriate means.

2. After studying the written submissions of the parties and all documents relied upon, the Arbitral Tribunal shall hear the parties together in person if any of them so requests or, failing such a request, it may of its own motion decide to hear them.

3. The Arbitral Tribunal may decide to hear witnesses, experts appointed by the parties or any other person, in the presence of the parties, or in their absence provided they have been duly summoned.

4. The Arbitral Tribunal, after having consulted the parties, may appoint one or more experts, define their terms of reference and receive their reports. At the request of a party, the parties shall be given the opportunity to question at a hearing any such expert appointed by the Tribunal.

5. At any time during the proceedings, the Arbitral Tribunal may summon any party to provide additional evidence.

6. The Arbitral Tribunal may decide the case solely on the documents submitted by the parties unless any of the parties requests a hearing.

7. The Arbitral Tribunal may take measures for protecting trade secrets and confidential information.

Article 21

Hearings

1. When a hearing is to be held, the Arbitral Tribunal, giving reasonable notice, shall summon the parties to appear before it on the day and at the place fixed by it.

2. If any of the parties, although duly summoned, fails to appear without valid excuse, the Arbitral Tribunal shall have the power to proceed with the hearing.

3. The Arbitral Tribunal shall be in full charge of the hearings, at which all the parties shall be entitled to be present. Save with the approval of the Arbitral Tribunal and the parties, persons not involved in the proceedings shall not be admitted.

4. The parties may appear in person or through duly authorized representatives. In addition, they may be assisted by advisers.

Article 22

Closing of the Proceedings

1. When it is satisfied that the parties have had a reasonable opportunity to present their cases, the Arbitral Tribunal shall declare the

proceedings closed. Thereafter, no further submission or argument may be made, or evidence produced, unless requested or authorized by the Arbitral Tribunal.

2. When the Arbitral Tribunal has declared the proceedings closed, it shall indicate to the Secretariat an approximate date by which the draft Award will be submitted to the Court for approval pursuant to Article 27. Any postponement of that date shall be communicated to the Secretariat by the Arbitral Tribunal.

Article 23

Conservatory and Interim Measures

1. Unless the parties have otherwise agreed, as soon as the file has been transmitted to it, the Arbitral Tribunal may, at the request of a party, order any interim or conservatory measure it deems appropriate. The Arbitral Tribunal may make the granting of any such measure subject to appropriate security being furnished by the requesting party. Any such measure shall take the form of an order, giving reasons, or of an Award, as the Arbitral Tribunal considers appropriate.

2. Before the file is transmitted to the Arbitral Tribunal, and in appropriate circumstances even thereafter, the parties may apply to any competent judicial authority for interim or conservatory measures. The application of a party to a judicial authority for such measures or for the implementation of any such measures ordered by an Arbitral Tribunal shall not be deemed to be an infringement or a waiver of the arbitration agreement and shall not affect the relevant powers reserved to the Arbitral Tribunal. Any such application and any measures taken by the judicial authority must be notified without delay to the Secretariat. The Secretariat shall inform the Arbitral Tribunal thereof.

AWARDS

Article 24

Time Limit for the Award

1. The time limit within which the Arbitral Tribunal must render its final Award is six months. Such time limit shall start to run from the

date of the last signature by the Arbitral Tribunal or of the parties of the Terms of Reference, or, in the case of application of Article 18(3), the date of the notification to the Arbitral Tribunal by the Secretariat of the approval of the Terms of Reference by the Court.

2. The Court may extend this time limit pursuant to a reasoned request from the Arbitral Tribunal or on its own initiative if it decides it is necessary to do so.

Article 25

Making of the Award

1. When the Arbitral Tribunal is composed of more than one arbitrator, an Award is given by a majority decision. If there be no majority, the Award shall be made by the chairman of the Arbitral Tribunal alone.
2. The Award shall state the reasons upon which it is based.
3. The Award shall be deemed to be made at the place of the arbitration and on the date stated therein.

Article 26

Award by Consent

If the parties reach a settlement after the file has been transmitted to the Arbitral Tribunal in accordance with Article 13, the settlement shall be recorded in the form of an Award made by consent of the parties if so requested by the parties and if the Arbitral Tribunal agrees to do so.

Article 27

Scrutiny of the Award by the Court

Before signing any Award, the Arbitral Tribunal shall submit it in draft form to the Court. The Court may lay down modifications as to the form of the Award and, without affecting the Arbitral Tribunal's liberty of decision, may also draw its attention to points of substance. No Award shall be rendered by the Arbitral Tribunal until it has been approved by the Court as to its form.

Article 28

Notification, Deposit and Enforceability of the Award

1. Once an Award has been made, the Secretariat shall notify to the parties the text signed by the Arbitral Tribunal, provided always that the costs of the arbitration have been fully paid to the ICC by the parties or by one of them.

2. Additional copies certified true by the Secretary General shall be made available on request and at any time to the parties, but to no one else.

3. By virtue of the notification made in accordance with Paragraph 1 of this Article, the parties waive any other form of notification or deposit on the part of the Arbitral Tribunal.

4. An original of each Award made in accordance with the present Rules shall be deposited with the Secretariat.

5. The Arbitral Tribunal and the Secretariat shall assist the parties in complying with whatever further formalities may be necessary.

6. Every Award shall be binding on the parties. By submitting the dispute to arbitration under these Rules, the parties undertake to carry out any Award without delay and shall be deemed to have waived their right to any form of recourse insofar as such waiver can validly be made.

Article 29

Correction and Interpretation of the Award

1. On its own initiative, the Arbitral Tribunal may correct a clerical, computational or typographical error, or any errors of similar nature contained in an Award, provided such correction is submitted for approval to the Court within 30 days of the date of such Award.

2. Any application of a party for the correction of an error of the kind referred to in Article 29(1), or for the interpretation of an Award, must be made to the Secretariat within 30 days of the receipt of the Award by such party, in a number of copies as stated in Article 3(1). After transmittal of the application to the Arbitral Tribunal, it shall grant the other party a short time limit, normally not exceeding 30 days, from the receipt of the application by that party to submit any comments

thereon. If the Arbitral Tribunal decides to correct or interpret the Award, it shall submit its decision in draft form to the Court not later than 30 days following the expiration of the time limit for the receipt of any comments from the other party or within such other period as the Court may decide.

3. The decision to correct or to interpret the Award shall take the form of an addendum and shall constitute part of the Award. The provisions of Articles 25, 27 and 28 shall apply mutatis mutandis.

COSTS

Article 30

Advance to Cover the Costs of the Arbitration

1. After receipt of the Request, the Secretary General may request the Claimant to pay a provisional advance in an amount intended to cover the costs of arbitration until the Terms of Reference have been drawn up.

2. As soon as practicable, the Court shall fix the advance on costs in an amount likely to cover the fees and expenses of the arbitrators and the ICC administrative costs for the claims and counterclaims which have been referred to it by the parties. This amount may be subject to readjustment at any time during the arbitration. Where, apart from the claims, counter- claims are submitted, the Court may fix separate advances on costs for the claims and the counterclaims.

3. The advance on costs fixed by the Court shall be payable in equal shares by the Claimant and the Respondent. Any provisional advance paid on the basis of Article 30(1) will be considered as a partial payment thereof. However, any party shall be free to pay the whole of the advance on costs in respect of the principal claim or the counterclaim should the other party fail to pay its share. When the Court has set separate advances on costs in accordance with Article 30(2), each of the parties shall pay the advance on costs corresponding to its claims.

4. When a request for an advance on costs has not been complied with, and after consultation with the Arbitral Tribunal, the Secretary General may direct the Arbitral Tribunal to suspend its work and set a time limit, which must be not less than 15 days, on the expiry of which the relevant claims, or counterclaims, shall be considered as

withdrawn. Should the party in question wish to object to this measure it must make a request within the aforementioned period for the matter to be decided by the Court. Such party shall not be prevented on the ground of such withdrawal from reintroducing the same claims or counterclaims at a later date in another proceeding.

5. If one of the parties claims a right to a set-off with regard to either claims or counterclaims, such set-off shall be taken into account in determining the advance to cover the costs of arbitration in the same way as a separate claim insofar as it may require the Arbitral Tribunal to consider additional matters.

Article 31

Decision as to the Costs of the Arbitration

1. The costs of the arbitration shall include the fees and expenses of the arbitrators and the ICC administrative costs fixed by the Court, in accordance with the scale in force at the time of the commencement of the arbitral proceedings, as well as the fees and expenses of any experts appointed by the Arbitral Tribunal and the reasonable legal and other costs incurred by the parties for the arbitration.

2. The Court may fix the fees of the arbitrators at a figure higher or lower than that which would result from the application of the relevant scale should this be deemed necessary due to the exceptional circumstances of the case. Decisions on costs other than those fixed by the Court may be taken by the Arbitral Tribunal at any time during the proceedings.

3. The final Award shall fix the costs of the arbitration and decide which of the parties shall bear them or in what proportion they shall be borne by the parties.

MISCELLANEOUS

Article 32

Modified Time Limits

1. The parties may agree to shorten the various time limits set out in these Rules. Any such agreement entered into subsequent to the constitution of an Arbitral Tribunal shall become effective only upon the approval of the Arbitral Tribunal.

2. The Court, on its own initiative, may extend any time limit which has been modified pursuant to Article 32(1) if it decides that it is necessary to do so in order that the Arbitral Tribunal or the Court may fulfill their responsibilities in accordance with these Rules.

Article 33

Waiver

A party which proceeds with the arbitration without raising its objection to a failure to comply with any provision of these Rules, or of any other rules applicable to the proceedings, any direction given by the Arbitral Tribunal, or any requirement under the arbitration agreement relating to the constitution of the Arbitral Tribunal, or to the conduct of the proceedings, shall be deemed to have waived its right to object.

Article 34

Exclusion of Liability

Neither the arbitrators, nor the Court and its members, nor the ICC and its employees, nor the ICC National Committees shall be liable to any person for any act or omission in connection with the arbitration.

Article 35

General Rule

In all matters not expressly provided for in these Rules, the Court and the Arbitral Tribunal shall act in the spirit of these Rules and shall make every effort to make sure that the Award is enforceable at law.

APPENDIX 34
LCIA ARBITRATION RULES

*(Adopted to take effect for arbitrations commencing on or after
1 January 1998)*

Where any agreement, submission or reference provides in writing and in whatsoever manner for arbitration under the rules of the LCIA or by the Court of the LCIA ("the LCIA Court"), the parties shall be taken to have agreed in writing that the arbitration shall be conducted in accordance with the following rules ("the Rules") or such amended rules as the LCIA may have adopted hereafter to take effect before the commencement of the arbitration. The Rules include the Schedule of Costs in effect at the commencement of the arbitration, as separately amended from time to time by the LCIA Court.

Article 1
The Request for Arbitration

1.1   Any party wishing to commence an arbitration under these Rules ("the Claimant") shall send to the Registrar of the LCIA Court ("the Registrar") a written request for arbitration ("the Request"), containing or accompanied by:

(a) the names, addresses, telephone, facsimile, telex and e-mail numbers (if known) of the parties to the arbitration and of their legal representatives;

(b) a copy of the written arbitration clause or separate written arbitration agreement invoked by the Claimant ("the Arbitration Agreement"), together with a copy of the contractual documentation in which the arbitration clause is contained or in respect of which the arbitration arises;

(c) a brief statement describing the nature and circumstances of the dispute, and specifying the claims advanced by the Claimant against another party to the arbitration ("the Respondent");

(d) a statement of any matters (such as the seat or language(s) of the arbitration, or the number of arbitrators, or their qualifications or identities) on which the parties have already agreed in writing for the arbitration or in respect of which the Claimant wishes to make a proposal;

(e) if the Arbitration Agreement calls for party nomination of arbitrators, the name, address, telephone, facsimile, telex and e-mail numbers (if known) of the Claimant's nominee;

(f) the fee prescribed in the Schedule of Costs (without which the Request shall be treated as not having been received by the Registrar and the arbitration as not having been commenced);

(g) confirmation to the Registrar that copies of the Request (including all accompanying documents) have been or are being served simultaneously on all other parties to the arbitration by one or more means of service to be identified in such confirmation.

1.2   The date of receipt by the Registrar of the Request shall be treated as the date on which the arbitration has commenced for all purposes. The Request (including all accompanying documents) should be submitted to the Registrar in two copies where a sole arbitrator should be appointed, or, if the parties have agreed or the Claimant considers that three arbitrators should be appointed, in four copies.

Article 2
The Response

2.1   Within 30 days of service of the Request on the Respondent, (or such lesser period fixed by the LCIA Court), the Respondent shall send to the Registrar a written response to the Request ("the Response"), containing or accompanied by:

(a) confirmation or denial of all or part of the claims advanced by the Claimant in the Request;

(b) a brief statement describing the nature and circumstances of any counterclaims advanced by the Respondent against the Claimant;

(c) comment in response to any statements contained in the Request, as called for under Article 1.1(d), on matters relating to the conduct of the arbitration;

(d) if the Arbitration Agreement calls for party nomination of arbitrators, the name, address, telephone, facsimile, telex and e-mail numbers (if known) of the Respondent's nominee; and

(e) confirmation to the Registrar that copies of the Response (including all accompanying documents) have been or are being served simultaneously on all other parties to the arbitration by one or more means of service to be identified in such confirmation.

2.2   The Response (including all accompanying documents) should be submitted to the Registrar in two copies, or if the parties have agreed or the Respondent considers that three arbitrators should be appointed, in four copies.

2.3   Failure to send a Response shall not preclude the Respondent from denying any claim or from advancing a counterclaim in the arbitration. However, if the Arbitration Agreement calls for party nomination of arbitrators, failure to send a Response or to nominate an arbitrator within time or at all shall constitute an irrevocable waiver of that party's opportunity to nominate an arbitrator.

Article 3
The LCIA Court and Registrar

3.1   The functions of the LCIA Court under these Rules shall be performed in its name by the President or a Vice President of the LCIA Court or by a division of three or five members of the LCIA Court appointed by the President or a Vice President of the LCIA Court, as determined by the President.

3.2   The functions of the Registrar under these Rules shall be performed by the Registrar or any deputy Registrar of the LCIA Court under the supervision of the LCIA Court.

3.3   All communications from any party or arbitrator to the LCIA Court shall be addressed to the Registrar.

Article 4
Notices and Periods of Time

4.1   Any notice or other communication that may be or is required to be given by a party under these Rules shall be in writing and shall be delivered by registered postal or courier service or transmitted by facsimile, telex, e-mail or any other means of telecommunication that provide a record of its transmission.

4.2   A party's last-known residence or place of business during the arbitration shall be a valid address for the purpose of any notice or other communication in the absence of any notification of a change to such address by that party to the other parties, the Arbitral Tribunal and the Registrar.

4.3   For the purpose of determining the date of commencement of a time limit, a notice or other communication shall be treated as having been received on the day it is delivered or, in the case of telecommunications, transmitted in accordance with Articles 4.1 and 4.2.

4.4   For the purpose of determining compliance with a time limit, a notice or other communication shall be treated as having been sent, made or transmitted if it is dispatched in accordance with Articles 4.1 and 4.2 prior to or on the date of the expiration of the time-limit.

4.5   Notwithstanding the above, any notice or communication by one party may be addressed to another party in the manner agreed in writing between them or, failing such agreement, according to the practice followed in the course of their previous dealings or in whatever manner ordered by the Arbitral Tribunal.

4.6   For the purpose of calculating a period of time under these Rules, such period shall begin to run on the day following the day when a notice or other communication is received. If the last day of such period is an official holiday or a non-business day at the residence or place of business of the addressee, the period is extended until the first business day which follows. Official holidays or non-business days occurring during the running of the period of time are included in calculating that period.

4.7   The Arbitral Tribunal may at any time extend (even where the period of time has expired) or abridge any period of time prescribed under these Rules or under the Arbitration Agreement for the conduct of the arbitration, including any notice or communication to be served by one party on any other party.

Article 5
Formation of the Arbitral Tribunal

5.1   The expression "the Arbitral Tribunal" in these Rules includes a sole arbitrator or all the arbitrators where more than one. All references to an arbitrator shall include the masculine and feminine. (References to the President, Vice President and members of the LCIA Court, the Registrar or deputy Registrar, expert, witness, party and legal representative shall be similarly understood).

5.2   All arbitrators conducting an arbitration under these Rules shall be and remain at all times impartial and independent of the parties; and none shall act in the arbitration as advocates for any party. No arbitrator, whether before or after appointment, shall advise any party on the merits or outcome of the dispute.

5.3   Before appointment by the LCIA Court, each arbitrator shall furnish to the Registrar a written résumé of his past and present professional positions; he shall agree in writing upon fee rates conforming to the Schedule of Costs; and he shall sign a declaration to the effect that there are no circumstances known to him likely to give rise to any justified doubts as to his impartiality or independence, other than any circumstances disclosed by him in the declaration. Each arbitrator shall thereby also assume a continuing duty forthwith to disclose any such circumstances to the LCIA Court, to any other members of the Arbitral Tribunal and to all the parties if such circumstances should arise after the date of such declaration and before the arbitration is concluded.

5.4   The LCIA Court shall appoint the Arbitral Tribunal as soon as practicable after receipt by the Registrar of the Response or after the expiry of 30 days following service of the Request upon the Respondent if no Response is received by the Registrar (or such lesser period fixed by the LCIA Court). The LCIA Court may proceed with the formation of the Arbitral Tribunal notwithstanding that the Request is incomplete or the Response is missing, late or incomplete. A sole arbitrator shall be appointed unless the parties have agreed in writing otherwise, or unless the LCIA Court determines that in view of all the circumstances of the case a three-member tribunal is appropriate.

5.5   The LCIA Court alone is empowered to appoint arbitrators. The LCIA Court will appoint arbitrators with due regard for any particular method or criteria of selection agreed in writing by the parties. In selecting arbitrators consideration will be given to the nature of the transaction, the nature and circumstances of the dispute, the nationality, location and languages of the parties and (if more than two) the number of parties.

5.6   In the case of a three-member Arbitral Tribunal, the chairman (who will not be a party-nominated arbitrator) shall be appointed by the LCIA Court.

Article 6
Nationality of Arbitrators

6.1   Where the parties are of different nationalities, a sole arbitrator or chairman of the Arbitral Tribunal shall not have the same nationality as any party unless the parties who are not of the same nationality as the proposed appointee all agree in writing otherwise.

6.2   The nationality of parties shall be understood to include that of controlling shareholders or interests.

6.3   For the purpose of this Article, a person who is a citizen of two or more states shall be treated as a national of each state; and citizens of the European Union shall be treated as nationals of its different Member States and shall not be treated as having the same nationality.

Article 7
Party and Other Nominations

7.1   If the parties have agreed that any arbitrator is to be appointed by one or more of them or by any third person, that agreement shall be treated as an agreement to nominate an arbitrator for all purposes.

Such nominee may only be appointed by the LCIA Court as arbitrator subject to his prior compliance with Article 5.3. The LCIA Court may refuse to appoint any such nominee if it determines that he is not suitable or independent or impartial.

7.2   Where the parties have howsoever agreed that the Respondent or any third person is to nominate an arbitrator and such nomination is not made within time or at all, the LCIA Court may appoint an arbitrator notwithstanding the absence of the nomination and without regard to any late nomination. Likewise, if the Request for Arbitration does not contain a nomination by the Claimant where the parties have howsoever agreed that the Claimant or a third person is to nominate an arbitrator, the LCIA Court may appoint an arbitrator notwithstanding the absence of the nomination and without regard to any late nomination.

Article 8
Three or More Parties

8.1   Where the Arbitration Agreement entitles each party howsoever to nominate an arbitrator, the parties to the dispute number more than two and such parties have not all agreed in writing that the disputant parties represent two separate sides for the formation of the Arbitral Tribunal as Claimant and Respondent respectively, the LCIA Court shall appoint the Arbitral Tribunal without regard to any party's nomination.

8.2   In such circumstances, the Arbitration Agreement shall be treated for all purposes as a written agreement by the parties for the appointment of the Arbitral Tribunal by the LCIA Court.

Article 9
Expedited Formation

9.1   In exceptional urgency, on or after the commencement of the arbitration, any party may apply to the LCIA Court for the expedited formation of the Arbitral Tribunal, including the appointment of any replacement arbitrator under Articles 10 and 11 of these Rules.

9.2   Such an application shall be made in writing to the LCIA Court, copied to all other parties to the arbitration; and it shall set out the specific grounds for exceptional urgency in the formation of the Arbitral Tribunal.

9.3   The LCIA Court may, in its complete discretion, abridge or curtail any time-limit under these Rules for the formation of the Arbitral Tribunal, including service of the Response and of any matters or documents adjudged to be missing from the Request. The LCIA Court shall not be entitled to abridge or curtail any other time-limit.

Article 10
Revocation of Arbitrator's Appointment

10.1   If either (a) any arbitrator gives written notice of his desire to resign as arbitrator to the LCIA Court, to be copied to the parties and the other arbitrators (if any) or (b) any arbitrator dies, falls seriously ill, refuses, or becomes unable or unfit to act, either upon challenge by a party or at the request of the remaining arbitrators, the LCIA Court may revoke that arbitrator's appointment and appoint another arbitrator. The LCIA Court shall decide upon the amount of fees and expenses to be paid for the former arbitrator's services (if any) as it may consider appropriate in all the circumstances.

10.2   If any arbitrator acts in deliberate violation of the Arbitration Agreement (including these Rules) or does not act fairly and impartially as between the parties or does not conduct or participate in the arbitration proceedings with reasonable diligence, avoiding unnecessary delay or expense, that arbitrator may be considered unfit in the opinion of the LCIA Court.

10.3   An arbitrator may also be challenged by any party if circumstances exist that give rise to justifiable doubts as to his impartiality or independence. A party may challenge an arbitrator it has nominated, or in whose appointment it has participated, only for reasons of which it becomes aware after the appointment has been made.

10.4   A party who intends to challenge an arbitrator shall, within 15 days of the formation of the Arbitral Tribunal or (if later) after becoming aware of any circumstances referred to in Article 10.1, 10.2 or 10.3, send a written statement of the reasons for its challenge to the LCIA Court, the Arbitral Tribunal and all other parties. Unless the challenged arbitrator withdraws or all other parties agree to the challenge within 15 days of receipt of the written statement, the LCIA Court shall decide on the challenge.

Article 11
Nomination and Replacement of Arbitrators

11.1 In the event that the LCIA Court determines that any nominee is not suitable or independent or impartial or if an appointed arbitrator is to be replaced for any reason, the LCIA Court shall have a complete discretion to decide whether or not to follow the original nominating process.

11.2 If the LCIA Court should so decide, any opportunity given to a party to make a re-nomination shall be waived if not exercised within 15 days (or such lesser time as the LCIA Court may fix), after which the LCIA Court shall appoint the replacement arbitrator.

Article 12
Majority Power to Continue Proceedings

12.1 If any arbitrator on a three-member Arbitral Tribunal refuses or persistently fails to participate in its deliberations, the two other arbitrators shall have the power, upon their written notice of such refusal or failure to the LCIA Court, the parties and the third arbitrator, to continue the arbitration (including the making of any decision, ruling or award), notwithstanding the absence of the third arbitrator.

12.2 In determining whether to continue the arbitration, the two other arbitrators shall take into account the stage of the arbitration, any explanation made by the third arbitrator for his non-participation and such other matters as they consider appropriate in the circumstances of the case. The reasons for such determination shall be stated in any award, order or other decision made by the two arbitrators without the participation of the third arbitrator.

12.3 In the event that the two other arbitrators determine at any time not to continue the arbitration without the participation of the third arbitrator missing from their deliberations, the two arbitrators shall notify in writing the parties and the LCIA Court of such determination; and in that event, the two arbitrators or any party may refer the matter to the LCIA Court for the revocation of that third arbitrator's appointment and his replacement under Article 10.

Article 13
Communications between Parties and the Arbitral Tribunal

13.1   Until the Arbitral Tribunal is formed, all communications between parties and arbitrators shall be made through the Registrar.

13.2   Thereafter, unless and until the Arbitral Tribunal directs that communications shall take place directly between the Arbitral Tribunal and the parties (with simultaneous copies to the Registrar), all written communications between the parties and the Arbitral Tribunal shall continue to be made through the Registrar.

13.3   Where the Registrar sends any written communication to one party on behalf of the Arbitral Tribunal, he shall send a copy to each of the other parties. Where any party sends to the Registrar any communication (including Written Statements and Documents under Article 15), it shall include a copy for each arbitrator; and it shall also send copies direct to all other parties and confirm to the Registrar in writing that it has done or is doing so.

Article 14
Conduct of the Proceedings

14.1   The parties may agree on the conduct of their arbitral proceedings and they are encouraged to do so, consistent with the Arbitral Tribunal's general duties at all times:

(i) to act fairly and impartially as between all parties, giving each a reasonable opportunity of putting its case and dealing with that of its opponent; and

(ii) to adopt procedures suitable to the circumstances of the arbitration, avoiding unnecessary delay or expense, so as to provide a fair and efficient means for the final resolution of the parties' dispute.

Such agreements shall be made by the parties in writing or recorded in writing by the Arbitral Tribunal at the request of and with the authority of the parties

14.2   Unless otherwise agreed by the parties under Article 14.1, the Arbitral Tribunal shall have the widest discretion to discharge its duties allowed under such law(s) or rules of law as the Arbitral Tribunal may determine to be applicable; and at all times the parties shall do everything necessary for the fair, efficient and expeditious conduct of the arbitration.

14.3   In the case of a three-member Arbitral Tribunal the chairman may, with the prior consent of the other two arbitrators, make procedural rulings alone.

Article 15
Submission of Written Statements and Documents

15.1   Unless the parties have agreed otherwise under Article 14.1 or the Arbitral Tribunal should determine differently, the written stage of the proceedings shall be as set out below.

15.2   Within 30 days of receipt of written notification from the Registrar of the formation of the Arbitral Tribunal, the Claimant shall send to the Registrar a Statement of Case setting out in sufficient detail the facts and any contentions of law on which it relies, together with the relief claimed against all other parties, save and insofar as such matters have not been set out in its Request.

15.3   Within 30 days of receipt of the Statement of Case or written notice from the Claimant that it elects to treat the Request as its Statement of Case, the Respondent shall send to the Registrar a Statement of Defence setting out in sufficient detail which of the facts and contentions of law in the Statement of Case or Request (as the case may be) it admits or denies, on what grounds and on what other facts and contentions of law it relies. Any counterclaims shall be submitted with the Statement of Defence in the same manner as claims are to be set out in the Statement of Case.

15.4   Within 30 days of receipt of the Statement of Defence, the Claimant shall send to the Registrar a Statement of Reply which, where there are any counterclaims, shall include a Defence to Counterclaim in the same manner as a defence is to be set out in the Statement of Defence.

15.5   If the Statement of Reply contains a Defence to Counterclaim, within 30 days of its receipt the Respondent shall send to the Registrar a Statement of Reply to Counterclaim.

15.6   All Statements referred to in this Article shall be accompanied by copies (or, if they are especially voluminous, lists) of all essential documents on which the party concerned relies and which have not previously been submitted by any party, and (where appropriate) by any relevant samples and exhibits.

15.7   As soon as practicable following receipt of the Statements specified in this Article, the Arbitral Tribunal shall proceed in such manner as has been agreed in writing by the parties or pursuant to its authority under these Rules.

15.8   If the Respondent fails to submit a Statement of Defence or the Claimant a Statement of Defence to Counterclaim, or if at any point any party fails to avail itself of the opportunity to present its case in the manner determined by Article 15.2 to 15.6 or directed by the Arbitral Tribunal, the Arbitral Tribunal may nevertheless proceed with the arbitration and make an award.

Article 16
Seat of Arbitration and Place of Hearings

16.1   The parties may agree in writing the seat (or legal place) of their arbitration. Failing such a choice, the seat of arbitration shall be London, unless and until the LCIA Court determines in view of all the circumstances, and after having given the parties an opportunity to make written comment, that another seat is more appropriate.

16.2   The Arbitral Tribunal may hold hearings, meetings and deliberations at any convenient geographical place in its discretion; and if elsewhere than the seat of the arbitration, the arbitration shall be treated as an arbitration conducted at the seat of the arbitration and any award as an award made at the seat of the arbitration for all purposes.

16.3   The law applicable to the arbitration (if any) shall be the arbitration law of the seat of arbitration, unless and to the extent that the parties have expressly agreed in writing on the application of another arbitration law and such agreement is not prohibited by the law of the arbitral seat.

Article 17
Language of Arbitration

17.1   The initial language of the arbitration shall be the language of the Arbitration Agreement, unless the parties have agreed in writing otherwise and providing always that a non-participating or defaulting party shall have no cause for complaint if communications to and from the Registrar and the arbitration proceedings are conducted in English.

17.2   In the event that the Arbitration Agreement is written in more than one language, the LCIA Court may, unless the Arbitration Agreement provides that the arbitration proceedings shall be conducted in more than one language, decide which of those languages shall be the initial language of the arbitration.

17.3   Upon the formation of the Arbitral Tribunal and unless the parties have agreed upon the language or languages of the arbitration, the Arbitration Tribunal shall decide upon the language(s) of the arbitration, after giving the parties an opportunity to make written comment and taking into account the initial language of the arbitration and any other matter it may consider appropriate in all the circumstances of the case.

17.4   If any document is expressed in a language other than the language(s) of the arbitration and no translation of such document is submitted by the party relying upon the document, the Arbitral Tribunal or (if the Arbitral Tribunal has not been formed) the LCIA Court may order that party to submit a translation in a form to be determined by the Arbitral Tribunal or the LCIA Court, as the case may be.

Article 18
Party Representation

18.1   Any party may be represented by legal practitioners or any other representatives.

18.2   At any time the Arbitral Tribunal may require from any party proof of authority granted to its representative(s) in such form as the Arbitral Tribunal may determine.

Article 19
Hearings

19.1   Any party which expresses a desire to that effect has the right to be heard orally before the Arbitral Tribunal on the merits of the dispute, unless the parties have agreed in writing on documents-only arbitration.

19.2   The Arbitral Tribunal shall fix the date, time and physical place of any meetings and hearings in the arbitration, and shall give the parties reasonable notice thereof.

19.3   The Arbitral Tribunal may in advance of any hearing submit to the parties a list of questions which it wishes them to answer with special attention.

19.4   All meetings and hearings shall be in private unless the parties agree otherwise in writing or the Arbitral Tribunal directs otherwise.

19.5   The Arbitral Tribunal shall have the fullest authority to establish time-limits for meetings and hearings, or for any parts thereof.

Article 20
Witnesses

20.1   Before any hearing, the Arbitral Tribunal may require any party to give notice of the identity of each witness that party wishes to call (including rebuttal witnesses), as well as the subject matter of that witness's testimony, its content and its relevance to the issues in the arbitration.

20.2   The Arbitral Tribunal may also determine the time, manner and form in which such materials should be exchanged between the parties and presented to the Arbitral Tribunal; and it has a discretion to allow, refuse, or limit the appearance of witnesses (whether witness of fact or expert witness).

20.3   Subject to any order otherwise by the Arbitral Tribunal, the testimony of a witness may be presented by a party in written form, either as a signed statement or as a sworn affidavit.

20.4   Subject to Article 14.1 and 14.2, any party may request that a witness, on whose testimony another party seeks to rely, should attend for oral questioning at a hearing before the Arbitral Tribunal. If the Arbitral Tribunal orders that other party to produce the witness and the witness fails to attend the oral hearing without good cause, the Arbitral Tribunal may place such weight on the written testimony (or exclude the same altogether) as it considers appropriate in the circumstances of the case.

20.5   Any witness who gives oral evidence at a hearing before the Arbitral Tribunal may be questioned by each of the parties under the control of the Arbitral Tribunal. The Arbitral Tribunal may put questions at any stage of his evidence.

20.6   Subject to the mandatory provisions of any applicable law, it shall not be improper for any party or its legal representatives to interview any witness or potential witness for the purpose of presenting his testimony in written form or producing him as an oral witness.

20.7   Any individual intending to testify to the Arbitral Tribunal on any issue of fact or expertise shall be treated as a witness under these Rules notwithstanding that the individual is a party to the arbitration or was or is an officer, employee or shareholder of any party.

Article 21
Experts to the Arbitral Tribunal

21.1   Unless otherwise agreed by the parties in writing, the Arbitral Tribunal:

(a) may appoint one or more experts to report to the Arbitral Tribunal on specific issues, who shall be and remain impartial and independent of the parties throughout the arbitration proceedings; and

(b) may require a party to give any such expert any relevant information or to provide access to any relevant documents, goods, samples, property or site for inspection by the expert.

21.2   Unless otherwise agreed by the parties in writing, if a party so requests or if the Arbitral Tribunal considers it necessary, the expert shall, after delivery of his written or oral report to the Arbitral Tribunal and the parties, participate in one or more hearings at which the parties shall have the opportunity to question the expert on his report and to present expert witnesses in order to testify on the points at issue.

21.3   The fees and expenses of any expert appointed by the Arbitral Tribunal under this Article shall be paid out of the deposits payable by the parties under Article 24 and shall form part of the costs of the arbitration.

Article 22
Additional Powers of the Arbitral Tribunal

22.1   Unless the parties at any time agree otherwise in writing, the Arbitral Tribunal shall have the power, on the application of any party or of its own motion, but in either case only after giving the parties a reasonable opportunity to state their views:

(a) to allow any party, upon such terms (as to costs and otherwise) as it shall determine, to amend any claim, counterclaim, defence and reply;

(b) to extend or abbreviate any time-limit provided by the Arbitration Agreement or these Rules for the conduct of the arbitration or by the Arbitral Tribunal's own orders;

(c) to conduct such enquiries as may appear to the Arbitral Tribunal to be necessary or expedient, including whether and to what extent the Arbitral Tribunal should itself take the initiative in identifying the issues and ascertaining the relevant facts and the law(s) or rules of law applicable to the arbitration, the merits of the parties' dispute and the Arbitration Agreement;

(d) to order any party to make any property, site or thing under its control and relating to the subject matter of the arbitration available for inspection by the Arbitral Tribunal, any other party, its expert or any expert to the Arbitral Tribunal;

(e) to order any party to produce to the Arbitral Tribunal, and to the other parties for inspection, and to supply copies of, any documents or classes of documents in their possession, custody or power which the Arbitral Tribunal determines to be relevant;

(f) to decide whether or not to apply any strict rules of evidence (or any other rules) as to the admissibility, relevance or weight of any material tendered by a party on any matter of fact or expert opinion; and to determine the time, manner and form in which such material should be exchanged between the parties and presented to the Arbitral Tribunal;

(g) to order the correction of any contract between the parties or the Arbitration Agreement, but only to the extent required to rectify any mistake which the Arbitral Tribunal determines to be common to the parties and then only if and to the extent to which the law(s) or rules of law applicable to the contract or Arbitration Agreement permit such correction; and

(h) to allow, only upon the application of a party, one or more third persons to be joined in the arbitration as a party provided any such third person and the applicant party have consented thereto in writing, and thereafter to make a single final award, or separate awards, in respect of all parties so implicated in the arbitration.

22.2   By agreeing to arbitration under these Rules, the parties shall be treated as having agreed not to apply to any state court or other judicial authority for any order available from the Arbitral Tribunal under Article 22.1, except with the agreement in writing of all parties.

22.3   The Arbitral Tribunal shall decide the parties' dispute in accordance with the law(s) or rules of law chosen by the parties as applicable to the merits of their dispute. If and to the extent that the Arbitral Tribunal determines that the parties have made no such choice, the Arbitral Tribunal shall apply the law(s) or rules of law which it considers appropriate.

22.4   The Arbitral Tribunal shall only apply to the merits of the dispute principles deriving from "ex aequo et bono", "amiable composition" or "honourable engagement" where the parties have so agreed expressly in writing.

Article 23
Jurisdiction of the Arbitral Tribunal

23.1   The Arbitral Tribunal shall have the power to rule on its own jurisdiction, including any objection to the initial or continuing existence, validity or effectiveness of the Arbitration Agreement. For that purpose, an arbitration clause which forms or was intended to form part of another agreement shall be treated as an arbitration agreement independent of that other agreement. A decision by the Arbitral Tribunal that such other agreement is non-existent, invalid or ineffective shall not entail ipso jure the non-existence, invalidity or ineffectiveness of the arbitration clause.

23.2   A plea by a Respondent that the Arbitral Tribunal does not have jurisdiction shall be treated as having been irrevocably waived unless it is raised not later than the Statement of Defence; and a like plea by a Respondent to Counterclaim shall be similarly treated unless it is raised no later than the Statement of Defence to Counterclaim. A plea that the Arbitral Tribunal is exceeding the scope of its authority shall be raised promptly after the Arbitral Tribunal has indicated its intention to decide on the matter alleged by any party to be beyond the scope of its authority, failing which such plea shall also be treated as having been waived irrevocably. In any case, the Arbitral Tribunal may nevertheless admit an untimely plea if it considers the delay justified in the particular circumstances.

23.3   The Arbitral Tribunal may determine the plea to its jurisdiction or authority in an award as to jurisdiction or later in an award on the merits, as it considers appropriate in the circumstances.

23.4   By agreeing to arbitration under these Rules, the parties shall be treated as having agreed not to apply to any state court or other judicial authority for any relief regarding the Arbitral Tribunal's jurisdiction or authority, except with the agreement in writing of all parties to the arbitration or the prior authorisation of the Arbitral Tribunal or following the latter's award ruling on the objection to its jurisdiction or authority.

Article 24
Deposits

24.1   The LCIA Court may direct the parties, in such proportions as it thinks appropriate, to make one or several interim or final payments on account of the costs of the arbitration. Such deposits shall be made to and held by the LCIA and from time to time may be released by the LCIA Court to the arbitrator(s), any expert appointed by the Arbitral Tribunal and the LCIA itself as the arbitration progresses.

24.2   The Arbitral Tribunal shall not proceed with the arbitration without ascertaining at all times from the Registrar or any deputy Registrar that the LCIA is in requisite funds.

24.3   In the event that a party fails or refuses to provide any deposit as directed by the LCIA Court, the LCIA Court may direct the other party or parties to effect a substitute payment to allow the arbitration to proceed (subject to any award on costs). In such circumstances, the party paying the substitute payment shall be entitled to recover that amount as a debt immediately due from the defaulting party.

24.4   Failure by a claimant or counterclaiming party to provide promptly and in full the required deposit may be treated by the LCIA Court and the Arbitral Tribunal as a withdrawal of the claim or counterclaim respectively.

Article 25
Interim and Conservatory Measures

25.1   The Arbitral Tribunal shall have the power, unless otherwise agreed by the parties in writing, on the application of any party:

(a) to order any respondent party to a claim or counterclaim to provide security for all or part of the amount in dispute, by way of deposit or bank guarantee or in any other manner and upon such terms as the Arbitral Tribunal considers appropriate. Such terms may include the provision by the claiming or counterclaiming party of a cross-indemnity, itself secured in such manner as the Arbitral Tribunal considers appropriate, for any costs or losses incurred by such respondent in providing security. The amount of any costs and losses payable under such cross-indemnity may be determined by the Arbitral Tribunal in one or more awards;

(b) to order the preservation, storage, sale or other disposal of any property or thing under the control of any party and relating to the subject matter of the arbitration; and

(c) to order on a provisional basis, subject to final determination in an award, any relief which the Arbitral Tribunal would have power to grant in an award, including a provisional order for the payment of money or the disposition of property as between any parties.

25.2   The Arbitral Tribunal shall have the power, upon the application of a party, to order any claiming or counterclaiming party to provide security for the legal or other costs of any other party by way of deposit or bank guarantee or in any other manner and upon such terms as the Arbitral Tribunal considers appropriate. Such terms may include the provision by that other party of a cross-indemnity, itself secured in such manner as the Arbitral Tribunal considers appropriate, for any costs and losses incurred by such claimant or counterclaimant in providing security. The amount of any costs and losses payable under such cross-indemnity may be determined by the Arbitral Tribunal in one or more awards. In the event that a claiming or counterclaiming party does not comply with any order to provide security , the Arbitral Tribunal may stay that party's claims or counterclaims or dismiss them in an award.

25.3   The power of the Arbitral Tribunal under Article 25.1 shall not prejudice howsoever any party's right to apply to any state court or other judicial authority for interim or conservatory measures before the formation of the Arbitral Tribunal and, in exceptional cases, thereafter. Any application and any order for such measures after the formation of the Arbitral Tribunal shall be promptly communicated by the applicant to the Arbitral Tribunal and all other parties. However, by agreeing to arbitration under these Rules, the parties shall be taken to have agreed not to apply to any state court or other judicial authority for any order for security for its legal or other costs available from the Arbitral Tribunal under Article 25.2.

Article 26
The Award

26.1   The Arbitral Tribunal shall make its award in writing and, unless all parties agree in writing otherwise, shall state the reasons upon which its award is based. The award shall also state the date when the award is made and the seat of the arbitration; and it shall be signed by the Arbitral Tribunal or those of its members assenting to it.

26.2   If any arbitrator fails to comply with the mandatory provisions of any applicable law relating to the making of the award, having been given a reasonable opportunity to do so, the remaining arbitrators may proceed in his absence and state in their award the circumstances of the other arbitrator's failure to participate in the making of the award.

26.3   Where there are three arbitrators and the Arbitral Tribunal fails to agree on any issue, the arbitrators shall decide that issue by a majority. Failing a majority decision on any issue, the chairman of the Arbitral Tribunal shall decide that issue.

26.4   If any arbitrator refuses or fails to sign the award, the signatures of the majority or (failing a majority) of the chairman shall be sufficient, provided that the reason for the omitted signature is stated in the award by the majority or chairman.

26.5   The sole arbitrator or chairman shall be responsible for delivering the award to the LCIA Court, which shall transmit certified copies to the parties provided that the costs of arbitration have been paid to the LCIA in accordance with Article 28.

26.6   An award may be expressed in any currency. The Arbitral Tribunal may order that simple or compound interest shall be paid by any party on any sum awarded at such rates as the Arbitral Tribunal determines to be appropriate, without being bound by legal rates of interest imposed by any state court, in respect of any period which the Arbitral Tribunal determines to be appropriate ending not later than the date upon which the award is complied with.

26.7   The Arbitral Tribunal may make separate awards on different issues at different times. Such awards shall have the same status and effect as any other award made by the Arbitral Tribunal.

26.8   In the event of a settlement of the parties' dispute, the Arbitral Tribunal may render an award recording the settlement if the parties so request in writing (a "Consent Award"), provided always that such award contains an express statement that it is an award made by the parties' consent. A Consent Award need not contain reasons. If the parties do not require a consent award, then on written confirmation by the parties to the LCIA Court that a settlement has been reached, the Arbitral Tribunal shall be discharged and the arbitration proceedings concluded, subject to payment by the parties of any outstanding costs of the arbitration under Article 28.

26.9   All awards shall be final and binding on the parties. By agreeing to arbitration under these Rules, the parties undertake to carry out any award immediately and without any delay (subject only to Article 27); and the parties also waive irrevocably their right to any form of appeal, review or recourse to any state court or other judicial authority, insofar as such waiver may be validly made.

Article 27
Correction of Awards and Additional Awards

27.1   Within 30 days of receipt of any award, or such lesser period as may be agreed in writing by the parties, a party may by written notice to the Registrar (copied to all other parties) request the Arbitral Tribunal to correct in the award any errors in computation, clerical or typographical errors or any errors of a similar nature. If the Arbitral Tribunal considers the request to be justified, it shall make the corrections within 30 days of receipt of the request. Any correction shall take the form of separate memorandum dated and signed by the Arbitral Tribunal or (if three arbitrators) those of its members assenting to it; and such memorandum shall become part of the award for all purposes.

27.2   The Arbitral Tribunal may likewise correct any error of the nature described in Article 27.1 on its own initiative within 30 days of the date of the award, to the same effect.

27.3   Within 30 days of receipt of the final award, a party may by written notice to the Registrar (copied to all other parties), request the Arbitral Tribunal to make an additional award as to claims or counterclaims presented in the arbitration but not determined in any award. If the Arbitral Tribunal considers the request to be justified, it shall make the additional award within 60 days of receipt of the request. The provisions of Article 26 shall apply to any additional award.

Article 28
Arbitration and Legal Costs

28.1   The costs of the arbitration (other than the legal or other costs incurred by the parties themselves) shall be determined by the LCIA

434

Court in accordance with the Schedule of Costs. The parties shall be jointly and severally liable to the Arbitral Tribunal and the LCIA for such arbitration costs.

28.2   The Arbitral Tribunal shall specify in the award the total amount of the costs of the arbitration as determined by the LCIA Court. Unless the parties agree otherwise in writing, the Arbitral Tribunal shall determine the proportions in which the parties shall bear all or part of such arbitration costs. If the Arbitral Tribunal has determined that all or any part of the arbitration costs shall be borne by a party other than a party which has already paid them to the LCIA, the latter party shall have the right to recover the appropriate amount from the former party.

28.3   The Arbitral Tribunal shall also have the power to order in its award that all or part of the legal or other costs incurred by a party be paid by another party, unless the parties agree otherwise in writing. The Arbitral Tribunal shall determine and fix the amount of each item comprising such costs on such reasonable basis as it thinks fit.

28.4   Unless the parties otherwise agree in writing, the Arbitral Tribunal shall make its orders on both arbitration and legal costs on the general principle that costs should reflect the parties' relative success and failure in the award or arbitration, except where it appears to the Arbitral Tribunal that in the particular circumstances this general approach is inappropriate. Any order for costs shall be made with reasons in the award containing such order.

28.5   If the arbitration is abandoned, suspended or concluded, by agreement or otherwise, before the final award is made, the parties shall remain jointly and severally liable to pay to the LCIA and the Arbitral Tribunal the costs of the arbitration as determined by the LCIA Court in accordance with the Schedule of Costs. In the event that such arbitration costs are less than the deposits made by the parties, there shall be a refund by the LCIA in such proportion as the parties may agree in writing, or failing such agreement, in the same proportions as the deposits were made by the parties to the LCIA.

Article 29
Decisions by the LCIA Court

29.1   The decisions of the LCIA Court with respect to all matters relating to the arbitration shall be conclusive and binding upon the parties and the Arbitral Tribunal. Such decisions are to be treated as administrative in nature and the LCIA Court shall not be required to give any reasons.

29.2   To the extent permitted by the law of the seat of the arbitration, the parties shall be taken to have waived any right of appeal or review in respect of any such decisions of the LCIA Court to any state court or other judicial authority. If such appeals or review remain possible due to mandatory provisions of any applicable law, the LCIA Court shall, subject to the provisions of that applicable law, decide whether the arbitral proceedings are to continue, notwithstanding an appeal or review.

Article 30
Confidentiality

30.1   Unless the parties expressly agree in writing to the contrary, the parties undertake as a general principle to keep confidential all awards in their arbitration, together with all materials in the proceedings created for the purpose of the arbitration and all other documents produced by another party in the proceedings not otherwise in the public domain - save and to the extent that disclosure may be required of a party by legal duty, to protect or pursue a legal right or to enforce or challenge an award in bona fide legal proceedings before a state court or other judicial authority.

30.2   The deliberations of the Arbitral Tribunal are likewise confidential to its members, save and to the extent that disclosure of an arbitrator's refusal to participate in the arbitration is required of the other members of the Arbitral Tribunal under Articles 10, 12 and 26.

30.3   The LCIA Court does not publish any award or any part of an award without the prior written consent of all parties and the Arbitral Tribunal.

Article 31
Exclusion of Liability

31.1   None of the LCIA, the LCIA Court (including its President, Vice Presidents and individual members), the Registrar, any deputy Registrar, any arbitrator and any expert to the Arbitral Tribunal shall be liable to any party howsoever for any act or omission in connection with any arbitration conducted by reference to these Rules, save where the act or omission is shown by that party to constitute conscious and deliberate wrongdoing committed by the body or person alleged to be liable to that party.

31.2   After the award has been made and the possibilities of correction and additional awards referred to in Article 27 have lapsed or been exhausted, neither the LCIA, the LCIA Court (including its President, Vice Presidents and individual members), the Registrar, any deputy Registrar, any arbitrator or expert to the Arbitral Tribunal shall be under any legal obligation to make any statement to any person about any matter concerning the arbitration, nor shall any party seek to make any of these persons a witness in any legal or other proceedings arising out of the arbitration.

Article 32
General Rules

32.1   A party who knows that any provision of the Arbitration Agreement (including these Rules) has not been complied with and yet proceeds with the arbitration without promptly stating its objection to such non-compliance, shall be treated as having irrevocably waived its right to object.

32.2   In all matters not expressly provided for in these Rules, the LCIA Court, the Arbitral Tribunal and the parties shall act in the spirit of these Rules and shall make every reasonable effort to ensure that an award is legally enforceable.

RECOMMENDED ARBITRATION CLAUSES

Future disputes

For contracting parties who wish to have future disputes referred to arbitration under the LCIA Rules, the following clause is recommended. Words/spaces in square brackets should be deleted/completed as appropriate.

"Any dispute arising out of or in connection with this contract, including any question regarding its existence, validity or termination, shall be referred to and finally resolved by arbitration under the LCIA Rules, which Rules are deemed to be incorporated by reference into this clause.

The number of arbitrators shall be [one/three].

The seat, or legal place, of arbitration shall be [City and/or Country].

The language to be used in the arbitral proceedings shall be [   ].

The governing law of the contract shall be the substantive law of [   ]."

Existing disputes

If a dispute has arisen, but there is no agreement between the parties to arbitrate, or if the parties wish to vary a dispute resolution clause to provide for LCIA arbitration, the following clause is recommended. Words/spaces in square brackets should be deleted/completed as appropriate.

"A dispute having arisen between the parties concerning [   ], the parties hereby agree that the dispute shall be referred to and finally resolved by arbitration under the LCIA Rules.

The number of arbitrators shall be [one/three].

The seat, or legal place, of arbitration shall be [City and/or Country].

The language to be used in the arbitral proceedings shall be [   ].

The governing law of the contract [is/shall be] the substantive law of [   ]."

SCHEDULE OF ARBITRATION COSTS

(effective 15 May 2009)

For all arbitrations in which the LCIA provides services, whether as administrator, or as appointing authority only, and whether under the LCIA Rules, UNCITRAL Rules or other, ad hoc, rules or procedures agreed by the parties to the arbitration.

1. Administrative charges under LCIA Rules, UNCITRAL Rules, or other, ad hoc, rules or procedures*

1(a) Registration Fee (payable in advance with Request for Arbitration non-refundable).   £1,500

1(b) Time spent** by the Secretariat of the LCIA in the administration of the arbitration.***

Registrar / Deputy Registrar / Counsel   £200 per hour

Other Secretariat personnel   £100 per hour

1(c) Time spent by members of the LCIA Court in carrying out their functions in deciding any challenge brought under the applicable rules.***

at hourly rates advised by members of the LCIA Court

1(d) A sum equivalent to 5% of the fees of the Tribunal (excluding expenses) in respect of the LCIA's general overhead.***

1(e) Expenses incurred by the Secretariat and by members of the LCIA Court, in connection with the arbitration (such as postage, telephone, facsimile, travel etc.), and additional arbitration support services, whether provided by the Secretariat or the members of the LCIA Court from their own resources or otherwise.***

at applicable hourly rates or at cost

1(f) The LCIA's fees and expenses will be invoiced in sterling, but may be paid in other convertible currencies, at rates prevailing at the time of payment, provided that any transfer and/or currency exchange charges shall be borne by the payer.

2. Request to act as Appointing Authority only*

2(a) Appointment Fee (payable in advance with request – non-refundable). £1,000

2(b) As for 1(b) and 1(e), above.

3. Request to act in deciding challenges to arbitrators in non-LCIA arbitrations*

3(a) As for 2(a) and 2(b), above; plus

3(b) Time spent by members of the LCIA Court in carrying out their functions in deciding the challenges.

at hourly rates advised by members of the LCIA Court

4. Fees and expenses of the Tribunal*

4(a) The Tribunal's fees will be calculated by reference to work done by its members in connection with the arbitration and will be charged at rates appropriate to the particular circumstances of the case, including its complexity and the special qualifications of the arbitrators. The Tribunal shall agree in writing upon fee rates conforming to this Schedule of Arbitration Costs prior to its appointment by the LCIA Court. The rates will be advised by the Registrar to the parties at the time of the appointment of the Tribunal, but may be reviewed annually if the duration of the arbitration requires.

Fees shall be at hourly rates not exceeding £350.

However, in exceptional cases, the rate may be higher provided that, in such cases, (a) the fees of the Tribunal shall be fixed by the LCIA Court on the recommendation of the Registrar, following consultations with the arbitrator(s), and (b) the fees shall be agreed expressly by all parties.

4(b) The Tribunal's fees may include a charge for time spent travelling.

4(c) The Tribunal's fees may also include a charge for time reserved but not used as a result of late postponement or cancellation, provided that the basis for such charge shall be advised in writing to, and approved by, the LCIA Court.

4(d) The Tribunal may also recover such expenses as are reasonably incurred in connection with the arbitration, and as are in a reasonable amount, provided that claims for expenses should be supported by invoices or receipts.

4(e) The Tribunal's fees may be invoiced either in the currency of account between the Tribunal and the parties, or in sterling. The Tribunal's expenses may be invoiced in the currency in which they were incurred, or in sterling.

4(f) In the event of the revocation of the appointment of any arbitrator, pursuant to the provisions of Article 10 of the LCIA Rules, the LCIA Court shall decide upon the amount of fees and expenses to be paid for the former arbitrator's services (if any) as it may consider appropriate in all the circumstances.

5. Deposits

5(a) The LCIA Court may direct the parties, in such proportions as it thinks appropriate, to make one or several interim or final payments on account of the costs of the arbitration. The LCIA Court may limit such payments to a sum sufficient to cover fees, expenses and costs for the next stage of the arbitration.

5(b) The Tribunal shall not proceed with the arbitration without ascertaining at all times from the Registrar or any deputy Registrar that the LCIA is in requisite funds.

5(c) In the event that a party fails or refuses to provide any deposit as directed by the LCIA Court, the LCIA Court may direct the other party or parties to effect a substitute payment to allow the arbitration to proceed (subject to any award on costs). In such circumstances, the party paying the substitute payment shall be entitled to recover that amount as a debt immediately due from the defaulting party.

5(d) Failure by a claimant or counterclaiming party to provide promptly and in full the required deposit may be treated by the LCIA Court and the Arbitral Tribunal as a withdrawal of the claim or counterclaim, respectively.

5(e) Funds lodged by the parties on account of the fees and expenses of the Tribunal and of the LCIA are held on trust in client bank accounts which are controlled by reference to each individual case and are disbursed by the LCIA, in accordance with the LCIA Rules and with this Schedule of Arbitration Fees and Costs. In the event that funds lodged by the parties exceed the costs of the arbitration at the conclusion of the arbitration, surplus monies will be returned to the parties as the ultimate default beneficiaries under the trust.

6. Interest on deposits

Interest on sums deposited shall be credited to the account of each party depositing them, at the rate applicable to an amount equal to the amount so credited.

7. Interim payments

7(a) When interim payments are required to cover the LCIA's administrative costs, or the fees or expenses of members of the LCIA Court, or the Tribunal's fees or expenses, including the fees or expenses of any expert appointed by the Tribunal, such payments may be made out of deposits held, upon the approval of the LCIA Court.

7(b) The LCIA may, in any event, submit interim invoices in respect of all current arbitrations, in March, June, September and December of each year, for payment direct by the parties or from funds held on deposit.

8. Registrar's authority

8(a) For the purposes of sections 5(a) and 5(c) above, and of Articles 24.1 and 24.3 of the LCIA Rules, the Registrar has the authority of the LCIA Court to make the directions referred to, under the supervision of the Court.

8(b) For the purposes of section 7(a) above, and of Article 24.1 of the LCIA Rules, the Registrar has the authority of the LCIA Court to approve the payments referred to.

8(c) Any request by an arbitrator for payment on account of his fees shall be supported by a fee note, which shall include, or be accompanied by, details of the time spent at the rates that have been advised to the parties by the LCIA.

8(d) Any dispute regarding administration costs or the fees and expenses of the Tribunal shall be determined by the LCIA Court.

9. Arbitration costs

9(a) The parties shall be jointly and severally liable to the Arbitral Tribunal and the LCIA for the arbitration costs (other than the legal or other costs incurred by the parties themselves).

9(b) The Tribunal's Award(s) shall be transmitted to the parties by the LCIA Court provided that the costs of the arbitration have been paid in accordance with Article 28 of the LCIA Rules.

* Charges may be subject to Value Added Tax at the prevailing rate.
** Minimum unit of time in all cases: 15 minutes.
*** Items 1(b), 1(c), 1(d) and 1(e) above, are payable on interim invoice; with the award, or as directed by the LCIA Court under Article 24.1 of the Rules.

APPENDIX 35
AAA-ICDR DISPUTE RESOLUTION PROCEDURES

Introduction

The international business community uses arbitration to resolve commercial disputes arising in the global marketplace. Supportive laws are in place. The New York Convention of 1958 has been widely adopted, providing a favorable legislative climate that enables the enforcement of arbitration clauses. International commercial arbitration awards are recognized by national courts in most parts of the world, even more than foreign court judgments. A key component to the successful resolution of an international commercial dispute is the role played by the administrative institution. The International Centre for Dispute Resolution ® (ICDR) is the international division of the American Arbitration Association (AAA) charged with the exclusive administration of all of the AAA's international matters. The ICDR's experience, international expertise and multilingual staff forms an integral part of the dispute resolution process. The ICDR's international system is premised on its ability to move the matter forward, facilitate communications, ensure that qualified arbitrators and mediators are appointed, control costs, understand cultural sensitivies, resolve procedural impasses and properly interpret and apply its International Mediation and Arbitration Rules. Additionally, the ICDR has many cooperative agreements with arbitral institutions around the world for facilitating the administration of its international cases.

International Mediation

The parties might wish to submit their dispute to an international mediation prior to arbitration. In mediation, an impartial and independent mediator assists the parties in reaching a settlement but does not have the authority to make a binding decision or award. International Mediation is administered by the ICDR in accordance with its International Mediation Rules. There is no additional administrative fee where parties to a pending arbitration attempt to mediate their dispute under the ICDR's auspices.

If the parties want to adopt mediation as a part of their contractual dispute settlement procedure, they can insert the following mediation clause into their contract in conjunction with a standard arbitration provision:

- *If a dispute arises out of or relates to this contract, or the breach thereof, and if the dispute cannot be settled through negotiation, the parties agree first to try in good faith to settle the dispute by mediation in accordance with the International Mediation Rules of the International Centre for Dispute Resolution before resorting to arbitration, litigation or some other dispute resolution procedure.*

If the parties want to use a mediator to resolve an existing dispute, they can enter into the following submission:

- *The parties hereby submit the following dispute to mediation administered by the International Centre for Dispute Resolution in accordance with its International Mediation Rules. (The clause may also provide for the qualifications of the mediator(s), method of payment, locale of meetings and any other item of concern to the parties.)*

The ICDR can schedule the mediation anywhere in the world and will propose a list of specialized international mediators.

International Arbitration

As the ICDR is a division of the AAA, parties can arbitrate future disputes under these Rules by inserting either of the following clauses into their contracts:

- *"Any controversy or claim arising out of or relating to this contract, or the breach thereof, shall be determined by arbitration administered by the International Centre for Dispute Resolution in accordance with its International Arbitration Rules."*

  or

- *"Any controversy or claim arising out of or relating to this contract, or the breach thereof, shall be determined by arbitration administered by the American Arbitration Association in accordance with its International Arbitration Rules."*

The parties may wish to consider adding:

(a) *"The number of arbitrators shall be (one or three)";*

(b) *"The place of arbitration shall be (city and/or country)"; or*

(c) *"The language(s) of the arbitration shall be* _____*."*

Parties are encouraged, when writing their contracts or when a dispute arises, to request a conference, in person or by telephone, with the ICDR, to discuss an appropriate method for selection of arbitrators or any other matter that might facilitate efficient arbitration of the dispute.

Under these Rules, the parties are free to adopt any mutually agreeable procedure for appointing arbitrators, or may designate arbitrators upon whom they agree. Parties can reach agreements concerning appointing arbitrators either when writing their contracts or after a dispute has arisen. This flexible procedure permits parties to utilize whatever method they consider best suits their needs. For example, parties may choose to have a sole arbitrator or a tribunal of three or more. They may agree that arbitrators shall be appointed by the ICDR, or that each side shall designate one arbitrator and those two shall name a third, with the ICDR making appointments if the tribunal is not promptly formed by that procedure. Parties may mutually request the ICDR to submit to them a list of arbitrators from which each can delete names not acceptable to it, or the parties may instruct the ICDR to appoint arbitrators without the submission of lists, or may leave that matter to the sole discretion of the ICDR. Parties also may agree on a variety of other methods for establishing the tribunal. In any event, if parties are unable to agree on a procedure for appointing arbitrators or on the designation of arbitrators, the ICDR, after inviting consultation by the parties, will appoint the arbitrators. The Rules thus provide for the fullest exercise of party autonomy, while assuring that the ICDR is available to act if the parties cannot reach mutual agreement. By providing for arbitration under these Rules, parties can avoid the uncertainty of having to petition a local court to resolve procedural impasses. These Rules, as administered by the IDCR, are intended to provide prompt, effective and economical arbitration services to the global business community.

Whenever a singular term is used in the Rules, such as "party," "claimant" or "arbitrator," that term shall include the plural if there is more than one such entity.

Parties filing an international case with the International Centre for Dispute Resolution, or the American Arbitration Association, may file online via AAAWebFile ® at www.adr.org. or by directly contacting the ICDR in New York, Dublin or Singapore. Parties can also file a case at any one of the AAA's regional offices.

Further information about these Rules can be secured by contacting the International Centre for Dispute Resolution at 212.484.4181 or by visiting the ICDR's Web site at www.icdr.org.

The English language version of the Rules is the official text for questions of interpretation.

International Mediation Rules

1. Agreement of Parties

Whenever parties have agreed in writing to mediate disputes under these International Mediation Rules, or have provided for mediation or conciliation of existing or future international disputes under the auspices of the International Centre for Dispute Resolution, the international division of the American Arbitration Association, or the American Arbitration Association without designating particular Rules, they shall be deemed to have made these Rules, as amended and in effect as of the date of the submission of the dispute, a part of their agreement.

The parties by mutual agreement may vary any part of these Rules including, but not limited to, agreeing to conduct the mediation via telephone or other electronic or technical means.

2. Initiation of Mediation

Any party or parties to a dispute may initiate mediation under the ICDR's auspices by making a request for mediation to any of the ICDR's regional offices or case management centers via telephone, email, regular mail or fax. Requests for mediation may also be filed online via AAA WebFile at www.adr.org.

The party initiating the mediation shall simultaneously notify the other party or parties of the request. The initiating party shall provide the following information to the ICDR and the other party or parties as applicable:

(i) A copy of the mediation provision of the parties' contract or the parties' stipulation to mediate.

(ii) The names, regular mail addresses, email addresses, and telephone numbers of all parties to the dispute and representatives, if any, in the mediation.

(iii) A brief statement of the nature of the dispute and the relief requested.

(iv) Any specific qualifications the mediator should possess.

Where there is no preexisting stipulation or contract by which the parties have provided for mediation of existing or future disputes under the auspices of the ICDR, a party may request the ICDR to invite another party to participate in "mediation by voluntary submission". Upon receipt of such a request, the ICDR will contact the other party or parties involved in the dispute and attempt to obtain a submission to mediation.

3. Representation

Subject to any applicable law, any party may be represented by persons of the party's choice. The names and addresses of such persons shall be communicated in writing to all parties and to the ICDR.

4. Appointment of the Mediator

Parties may search the online profiles of the ICDR's Panel of Mediators at www.aaamediation.comin an effort to agree on a mediator. If the parties have not agreed to the appointment of a mediator and have not provided any other method of appointment, the mediator shall be appointed in the following manner:

a. Upon receipt of a request for mediation, the ICDR will send to each party a list of mediators from the ICDR's Panel of Mediators. The parties are encouraged to agree to a mediator from the submitted list and to advise the ICDR of their agreement.

b. If the parties are unable to agree upon a mediator, each party shall strike unacceptable names from the list, number the remaining names in order of preference, and return the list to the ICDR. If a party does not return the list within the time specified, all mediators on the list shall be deemed acceptable. From among the mediators who have been mutually approved by the parties, and in accordance with the designated order of mutual preference, the ICDR shall invite a mediator to serve.

c. If the parties fail to agree on any of the mediators listed, or if acceptable mediators are unable to serve, or if for any other reason the appointment cannot be made from the submitted list, the ICDR shall have the authority to make the appointment from among other members of the Panel of Mediators without the submission of additional lists.

5. Mediator's Impartiality and Duty to Disclose

ICDR mediators are required to abide by the Model Standards of Conduct for Mediators in effect at the time a mediator is appointed to a case. Where there is a conflict between the Model Standards and any provision of these Mediation Rules, these Mediation Rules shall govern. The Standards require mediators to (i) decline a mediation if the mediator cannot conduct it in an impartial manner, and (ii) disclose, as soon as practicable, all actual and potential conflicts of interest that are reasonably known to the mediator and could reasonably be seen as raising a question about the mediator's impartiality.

Prior to accepting an appointment, ICDR mediators are required to make a reasonable inquiry to determine whether there are any facts that a reasonable individual would consider likely to create a potential or actual conflict of interest for the mediator. ICDR mediators are required to disclose any circumstance likely to create a presumption of bias or prevent a resolution of the parties' dispute within the time frame desired by the parties. Upon receipt of such disclosures, the ICDR shall immediately communicate the disclosures to the parties for their comments.

The parties may, upon receiving disclosure of actual or potential conflicts of interest of the mediator, waive such conflicts and proceed with the mediation. In the event that a party disagrees as to whether the mediator shall serve, or in the event that the mediator's conflict of interest might reasonably be viewed as undermining the integrity of the mediation, the mediator shall be replaced.

6. Vacancies

If any mediator shall become unwilling or unable to serve, the ICDR will appoint another mediator, unless the parties agree otherwise, in accordance with section 4.

7. Duties and Responsibilities of the Mediator

i. The mediator shall conduct the mediation based on the principle of party self-determination. Self-determination is the act of coming to a voluntary, uncoerced decision in which each party makes free and informed choices as to process and outcome.

ii. The mediator is authorized to conduct separate or ex parte meetings and other communications with the parties and/or their representatives, before, during, and after any scheduled mediation conference. Such communications may be conducted via telephone, in writing, via email, online, in person or otherwise.

iii. The parties are encouraged to exchange all documents pertinent to the relief requested. The mediator may request the exchange of memoranda on issues, including the underlying interests and the history of the parties' negotiations. Information that a party wishes to keep confidential may be sent to the mediator, as necessary, in a separate communication with the mediator.

iv. The mediator does not have the authority to impose a settlement on the parties but will attempt to help them reach a satisfactory resolution of their dispute. Subject to the discretion of the mediator, the mediator may make oral or written recommendations for settlement to a party privately or, if the parties agree, to all parties jointly.

v. In the event that a complete settlement of all or some issues in dispute is not achieved within the scheduled mediation conference(s), the mediator may continue to communicate with the parties, for a period of time, in an ongoing effort to facilitate a complete settlement.

vi. The mediator is not a legal representative of any party and has no fiduciary duty to any party.

8. Responsibilities of the Parties

The parties shall ensure that appropriate representatives of each party, having authority to consummate a settlement, attend the mediation conference.

Prior to and during the scheduled mediation conference(s) the parties and their representatives shall, as appropriate to each party's circumstances, exercise their best efforts to prepare for and engage in a meaningful and productive mediation.

9. Privacy

Mediation conferences and related mediation communications are private proceedings. The parties and their representatives may attend mediation conferences. Other persons may attend only with the permission of the parties and with the consent of the mediator.

10. Confidentiality

Subject to applicable law or the parties' agreement, confidential information disclosed to a mediator by the parties or by other participants (witnesses) in the course of the mediation shall not be divulged by the mediator. The mediator shall maintain the confidentiality of all information obtained in the mediation, and all records, reports, or other documents received by a mediator while serving in that capacity shall be confidential.

The mediator shall not be compelled to divulge such records or to testify in regard to the mediation in any adversary proceeding or judicial forum.

The parties shall maintain the confidentiality of the mediation and shall not rely on, or introduce as evidence in any arbitral, judicial, or other proceeding the following, unless agreed to by the parties or required by applicable law:

a. Views expressed or suggestions made by a party or other participant with respect to a possible settlement of the dispute;

b. Admissions made by a party or other participant in the course of the mediation proceedings;

c. Proposals made or views expressed by the mediator; or

d. The fact that a party had or had not indicated willingness to accept a proposal for settlement made by the mediator.

11. No Stenographic Record

There shall be no stenographic record of the mediation process.

12. Termination of Mediation

The mediation shall be terminated:

a. By the execution of a settlement agreement by the parties; or

b. By a written or verbal declaration of the mediator to the effect that further efforts at mediation would not contribute to a resolution of the parties' dispute; or

c. By a written or verbal declaration of all parties to the effect that the mediation proceedings are terminated; or

d. When there has been no communication between the mediator and any party or party's representative for 21 days following the conclusion of the mediation conference.

13. Exclusion of Liability

Neither the ICDR nor any mediator is a necessary party in judicial proceedings relating to the mediation. Neither the ICDR nor any mediator shall be liable to any party for any error, act or omission in connection with any mediation conducted under these Rules.

14. Interpretation and Application of Rules

The mediator shall interpret and apply these Rules insofar as they relate to the mediator's duties and responsibilities. All other Rules shall be interpreted and applied by the ICDR.

15. Deposits

Unless otherwise directed by the mediator, the ICDR will require the parties to deposit in advance of the mediation conference such sums of money as it, in consultation with the mediator, deems necessary to cover the costs and expenses of the mediation and shall render an accounting to the parties and return any unexpended balance at the conclusion of the mediation.

16. Expenses

All expenses of the mediation, including required traveling and other expenses or charges of the mediator, shall be borne equally by the parties unless they agree otherwise. The expenses of participants for either side shall be paid by the party requesting the attendance of such participants.

17. Cost of the Mediation

There is no filing fee to initiate a mediation or a fee to request the ICDR to invite parties to mediate.

The cost of mediation is based on the hourly mediation rate published on the mediator's ICDR profile. This rate covers both mediator compensation and an allocated portion for the ICDR's services. There is a four-hour minimum charge for a mediation conference. Expenses referenced in Section M-16 may also apply.

If a matter submitted for mediation is withdrawn or cancelled or results in a settlement after the agreement to mediate is filed but prior to the mediation conference the cost is $250 plus any mediator time and charges incurred.

The parties will be billed equally for all costs unless they agree otherwise.

If you have questions about mediation costs or services visit our website at www.icdr.org or contact us at + 1 212.484.4181.

18. Language

If the parties have not agreed otherwise, the language(s) of the mediation shall be that of the documents containing the mediation agreement.

Conference Room Rental

The costs described above do not include the use of ICDR conference rooms. Conference rooms are available on a rental basis. Please contact your local ICDR office for availability and rates.

International Arbitration Rules

Article 1

a. Where parties have agreed in writing to arbitrate disputes under these International Arbitration Rules or have provided for arbitration of an international dispute by the International Centre for Dispute Resolution or the American Arbitration Association without designating particular Rules, the arbitration shall take place in accordance with these Rules, as in effect at the date of commencement of the arbitration, subject to whatever modifications the parties may adopt in writing.

b. These Rules govern the arbitration, except that, where any such rule is in conflict with any provision of the law applicable to the arbitration from which the parties cannot derogate, that provision shall prevail.

c. These Rules specify the duties and responsibilities of the administrator, the International Centre for Dispute Resolution, a division of the American Arbitration Association. The administrator may provide services through its Centre, located in New York, or through the facilities of arbitral institutions with which it has agreements of cooperation.

Commencing the Arbitration
Notice of Arbitration and Statement of Claim

Article 2

1. The party initiating arbitration ("claimant") shall give written notice of arbitration to the administrator and at the same time to the party against whom a claim is being made ("respondent").

2. Arbitral proceedings shall be deemed to commence on the date on which the administrator receives the notice of arbitration.

3. The notice of arbitration shall contain a statement of claim including the following:

   (a) a demand that the dispute be referred to arbitration;

   (b) the names, addresses and telephone numbers of the parties;

   (c) a reference to the arbitration clause or agreement that is invoked;

(d) a reference to any contract out of or in relation to which the dispute arises;

(e) a description of the claim and an indication of the facts supporting it;

(f) the relief or remedy sought and the amount claimed; and

(g) may include proposals as to the means of designating and the number of arbitrators, the place of arbitration and the language(s) of the arbitration.

4. Upon receipt of the notice of arbitration, the administrator shall communicate with all parties with respect to the arbitration and shall acknowledge the commencement of the arbitration.

Statement of Defense and Counterclaim

Article 3

1. Within 30 days after the commencement of the arbitration, a respondent shall submit a written statement of defense, responding to the issues raised in the notice of arbitration, to the claimant and any other parties, and to the administrator.

2. At the time a respondent submits its statement of defense, a respondent may make counterclaims or assert setoffs as to any claim covered by the agreement to arbitrate, as to which the claimant shall within 30 days submit a written statement of defense to the respondent and any other parties and to the administrator.

3. A respondent shall respond to the administrator, the claimant and other parties within 30 days after the commencement of the arbitration as to any proposals the claimant may have made as to the number of arbitrators, the place of the arbitration or the language(s) of the arbitration, except to the extent that the parties have previously agreed as to these matters.

4. The arbitral tribunal, or the administrator if the arbitral tribunal has not yet been formed, may extend any of the time limits established in this article if it considers such an extension justified.

Amendments to Claims

Article 4

During the arbitral proceedings, any party may amend or supplement its claim, counterclaim or defense, unless the tribunal considers it inappropriate to allow such amendment or supplement because of the party's delay in making it, prejudice to the other parties or any other circumstances. A party may not amend or supplement a claim or counterclaim if the amendment or supplement would fall outside the scope of the agreement to arbitrate.

THE TRIBUNAL

Number of Arbitrators

Article 5

If the parties have not agreed on the number of arbitrators, one arbitrator shall be appointed unless the administrator determines in its discretion that three arbitrators are appropriate because of the large size, complexity or other circumstances of the case.

Appointment of Arbitrators

Article 6

1. The parties may mutually agree upon any procedure for appointing arbitrators and shall inform the administrator as to such procedure.

2. The parties may mutually designate arbitrators, with or without the assistance of the administrator. When such designations are made, the parties shall notify the administrator so that notice of the appointment can be communicated to the arbitrators, together with a copy of these Rules.

3. If within 45 days after the commencement of the arbitration, all of the parties have not mutually agreed on a procedure for appointing the arbitrator(s) or have not mutually agreed on the designation of the arbitrator(s), the administrator shall, at the written request of any party, appoint the arbitrator(s) and designate the presiding arbitrator. If all of the parties have mutually agreed upon a procedure for

457

appointing the arbitrator(s), but all appointments have not been made within the time limits provided in that procedure, the administrator shall, at the written request of any party, perform all functions provided for in that procedure that remain to be performed.

4. In making such appointments, the administrator, after inviting consultation with the parties, shall endeavor to select suitable arbitrators. At the request of any party or on its own initiative, the administrator may appoint nationals of a country other than that of any of the parties.

5. Unless the parties have agreed otherwise no later than 45 days after the commencement of the arbitration, if the notice of arbitration names two or more claimants or two or more respondents, the administrator shall appoint all the arbitrators.

Impartiality and Independence of Arbitrators

Article 7

1. Arbitrators acting under these Rules shall be impartial and independent. Prior to accepting appointment, a prospective arbitrator shall disclose to the administrator any circumstance likely to give rise to justifiable doubts as to the arbitrator's impartiality or independence. If, at any stage during the arbitration, new circumstances arise that may give rise to such doubts, an arbitrator shall promptly disclose such circumstances to the parties and to the administrator. Upon receipt of such information from an arbitrator or a party, the administrator shall communicate it to the other parties and to the tribunal.

2. No party or anyone acting on its behalf shall have any ex parte communication relating to the case with any arbitrator, or with any candidate for appointment as party-appointed arbitrator except to advise the candidate of the general nature of the controversy and of the anticipated proceedings and to discuss the candidate's qualifications, availability or independence in relation to the parties, or to discuss the suitability of candidates for selection as a third arbitrator where the parties or party designated arbitrators are to participate in that selection. No party or anyone acting on its behalf shall have any ex parte communication relating to the case with any candidate for presiding arbitrator.

Challenge of Arbitrators

Article 8

1. A party may challenge any arbitrator whenever circumstances exist that give rise to justifiable doubts as to the arbitrator's impartiality or independence. A party wishing to challenge an arbitrator shall send notice of the challenge to the administrator within 15 days after being notified of the appointment of the arbitrator or within 15 days after the circumstances giving rise to the challenge become known to that party.

2. The challenge shall state in writing the reasons for the challenge.

3. Upon receipt of such a challenge, the administrator shall notify the other parties of the challenge. When an arbitrator has been challenged by one party, the other party or parties may agree to the acceptance of the challenge and, if there is agreement, the arbitrator shall withdraw. The challenged arbitrator may also withdraw from office in the absence of such agreement. In neither case does withdrawal imply acceptance of the validity of the grounds for the challenge.

Article 9

If the other party or parties do not agree to the challenge or the challenged arbitrator does not withdraw, the administrator in its sole discretion shall make the decision on the challenge.

Replacement of an Arbitrator

Article 10

If an arbitrator withdraws after a challenge, or the administrator sustains the challenge, or the administrator determines that there are sufficient reasons to accept the resignation of an arbitrator, or an arbitrator dies, a substitute arbitrator shall be appointed pursuant to the provisions of Article 6, unless the parties otherwise agree.

Article 11

1. If an arbitrator on a three-person tribunal fails to participate in the arbitration for reasons other than those identified in Article 10, the two other arbitrators shall have the power in their sole discretion to continue the arbitration and to make any decision, ruling or award,

notwithstanding the failure of the third arbitrator to participate. In determining whether to continue the arbitration or to render any decision, ruling or award without the participation of an arbitrator, the two other arbitrators shall take into account the stage of the arbitration, the reason, if any, expressed by the third arbitrator for such nonparticipation and such other matters as they consider appropriate in the circumstances of the case. In the event that the two other arbitrators determine not to continue the arbitration without the participation of the third arbitrator, the administrator on proof satisfactory to it shall declare the office vacant, and a substitute arbitrator shall be appointed pursuant to the provisions of Article 6, unless the parties otherwise agree.

2. If a substitute arbitrator is appointed under either Article 10 or Article 11, the tribunal shall determine at its sole discretion whether all or part of any prior hearings shall be repeated.

GENERAL CONDITIONS

Representation

Article 12

Any party may be represented in the arbitration. The names, addresses and telephone numbers of representatives shall be communicated in writing to the other parties and to the administrator. Once the tribunal has been established, the parties or their representatives may communicate in writing directly with the tribunal.

Place of Arbitration

Article 13

1. If the parties disagree as to the place of arbitration, the administrator may initially determine the place of arbitration, subject to the power of the tribunal to determine finally the place of arbitration within 60 days after its constitution. All such determinations shall be made having regard for the contentions of the parties and the circumstances of the arbitration.

2. The tribunal may hold conferences or hear witnesses or inspect property or documents at any place it deems appropriate. The parties

shall be given sufficient written notice to enable them to be present at any such proceedings.

Language

Article 14

If the parties have not agreed otherwise, the language(s) of the arbitration shall be that of the documents containing the arbitration agreement, subject to the power of the tribunal to determine otherwise based upon the contentions of the parties and the circumstances of the arbitration. The tribunal may order that any documents delivered in another language shall be accompanied by a translation into the language(s) of the arbitration.

Pleas as to Jurisdiction

Article 15

1. The tribunal shall have the power to rule on its own jurisdiction, including any objections with respect to the existence, scope or validity of the arbitration agreement.

2. The tribunal shall have the power to determine the existence or validity of a contract of which an arbitration clause forms a part. Such an arbitration clause shall be treated as an agreement independent of the other terms of the contract. A decision by the tribunal that the contract is null and void shall not for that reason alone render invalid the arbitration clause.

3. A party must object to the jurisdiction of the tribunal or to the arbitrability of a claim or counterclaim no later than the filing of the statement of defense, as provided in Article 3, to the claim or counterclaim that gives rise to the objection. The tribunal may rule on such objections as a preliminary matter or as part of the final award.

Conduct of the Arbitration

Article 16

1. Subject to these Rules, the tribunal may conduct the arbitration in whatever manner it considers appropriate, provided that the parties

are treated with equality and that each party has the right to be heard and is given a fair opportunity to present its case.

2. The tribunal, exercising its discretion, shall conduct the proceedings with a view to expediting the resolution of the dispute. It may conduct a preparatory conference with the parties for the purpose of organizing, scheduling and agreeing to procedures to expedite the subsequent proceedings.

3. The tribunal may in its discretion direct the order of proof, bifurcate proceedings, exclude cumulative or irrelevant testimony or other evidence and direct the parties to focus their presentations on issues the decision of which could dispose of all or part of the case.

4. Documents or information supplied to the tribunal by one party shall at the same time be communicated by that party to the other party or parties.

Further Written Statements

Article 17

1. The tribunal may decide whether the parties shall present any written statements in addition to statements of claims and counterclaims and statements of defense, and it shall fix the periods of time for submitting any such statements.

2. The periods of time fixed by the tribunal for the communication of such written statements should not exceed 45 days. However, the tribunal may extend such time limits if it considers such an extension justified.

Notices

Article 18

1. Unless otherwise agreed by the parties or ordered by the tribunal, all notices, statements and written communications may be served on a party by air mail, air courier, facsimile transmission, telex, telegram or other written forms of electronic communication addressed to the party or its representative at its last known address or by personal service.

2. For the purpose of calculating a period of time under these Rules, such period shall begin to run on the day following the day when a

notice, statement or written communication is received. If the last day of such period is an official holiday at the place received, the period is extended until the first business day which follows. Official holidays occurring during the running of the period of time are included in calculating the period.

Evidence

Article 19

1. Each party shall have the burden of proving the facts relied on to support its claim or defense.
2. The tribunal may order a party to deliver to the tribunal and to the other parties a summary of the documents and other evidence which that party intends to present in support of its claim, counterclaim or defense.
3. At any time during the proceedings, the tribunal may order parties to produce other documents, exhibits or other evidence it deems necessary or appropriate.

Hearings

Article 20

1. The tribunal shall give the parties at least 30 days advance notice of the date, time and place of the initial oral hearing. The tribunal shall give reasonable notice of subsequent hearings.
2. At least 15 days before the hearings, each party shall give the tribunal and the other parties the names and addresses of any witnesses it intends to present, the subject of their testimony and the languages in which such witnesses will give their testimony.
3. At the request of the tribunal or pursuant to mutual agreement of the parties, the administrator shall make arrangements for the interpretation of oral testimony or for a record of the hearing.
4. Hearings are private unless the parties agree otherwise or the law provides to the contrary. The tribunal may require any witness or witnesses to retire during the testimony of other witnesses. The tribunal may determine the manner in which witnesses are examined.

5. Evidence of witnesses may also be presented in the form of written statements signed by them.

6. The tribunal shall determine the admissibility, relevance, materiality and weight of the evidence offered by any party. The tribunal shall take into account applicable principles of legal privilege, such as those involving the confidentiality of communications between a lawyer and client.

Interim Measures of Protection

Article 21

1. At the request of any party, the tribunal may take whatever interim measures it deems necessary, including injunctive relief and measures for the protection or conservation of property.

2. Such interim measures may take the form of an interim award, and the tribunal may require security for the costs of such measures.

3. A request for interim measures addressed by a party to a judicial authority shall not be deemed incompatible with the agreement to arbitrate or a waiver of the right to arbitrate.

4. The tribunal may in its discretion apportion costs associated with applications for interim relief in any interim award or in the final award.

Experts

Article 22

1. The tribunal may appoint one or more independent experts to report to it, in writing, on specific issues designated by the tribunal and communicated to the parties.

2. The parties shall provide such an expert with any relevant information or produce for inspection any relevant documents or goods that the expert may require. Any dispute between a party and the expert as to the relevance of the requested information or goods shall be referred to the tribunal for decision.

3. Upon receipt of an expert's report, the tribunal shall send a copy of the report to all parties and shall give the parties an opportunity to express, in writing, their opinion on the report. A party may examine any document on which the expert has relied in such a report.

4. At the request of any party, the tribunal shall give the parties an opportunity to question the expert at a hearing. At this hearing, parties may present expert witnesses to testify on the points at issue.

Default

Article 23

1. If a party fails to file a statement of defense within the time established by the tribunal without showing sufficient cause for such failure, as determined by the tribunal, the tribunal may proceed with the arbitration.

2. If a party, duly notified under these Rules, fails to appear at a hearing without showing sufficient cause for such failure, as determined by the tribunal, the tribunal may proceed with the arbitration.

3. If a party, duly invited to produce evidence or take any other steps in the proceedings, fails to do so within the time established by the tribunal without showing sufficient cause for such failure, as determined by the tribunal, the tribunal may make the award on the evidence before it.

Closure of Hearing

Article 24

1. After asking the parties if they have any further testimony or evidentiary submissions and upon receiving negative replies or if satisfied that the record is complete, the tribunal may declare the hearings closed.

2. The tribunal in its discretion, on its own motion or upon application of a party, may reopen the hearings at any time before the award is made.

Waiver of Rules

Article 25

A party who knows that any provision of the Rules or requirement under the Rules has not been complied with, but proceeds with the arbitration without promptly stating an objection in writing thereto, shall be deemed to have waived the right to object.

Awards, Decisions and Rulings

Article 26

1. When there is more than one arbitrator, any award, decision or ruling of the arbitral tribunal shall be made by a majority of the arbitrators. If any arbitrator fails to sign the award, it shall be accompanied by a statement of the reason for the absence of such signature.

2. When the parties or the tribunal so authorize, the presiding arbitrator may make decisions or rulings on questions of procedure, subject to revision by the tribunal.

Form and Effect of the Award

Article 27

1. Awards shall be made in writing, promptly by the tribunal, and shall be final and binding on the parties. The parties undertake to carry out any such award without delay.

2. The tribunal shall state the reasons upon which the award is based, unless the parties have agreed that no reasons need be given.

3. The award shall contain the date and the place where the award was made, which shall be the place designated pursuant to Article 13.

4. An award may be made public only with the consent of all parties or as required by law.

5. Copies of the award shall be communicated to the parties by the administrator.

6. If the arbitration law of the country where the award is made requires the award to be filed or registered, the tribunal shall comply with such requirement.

7. In addition to making a final award, the tribunal may make interim, interlocutory or partial orders and awards.

8. Unless otherwise agreed by the parties, the administrator may publish or otherwise make publicly available selected awards, decisions and rulings that have been edited to conceal the names of the parties and other identifying details or that have been made publicly available in the course of enforcement or otherwise.

Applicable Laws and Remedies

Article 28

1. The tribunal shall apply the substantive law(s) or rules of law designated by the parties as applicable to the dispute. Failing such a designation by the parties, the tribunal shall apply such law(s) or rules of law as it determines to be appropriate.

2. In arbitrations involving the application of contracts, the tribunal shall decide in accordance with the terms of the contract and shall take into account usages of the trade applicable to the contract.

3. The tribunal shall not decide as amiable *compositeur* or *ex aequo et bono* unless the parties have expressly authorized it to do so.

4. A monetary award shall be in the currency or currencies of the contract unless the tribunal considers another currency more appropriate, and the tribunal may award such pre-award and post-award interest, simple or compound, as it considers appropriate, taking into consideration the contract and applicable law.

5. Unless the parties agree otherwise, the parties expressly waive and forego any right to punitive, exemplary or similar damages unless a statute requires that compensatory damages be increased in a specified manner. This provision shall not apply to any award of arbitration costs to a party to compensate for dilatory or bad faith conduct in the arbitration.

Settlement or Other Reasons for Termination

Article 29

1. If the parties settle the dispute before an award is made, the tribunal shall terminate the arbitration and, if requested by all parties, may record the settlement in the form of an award on agreed terms. The tribunal is not obliged to give reasons for such an award.

2. If the continuation of the proceedings becomes unnecessary or impossible for any other reason, the tribunal shall inform the parties of its intention to terminate the proceedings. The tribunal shall thereafter issue an order terminating the arbitration, unless a party raises justifiable grounds for objection.

Interpretation or Correction of the Award

Article 30

1. Within 30 days after the receipt of an award, any party, with notice to the other parties, may request the tribunal to interpret the award or correct any clerical, typographical or computation errors or make an additional award as to claims presented but omitted from the award.

2. If the tribunal considers such a request justified, after considering the contentions of the parties, it shall comply with such a request within 30 days after the request.

Costs

Article 31

The tribunal shall fix the costs of arbitration in its award. The tribunal may apportion such costs among the parties if it determines that such apportionment is reasonable, taking into account the circumstances of the case.

Such costs may include:

(a) the fees and expenses of the arbitrators;

(b) the costs of assistance required by the tribunal, including its experts;

(c) the fees and expenses of the administrator;

(d) the reasonable costs for legal representation of a successful party; and

(e) any such costs incurred in connection with an application for interim or emergency relief pursuant to Article 21.

Compensation of Arbitrators

Article 32

Arbitrators shall be compensated based upon their amount of service, taking into account their stated rate of compensation and the size and complexity of the case. The administrator shall arrange an appropriate daily or hourly rate, based on such considerations, with the parties and with each of the arbitrators as soon as practicable after the commencement of the arbitration. If the parties fail to agree on the terms of compensation, the administrator shall establish an appropriate rate and communicate it in writing to the parties.

Deposit of Costs

Article 33

1. When a party files claims, the administrator may request the filing party to deposit appropriate amounts as an advance for the costs referred to in Article 31, paragraphs (a.), (b.) and (c.).

2. During the course of the arbitral proceedings, the tribunal may request supplementary deposits from the parties.

3. If the deposits requested are not paid in full within 30 days after the receipt of the request, the administrator shall so inform the parties, in order that one or the other of them may make the required payment. If such payments are not made, the tribunal may order the suspension or termination of the proceedings.

4. After the award has been made, the administrator shall render an accounting to the parties of the deposits received and return any unexpended balance to the parties.

Confidentiality

Article 34

Confidential information disclosed during the proceedings by the parties or by witnesses shall not be divulged by an arbitrator or by the administrator. Except as provided in Article 27, unless otherwise agreed by the parties, or required by applicable law, the members of the tribunal and the administrator shall keep confidential all matters relating to the arbitration or the award.

Exclusion of Liability

Article 35

The members of the tribunal and the administrator shall not be liable to any party for any act or omission in connection with any arbitration conducted under these Rules, except that they may be liable for the consequences of conscious and deliberate wrongdoing.

Interpretation of Rules

Article 36

The tribunal shall interpret and apply these Rules insofar as they relate to its powers and duties. The administrator shall interpret and apply all other Rules.

Emergency Measures of Protection

Article 37

1. Unless the parties agree otherwise, the provisions of this Article 37 shall apply to arbitrations conducted under arbitration clauses or agreements entered on or after May 1, 2006.

2. A party in need of emergency relief prior to the constitution of the tribunal shall notify the administrator and all other parties in writing of the nature of the relief sought and the reasons why such relief is required on an emergency basis. The application shall also set forth the reasons why the party is entitled to such relief. Such notice may be given by e-mail, facsimile transmission or other reliable means, but must include a statement certifying that all other parties have been notified or an explanation of the steps taken in good faith to notify other parties.

3. Within one business day of receipt of notice as provided in paragraph 2, the administrator shall appoint a single emergency arbitrator from a special panel of emergency arbitrators designated to rule on emergency applications. Prior to accepting appointment, a prospective emergency arbitrator shall disclose to the administrator any circumstance likely to give rise to justifiable doubts to the arbitrator's impartiality or independence. Any challenge to the appointment of the emergency arbitrator must be made within one business day of the communication by the administrator to the parties of the appointment of the emergency arbitrator and the circumstances disclosed.

4. The emergency arbitrator shall as soon as possible, but in any event within two business days of appointment, establish a schedule for

consideration of the application for emergency relief. Such schedule shall provide a reasonable opportunity to all parties to be heard, but may provide for proceedings by telephone conference or on written submissions as alternatives to a formal hearing. The emergency arbitrator shall have the authority vested in the tribunal under Article 15, including the authority to rule on her/his own jurisdiction, and shall resolve any disputes over the applicability of this Article 37.

5. The emergency arbitrator shall have the power to order or award any interim or conservancy measure the emergency arbitrator deems necessary, including injunctive relief and measures for the protection or conservation of property. Any such measure may take the form of an interim award or of an order. The emergency arbitrator shall give reasons in either case. The emergency arbitrator may modify or vacate the interim award or order for good cause shown.

6. The emergency arbitrator shall have no further power to act after the tribunal is constituted. Once the tribunal has been constituted, the tribunal may reconsider, modify or vacate the interim award or order of emergency relief issued by the emergency arbitrator. The emergency arbitrator may not serve as a member of the tribunal unless the parties agree otherwise.

7. Any interim award or order of emergency relief may be conditioned on provision by the party seeking such relief of appropriate security.

8. A request for interim measures addressed by a party to a judicial authority shall not be deemed incompatible with this Article 37 or with the agreement to arbitrate or a waiver of the right to arbitrate. If the administrator is directed by a judicial authority to nominate a special master to consider and report on an application for emergency relief, the administrator shall proceed as in Paragraph 2 of this article and the references to the emergency arbitrator shall be read to mean the special master, except that the special master shall issue a report rather than an interim award.

9. The costs associated with applications for emergency relief shall initially be apportioned by the emergency arbitrator or special master, subject to the power of the tribunal to determine finally the apportionment of such costs.

ADMINISTRATIVE FEES

The administrative fees of the ICDR are based on the amount of the claim or counterclaim. Arbitrator compensation is not included in this schedule. Unless the parties agree otherwise, arbitrator compensation and administrative fees are subject to allocation by the arbitrator in the award.

Pilot Flexible Fee Schedule

Recognizing the continued fragility of the business environment and wishing to provide cost-saving alternatives to parties filing an arbitration case, the American Arbitration Association is offering an optional fee payment schedule that parties may choose instead of the Standard Fee Schedule. It is a pilot that will be available on cases filed through May 30, 2010,[1] and is intended to give parties added flexibility in both filing and in selection of arbitrators. Please call 1-800-778-7879 or your nearest office if you have questions.

A non-refundable Initial Filing Fee is payable in full by a filing party when a claim, counterclaim, or additional claim is filed. Upon receipt of the Demand for Arbitration, the AAA will promptly initiate the case and notify all parties as well as establish the due date for filing of an Answer, which may include a Counterclaim. In order to proceed with the further administration of the arbitration and appointment of the arbitrator(s), the appropriate, non-refundable Proceed Fee outlined below must be paid. If a Proceed Fee is not submitted within ninety (90) days of the filing of the Claimant's Demand for Arbitration, the Association will administratively close the file and notify all parties. *No refunds or refund schedule will apply to the Filing or Proceed Fees once received.*

Savings for Mutual Arbitrator Appointment by Parties: Proceed Fees may be reduced by fifty (50) percent where parties mutually select and appoint their arbitrator(s) without the AAA providing a list of arbitrators and an appointment process. Parties must provide the Case Manager with the appropriate stipulations and information pertaining to arbitrator(s) that have been mutually selected and have accepted their appointment(s). Forms for confirmation of arbitrators mutually selected and appointed by the parties are available through the Case Manager or AAA regional office.

---

[1] The Pilot Flexible Fee Schedule is subject to change or cancellation at any time prior to the date of May 30, 2010.

The Flexible Fee Schedule below also may be utilized for the filing of counterclaims. However, as with the Claimant's claim, the counterclaim will not be presented to the arbitrator until the Proceed Fee is paid.

A Final Fee will be incurred for all claims and/or counterclaims that proceed to their first hearing. This fee will be payable in advance when the first hearing is scheduled, but will be refunded at the conclusion of the case if no hearings have occurred. However, if the Association is not notified of a cancellation at least 24 hours before the time of the scheduled hearing, the Final Fee will remain due and will not be refunded.

All fees will be billed in accordance with the following schedule:

Amount of Claim	Initial Filing Fee	Proceed Fee	Final Fee
Above $0 to $10,000	$300	$550*	$200
Above $10,000 to $75,000	$500	$600*	$300
Above $75,000 to $150,000	$500	$1,500*	$750
Above $150,000 to $300,000	$500	$2,525*	$1,250
Above $300,000 to $500,000	$1,000	$3,750*	$1,750
Above $500,000 $1,000,000	$1,000	$5,600*	$2,500
Above $1,000,000 to $5,000,000	$1,000	$7,800*	$3,250
Above $5,000,000 to $10,000,000	$2,000	$9,000*	$4,000
Above $10,000,000	$2,500	$11,500* plus .01% of claim amount over $10,000,000 up to $65,000	$6,000
Non-Monetary**	$1,000	$2,750*	$1,250
Consent Award***			

* Where an arbitrator has been pre-selected and appointed by the parties, the Proceed Fee will be reduced by fifty percent (50%).

** This fee is applicable only when a claim or counterclaim is not for a monetary amount. Where a monetary claim amount is not known, parties will be required to state a range of claims or be subject to the highest possible filing fee (see fee range for claims above $10,000,000.00).

*** The AAA may assist the parties with the appointment of an arbitrator for the sole purpose of having their Consent Award signed. For more information, please contact your local AAA office, case management center, or our Customer Service desk at 1-800-778-7879.

All fees are subject to increase if the amount of a claim or counterclaim is modified after the initial filing date. Fees are subject to decrease if the amount of a claim or counterclaim is modified before the first hearing.

The minimum fees for any case having three or more arbitrators are $1,000 for the Initial Filing Fee; $3,750 for the Proceed Fee; and $1,750 for the Final Fee.

Under the Flexible Fee Schedule, a party's obligation to pay the Proceed Fee shall remain in effect regardless of any agreement of the parties to stay, postpone or otherwise modify the arbitration proceedings. Parties that, through mutual agreement, have held their case in abeyance for one year will be assessed an annual abeyance fee of $300. If a party refuses to pay the assessed fee, the other party or parties may pay the entire fee on behalf of all parties, otherwise the matter will be closed.

Note: The date of receipt by the AAA of the demand/notice for arbitration will be used to calculate the ninety(90)-day time limit for payment of the Proceed Fee.

Standard Fee Schedule

An initial filing fee is payable in full by a filing party when a claim, counterclaim, or additional claim is filed. A case service fee will be incurred for all cases that proceed to their first hearing. This fee will be payable in advance at the time that the first hearing is scheduled. This fee will be refunded at the conclusion of the case if no hearings have occurred.

However, if the administrator is not notified at least 24 hours before the time of the scheduled hearing, the case service fee will remain due and will not be refunded.

These fees will be billed in accordance with the following schedule:

Amount of Claim	Initial Filing Fee	Case Service Fee
Above $0 to $10,000	$750	$200
Above $10,000 to $75,000	$950	$300
Above $75,000 to $150,000	$1,800	$750
Above $150,000 to $300,000	$2,750	$1,250
Above $300,000 to $500,000	$4,250	$1,750
Above $500,000 to $1,000,000	$6,000	$2,500
Above $1,000,000 to $5,000,000	$8,000	$3,250
Above $5,000,000 to $10,000,000	$10,000	$4,000
Above $10,000,000	Base fee of $ 12,500 plus .01% of the amount of claim above $ 10 million.	$6000
Nonmonetary Claims*	$3,250	$1,250
	Filing fees capped at $65,000	

Fees are subject to increase if the amount of a claim or counterclaim is modified after the initial filing date. Fees are subject to decrease if the amount of a claim or counterclaim is modified before the first hearing.

The minimum fees for any case having three or more arbitrators are $2,750 for the filing fee, plus a $1,250 case service fee.

Parties on cases filed under either the Pilot Flexible Fee Schedule or the Standard Fee Schedule that are held in abeyance for one year by agreement, will be assessed an annual abeyance fee of $300. If a party refuses to pay the assessed fee, the other party or parties may pay the entire fee on behalf of all parties, otherwise the matter will be closed.

Refund Schedule

The ICDR offers a refund schedule on filing fees connected with the Standard Fee Schedule. For cases with claims up to $75,000, a minimum filing fee of $300 will not be refunded. For all other cases, a minimum fee of $500 will not be refunded. Subject to the minimum fee requirements, refunds will be calculated as follows:

---

* *This fee is applicable only when a claim or counterclaim is not for a monetary amount. Where a monetary claim amount is not known, parties will be required to state a range of claims or be subject to the highest possible filing fee.*

- 100% of the filing fee, above the minimum fee, will be refunded if the case is settled or withdrawn within five calendar days of filing.
- 50% of the filing fee will be refunded if the case is settled or withdrawn between six and 30 calendar days of filing.
- 25% of the filing fee will be refunded if the case is settled or withdrawn between 31 and 60 calendar days of filing. No refund will be made once an arbitrator has been appointed (this includes one arbitrator on a three-arbitrator panel). No refunds will be granted on awarded cases.

Note: The date of receipt of the demand for arbitration with the ICDR will be used to calculate refunds of filing fees for both claims and counterclaims.

Suspension for Nonpayment

If arbitrator compensation or administrative charges have not been paid in full, the administrator may so inform the parties in order that one of them may advance the required payment. If such payments are not made, the tribunal may order the suspension or termination of the proceedings. If no arbitrator has yet been appointed, the ICDR may suspend the proceedings.

Hearing Room Rental

The fees described above do not cover the cost of hearing rooms, which are available on a rental basis. Check with the ICDR for availability and rates.

APPENDIX 36
UNCITRAL ARBITRATION RULES

SECTION I. INTRODUCTORY RULES
Scope of Application

Article 1

1. Where the parties to a contract have agreed in writing that disputes in relation to that contract shall be referred to arbitration under the UNCITRAL Arbitration Rules, then such disputes shall be settled in accordance with these Rules subject to such modification as the parties may agree in writing.

2. These Rules shall govern the arbitration except that where any of these Rules is in conflict with a provision of the law applicable to the arbitration form which the parties cannot derogate, that provision shall prevail.

Notice, Calculation of Periods of Time

Article 2

1. For the purposes of these Rules, any notice, including a notification, communication or proposal, is deemed to have been received if it is physically delivered to the addressee or if it is delivered at his habitual residence, place of business or mailing address, or, if none of these can be found after making reasonable inquiry, then at the addressee's last known residence or place of business. Notice shall be deemed to have been received on the day it is so delivered.

2. For the purposes of calculating a period of time under these Rules, such period shall begin to run on the day following the day when a notice, notification, communication or proposal is received. If the last day of such period is an official holiday or a non-business day at the residence or place of business of the addressee, the period is extended until the first business day which follows. Official holidays or non-business days occurring during the running of the period of time are included in calculating the period.

Notice of Arbitration

Article 3

1. The party initiating recourse to arbitration (hereinafter called the "claimant") shall give to the other party (hereinafter called the "respondent") a notice of arbitration.

2. Arbitral proceedings shall be deemed to commence on the date on which the notice of arbitration is received by the respondent.

3. The notice of arbitration shall include the following:

    (a) A demand that the dispute be referred to arbitration;

    (b) The names and addresses of the parties;

    (c) A reference to the arbitration clause or the separate arbitration agreement that is invoked;

    (d) A reference to the contract out of or in relation to which the dispute arises;

    (e) The general nature of the claim and an indication of the amount involved, if any;

    (f) The relief or remedy sought;

    (g) A proposal as to the number of arbitrators (i.e. one or three). if the parties have not previously agreed thereon.

4. The notice of arbitration may also include:

    (a) The proposal for the appointments of a sole arbitrator and an appointing authority referred to in article 6, paragraph 1;

    (b) The notification of the appointment of an arbitrator referred to in article 7;

    (c) The statement of claim referred to in article 18.

Representation and Assistance

Article 4

The parties may be represented or assisted by persons of their choice. The names and addresses of such persons must be communicated in writing to the other party; such communication must specify whether the appointment is being made for purposes of representation or assistance.

SECTION II. COMPOSITION OF THE ARBITRAL TRIBUNAL

Number of Arbitrators

Article 5

If the parties have not previously agreed on the number of arbitrators (i.e. one or three), and if within 15 days after the receipt by the respondent of the notice of arbitration the parties have not agreed that there shall be only one arbitrator, three arbitrators shall be appointed.

Appointment of Arbitrators (Articles 6 to 8)

Article 6

1. If a sole arbitrator is to be appointed, either party may propose to the other:

    (a) The names of one or more persons, one of whom would serve as the sole arbitrator; and

    (b) If no appointing authority has been agreed upon by the parties, the name or names of one or more institutions or persons, one of whom would serve as appointing authority.

2. If within 30 days after receipt by a party of a proposal made in accordance with paragraph 1 the parties have not reached agreement on the choice of a sole arbitrator, the sole arbitrator shall be appointed by the appointing authority agreed upon by the parties. If no appointing authority has been agreed upon by the parties, or if the appointing authority agreed upon refuses to act or fails to appoint the arbitrator within 60 days of the receipt of a party's request therefore, either party may request the Secretary-General of the Permanent Court of Arbitration at The Hague to designate and appointing authority.

3. The appointing authority shall, at the request of one of the parties, appoint the sole arbitrator as promptly as possible. In making the appointment the appointing authority shall use the following list-procedure, unless both parties agree that the list-procedure should not be used or unless the appointing authority determines in its discretion that the use of the list-procedure is not appropriate for the case:

    (a) At the request of one of the parties the appointing authority shall communicate to both parties an identical list containing at least three names;

   (b) Within 15 days after the receipt of this list, each party may return the list to the appointing authority after having deleted the name or names to which he objects and numbered the remaining names on the list in the order of his preference;

   (c) After the expiration of the above period of time the appointing authority shall appoint the sole arbitrator from among the names approved on the lists returned to it and in accordance with the order of preference indicated by the parties;

   (d) If for any reason the appointment cannot be made according to this procedure, the appointing authority may exercise its discretion in appointing the sole arbitrator.

4. In making the appointment, the appointing authority shall have regard to such considerations as are likely to secure the appointment of an independent and impartial arbitrator and shall take into account as well the advisability of appointing and arbitrator of a nationality other than the nationalities of the parties.

Article 7

1. If three arbitrators are to be appointed, each party shall appoint one arbitrator. The two arbitrators thus appointed shall choose the third arbitrator who will act as the presiding arbitrator of the tribunal.

2. If within 30 days after the receipt of a party's notification of the appointment of an arbitrator the other party has not notified the first party of the arbitrator he has appointed:

   (a) The first party may request the appointing authority previously designated by the parties to appoint the second arbitrator; or

   (b) If no such authority has been previously designated by the parties, or if the appointing authority previously designated refuses to act or fails to appoint the arbitrator within 30 days after receipt of a party's request therefor, the first party may request the Secretary-General of the Permanent Court of Arbitration at The Hague to designate the appointing authority. The first party may then request the appointing authority so designated to appoint the second arbitrator. In either case, the appointing authority may exercise its discretion in appointing the arbitrator.

3. If within 30 days after the appointment of the second arbitrator the two arbitrators have not agreed on the choice of the presiding

arbitrator, the presiding arbitrator shall be appointed by an appointing authority in the same way as a sole arbitrator would be appointed under article 6.

Article 8

1. When an appointing authority is requested to appoint and arbitrator pursuant to article 6 or article 7, the party which makes the request shall send to the appointing authority a copy of the notice of arbitration, a copy of the contract out of or in relation to which the dispute has arisen and a copy of the arbitration agreement if it is not contained in the contract. The appointing authority may require from either party such information as it deems necessary to fulfill its function.

2. Where the names of one or more persons are proposed for appointment as arbitrators, their full names, addresses and nationalities shall be indicated, together with a description of their qualifications.

Challenge of Arbitrators (Articles 9 to 12)

Article 9

A prospective arbitrator shall disclose to those who approach him in connection with his possible appointment any circumstances likely to give rise to justifiable doubts as to his impartiality or independence. An arbitrator, once appointed or chosen, shall disclose such circumstances to the parties unless they have already been informed by him of these circumstances.

Article 10

1. Any arbitrator may be challenged if circumstance exist that give rise to justifiable doubts as to the arbitrator's impartiality or independence.

2. A party may challenge the arbitrator appointed by him only for reasons of which he becomes aware after the appointment has been made.

Article 11

1. A party who intends to challenge an arbitrator shall send notice of his challenge within 15 days after the appointment of the challenged arbitrator has been notified to the challenging party or within 15 days after the circumstances mentioned in articles 9 and 10 became known to that party.

2. The challenge shall be notified to the other party, to the arbitrator who is challenged and to the other members of the arbitral tribunal. The notification shall be in writing and shall state the reasons for the challenge.

3. When an arbitrator has been challenged by one party, the other party may agree to the challenge. The arbitrator may also, after the challenge, withdraw from his office. In neither case does this imply acceptance of the validity of the grounds for the challenge. In both cease the procedure provided in article 6 or 7 shall be used in full for the appointment of the substitute arbitrator, even if during the process of appointing the challenged arbitrator a party had failed to exercise his right to appoint or to participate in the appointment.

Article 12

1. If the other party does not agree to the challenge and the challenged arbitrator does not withdraw, the decision on the challenge will be made:

    (a) When the initial appointment was made by an appointing authority, by that authority:

    (b) When the initial appointment was not made by an appointing authority but an appointing authority has been previously designated, by that authority;

    (c) In all other cases, by the appointing authority to be designated in accordance with the procedure for designating an appointing authority as provided for in article 6.

2. If the appointing authority sustains the challenge, a substitute arbitrator shall be appointed or chosen pursuant to the procedure applicable to the appointment or choice of an arbitrator as provided in articles 6 to 9 except that, when this procedure would call for the designation of an appointing authority, the appointment of the

arbitrator shall be made by the appointing authority which decided on the challenge.

Replacement of an Arbitrator

Article 13

1. In the event of the death or resignation of an arbitrator during the course of the arbitral proceedings, a substitute arbitrator shall be appointed or chosen pursuant to the procedure provided for in articles 6 to 9 that was applicable to the appointment or choice of the arbitrator being replaced.

2. In the event that an arbitrator fails to act or in the event of the *de jure* or *de facto* impossibility of his performing his functions, the procedure in respect of the challenge and replacement of an arbitrator as provided in the preceding articles shall apply.

Repetition of Hearings in the Event of the Replacement of an Arbitrator

Article 14

If under articles 11 to 13 the sole or presiding arbitrator is replaced, any hearings held previously shall be repeated; if any other arbitrator is replaced, such prior hearings may be repeated at the discretion of the arbitral tribunal.

SECTION III. ARBITRAL PROCEEDINGS

General Provisions

Article 15

1. Subject to these Rules, the arbitral tribunal may conduct the arbitration in such manner as it considers appropriate, provided that the parties are treated with equality and that at any stage of the proceedings each party is given a full opportunity of presenting his case.

2. If either party so requests at any stage of the proceedings, the arbitral tribunal shall hold hearings for the presentation of evidence by witnesses, including expert witnesses, or for oral argument. In the absence of such a request, the arbitral tribunal shall decide whether

to hold such hearings or whether the proceedings shall be conducted on the basis of documents and other materials.

3. All documents or information supplied to the arbitral tribunal by one party shall at the same time be communicated by that party to the other party.

Place of Arbitration

Article 16

1. Unless the parties have agreed upon the place where the arbitration is to be held, such place shall be determined by the arbitral tribunal, having regard to the circumstances of the arbitration.

2. The arbitral tribunal may determine the locale of the arbitration within the country agreed upon by the parties. It may hear witnesses and hold meetings for consultation among its members at any place it deems appropriate, having regard to the circumstances of the arbitration.

3. The arbitral tribunal may meet at anyplace it deems appropriate for the inspection of goods, other property or documents. The parties shall be given sufficient notice to enable them to be present at such inspection.

4. The award shall be made at the place of arbitration.

Language

Article 17

1. Subject to an agreement by the parties, the arbitral tribunal shall, promptly after its appointment, determine the language or languages to be used in the proceedings. This determination shall apply to the statements of claim, the statement of defence, and any further written statements and, if oral hearings take place, to the language or languages to be used in such hearings.

2. The arbitral tribunal may order that any documents annexed to the statement of claim or statement of defence, and any supplementary documents or exhibits submitted in the course of the proceedings, delivered in their original language, shall be accompanied by a translation into the language or languages agreed upon by the parties or determined by the arbitral tribunal.

Statement of Claim

Article 18

1. Unless the statement of claim was contained in the notice of arbitration, within a period of time to be determined by the arbitral tribunal, the claimant shall communicate his statement of claim in writing to the respondent and to each of the arbitrators. A copy of the contract, and of the arbitration agreement if not contained in the contract, shall be annexed thereto.

2. The statement of claim shall include the following particulars:

   (a) The names and addresses of the parties;

   (b) A statement of the facts supporting the claim;

   (c) The points at issue;

   (d) The relief or remedy sought.

   The claimant may annex to his statement of claim all documents he deems relevant or may add a reference to the documents or other evidence he will submit.

Statement of Defence

Article 19

1. Within a period of time to be determined by the arbitral tribunal, the respondent shall communicate his statement of defence in writing to the claimant and to each of the arbitrators.

2. The statement of defence shall reply to the particulars (b), (c) and (d) of the statement of claim (article 18, para. 2). The respondent may annex to his statement the documents on which he relies for his defence or may add a reference to the documents or other evidence he will submit.

3. In his statement of defence, or at a later stage in the arbitral proceedings if the arbitral tribunal decides that the delay was justified under the circumstances, the respondent may make a counter-claim arising out of the same contract or rely on a claim arising out of the same contract for the purpose of a set-off.

4. The provisions of article 18, paragraph 2, shall apply to a counter-claim and a claim relied on for the purpose of a set-off.

Amendments to the Claim or Defence

Article 20

During the course of the arbitral proceedings either party may amend or supplement his claim of defence unless the arbitral tribunal considers it inappropriate to allow such amendment having regard to the delay in making it or prejudice to the other party or any other circumstances. However, a claim may not be amended in such a manner that the amended claim falls outside the scope of the arbitration clause or separate arbitration agreement.

Pleas as to the Jurisdiction of the Arbitral Tribunal

Article 21

1. The arbitral tribunal shall have the power to rule on objections that it has no jurisdiction, including any objections with respect to the existence or validity of the arbitration clause or of the separate arbitration agreement.

2. The arbitral tribunal shall have the power to determine the existence or the validity of the contract of which an arbitration clause forms a part. For the purposes of article 21, and arbitration clause which forms part of a contract and which provides for arbitration under these Rules shall be treated as an agreement independent of the other terms of the contract. A decision by the arbitral tribunal that the contract is null and void shall not entail *ipso jure* the invalidity of the arbitration clause.

3. A plea that the arbitral tribunal does not have jurisdiction shall be raised not later than in the statement of defence or, with respect to a counter-claim, in the reply to the counter-claim.

4. In general, the arbitral tribunal should rule on a plea concerning its jurisdiction as a preliminary question. However, the arbitral tribunal may proceed with the arbitration and rule on such a plea in their final award.

Further Written Statements

Article 22

The arbitral tribunal shall decide which further written statements, in addition to the statement of claim and the statement of defence, shall be required from the parties or may be presented by them and shall fix the periods of time for communicating such statements.

Periods of Time

Article 23

The periods of time fixed by the arbitral tribunal for the communication of written statements (including the statement of claim and statement of defence) should not exceed 45 days. However, the arbitral tribunal may extend the time-limits if it concludes that an extension is justified.

Evidence and Hearings (Articles 24 and 25)

Article 24

1. Each party shall have the burden of proving the facts relied on to support his claim or defence.

2. The arbitral tribunal may, if it considers it appropriate, require a party to deliver to the tribunal and to the other party, within such a period of time as the arbitral tribunal shall decide, a summary of the documents and other evidence which that party intends to present in support of the facts in issue set out in his statement of claim or statement of defence.

3. At any time during the arbitral proceeding the arbitral tribunal may require the parties to produce documents, exhibits or other evidence within such period of time as the tribunal shall determine.

Article 25

1. In the event of an oral hearing, the arbitral tribunal shall give the parties adequate advance notice of the date, time and place thereof.

2. If witnesses are to be heard, at least 15 days before the hearing each party shall communicate to the arbitral tribunal and to the other party the names and addresses of the witnesses he intends to present, the subject upon and the languages in which such witnesses will give their testimony.

3. The arbitral tribunal shall make arrangements for the translation of oral statements made at a hearing and for a record of the hearing if either is deemed necessary by the tribunal under the circumstances of

the case, or if the parties have agreed thereto and have communicated such agreement to the tribunal at least 15 days before the hearing.

4. Hearings shall be held *in camera* unless the parties agree otherwise. The arbitral tribunal may require the retirement of any witness or witnesses during the testimony of other witnesses. The arbitral tribunal is free to determine the manner in which witnesses are examined.

5. Evidence of witnesses may also be presented in the form of written statements signed by them.

6. The arbitral tribunal shall determine the admissibility, relevance, materiality and weight of the evidence offered.

Interim Measures of Protection

Article 26

1. At the request of either party, the arbitral tribunal may take any interim measures it deems necessary in respect of the subject-matter of the dispute, including measures for the conservation of the goods forming the subject matter in dispute, such as ordering their deposit with a third person or the sale of perishable goods.

2. Such interim measures may be established in the form of an interim award. The arbitral tribunal shall be entitled to require security for the costs of such measures.

3. A request for interim measures addressed by any party to a judicial authority shall not be deemed incompatible with the agreement to arbitrate, or as a waiver of that agreement.

Experts

Article 27

1. The arbitral tribunal may appoint one or more experts to report to it, in writing, on specific issues to be determined by the tribunal. A copy of the expert's terms of reference, established by the arbitral tribunal, shall be communicated to the parties.

2. The parties shall give the expert any relevant information or produce for his inspection any relevant documents or goods that he may require of them. Any dispute between a party and such expert as to the relevance of the required information or production shall be referred to the arbitral tribunal for decision.

3. Upon receipt of the expert's report, the arbitral tribunal shall communicate a copy of the report to the parties who shall be given the opportunity to express, in writing, their opinion on the report. A party shall be entitled to examine any document on which the expert has relied in his report.

4. At the request of either party the expert, after delivery of the report, may be heard at a hearing where the parties shall have the opportunity to be present and to interrogate the expert. At this hearing either party may present expert witnesses in order to testify on the points at issue. The provisions of article 25 shall be applicable to such proceedings.

Default

Article 28

1. If, within the period of time fixed by the arbitral tribunal, the claimant has failed to communicate his claim without showing sufficient cause for such failure, the arbitral tribunal shall issue an order for the termination of the arbitral proceedings. If, within the period of time fixed by the arbitral tribunal, the respondent has failed to communicate his statement of defence without showing sufficient cause for such failures, the arbitral tribunal shall order that the proceedings continue.

2. If one of the parties, duly notified under these Rules, fails to appear at a hearing, without showing sufficient cause for such failure, the arbitral tribunal may proceed with the arbitration.

3. If one of the parties, duly invited to produce documentary evidence, fails to do so within the established period of time., without showing sufficient cause for such failure, the arbitral tribunal may make the award on the evidence before it.

Closure of Hearings

Article 29

1. The arbitral tribunal may inquire of the parties if they have any further proof to offer or witnesses to be heard or submissions to make and, if there are none, it may declare the hearings closed.

2. The arbitral tribunal may, if it considers it necessary owing to exceptional circumstances, decide, on its own motion or upon application of a party, to reopen the hearings at any time before the award is made.

Waiver of Rules

Article 30

A party who knows that any provision of, or requirement under, these Rules has not been complied with and yet proceeds with the arbitration without promptly stating his objection to such non-compliance, shall be deemed to have waived his right to object.

SECTION IV. THE AWARD

Decisions

Article 31

1. When there are three arbitrators, any award or other decision of the arbitral tribunal shall be made by a majority of the arbitrators.
2. In the case of questions of procedure, when there is no majority or when the arbitral tribunal so authorized, the presiding arbitrator may decide on his own, subject to revision, if any, by the arbitral tribunal.

Form and Effect of the Award

Article 32

1. In addition to making a final award, the arbitral tribunal shall be entitled to make interim, interlocutory, or partial awards.
2. The award shall be made in writing and shall be final and binding on the parties. The parties undertake to carry out the award without delay.
3. The arbitral tribunal shall state the reasons upon which the award is based, unless the parties have agreed that no reasons are to be given.
4. An award shall be signed by the arbitrator and it shall contain the date on which and the place where the award was made. Where there are three arbitrators and one of them fails to sign, the award shall state the reason for the absence of the signature.

5. The award may be made public only with the consent of both parties.

6. Copies of the award signed by the arbitrators shall be communicated to the parties by the arbitral tribunal.

7. If the arbitration law of the country where the award is made requires that the award be filed or registered by the arbitral tribunal, the tribunal shall comply with this requirement within the period of time required by law.

Applicable Law, *Amiable Compositeur*

Article 33

1. The arbitral tribunal shall apply the law designated by the parties as applicable to the substance of the dispute. Failing such designation by the parties, the arbitral tribunal shall apply the law determined by the conflict of laws rules which it considers applicable.

2. The arbitral tribunal shall decide as *amiable compositeur* or *ex aequo et bono* only if the parties have expressly authorized the arbitral tribunal to do so and if the law applicable to the arbitral procedure permits such arbitration.

3. In all cases, the arbitral tribunal shall decide in accordance with the terms of the contract and shall take into account the usages of the trade applicable to the transaction.

Settlement or Other Grounds for Termination

Article 34

1. If, before the award is made, the parties agree on a settlement of the dispute, the arbitral tribunal shall either issue an order for the termination of the arbitral proceedings or, if requested by both parties and accepted by the tribunal, record the settlement in the form of an arbitral award on agreed terms. The arbitral tribunal is not obliged to give reasons for such an award.

2. If, before the award is made, the continuation of the arbitral proceedings becomes unnecessary or impossible for any reason not mentioned in paragraph 1, the arbitral tribunal shall inform the parties of its intention to issue an order for the termination of the proceeding. The arbitral tribunal shall have the power to issue such an order unless a party raises justifiable grounds for objection.

3. Copies of the order for termination of the arbitral proceedings or of the arbitral award on agreed terms, signed by the arbitrators, shall be communicated by the arbitral tribunal to the parties. Where an arbitral award on agreed terms is made, the provisions of article 32, paragraphs 2 and 4 to 7, shall apply.

Interpretation of the Award

Article 35

1. Within 30 days after the receipt of the award, either party, with notice to the other party, may request that the arbitral tribunal give an interpretation of the award.

2. The interpretation shall be given in writing within 45 days after the receipt of the request. The interpretation shall form part of the award and the provisions of article 32, paragraphs 2 to 7, shall apply.

Correction of the Award

Article 36

1. Within 30 days after the receipt of the award, either party, with notice to the other party, may request the arbitral tribunal to correct in the award any errors in computation, any clerical or typographical errors, or any errors of similar nature. The arbitral tribunal may within 30 days after the communication of the award make such corrections on its own initiative.

2. Such corrections shall be in writing, and provisions of article 32, paragraphs 2 to 7, shall apply.

Additional Award

Article 37

1. Within 30 days after the receipt of the award, either party, with notice to the other party, may request the arbitral tribunal to make an additional award as to claims presented in the arbitral proceedings but omitted from the award.

2. If the arbitral tribunal considers the request for an additional award to be justified and considers that the omission can be rectified without any further hearings or evidence, it shall complete its award within 60 days after the receipt of the request.

3. When an additional award is made, the provisions of article 32, paragraphs 2 to 7, shall apply.

Costs (Articles 38 to 40)

Article 38

The arbitral tribunal shall fix the costs of arbitration in its award. The term "costs" includes only:

(a) The fees of the arbitral tribunal to be stated separately as to each arbitrator and to be fixed by the tribunal itself in accordance with article 39;

(b) The travel and other expenses incurred by the arbitrators;

(c) The costs of expert advice and of other assistance required by the arbitral tribunal;

(d) The travel and other expenses of witnesses to the extent such expenses are approved by the arbitral tribunal;

(e) The costs for legal representation and assistance of the successful party if such costs were claimed during the arbitral proceedings, and only to the extent that the arbitral tribunal determines that the amount of such costs is reasonable;

(f) Any fees and expenses of the appointing authority as well as the expenses of the Secretary-General of the Permanent Court of Arbitration at The Hague.

Article 39

1. The fees of the arbitral tribunal shall be reasonable in amount, taking into account the amount in dispute, the complexity of the subject matter, the time spent by the arbitrators and any other relevant circumstances of the case.

2. If an appointing authority has been agreed upon by the parties or designated by the Secretary-General of the Permanent Court of Arbitration at The Hague, and if that authority has issued a schedule of fees for arbitrators in international cases which it administers, the arbitral tribunal in fixing its fees shall take that schedule of fees into account to the extent that it considers appropriate in the circumstances of the case.

3. If such appointing authority has not issued a schedule of fees for arbitrators in international cases, any party may at any time request the appointing authority to furnish a statement setting forth the basis for establishing fees which is customarily followed in international cases in which the authority appoints arbitrators. If the appointing authority consents to provide such a statement, the arbitral tribunal in fixing its fees shall take such information into account to the extent that it considers appropriate in the circumstances of the case.

4. In cases referred to in paragraphs 2 and 3, when a party so requests and the appointing authority consents to perform the function, the arbitral tribunal shall fix its fees only after consultation with the appointing authority, which may make any comment it deems appropriate to the arbitral tribunal concerning the fees.

Article 40

1. Except as provided in paragraph 2, the costs of arbitration shall in principle be borne by the unsuccessful party. However, the arbitral tribunal may apportion each of such costs between the parties if it determines that apportionment is reasonable, taking into account the circumstances of the case.

2. With respect to the costs of legal representation and assistance referred to in article 38, paragraph (e), the arbitral tribunal, taking into account the circumstances of the case, shall be free to determine which party shall bear such costs or may apportion such costs between the parties if it determines that apportionment is reasonable.

3. When the arbitral tribunal issues an order for the termination of the arbitral proceedings or makes an award on agreed terms it shall fix the costs of arbitration referred to in article 38 and article 39, paragraph 1, in the text of that order or award.

4. No additional fees may be charged by an arbitral tribunal for interpretation or correction or completion of its award under articles 35 to 37.

Deposit of Costs

Article 41

1. The arbitral tribunal, on its establishment, may request each party to deposit an equal amount as an advance for the costs referred to in article 38, paragraphs (a), (b) and (c).

2. During the course of the arbitral proceedings the arbitral tribunal may request supplementary deposits form the parties.

3. If an appointing authority has been agreed upon by the parties or designated by the Secretary-General of the Permanent Court of Arbitration at The Hague, and when a party so requests and the appointing authority consents to perform the function, the arbitral tribunal shall fix the amounts of any deposits or supplementary deposits only after consultation with the appointing authority which may make any comments to the arbitral tribunal which it deems appropriate concerning the amount of such deposits and supplementary deposits.

4. If the required deposits are not paid in full within 30 days after the receipt of the request, the arbitral tribunal shall so inform the parties in order that one or another of them may make the required payment. If such payment is not made, the arbitral tribunal may order the suspension or termination of the arbitral proceedings.

5. After the award has been made, the arbitral tribunal shall render an accounting to the parties of the deposits received and return any unexpended balance to the parties.

APPENDIX 37
UNCITRAL NOTES ON ORGANIZING ARBITRAL PROCEEDINGS

INTRODUCTION

Purpose of the Notes

1. The purpose of the Notes is to assist arbitration practitioners by listing and briefly describing questions on which appropriately timed decisions on organizing arbitral proceedings may be useful. The text, prepared with a particular view to international arbitrations, may be used whether or not the arbitration is administered by an arbitral institution.

Non-binding character of the Notes

2. No legal requirement binding on the arbitrators or the parties is imposed by the Notes. The arbitral tribunal remains free to use the Notes as it sees fit and is not required to give reasons for disregarding them.

3. The Notes are not suitable to be used as arbitration rules, since they do not establish any obligation of the arbitral tribunal or the parties to act in a particular way. Accordingly, the use of the Notes cannot imply any modification of the arbitration rules that the parties may have agreed upon.

Discretion in conduct of proceedings and usefulness of timely decisions on organizing proceedings

4. Laws governing the arbitral procedure and arbitration rules that parties may agree upon typically allow the arbitral tribunal broad discretion and flexibility in the conduct of arbitral proceedings.[1] This is useful in that it enables the arbitral tribunal to take decisions on the organization of proceedings that take into account the circumstances of

---

[1] A prominent example of such rules are the UNCITRAL Arbitration Rules, which provide in article 15(1): "Subject to these Rules, the arbitral tribunal may conduct the arbitration in such manner as it considers appropriate, provided that the parties are treated with equality and that at any stage of the proceedings each party is given a full opportunity of presenting his case."

the case, the expectations of the parties and of the members of the arbitral tribunal, and the need for a just and cost-efficient resolution of the dispute.

5.   Such discretion may make it desirable for the arbitral tribunal to give the parties a timely indication as to the organization of the proceedings and the manner in which the tribunal intends to proceed. This is particularly desirable in international arbitrations, where the participants may be accustomed to differing styles of conducting arbitrations. Without such guidance, a party may find aspects of the proceedings unpredictable and difficult to prepare for. That may lead to misunderstandings, delays and increased costs.

Multi-party arbitration

6.   These Notes are intended for use not only in arbitrations with two parties but also in arbitrations with three or more parties. Use of the Notes in multi-party arbitration is referred to below in paragraphs 86-88 (item 18).

Process of making decisions on organizing arbitral proceedings

7.   Decisions by the arbitral tribunal on organizing arbitral proceedings may be taken with or without previous consultations with the parties. The method chosen depends on whether, in view of the type of the question to be decided, the arbitral tribunal considers that consultations are not necessary or that hearing the views of the parties would be beneficial for increasing the predictability of the proceedings or improving the procedural atmosphere.

8.   The consultations, whether they involve only the arbitrators or also the parties, can be held in one or more meetings, or can be carried out by correspondence or telecommunications such as telefax or conference telephone calls or other electronic means. Meetings may be held at the venue of arbitration or at some other appropriate location.

9.   In some arbitrations a special meeting may be devoted exclusively to such procedural consultations; alternatively, the consultations may be held in conjunction with a hearing on the substance of the dispute. Practices differ as to whether such special meetings should be held and how they should be organized. Special procedural meetings of the arbitrators and the parties separate from hearings are in practice referred to by expressions such as "preliminary meeting", "pre-hearing

conference", "preparatory conference", "pre-hearing review", or terms of similar meaning. The terms used partly depend on the stage of the proceedings at which the meeting is taking place.

List of matters for possible consideration in organizing arbitral proceedings

10. The Notes provide a list, followed by annotations, of matters on which the arbitral tribunal may wish to formulate decisions on organizing arbitral proceedings.

11. Given that procedural styles and practices in arbitration vary widely, that the purpose of the Notes is not to promote any practice as best practice, and that the Notes are designed for universal use, it is not attempted in the Notes to describe in detail different arbitral practices or express a preference for any of them.

12. The list, while not exhaustive, covers a broad range of situations that may arise in an arbitration. In many arbitrations, however, only a limited number of the matters mentioned in the list need to be considered. It also depends on the circumstances of the case at which stage or stages of the proceedings it would be useful to consider matters concerning the organization of the proceedings. Generally, in order not to create opportunities for unnecessary discussions and delay, it is advisable not to raise a matter prematurely, i.e. before it is clear that a decision is needed.

13. When the Notes are used, it should be borne in mind that the discretion of the arbitral tribunal in organizing the proceedings may be limited by arbitration rules, by other provisions agreed to by the parties and by the law applicable to the arbitral procedure. When an arbitration is administered by an arbitral institution, various matters discussed in the Notes may be covered by the rules and practices of that institution.

LIST OF MATTERS FOR POSSIBLE CONSIDERATION IN ORGANIZING ARBITRAL PROCEEDINGS

1. Set of arbitration rules: paras. 14 - 16

    If the parties have not agreed on a set of arbitration rules, would they wish to do so: paras. 14 - 16

2. Language of proceedings 17-20

    (a) Possible need for translation of documents, in full or in part 18

ANNOTATIONS

1. Set of arbitration rules

If the parties have not agreed on a set of arbitration rules, would they wish to do so

14. Sometimes parties who have not included in their arbitration agreement a stipulation that a set of arbitration rules will govern their arbitral proceedings might wish to do so after the arbitration has begun. If that occurs, the UNCITRAL Arbitration Rules may be used either without modification or with such modifications as the parties might wish to agree upon. In the alternative, the parties might wish to adopt the rules of an arbitral institution; in that case, it may be necessary to secure the agreement of that institution and to stipulate the terms under which

the arbitration could be carried out in accordance with the rules of that institution.

15. However, caution is advised as consideration of a set of arbitration rules might delay the proceedings or give rise to unnecessary controversy.

16. It should be noted that agreement on arbitration rules is not a necessity and that, if the parties do not agree on a set of arbitration rules, the arbitral tribunal has the power to continue the proceedings and determine how the case will be conducted.

2. Language of proceedings

17. Many rules and laws on arbitral procedure empower the arbitral tribunal to determine the language or languages to be used in the proceedings, if the parties have not reached an agreement thereon.

(a) Possible need for translation of documents, in full or in part

18. Some documents annexed to the statements of claim and defence or submitted later may not be in the language of the proceedings. Bearing in mind the needs of the proceedings and economy, it may be considered whether the arbitral tribunal should order that any of those documents or parts thereof should be accompanied by a translation into the language of the proceedings.

(b) Possible need for interpretation of oral presentations

19. If interpretation will be necessary during oral hearings, it is advisable to consider whether the interpretation will be simultaneous or consecutive and whether the arrangements should be the responsibility of a party or the arbitral tribunal. In an arbitration administered by an institution, interpretation as well as translation services are often arranged by the arbitral institution.

(c) Cost of translation and interpretation

20. In taking decisions about translation or interpretation, it is advisable to decide whether any or all of the costs are to be paid directly by a party or whether they will be paid out of the deposits and apportioned between the parties along with the other arbitration costs.

3. Place of arbitration

*(a) Determination of the place of arbitration, if not already
agreed upon by the parties*

21. Arbitration rules usually allow the parties to agree on the place of arbitration, subject to the requirement of some arbitral institutions that arbitrations under their rules be conducted at a particular place, usually the location of the institution. If the place has not been so agreed upon, the rules governing the arbitration typically provide that it is in the power of the arbitral tribunal or the institution administering the arbitration to determine the place. If the arbitral tribunal is to make that determination, it may wish to hear the views of the parties before doing so.

22. Various factual and legal factors influence the choice of the place of arbitration, and their relative importance varies from case to case. Among the more prominent factors are: (a) suitability of the law on arbitral procedure of the place of arbitration; (b) whether there is a multilateral or bilateral treaty on enforcement of arbitral awards between the State where the arbitration takes place and the State or States where the award may have to be enforced; (c) convenience of the parties and the arbitrators, including the travel distances; (d) availability and cost of support services needed; and (e) location of the subjectmatter in dispute and proximity of evidence.

(b) Possibility of meetings outside the place of arbitration

23. Many sets of arbitration rules and laws on arbitral procedure expressly allow the arbitral tribunal to hold meetings elsewhere than at the place of arbitration. For example, under the UNCITRAL Model Law on International Commercial Arbitration "the arbitral tribunal may, unless otherwise agreed by the parties, meet at any place it considers appropriate for consultation among its members, for hearing witnesses, experts or the parties, or for inspection of goods, other property or documents" (article 20(2)). The purpose of this discretion is to permit arbitral proceedings to be carried out in a manner that is most efficient and economical.

4. Administrative services that may be needed for the arbitral tribunal to carry out its functions

24. Various administrative services (e.g. hearing rooms or secretarial services) may need to be procured for the arbitral tribunal to be able to carry out its functions. When the arbitration is administered by an arbitral institution, the institution will usually provide all or a good part of the required administrative support to the arbitral tribunal. When an arbitration administered by an arbitral institution takes place away from the seat of the institution, the institution may be able to arrange for administrative services to be obtained from another source, often an arbitral institution; some arbitral institutions have entered into cooperation agreements with a view to providing mutual assistance in servicing arbitral proceedings.

25. When the case is not administered by an institution, or the involvement of the institution does not include providing administrative support, usually the administrative arrangements for the proceedings will be made by the arbitral tribunal or the presiding arbitrator; it may also be acceptable to leave some of the arrangements to the parties, or to one of the parties subject to agreement of the other party or parties. Even in such cases, a convenient source of administrative support might be found in arbitral institutions, which often offer their facilities to arbitrations not governed by the rules of the institution. Otherwise, some services could be procured from entities such as chambers of commerce, hotels or specialized firms providing secretarial or other support services.

26. Administrative services might be secured by engaging a secretary of the arbitral tribunal (also referred to as registrar, clerk, administrator or rapporteur), who carries out the tasks under the direction of the arbitral tribunal. Some arbitral institutions routinely assign such persons to the cases administered by them. In arbitrations not administered by an institution or where the arbitral institution does not appoint a secretary, some arbitrators frequently engage such persons, at least in certain types of cases, whereas many others normally conduct the proceedings without them.

27. To the extent the tasks of the secretary are purely organizational (e.g. obtaining meeting rooms and providing or coordinating secretarial services), this is usually not controversial. Differences in views, however, may arise if the tasks include legal research and other professional assistance to the arbitral tribunal (e.g. collecting case law or published commentaries on legal issues defined by the arbitral tribunal,

preparing summaries from case law and publications, and sometimes also preparing drafts of procedural decisions or drafts of certain parts of the award, in particular those concerning the facts of the case). Views or expectations may differ especially where a task of the secretary is similar to professional functions of the arbitrators. Such a role of the secretary is in the view of some commentators inappropriate or is appropriate only under certain conditions, such as that the parties agree thereto. However, it is typically recognized that it is important to ensure that the secretary does not perform any decision-making function of the arbitral tribunal.

5. Deposits in respect of costs

(a) Amount to be deposited

28. In an arbitration administered by an institution, the institution often sets, on the basis of an estimate of the costs of the proceedings, the amount to be deposited as an advance for the costs of the arbitration. In other cases it is customary for the arbitral tribunal to make such an estimate and request a deposit. The estimate typically includes travel and other expenses by the arbitrators, expenditures for administrative assistance required by the arbitral tribunal, costs of any expert advice required by the arbitral tribunal, and the fees for the arbitrators. Many arbitration rules have provisions on this matter, including on whether the deposit should be made by the two parties (or all parties in a multi-party case) or only by the claimant.

(b) Management of deposits

29. When the arbitration is administered by an institution, the institution's services may include managing and accounting for the deposited money. Where that is not the case, it might be useful to clarify matters such as the type and location of the account in which the money will be kept and how the deposits will be managed.

(c) Supplementary deposits

30. If during the course of proceedings it emerges that the costs will be higher than anticipated, supplementary deposits may be required (e.g. because the arbitral tribunal decides pursuant to the arbitration rules to appoint an expert).

6. Confidentiality of information relating to the arbitration; possible agreement thereon

31. It is widely viewed that confidentiality is one of the advantageous and helpful features of arbitration. Nevertheless, there is no uniform answer in national laws as to the extent to which the participants in an arbitration are under the duty to observe the confidentiality of information relating to the case. Moreover, parties that have agreed on arbitration rules or other provisions that do not expressly address the issue of confidentiality cannot assume that all jurisdictions would recognize an implied commitment to confidentiality. Furthermore, the participants in an arbitration might not have the same understanding as regards the extent of confidentiality that is expected. Therefore, the arbitral tribunal might wish to discuss that with the parties and, if considered appropriate, record any agreed principles on the duty of confidentiality.

32. An agreement on confidentiality might cover, for example, one or more of the following matters: the material or information that is to be kept confidential (e.g. pieces of evidence, written and oral arguments, the fact that the arbitration is taking place, identity of the arbitrators, content of the award); measures for maintaining confidentiality of such information and hearings; whether any special procedures should be employed for maintaining the confidentiality of information transmitted by electronic means (e.g. because communication equipment is shared by several users, or because electronic mail over public networks is considered not sufficiently protected against unauthorized access); circumstances in which confidential information may be disclosed in part or in whole (e.g. in the context of disclosures of information in the public domain, or if required by law or a regulatory body).

7. Routing of written communications among the parties and the arbitrators

33. To the extent the question how documents and other written communications should be routed among the parties and the arbitrators is not settled by the agreed rules, or, if an institution administers the case, by the practices of the institution, it is useful for the arbitral tribunal to clarify the question suitably early so as to avoid misunderstandings and delays.

34. Among various possible patterns of routing, one example is that a party transmits the appropriate number of copies to the arbitral tribunal, or to the arbitral institution, if one is involved, which then forwards them as appropriate. Another example is that a party is to send copies simultaneously to the arbitrators and the other party or parties. Documents and other written communications directed by the arbitral tribunal or the presiding arbitrator to one or more parties may also follow a determined pattern, such as through the arbitral institution or by direct transmission. For some communications, in particular those on organizational matters (e.g. dates for hearings), more direct routes of communication may be agreed, even if, for example, the arbitral institution acts as an intermediary for documents such as the statements of claim and defence, evidence or written arguments.

8. Telefax and other electronic means of sending documents

(a) Telefax

35. Telefax, which offers many advantages over traditional means of communication, is widely used in arbitral proceedings. Nevertheless, should it be thought that, because of the characteristics of the equipment used, it would be preferable not to rely only on a telefacsimile of a document, special arrangements may be considered, such as that a particular piece of written evidence should be mailed or otherwise physically delivered, or that certain telefax messages should be confirmed by mailing or otherwise delivering documents whose facsimile were transmitted by electronic means. When a document should not be sent by telefax, it may, however, be appropriate, in order to avoid an unnecessarily rigid procedure, for the arbitral tribunal to retain discretion to accept an advance copy of a document by telefax for the purposes of meeting a deadline, provided that the document itself is received within a reasonable time thereafter.

(b) Other electronic means (e.g. electronic mail and magnetic or optical disk)

36. It might be agreed that documents, or some of them, will be exchanged not only in paper-based form, but in addition also in an electronic form other than telefax (e.g. as electronic mail, or on a magnetic or optical disk), or only in electronic form. Since the use of electronic means depends on the aptitude of the persons involved and the

availability of equipment and computer programs, agreement is necessary for such means to be used. If both paper-based and electronic means are to be used, it is advisable to decide which one is controlling and, if there is a time-limit for submitting a document, which act constitutes submission.

37. When the exchange of documents in electronic form is planned, it is useful, in order to avoid technical difficulties, to agree on matters such as: data carriers (e.g. electronic mail or computer disks) and their technical characteristics; computer programs to be used in preparing the electronic records; instructions for transforming the electronic records into human-readable form; keeping of logs and backup records of communications sent and received; information in human-readable form that should accompany the disks (e.g. the names of the originator and recipient, computer program, titles of the electronic files and the back-up methods used); procedures when a message is lost or the communication system otherwise fails; and identification of persons who can be contacted if a problem occurs.

9. Arrangements for the exchange of written submissions

38. After the parties have initially stated their claims and defences, they may wish, or the arbitral tribunal might request them, to present further written submissions so as to prepare for the hearings or to provide the basis for a decision without hearings. In such submissions, the parties, for example, present or comment on allegations and evidence, cite or explain law, or make or react to proposals. In practice such submissions are referred to variously as, for example, statement, memorial, counter-memorial, brief, counter-brief, reply, réplique, duplique, rebuttal or rejoinder; the terminology is a matter of linguistic usage and the scope or sequence of the submission.

(a) Scheduling of written submissions

39. It is advisable that the arbitral tribunal set time-limits for written submissions. In enforcing the timelimits, the arbitral tribunal may wish, on the one hand, to make sure that the case is not unduly protracted and, on the other hand, to reserve a degree of discretion and allow late submissions if appropriate under the circumstances. In some cases the arbitral tribunal might prefer not to plan the written submissions in advance, thus leaving such matters, including time-limits, to be decided

in light of the developments in the proceedings. In other cases, the arbitral tribunal may wish to determine, when scheduling the first written submissions, the number of subsequent submissions.

40. Practices differ as to whether, after the hearings have been held, written submissions are still acceptable. While some arbitral tribunals consider post-hearing submissions unacceptable, others might request or allow them on a particular issue. Some arbitral tribunals follow the procedure according to which the parties are not requested to present written evidence and legal arguments to the arbitral tribunal before the hearings; in such a case, the arbitral tribunal may regard it as appropriate that written submissions be made after the hearings.

(b) Consecutive or simultaneous submissions

41. Written submissions on an issue may be made consecutively, i.e. the party who receives a submission is given a period of time to react with its counter-submission. Another possibility is to request each party to make the submission within the same time period to the arbitral tribunal or the institution administering the case; the received submissions are then forwarded simultaneously to the respective other party or parties. The approach used may depend on the type of issues to be commented upon and the time in which the views should be clarified. With consecutive submissions, it may take longer than with simultaneous ones to obtain views of the parties on a given issue. Consecutive submissions, however, allow the reacting party to comment on all points raised by the other party or parties, which simultaneous submissions do not; thus, simultaneous submissions might possibly necessitate further submissions.

10. Practical details concerning written submissions and evidence (e.g. method of submission, copies, numbering, references)

42. Depending on the volume and kind of documents to be handled, it might be considered whether practical arrangements on details such as the following would be helpful:

- Whether the submissions will be made as paper documents or by electronic means, or both (see paragraphs 35-37);
- The number of copies in which each document is to be submitted;

- A system for numbering documents and items of evidence, and a method for marking them, including by tabs;
- The form of references to documents (e.g. by the heading and the number assigned to the document or its date);
- Paragraph numbering in written submissions, in order to facilitate precise references to parts of a text;
- When translations are to be submitted as paper documents, whether the translations are to be contained in the same volume as the original texts or included in separate volumes.

11. Defining points at issue; order of deciding issues; defining relief or remedy sought

(a) Should a list of points at issue be prepared

43. In considering the parties' allegations and arguments, the arbitral tribunal may come to the conclusion that it would be useful for it or for the parties to prepare, for analytical purposes and for ease of discussion, a list of the points at issue, as opposed to those that are undisputed. If the arbitral tribunal determines that the advantages of working on the basis of such a list outweigh the disadvantages, it chooses the appropriate stage of the proceedings for preparing a list, bearing in mind also that subsequent developments in the proceedings may require a revision of the points at issue. Such an identification of points at issue might help to concentrate on the essential matters, to reduce the number of points at issue by agreement of the parties, and to select the best and most economical process for resolving the dispute. However, possible disadvantages of preparing such a list include delay, adverse effect on the flexibility of the proceedings, or unnecessary disagreements about whether the arbitral tribunal has decided all issues submitted to it or whether the award contains decisions on matters beyond the scope of the submission to arbitration. The terms of reference required under some arbitration rules, or in agreements of parties, may serve the same purpose as the above-described list of points at issue.

(b) In which order should the points at issue be decided

44. While it is often appropriate to deal with all the points at issue collectively, the arbitral tribunal might decide to take them up during the

proceedings in a particular order. The order may be due to a point being preliminary relative to another (e.g. a decision on the jurisdiction of the arbitral tribunal is preliminary to consideration of substantive issues, or the issue of responsibility for a breach of contract is preliminary to the issue of the resulting damages). A particular order may be decided also when the breach of various contracts is in dispute or when damages arising from various events are claimed.

45. If the arbitral tribunal has adopted a particular order of deciding points at issue, it might consider it appropriate to issue a decision on one of the points earlier than on the other ones. This might be done, for example, when a discrete part of a claim is ready for decision while the other parts still require extensive consideration, or when it is expected that after deciding certain issues the parties might be more inclined to settle the remaining ones. Such earlier decisions are referred to by expressions such as "partial", "interlocutory" or "interim" awards or decisions, depending on the type of issue dealt with and on whether the decision is final with respect to the issue it resolves. Questions that might be the subject of such decisions are, for example, jurisdiction of the arbitral tribunal, interim measures of protection, or the liability of a party.

(c) Is there a need to define more precisely the relief or remedy sought

46. If the arbitral tribunal considers that the relief or remedy sought is insufficiently definite, it may wish to explain to the parties the degree of definiteness with which their claims should be formulated. Such an explanation may be useful since criteria are not uniform as to how specific the claimant must be in formulating a relief or remedy.

12. Possible settlement negotiations and their effect on scheduling proceedings

47. Attitudes differ as to whether it is appropriate for the arbitral tribunal to bring up the possibility of settlement. Given the divergence of practices in this regard, the arbitral tribunal should only suggest settlement negotiations with caution. However, it may be opportune for the arbitral tribunal to schedule the proceedings in a way that might facilitate the continuation or initiation of settlement negotiations.

13. Documentary evidence

(a) Time-limits for submission of documentary evidence intended to be submitted by the parties;consequences of late submission

48. Often the written submissions of the parties contain sufficient information for the arbitral tribunal to fix the time-limit for submitting evidence. Otherwise, in order to set realistic time periods, the arbitral tribunal may wish to consult with the parties about the time that they would reasonably need.

49. The arbitral tribunal may wish to clarify that evidence submitted late will as a rule not be accepted. It may wish not to preclude itself from accepting a late submission of evidence if the party shows sufficient cause for the delay.

(b) Whether the arbitral tribunal intends to require a party to produce documentary evidence

50. Procedures and practices differ widely as to the conditions under which the arbitral tribunal may require a party to produce documents. Therefore, the arbitral tribunal might consider it useful, when the agreed arbitration rules do not provide specific conditions, to clarify to the parties the manner in which it intends to proceed.

51. The arbitral tribunal may wish to establish time-limits for the production of documents. The parties might be reminded that, if the requested party duly invited to produce documentary evidence fails to do so within the established period of time, without showing sufficient cause for such failure, the arbitral tribunal is free to draw its conclusions from the failure and may make the award on the evidence before it.

(c) Should assertions about the origin and receipt of documents and about the correctness of photocopies be assumed as accurate

52. It may be helpful for the arbitral tribunal to inform the parties that it intends to conduct the proceedings on the basis that, unless a party raises an objection to any of the following conclusions within a specified period of time: (a) a document is accepted as having originated from the source indicated in the document; (b) a copy of a dispatched communication (e.g. letter, telex, telefax or other electronic message) is accepted without further proof as having been received by the addressee; and (c) a copy is accepted as correct. A statement by the arbitral tribunal

to that effect can simplify the introduction of documentary evidence and discourage unfounded and dilatory objections, at a late stage of the proceedings, to the probative value of documents. It is advisable to provide that the time-limit for objections will not be enforced if the arbitral tribunal considers the delay justified.

(d) Are the parties willing to submit jointly a single set of documentary evidence

53. The parties may consider submitting jointly a single set of documentary evidence whose authenticity is not disputed. The purpose would be to avoid duplicate submissions and unnecessary discussions concerning the authenticity of documents, without prejudicing the position of the parties concerning the content of the documents. Additional documents may be inserted later if the parties agree. When a single set of documents would be too voluminous to be easily manageable, it might be practical to select a number of frequently used documents and establish a set of "working" documents. A convenient arrangement of documents in the set may be according to chronological order or subject-matter. It is useful to keep a table of contents of the documents, for example, by their short headings and dates, and to provide that the parties will refer to documents by those headings and dates.

(e) Should voluminous and complicated documentary evidence be presented through summaries, tabulations, charts, extracts or samples

54. When documentary evidence is voluminous and complicated, it may save time and costs if such evidence is presented by a report of a person competent in the relevant field (e.g. public accountant or consulting engineer). The report may present the information in the form of summaries, tabulations, charts, extracts or samples. Such presentation of evidence should be combined with arrangements that give the interested party the opportunity to review the underlying data and the methodology of preparing the report.

14. Physical evidence other than documents

55. In some arbitrations the arbitral tribunal is called upon to assess physical evidence other than documents, for example, by inspecting samples of goods, viewing a video recording or observing the functioning of a machine.

(a) What arrangements should be made if physical evidence will be submitted

56. If physical evidence will be submitted, the arbitral tribunal may wish to fix the time schedule for presenting the evidence, make arrangements for the other party or parties to have a suitable opportunity to prepare itself for the presentation of the evidence, and possibly take measures for safekeeping the items of evidence.

(b) What arrangements should be made if an on-site inspection is necessary

57. If an on-site inspection of property or goods will take place, the arbitral tribunal may consider matters such as timing, meeting places, other arrangements to provide the opportunity for all parties to be present, and the need to avoid communications between arbitrators and a party about points at issue without the presence of the other party or parties.

58. The site to be inspected is often under the control of one of the parties, which typically means that employees or representatives of that party will be present to give guidance and explanations. It should be borne in mind that statements of those representatives or employees made during an on-site inspection, as contrasted with statements those persons might make as witnesses in a hearing, should not be treated as evidence in the proceedings.

15. Witnesses

59. While laws and rules on arbitral procedure typically leave broad freedom concerning the manner of taking evidence of witnesses, practices on procedural points are varied. In order to facilitate the preparations of the parties for the hearings, the arbitral tribunal may consider it appropriate to clarify, in advance of the hearings, some or all of the following issues.

(a) Advance notice about a witness whom a party intends to present; written witnesses' statements

60. To the extent the applicable arbitration rules do not deal with the matter, the arbitral tribunal may wish to require that each party give advance notice to the arbitral tribunal and the other party or parties of

any witness it intends to present. As to the content of the notice, the following is an example of what might be required, in addition to the names and addresses of the witnesses: (a) the subject upon which the witnesses will testify; (b) the language in which the witnesses will testify; and (c) the nature of the relationship with any of the parties, qualifications and experience of the witnesses if and to the extent these are relevant to the dispute or the testimony, and how the witnesses learned about the facts on which they will testify. However, it may not be necessary to require such a notice, in particular if the thrust of the testimony can be clearly ascertained from the party's allegations.

61. Some practitioners favour the procedure according to which the party presenting witness evidence submits a signed witness's statement containing testimony itself. It should be noted, however, that such practice, which implies interviewing the witness by the party presenting the testimony, is not known in all parts of the world and, moreover, that some practitioners disapprove of it on the ground that such contacts between the party and the witness may compromise the credibility of the testimony and are therefore improper (see paragraph 67). Notwithstanding these reservations, signed witness's testimony has advantages in that it may expedite the proceedings by making it easier for the other party or parties to prepare for the hearings or for the parties to identify uncontested matters. However, those advantages might be outweighed by the time and expense involved in obtaining the written testimony.

62. If a signed witness's statement should be made under oath or similar affirmation of truthfulness, it may be necessary to clarify by whom the oath or affirmation should be administered and whether any formal authentication will be required by the arbitral tribunal.

(b) Manner of taking oral evidence of witnesses

(i) Order in which questions will be asked and the manner in which the hearing of witnesses will be conducted

63. To the extent that the applicable rules do not provide an answer, it may be useful for the arbitral tribunal to clarify how witnesses will be heard. One of the various possibilities is that a witness is first questioned by the arbitral tribunal, whereupon questions are asked by the parties, first by the party who called the witness. Another possibility is for the witness to be questioned by the party presenting

the witness and then by the other party or parties, while the arbitral tribunal might pose questions during the questioning or after the parties on points that in the tribunal's view have not been sufficiently clarified. Differences exist also as to the degree of control the arbitral tribunal exercises over the hearing of witnesses. For example, some arbitrators prefer to permit the parties to pose questions freely and directly to the witness, but may disallow a question if a party objects; other arbitrators tend to exercise more control and may disallow a question on their initiative or even require that questions from the parties be asked through the arbitral tribunal.

(ii) Whether oral testimony will be given under oath or affirmation and, if so, in what form an oath or affirmation should be made

64. Practices and laws differ as to whether or not oral testimony is to be given under oath or affirmation. In some legal systems, the arbitrators are empowered to put witnesses on oath, but it is usually in their discretion whether they want to do so. In other systems, oral testimony under oath is either unknown or may even be considered improper as only an official such as a judge or notary may have the authority to administer oaths.

(iii) May witnesses be in the hearing room when they are not testifying

65. Some arbitrators favour the procedure that, except if the circumstances suggest otherwise, the presence of a witness in the hearing room is limited to the time the witness is testifying; the purpose is to prevent the witness from being influenced by what is said in the hearing room, or to prevent that the presence of the witness would influence another witness. Other arbitrators consider that the presence of a witness during the testimony of other witnesses may be beneficial in that possible contradictions may be readily clarified or that their presence may act as a deterrent against untrue statements. Other possible approaches may be that witnesses are not present in the hearing room before their testimony, but stay in the room after they have testified, or that the arbitral tribunal decides the question for each witness individually depending on what the arbitral tribunal considers most appropriate. The arbitral tribunal may leave the procedure to be decided during the hearings, or may give guidance on the question in advance of the hearings.

(c) The order in which the witnesses will be called

66. When several witnesses are to be heard and longer testimony is expected, it is likely to reduce costs if the order in which they will be called is known in advance and their presence can be scheduled accordingly. Each party might be invited to suggest the order in which it intends to present the witnesses, while it would be up to the arbitral tribunal to approve the scheduling and to make departures from it.

(d) Interviewing witnesses prior to their appearance at a hearing

67. In some legal systems, parties or their representatives are permitted to interview witnesses, prior to their appearance at the hearing, as to such matters as their recollection of the relevant events, their experience, qualifications or relation with a participant in the proceedings. In those legal systems such contacts are usually not permitted once the witness's oral testimony has begun. In other systems such contacts with witnesses are considered improper. In order to avoid misunderstandings, the arbitral tribunal may consider it useful to clarify what kind of contacts a party is permitted to have with a witness in the preparations for the hearings.

(e) Hearing representatives of a party

68. According to some legal systems, certain persons affiliated with a party may only be heard as representatives of the party but not as witnesses. In such a case, it may be necessary to consider ground rules for determining which persons may not testify as witnesses (e.g. certain executives, employees or agents) and for hearing statements of those persons and for questioning them.

16. Experts and expert witnesses

69. Many arbitration rules and laws on arbitral procedure address the participation of experts in arbitral proceedings. A frequent solution is that the arbitral tribunal has the power to appoint an expert to report on issues determined by the tribunal; in addition, the parties may be permitted to present expert witnesses on points at issue. In other cases, it is for the parties to present expert testimony, and it is not expected that the arbitral tribunal will appoint an expert.

(a) Expert appointed by the arbitral tribunal

70. If the arbitral tribunal is empowered to appoint an expert, one possible approach is for the tribunal to proceed directly to selecting the expert. Another possibility is to consult the parties as to who should be the expert; this may be done, for example, without mentioning a candidate, by presenting to the parties a list of candidates, soliciting proposals from the parties, or by discussing with the parties the "profile" of the expert the arbitral tribunal intends to appoint, i.e. the qualifications, experience and abilities of the expert.

(i) The expert's terms of reference

71. The purpose of the expert's terms of reference is to indicate the questions on which the expert is to provide clarification, to avoid opinions on points that are not for the expert to assess and to commit the expert to a time schedule. While the discretion to appoint an expert normally includes the determination of the expert's terms of reference, the arbitral tribunal may decide to consult the parties before finalizing the terms. It might also be useful to determine details about how the expert will receive from the parties any relevant information or have access to any relevant documents, goods or other property, so as to enable the expert to prepare the report. In order to facilitate the evaluation of the expert's report, it is advisable to require the expert to include in the report information on the method used in arriving at the conclusions and the evidence and information used in preparing the report.

(ii) The opportunity of the parties to comment on the expert's report, including by presenting expert testimony

72. Arbitration rules that contain provisions on experts usually also have provisions on the right of a party to comment on the report of the expert appointed by the arbitral tribunal. If no such provisions apply or more specific procedures than those prescribed are deemed necessary, the arbitral tribunal may, in light of those provisions, consider it opportune to determine, for example, the time period for presenting written comments of the parties, or, if hearings are to be held for the purpose of hearing the expert, the procedures for interrogating the expert by the parties or for the participation of any expert witnesses presented by the parties.

(b) Expert opinion presented by a party (expert witness)

73. If a party presents an expert opinion, the arbitral tribunal might consider requiring, for example, that the opinion be in writing, that the expert should be available to answer questions at hearings, and that, if a party will present an expert witness at a hearing, advance notice must be given or that the written opinion must be presented in advance, as in the case of other witnesses (see paragraphs 60-62).

17. Hearings

(a) Decision whether to hold hearings

74. Laws on arbitral procedure and arbitration rules often have provisions as to the cases in which oral hearings must be held and as to when the arbitral tribunal has discretion to decide whether to hold hearings.

75. If it is up to the arbitral tribunal to decide whether to hold hearings, the decision is likely to be influenced by factors such as, on the one hand, that it is usually quicker and easier to clarify points at issue pursuant to a direct confrontation of arguments than on the basis of correspondence and, on the other hand, the travel and other cost of holding hearings, and that the need of finding acceptable dates for the hearings might delay the proceedings. The arbitral tribunal may wish to consult the parties on this matter.

(b) Whether one period of hearings should be held or separate periods of hearings

76. Attitudes vary as to whether hearings should be held in a single period of hearings or in separate periods, especially when more than a few days are needed to complete the hearings. According to some arbitrators, the entire hearings should normally be held in a single period, even if the hearings are to last for more than a week. Other arbitrators in such cases tend to schedule separate periods of hearings. In some cases issues to be decided are separated, and separate hearings set for those issues, with the aim that oral presentation on those issues will be completed within the allotted time. Among the advantages of one period of hearings are that it involves less travel costs, memory will not fade, and it is unlikely that people representing a party will change. On the other hand, the longer the hearings, the more difficult it may be to find early dates acceptable to all participants. Furthermore, separate periods

of hearings may be easier to schedule, the subsequent hearings may be tailored to the development of the case, and the period between the hearings leaves time for analysing the records and negotiations between the parties aimed at narrowing the points at issue by agreement.

(c) Setting dates for hearings

77. Typically, firm dates will be fixed for hearings. Exceptionally, the arbitral tribunal may initially wish to set only "target dates" as opposed to definitive dates. This may be done at a stage of the proceedings when not all information necessary to schedule hearings is yet available, with the understanding that the target dates will either be confirmed or rescheduled within a reasonably short period. Such provisional planning can be useful to participants who are generally not available on short notice.

(d) Whether there should be a limit on the aggregate amount of time each party will have for oral arguments and questioning witnesses

78. Some arbitrators consider it useful to limit the aggregate amount of time each party has for any of the following: (a) making oral statements; (b) questioning its witnesses; and (c) questioning the witnesses of the other party or parties. In general, the same aggregate amount of time is considered appropriate for each party, unless the arbitral tribunal considers that a different allocation is justified. Before deciding, the arbitral tribunal may wish to consult the parties as to how much time they think they will need.

79. Such planning of time, provided it is realistic, fair and subject to judiciously firm control by the arbitral tribunal, will make it easier for the parties to plan the presentation of the various items of evidence and arguments, reduce the likelihood of running out of time towards the end of the hearings and avoid that one party would unfairly use up a disproportionate amount of time.

(e) The order in which the parties will present their arguments and evidence

80. Arbitration rules typically give broad latitude to the arbitral tribunal to determine the order of presentations at the hearings. Within that latitude, practices differ, for example, as to whether opening or closing

statements are heard and their level of detail; the sequence in which the claimant and the respondent present their opening statements, arguments, witnesses and other evidence; and whether the respondent or the claimant has the last word. In view of such differences, or when no arbitration rules apply, it may foster efficiency of the proceedings if the arbitral tribunal clarifies to the parties, in advance of the hearings, the manner in which it will conduct the hearings, at least in broad lines.

(f) Length of hearings

81. The length of a hearing primarily depends on the complexity of the issues to be argued and the amount of witness evidence to be presented. The length also depends on the procedural style used in the arbitration. Some practitioners prefer to have written evidence and written arguments presented before the hearings, which thus can focus on the issues that have not been sufficiently clarified. Those practitioners generally tend to plan shorter hearings than those practitioners who prefer that most if not all evidence and arguments are presented to the arbitral tribunal orally and in full detail. In order to facilitate the parties' preparations and avoid misunderstandings, the arbitral tribunal may wish to clarify to the parties, in advance of the hearings, the intended use of time and style of work at the hearings.

(g) Arrangements for a record of the hearings

82. The arbitral tribunal should decide, possibly after consulting with the parties, on the method of preparing a record of oral statements and testimony during hearings. Among different possibilities, one method is that the members of the arbitral tribunal take personal notes. Another is that the presiding arbitrator during the hearing dictates to a typist a summary of oral statements and testimony. A further method, possible when a secretary of the arbitral tribunal has been appointed, may be to leave to that person the preparation of a summary record. A useful, though costly, method is for professional stenographers to prepare verbatim transcripts, often within the next day or a similarly short time period. A written record may be combined with tape-recording, so as to enable reference to the tape in case of a disagreement over the written record.

83. If transcripts are to be produced, it may be considered how the persons who made the statements will be given an opportunity to check

the transcripts. For example, it may be determined that the changes to the record would be approved by the parties or, failing their agreement, would be referred for decision to the arbitral tribunal.

(h) Whether and when the parties are permitted to submit notes summarizing their oral arguments

84. Some legal counsel are accustomed to giving notes summarizing their oral arguments to the arbitral tribunal and to the other party or parties. If such notes are presented, this is usually done during the hearings or shortly thereafter; in some cases, the notes are sent before the hearing. In order to avoid surprise, foster equal treatment of the parties and facilitate preparations for the hearings, advance clarification is advisable as to whether submitting such notes is acceptable and the time for doing so.

85. In closing the hearings, the arbitral tribunal will normally assume that no further proof is to be offered or submission to be made. Therefore, if notes are to be presented to be read after the closure of the hearings, the arbitral tribunal may find it worthwhile to stress that the notes should be limited to summarizing what was said orally and in particular should not refer to new evidence or new argument.

18. Multi-party arbitration

86. When a single arbitration involves more than two parties (multi-party arbitration), considerations regarding the need to organize arbitral proceedings, and matters that may be considered in that connection, are generally not different from two-party arbitrations. A possible difference may be that, because of the need to deal with more than two parties, multi-party proceedings can be more complicated to manage than bilateral proceedings. The Notes, notwithstanding a possible greater complexity of multi-party arbitration, can be used in multi-party as well as in two-party proceedings.

87. The areas of possibly increased complexity in multi-party arbitration are, for example, the flow of communications among the parties and the arbitral tribunal (see paragraphs 33, 34 and 38-41); if points at issue are to be decided at different points in time, the order of deciding them (paragraphs 44-45); the manner in which the parties will participate in hearing witnesses (paragraph 63); the appointment of experts and the participation of the parties in considering their reports (paragraphs 70-72);

the scheduling of hearings (paragraph 76); the order in which the parties will present their arguments and evidence at hearings (paragraph 80).

88. The Notes, which are limited to pointing out matters that may be considered in organizing arbitral proceedings in general, do not cover the drafting of the arbitration agreement or the constitution of the arbitral tribunal, both issues that give rise to special questions in multi-party arbitration as compared to two-party arbitration.

19. Possible requirements concerning filing or delivering the award

89. Some national laws require that arbitral awards be filed or registered with a court or similar authority, or that they be delivered in a particular manner or through a particular authority. Those laws differ with respect to, for example, the type of award to which the requirement applies (e.g. to all awards or only to awards not rendered under the auspices of an arbitral institution); time periods for filing, registering or delivering the award (in some cases those time periods may be rather short); or consequences for failing to comply with the requirement (which might be, for example, invalidity of the award or inability to enforce it in a particular manner).

Who should take steps to fulfil any requirement

90. If such a requirement exists, it is useful, some time before the award is to be issued, to plan who should take the necessary steps to meet the requirement and how the costs are to be borne.

APPENDIX 38
IBA RULES ON THE TAKING OF EVIDENCE IN INTERNATIONAL COMMERCIAL ARBITRATION

The Rules

Preamble

1. These IBA Rules on the Taking of Evidence in International Commercial Arbitration (the "IBA Rules of Evidence") are intended to govern in an efficient and economical manner the taking of evidence in international commercial arbitrations, particularly those between Parties from different legal traditions. They are designed to supplement the legal provisions and the institutional or *ad hoc* rules according to which the Parties are conducting their arbitration.

2. Parties and Arbitral Tribunals may adopt the IBA Rules of Evidence, in whole or in part, to govern arbitration proceedings, or they may vary them or use them as guidelines in developing their own procedures. The Rules are not intended to limit the flexibility that is inherent in, and an advantage of, international arbitration, and Parties and Arbitral Tribunals are free to adapt them to the particular circumstances of each arbitration.

3. Each Arbitral Tribunal is encouraged to identify to the Parties, as soon as it considers it to be appropriate, the issues that it may regard as relevant and material to the outcome of the case, including issues where a preliminary determination may be appropriate.

4. The taking of evidence shall be conducted on the principle that each Party shall be entitled to know, reasonably in advance of any Evidentiary Hearing, the evidence on which the other Parties rely.

The Rules

Article 1
Definitions

In the IBA Rules of Evidence:

"Arbitral Tribunal" means a sole arbitrator or a panel of arbitrators validly deciding by majority or otherwise;

"Claimant" means the Party or Parties who commenced the arbitration and any Party who, through joinder or otherwise, becomes aligned with such Party or Parties;

"Document" means a writing of any kind, whether recorded on paper, electronic means, audio or visual recordings or any other mechanical or electronic means of storing or recording information;

"Evidentiary Hearing" means any hearing, whether or not held on consecutive days, at which the Arbitral Tribunal receives oral evidence;

"Expert Report" means a written statement by a Tribunal-Appointed Expert or a Party-Appointed Expert submitted pursuant to the IBA Rules of Evidence;

"General Rules" mean the institutional or *ad hoc* rules according to which the Parties are conducting their arbitration;

"Party" means a party to the arbitration;

"Party-Appointed Expert" means an expert witness presented by a Party;

"Request to Produce" means a request by a Party for a procedural order by which the Arbitral Tribunal would direct another Party to produce documents;

"Respondent" means the Party or Parties against whom the Claimant made its claim, and any Party who, through joinder or otherwise, becomes aligned with such Party or Parties, and includes a Respondent making a counter-claim;

"Tribunal-Appointed Expert" means a person or organization appointed by the Arbitral Tribunal in order to report to it on specific issues determined by the Arbitral Tribunal.

Article 2
Scope of Application

1. Whenever the Parties have agreed or the Arbitral Tribunal has determined to apply the IBA Rules of Evidence, the Rules shall govern the taking of evidence, except to the extent that any specific provision of them may be found to be in conflict with any mandatory provision of law determined to be applicable to the case by the Parties or by the Arbitral Tribunal.

2. In case of conflict between any provisions of the IBA Rules of Evidence and the General Rules, the Arbitral Tribunal shall apply the IBA Rules of Evidence in the manner that it determines best in order to accomplish the purposes of both the General Rules and the IBA Rules of Evidence, unless the Parties agree to the contrary.

3. In the event of any dispute regarding the meaning of the IBA Rules of Evidence, the Arbitral Tribunal shall interpret them according to their purpose and in the manner most appropriate for the particular arbitration.

4. Insofar as the IBA Rules of Evidence and the General Rules are silent on any matter concerning the taking of evidence and the Parties have not agreed otherwise, the Arbitral Tribunal may conduct the taking of evidence as it deems appropriate, in accordance with the general principles of the IBA Rules of Evidence.

Article 3
Documents

1. Within the time ordered by the Arbitral Tribunal, each Party shall submit to the Arbitral Tribunal and to the other Parties all documents available to it on which it relies, including public documents and those in the public domain, except for any documents that have already been submitted by another Party.

2. Within the time ordered by the Arbitral Tribunal, any Party may submit to the Arbitral Tribunal a Request to Produce.

3. A Request to Produce shall contain:

(a) *(i)* a description of a requested document sufficient to identify it, or *(ii)* a description in sufficient detail (including subject matter) of a narrow and specific requested category of documents that are reasonably believed to exist;

(b) a description of how the documents requested are relevant and material to the outcome of the case; and

(c) a statement that the documents requested are not in the possession, custody or control of the requesting Party, and of the reason why that Party assumes the documents requested to be in the possession, custody or control of the other Party.

4. Within the time ordered by the Arbitral Tribunal, the Party to whom the Request to Produce is addressed shall produce to the Arbitral

Tribunal and to the other Parties all the documents requested in its possession, custody or control as to which no objection is made.

5. If the Party to whom the Request to Produce is addressed has objections to some or all of the documents requested, it shall state them in writing to the Arbitral Tribunal within the time ordered by the Arbitral Tribunal. The reasons for such objections shall be any of those set forth in Article 9.2.

6. The Arbitral Tribunal shall, in consultation with the Parties and in timely fashion, consider the Request to Produce and the objections. The Arbitral Tribunal may order the Party to whom such Request is addressed to produce to the Arbitral Tribunal and to the other Parties those requested documents in its possession, custody or control as to which the Arbitral Tribunal determines that *(i)* the issues that the requesting Party wishes to prove are relevant and material to the outcome of the case, and *(ii)* none of the reasons for objection set forth in Article 9.2 apply.

7. In exceptional circumstances, if the propriety of an objection can only be determined by review of the document, the Arbitral Tribunal may determine that it should not review the document. In that event, the Arbitral Tribunal may, after consultation with the Parties, appoint an independent and impartial expert, bound to confidentiality, to review any such document and to report on the objection. To the extent that the objection is upheld by the Arbitral Tribunal, the expert shall not disclose to the Arbitral Tribunal and to the other Parties the contents of the document reviewed.

8. If a Party wishes to obtain the production of documents from a person or organization who is not a Party to the arbitration and from whom the Party cannot obtain the documents on its own, the Party may, within the time ordered by the Arbitral Tribunal, ask it to take whatever steps are legally available to obtain the requested documents. The Party shall identify the documents in sufficient detail and state why such documents are relevant and material to the outcome of the case. The Arbitral Tribunal shall decide on this request and shall take the necessary steps if in its discretion it determines that the documents would be relevant and material.

9. The Arbitral Tribunal, at any time before the arbitration is concluded, may request a Party to produce to the Arbitral Tribunal and to the other Parties any documents that it believes to be relevant and material to the outcome of the case. A Party may object to such a request

based on any of the reasons set forth in Article 9.2. If a Party raises such an objection, the Arbitral Tribunal shall decide whether to order the production of such documents based upon the considerations set forth in Article 3.6 and, if the Arbitral Tribunal considers it appropriate, through the use of the procedures set forth in Article 3.7.

10. Within the time ordered by the Arbitral Tribunal, the Parties may submit to the Arbitral Tribunal and to the other Parties any additional documents which they believe have become relevant and material as a consequence of the issues raised in documents, Witness Statements or Expert Reports submitted or produced by another Party or in other submissions of the Parties.

11. If copies are submitted or produced, they must conform fully to the originals. At the request of the Arbitral Tribunal, any original must be presented for inspection.

12. All documents produced by a Party pursuant to the IBA Rules of Evidence (or by a non-Party pursuant to Article 3.8) shall be kept confidential by the Arbitral Tribunal and by the other Parties, and they shall be used only in connection with the arbitration. The Arbitral Tribunal may issue orders to set forth the terms of this confidentiality. This requirement is without prejudice to all other obligations of confidentiality in arbitration.

Article 4
Witnesses of Fact

1. Within the time ordered by the Arbitral Tribunal, each Party shall identify the witnesses on whose testimony it relies and the subject matter of that testimony.

2. Any person may present evidence as a witness, including a Party or a Party's officer, employee or other representative.

3. It shall not be improper for a Party, its officers, employees, legal advisors or other representatives to interview its witnesses or potential witnesses.

4. The Arbitral Tribunal may order each Party to submit within a specified time to the Arbitral Tribunal and to the other Parties a written statement by each witness on whose testimony it relies, except for those witnesses whose testimony is sought pursuant to Article 4.10 (the "Witness Statement"). If Evidentiary Hearings are organized on separate

issues (such as liability and damages), the Arbitral Tribunal or the Parties by agreement may schedule the submission of Witness Statements separately for each Evidentiary Hearing.

5.   Each Witness Statement shall contain:

  (a) the full name and address of the witness, his or her present and past relationship (if any) with any of the Parties, and a description of his or her background, qualifications, training and experience, if such a description may be relevant and material to the dispute or to the contents of the statement;

  (b) a full and detailed description of the facts, and the source of the witness's information as to those facts, sufficient to serve as that witness's evidence in the matter in dispute;

  (c) an affirmation of the truth of the statement; and

  (d) the signature of the witness and its date and place.

6.   If Witness Statements are submitted, any Party may, within the time ordered by the Arbitral Tribunal, submit to the Arbitral Tribunal and to the other Parties revised or additional Witness Statements, including statements from persons not previously named as witnesses, so long as any such revisions or additions only respond to matters contained in another Party's Witness Statement or Expert Report and such matters have not been previously presented in the arbitration.

7.   Each witness who has submitted a Witness Statement shall appear for testimony at an Evidentiary Hearing, unless the Parties agree otherwise.

8.   If a witness who has submitted a Witness Statement does not appear without a valid reason for testimony at an Evidentiary Hearing, except by agreement of the Parties, the Arbitral Tribunal shall disregard that Witness Statement unless, in exceptional circumstances, the Arbitral Tribunal determines otherwise.

9.   If the Parties agree that a witness who has submitted a Witness Statement does not need to appear for testimony at an Evidentiary Hearing, such an agreement shall not be considered to reflect an agreement as to the correctness of the content of the Witness Statement.

10. If a Party wishes to present evidence from a person who will not appear voluntarily at its request, the Party may, within the time ordered by the Arbitral Tribunal, ask it to take whatever steps are legally available to obtain the testimony of that person. The Party shall identify

the intended witness, shall describe the subjects on which the witness's testimony is sought and shall state why such subjects are relevant and material to the outcome of the case. The Arbitral Tribunal shall decide on this request and shall take the necessary steps if in its discretion

it determines that the testimony of that witness would be relevant and material.

11. The Arbitral Tribunal may, at any time before the arbitration is concluded, order any Party to provide, or to use its best efforts to provide, the appearance for testimony at an Evidentiary Hearing of any person, including one whose testimony has not yet been offered.

Article 5
Party-Appointed Experts

1. A Party may rely on a Party-Appointed Expert as a means of evidence on specific issues. Within the time ordered by the Arbitral Tribunal, a Party-Appointed Expert shall submit an Expert Report.

2. The Expert Report shall contain:

   (a) the full name and address of the Party-Appointed Expert, his or her present and past relationship (if any) with any of the Parties, and a description of his or her background, qualifications, training and experience;

   (b) a statement of the facts on which he or she is basing his or her expert opinions and conclusions;

   (c) his or her expert opinions and conclusions, including a description of the method, evidence and information used in arriving at the conclusions;

   (d) an affirmation of the truth of the Expert Report; and

   (e) the signature of the Party-Appointed Expert and its date and place.

3. The Arbitral Tribunal in its discretion may order that any Party-Appointed Experts who have submitted Expert Reports on the same or related issues meet and confer on such issues. At such meeting, the Party-Appointed Experts shall attempt to reach agreement on those issues as to which they had differences of opinion in their Expert Reports, and they shall record in writing any such issues on which they reach agreement.

4. Each Party-Appointed Expert shall appear for testimony at an Evidentiary Hearing, unless the Parties agree otherwise and the Arbitral Tribunal accepts this agreement.

5. If a Party-Appointed Expert does not appear without a valid reason for testimony at an Evidentiary Hearing, except by agreement of the Parties accepted by the Arbitral Tribunal, the Arbitral Tribunal shall disregard his or her Expert Report unless, in exceptional circumstances, the Arbitral Tribunal determines otherwise.

6. If the Parties agree that a Party-Appointed Expert does not need to appear for testimony at an Evidentiary Hearing, such an agreement shall not be considered to reflect an agreement as to the correctness of the content of the Expert Report.

Article 6
Tribunal-Appointed Experts

1. The Arbitral Tribunal, after having consulted with the Parties, may appoint one or more independent Tribunal-Appointed Experts to report to it on specific issues designated by the Arbitral Tribunal. The Arbitral Tribunal shall establish the terms of reference for any Tribunal-Appointed Expert report after having consulted with the Parties. A copy of the final terms of reference shall be sent by the Arbitral Tribunal to the Parties.

2. The Tribunal-Appointed Expert shall, before accepting appointment, submit to the Arbitral Tribunal and to the Parties a statement of his or her independence from the Parties and the Arbitral Tribunal. Within the time ordered by the Arbitral Tribunal, the Parties shall inform the Arbitral Tribunal whether they have any objections to the Tribunal-Appointed Expert's independence. The Arbitral Tribunal shall decide promptly whether to accept any such objection.

3. Subject to the provisions of Article 9.2, the Tribunal-Appointed Expert may request a Party to provide any relevant and material information or to provide access to any relevant documents, goods, samples, property or site for inspection. The authority of a Tribunal-Appointed Expert to request such information or access shall be the same as the authority of the Arbitral Tribunal. The Parties and their representatives shall have the right to receive any such information and to attend any such inspection. Any disagreement between a Tribunal-Appointed Expert and a Party as to the relevance, materiality or

appropriateness of such a request shall be decided by the Arbitral Tribunal, in the manner provided in Articles 3.5 through 3.7. The Tribunal-Appointed Expert shall record in the report any non-compliance by a Party with an appropriate request or decision by the Arbitral Tribunal and shall describe its effects on the determination of the specific issue.

4.   The Tribunal-Appointed Expert shall report in writing to the Arbitral Tribunal. The Tribunal-Appointed Expert shall describe in the report the method, evidence and information used in arriving at the conclusions.

5.   The Arbitral Tribunal shall send a copy of such Expert Report to the Parties. The Parties may examine any document that the Tribunal-Appointed Expert has examined and any correspondence between the Arbitral Tribunal and the Tribunal, Appointed Expert. Within the time ordered by the Arbitral Tribunal, any Party shall have the opportunity to respond to the report in a submission by the Party or through an Expert Report by a Party-Appointed Expert. The Arbitral Tribunal shall send the submission or Expert Report to the Tribunal-Appointed Expert and to the other Parties.

6.   At the request of a Party or of the Arbitral Tribunal, the Tribunal-Appointed Expert shall be present at an Evidentiary Hearing. The Arbitral Tribunal may question the Tribunal-Appointed Expert, and he or she may be questioned by the Parties or by any Party-Appointed Expert on issues raised in the Parties' submissions or in the Expert Reports made by the Party-Appointed Experts pursuant to Article 6.5.

7.   Any Expert Report made by a Tribunal-Appointed Expert and its conclusions shall be assessed by the Arbitral Tribunal with due regard to all circumstances of the case.

8.   The fees and expenses of a Tribunal-Appointed Expert, to be funded in a manner determined by the Arbitral Tribunal, shall form part of the costs of the arbitration.

Article 7
On Site Inspection

Subject to the provisions of Article 9.2, the Arbitral Tribunal may, at the request of a Party or on its own motion, inspect or require the inspection by a Tribunal-Appointed Expert of any site, property, machinery or any other goods or process, or documents, as it deems appropriate. The Arbitral Tribunal shall, in consultation with the Parties, determine the timing and arrangement for the inspection. The Parties and their representatives shall have the right to attend any such inspection.

Article 8
Evidentiary Hearing

1. The Arbitral Tribunal shall at all times have complete control over the Evidentiary Hearing. The Arbitral Tribunal may limit or exclude any question to, answer by or appearance of a witness (which term includes, for the purposes of this Article, witnesses of fact and any Experts), if it considers such question, answer or appearance to be irrelevant, immaterial, burdensome, duplicative or covered by a reason for objection set forth in Article 9.2. Questions to a witness during direct and redirect testimony may not be unreasonably leading.

2. The Claimant shall ordinarily first present the testimony of its witnesses, followed by the Respondent presenting testimony of its witnesses, and then by the presentation by Claimant of rebuttal witnesses, if any. Following direct testimony, any other Party may question such witness, in an order to be determined by the Arbitral Tribunal. The Party who initially presented the witness shall subsequently have the opportunity to ask additional questions on the matters raised in the other Parties' questioning. The Arbitral Tribunal, upon request of a Party or on its own motion, may vary this order of proceeding, including the arrangement of testimony by particular issues or in such a manner that witnesses presented by different Parties be questioned at the same time and in confrontation with each other. The Arbitral Tribunal may ask questions to a witness at any time.

3. Any witness providing testimony shall first affirm, in a manner determined appropriate by the Arbitral Tribunal, that he or she is telling the truth. If the witness has submitted a Witness Statement or an Expert Report, the witness shall confirm it. The Parties may agree or the Arbitral Tribunal may order that the Witness Statement or Expert Report shall serve as that witness's direct testimony.

4. Subject to the provisions of Article 9.2, the Arbitral Tribunal may request any person to give oral or written evidence on any issue that the Arbitral Tribunal considers to be relevant and material. Any witness called and questioned by the Arbitral Tribunal may also be questioned by the Parties.

Article 9
Admissibility and Assessment of Evidence

1. The Arbitral Tribunal shall determine the admissibility, relevance, materiality and weight of evidence.

2. The Arbitral Tribunal shall, at the request of a Party or on its own motion, exclude from evidence or production any document, statement, oral testimony or inspection for any of the following reasons:

(a) lack of sufficient relevance or materiality;

(b) legal impediment or privilege under the legal or ethical rules determined by the Arbitral Tribunal to be applicable;

(c) unreasonable burden to produce the requested evidence;

(d) loss or destruction of the document that has been reasonably shown to have occurred;

(e) grounds of commercial or technical confidentiality that the Arbitral Tribunal determines to be compelling;

(f) grounds of special political or institutional sensitivity (including evidence that has been classified as secret by a government or a public international institution) that the Arbitral Tribunal determines to be compelling; or

(g) considerations of fairness or equality of the Parties that the Arbitral Tribunal determines to be compelling.

3. The Arbitral Tribunal may, where appropriate, make necessary arrangements to permit evidence to be considered subject to suitable confidentiality protection.

4. If a Party fails without satisfactory explanation to produce any document requested in a Request to Produce to which it has not objected in due time or fails to produce any document ordered to be produced by the Arbitral Tribunal, the Arbitral Tribunal may infer that such document would be adverse to the interests of that Party.

5. If a Party fails without satisfactory explanation to make available any other relevant evidence, including testimony, sought by one Party to which the Party to whom the request was addressed has not objected in due time or fails to make available any evidence, including testimony, ordered by the Arbitral Tribunal to be produced, the Arbitral Tribunal may infer that such evidence would be adverse to the interests of that Party.

APPENDIX 39
IBA GUIDELINES ON CONFLICTS OF INTEREST IN INTERNATIONAL ARBITRATION

Introduction

1. Problems of conflicts of interest increasingly challenge international arbitration. Arbitrators are often unsure about what facts need to be disclosed, and they may make different choices about disclosures than other arbitrators in the same situation. The growth of international business and the manner in which it is conducted, including interlocking corporate relationships and larger international law firms, have caused more disclosures and have created more difficult conflict of interest issues to determine. Reluctant parties have more opportunities to use challenges of arbitrators to delay arbitrations or to deny the opposing party the arbitrator of its choice. Disclosure of any relationship, no matter how minor or serious, has too often led to objections, challenge and withdrawal or removal of the arbitrator.

2. Thus, parties, arbitrators, institutions and courts face complex decisions about what to disclose and what standards to apply. In addition, institutions and courts face difficult decisions if an objection or a challenge is made after a disclosure. There is a tension between, on the one hand, the parties' right to disclosure of situations that may reasonably call into question an arbitrator's impartiality or independence and their right to a fair hearing and, on the other hand, the parties' right to select arbitrators of their choosing. Even though laws and arbitration rules provide some standards, there is a lack of detail in their guidance and of uniformity in their application. As a result, quite often members of the international arbitration community apply different standards in making decisions concerning disclosure, objections and challenges.

3. It is in the interest of everyone in the international arbitration community that international arbitration proceedings not be hindered by these growing conflicts of interest issues. The Committee on Arbitration and ADR of the International Bar Association appointed a Working Group of 19 experts[1] in international arbitration from 14

---

[1] The members of the Working Group are: (1) Henri Alvarez, Canada; (2) John Beechey, England; (3) Jim Carter, United States; (4) Emmanuel Gaillard, France,

countries to study, with the intent of helping this decision-making process, national laws, judicial decisions, arbitration rules and practical considerations and applications regarding impartiality and independence and disclosure in international arbitration. The Working Group has determined that existing standards lack sufficient clarity and uniformity in their application. It has therefore prepared these Guidelines, which set forth some General Standards and Explanatory Notes on the Standards. Moreover, the Working Group believes that greater consistency and fewer unnecessary challenges and arbitrator withdrawals and removals could be achieved by providing lists of specific situations that, in the view of the Working Group, do or do not warrant disclosure or disqualification of an arbitrator. Such lists – designated Red, Orange and Green (the 'Application Lists') – appear at the end of these Guidelines.[2]

4. The Guidelines reflect the Working Group's understanding of the best current international practice firmly rooted in the principles expressed in the General Standards. The Working Group has based the General Standards and the Application Lists upon statutes and case law in jurisdictions and upon the judgment and experience of members of the Working Group and others involved in international commercial arbitration. The Working Group has attempted to balance the various interests of parties, representatives, arbitrators and arbitration institutions, all of whom have a responsibility for ensuring the integrity, reputation and efficiency of international commercial arbitration. In particular, the Working Group has sought and considered the views of many leading arbitration institutions, as well as corporate counsel and other persons involved in international arbitration. The Working Group also published drafts of the Guidelines and sought comments at two annual meetings of the International Bar Association and other meetings of arbitrators.

---

(5) Emilio Gonzales de Castilla, Mexico; (6) Bernard Hanotiau, Belgium; (7) Michael Hwang, Singapore; (8) Albert Jan van den Berg, Belgium; (9) Doug Jones, Australia; (10) Gabrielle Kaufmann-Kohler, Switzerland; (11) Arthur Marriott, England; (12) Tore Wiwen Nilsson, Sweden; (13) Hilmar Raeschke-Kessler, Germany; (14) David W. Rivkin, United States; (15) Klaus Sachs, Germany; (16) Nathalie Voser, Switzerland (Rapporteur); (17) David Williams, New Zealand; (18) Des Williams, South Africa; (19) Otto de Witt Wijnen, The Netherlands (Chair).

[2] Detailed Background Information to the Guidelines has been published in *Business Law International* at BLI Vol 5, No 3, September 2004, pp 433-458 and is available at the IBA website www.ibanet.org.

While the comments received by the Working Group varied, and included some points of criticisms, the arbitration community generally supported and encouraged these efforts to help reduce the growing problems of conflicts of interests. The Working Group has studied all the comments received and has adopted many of the proposals that it has received. The Working Group is very grateful indeed for the serious considerations given to its proposals by so many institutions and individuals all over the globe and for the comments and proposals received.

5. Originally, the Working Group developed the Guidelines for international commercial arbitration. However, in the light of comments received, it realized that the Guidelines should equally apply to other types of arbitration, such as investment arbitrations (insofar as these may not be considered as commercial arbitrations).[3]

6. These Guidelines are not legal provisions and do not override any applicable national law or arbitral rules chosen by the parties. However, the Working Group hopes that these Guidelines will find general acceptance within the international arbitration community (as was the case with the IBA Rules on the Taking of Evidence in International Commercial Arbitration) and that they thus will help parties, practitioners, arbitrators, institutions and the courts in their decision-making process on these very important questions of impartiality, independence, disclosure, objections and challenges made in that connection. The Working Group trusts that the Guidelines will be applied with robust common sense and without pedantic and unduly formalistic interpretation. The Working Group is also publishing a Background and History, which describes the studies made by the Working Group and may be helpful in interpreting the Guidelines.

7. The IBA and the Working Group view these Guidelines as a beginning, rather than an end, of the process. The Application Lists cover many of the varied situations that commonly arise in practice, but they do not purport to be comprehensive, nor could they be. Nevertheless, the Working Group is confident that the Application Lists provide better concrete guidance than the General Standards (and certainly more than existing standards). The IBA and the

---

[3] Similarly, the Working Group is of the opinion that these Guidelines should apply by analogy to civil servants and government officers who are appointed as arbitrators by States or State entities that are parties to arbitration proceedings.

Working Group seek comments on the actual use of the Guidelines, and they plan to supplement, revise and refine the Guidelines based on that practical experience.

8. In 1987, the IBA published Rules of Ethics for International Arbitrators. Those Rules cover more topics than these Guidelines, and they remain in effect as to subjects that are not discussed in the Guidelines. The Guidelines supersede the Rules of Ethics as to the matters treated here.

PART I: General Standards Regarding Impartiality, Independence and Disclosure

(1) General Principle

Every arbitrator shall be impartial and independent of the parties at the time of accepting an appointment to serve and shall remain so during the entire arbitration proceeding until the final award has been rendered or the proceeding has otherwise finally terminated.

Explanation to General Standard 1:

The Working Group is guided by the fundamental principle in international arbitration that each arbitrator must be impartial and independent of the parties at the time he or she accepts an appointment to act as arbitrator and must remain so during the entire course of the arbitration proceedings. The Working Group considered whether this obligation should extend even during the period that the award may be challenged but has decided against this. The Working Group takes the view that the arbitrator's duty ends when the Arbitral Tribunal has rendered the final award or the proceedings have otherwise been finally terminated (eg, because of a settlement). If, after setting aside or other proceedings, the dispute is referred back to the same arbitrator, a fresh round of disclosure may be necessary.

(2) Conflicts of Interest

(a) *An arbitrator shall decline to accept an appointment or, if the arbitration has already been commenced, refuse to continue to act as an arbitrator if he or she has any doubts as to his or her ability to be impartial or independent.*

(b) *The same principle applies if facts or circumstances exist, or have arisen since the appointment, that, from a reasonable third person's point of view having knowledge of the relevant facts, give rise to justifiable doubts as to the arbitrator's impartiality or independence, unless the parties have accepted the arbitrator in accordance with the requirements set out in General Standard (4).*

(c) *Doubts are justifiable if a reasonable and informed third party would reach the conclusion that there was a likelihood that the arbitrator may be influenced by factors other than the merits of the case as presented by the parties in reaching his or her decision.*

(d) *Justifiable doubts necessarily exist as to the arbitrator's impartiality or independence if there is an identity between a party and the arbitrator, if the arbitrator is a legal representative of a legal entity that is a party in the arbitration, or if the arbitrator has a significant financial or personal interest in the matter at stake.*

Explanation to General Standard 2:

(a) It is the main ethical guiding principle of every arbitrator that actual bias from the arbitrator's own point of view must lead to that arbitrator declining his or her appointment. This standard should apply regardless of the stage of the proceedings. This principle is so selfevident that many national laws do not explicitly say so. See eg Article 12, UNCITRAL Model Law. The Working Group, however, has included it in the General Standards because explicit expression in these Guidelines helps to avoid confusion and to create confidence in procedures before arbitral tribunals. In addition, the Working Group believes that the broad standard of 'any doubts as to an ability to be impartial and independent' should lead to the arbitrator declining the appointment.

(b) In order for standards to be applied as consistently as possible, the Working Group believes that the test for disqualification should be an objective one. The Working Group uses the wording 'impartiality or independence' derived from the broadly adopted Article 12 of the UNCITRAL Model Law, and the use of an appearance test, based on justifiable doubts as to the impartiality or independence of the arbitrator, as provided in Article 12(2) of the UNCITRAL Model Law, to be applied objectively (a 'reasonable third person test'). As described in the Explanation to General Standard 3(d), this standard should apply regardless of the stage of the proceedings.

(c) Most laws and rules that apply the standard of justifiable doubts do not further define that standard. The Working Group believes that this General Standard provides some context for making this determination.

(d) The Working Group supports the view that no one is allowed to be his or her own judge; ie, there cannot be identity between an arbitrator and a party. The Working Group believes that this situation cannot be waived by the parties. The same principle should apply to persons who are legal representatives of a legal entity that is a party in the arbitration, like board members, or who have a significant economic interest in the matter at stake. Because of the importance of this principle, this nonwaivable situation is made a General Standard, and examples are provided in the non-waivable Red List.

The General Standard purposely uses the terms 'identity' and 'legal representatives.' In the light of comments received, the Working Group considered whether these terms should be extended or further defined, but decided against doing so. It realizes that there are situations in which an employee of a party or a civil servant can be in a position similar, if not identical, to the position of an official legal representative. The Working Group decided that it should suffice to state the principle.

(3) Disclosure by the Arbitrator

(a) *If facts or circumstances exist that may, in the eyes of the parties, give rise to doubts as to the arbitrator's impartiality or independence, the arbitrator shall disclose such facts or circumstances to the parties, the arbitration institution or other appointing authority (if any, and if so required by the applicable institutional rules) and to the co-arbitrators, if any, prior to accepting his or her appointment or, if thereafter, as soon as he or she learns about them.*

(b) *It follows from General Standards 1 and 2(a) that an arbitrator who has made a disclosure considers himself or herself to be impartial and independent of the parties despite the disclosed facts and therefore capable of performing his or her duties as arbitrator. Otherwise, he or she would have declined the nomination or appointment at the outset or resigned.*

(c) *Any doubt as to whether an arbitrator should disclose certain facts or circumstances should be resolved in favour of disclosure.*

(d) *When considering whether or not facts or circumstances exist that should be disclosed, the arbitrator shall not take into account whether the arbitration proceeding is at the beginning or at a later stage.*

Explanation to General Standard 3:

(a) General Standard 2(b) above sets out an objective test for disqualification of an arbitrator. However, because of varying considerations with respect to disclosure, the proper standard for disclosure may be different. A purely objective test for disclosure exists in the majority of the jurisdictions analyzed and in the UNCITRAL Model Law. Nevertheless, the Working Group recognizes that the parties have an interest in being fully informed about any circumstances that may be relevant in their view. Because of the strongly held views of many arbitration institutions (as reflected in their rules and as stated to the Working Group) that the disclosure test should reflect the perspectives of the parties, the Working Group in principle accepted, after much debate, a subjective approach for disclosure. The Working Group has adapted the language of Article 7(2) of the ICC Rules for this standard.

However, the Working Group believes that this principle should not be applied without limitations. Because some situations should never lead to disqualification under the objective test, such situations need not be disclosed, regardless of the parties' perspective. These limitations to the subjective test are reflected in the Green List, which lists some situations in which disclosure is not required. Similarly, the Working Group emphasizes that the two tests (objective test for disqualification and subjective test for disclosure) are clearly distinct from each other, and that a disclosure shall not automatically lead to disqualification, as reflected in General Standard 3(b). In determining what facts should be disclosed, an arbitrator should take into account all circumstances known to him or her, including to the extent known the culture and the customs of the country of which the parties are domiciled or nationals.

(b) Disclosure is not an admission of a conflict of interest. An arbitrator who has made a disclosure to the parties considers himself or herself to be impartial and independent of the parties, despite the disclosed facts, or else he or she would have declined the nomination or resigned. An arbitrator making disclosure thus feels capable of performing his or her duties. It is the purpose of disclosure to allow the parties to judge whether or not they agree with the evaluation of the arbitrator and, if they so wish, to explore the situation further. The Working Group hopes that the promulgation of this General Standard will eliminate the misunderstanding that disclosure demonstrates doubts sufficient to disqualify the arbitrator. Instead, any challenge should be successful only if an objective test, as set forth above, is met.

(c) Unnecessary disclosure sometimes raises an incorrect implication in the minds of the parties that the disclosed circumstances would affect his or her impartiality or independence. Excessive disclosures thus unnecessarily undermine the parties' confidence in the process. Nevertheless, after some debate, the Working Group believes it important to provide expressly in the General Standards that in case of doubt the arbitrator should disclose. If the arbitrator feels that he or she should disclose but that professional secrecy rules or other rules of practice prevent such disclosure, he or she should not accept the appointment or should resign.

(d) The Working Group has concluded that disclosure or disqualification (as set out in General Standard 2) should not depend on the particular stage of the arbitration. In order to determine whether the arbitrator should disclose, decline the appointment or refuse to continue to act or whether a challenge by a party should be successful, the facts and circumstances alone are relevant and not the current stage of the procedure or the consequences of the withdrawal. As a practical matter, institutions make a distinction between the commencement of an arbitration proceeding and a later stage. Also, courts tend to apply different standards. Nevertheless, the Working Group believes it important to clarify that no distinction should be made regarding the stage of the arbitral procedure. While there are practical concerns if an arbitrator must withdraw after an arbitration has commenced, a distinction based on the stage of arbitration would be inconsistent with the General Standards.

(4) Waiver by the Parties

(a) *If, within 30 days after the receipt of any disclosure by the arbitrator or after a party learns of facts or circumstances that could constitute a potential conflict of interest for an arbitrator, a party does not raise an express objection with regard to that arbitrator, subject to paragraphs (b) and (c) of this General Standard, the party is deemed to have waived any potential conflict of interest by the arbitrator based on such facts or circumstances and may not raise any objection to such facts or circumstances at a later stage.*

(b) *However, if facts or circumstances exist as described in General Standard 2(d), any waiver by a party or any agreement by the parties to have such a person serve as arbitrator shall be regarded as invalid.*

(c) *A person should not serve as an arbitrator when a conflict of interest, such as those exemplified in the waivable Red List, exists. Nevertheless, such a person may accept appointment as arbitrator or continue to act as an arbitrator, if the following conditions are met:*

    (i) *All parties, all arbitrators and the arbitration institution or other appointing authority (if any) must have full knowledge of the conflict of interest; and*

    (ii) *All parties must expressly agree that such person may serve as arbitrator despite the conflict of interest.*

(d) *An arbitrator may assist the parties in reaching a settlement of the dispute at any stage of the proceedings. However, before doing so, the arbitrator should receive an express agreement by the parties that acting in such a manner shall not disqualify the arbitrator from continuing to serve as arbitrator. Such express agreement shall be considered to be an effective waiver of any potential conflict of interest that may arise from the arbitrator's participation in such process or from information that the arbitrator may learn in the process. If the assistance by the arbitrator does not lead to final settlement of the case, the parties remain bound by their waiver. However, consistent with General Standard 2(a) and notwithstanding such agreement, the arbitrator shall resign if, as a consequence of his or her involvement in the settlement process, the arbitrator develops doubts as to his or her ability to remain impartial or independent in the future course of the arbitration proceedings.*

Explanation to General Standard 4:

(a) The Working Group suggests a requirement of an explicit objection by the parties within a certain time limit. In the view of the Working Group, this time limit should also apply to a party who refuses to be involved.

(b) This General Standard is included to make General Standard 4(a) consistent with the non-waivable provisions of General Standard 2(d).

Examples of such circumstances are described in the non-waivable Red List.

(c) In a serious conflict of interest, such as those that are described by way of example in the waivable Red List, the parties may nevertheless wish to use such a person as an arbitrator. Here, party autonomy and the desire to have only impartial and independent arbitrators must be balanced. The Working Group believes persons with such a serious conflict of interests may serve as arbitrators only if the parties make fully informed, explicit waivers.

(d) The concept of the Arbitral Tribunal assisting the parties in reaching a settlement of their dispute in the course of the arbitration proceedings is well established in some jurisdictions but not in others. Informed consent by the parties to such a process prior to its beginning should be regarded as effective waiver of a potential conflict of interest. Express consent is generally sufficient, as opposed to a consent made in writing which in certain jurisdictions requires signature. In practice, the requirement of an express waiver allows such consent to be made in the minutes or transcript of a hearing. In addition, in order to avoid parties using an arbitrator as mediator as a means of disqualifying the arbitrator, the General Standard makes clear that the waiver should remain effective if the mediation is unsuccessful. Thus, parties assume the risk of what the arbitrator may learn in the settlement process. In giving their express consent, the parties should realize the consequences of the arbitrator assisting the parties in a settlement process and agree on regulating this special position further where appropriate.

(5) Scope

These Guidelines apply equally to tribunal chairs, sole arbitrators and party-appointed arbitrators. These Guidelines do not apply to nonneutral arbitrators, who do not have an obligation to be independent and impartial, as may be permitted by some arbitration rules or national laws.

Explanation to General Standard 5:

Because each member of an Arbitral Tribunal has an obligation to be impartial and independent, the General Standards should not distinguish among sole arbitrators, party-appointed arbitrators and tribunal chairs. With regard to secretaries of Arbitral Tribunals, the Working Group takes the view that it is the responsibility of the arbitrator to ensure that the secretary is and remains impartial and independent. Some arbitration rules and domestic laws permit partyappointed arbitrators to be non-neutral. When an arbitrator is serving in such a role, these Guidelines should not apply to him or her, since their purpose is to protect impartiality and independence.

(6) Relationships

(a) *When considering the relevance of facts or circumstances to determine whether a potential conflict of interest exists or whether disclosure should be made, the activities of an arbitrator's law firm, if any, should be reasonably considered in each individual case. Therefore, the fact that the activities of the arbitrator's firm involve one of the parties shall not automatically constitute a source of such conflict or a reason for disclosure.*

(b) *Similarly, if one of the parties is a legal entity which is a member of a group with which the arbitrator's firm has an involvement, such facts or circumstances should be reasonably considered in each individual case. Therefore, this fact alone shall not automatically constitute a source of a conflict of interest or a reason for disclosure.*

(c) *If one of the parties is a legal entity, the managers, directors and members of a supervisory board of such legal entity and any person having a similar controlling influence on the legal entity shall be considered to be the equivalent of the legal entity.*

Explanation to General Standard 6:

(a) The growing size of law firms should be taken into account as part of today's reality in international arbitration. There is a need to balance the interests of a party to use the arbitrator of its choice and the importance of maintaining confidence in the impartiality and independence of international arbitration. In the opinion of the Working Group, the arbitrator must in principle be considered as identical to his or her law firm, but nevertheless the activities of the arbitrator's firm should not automatically constitute a conflict of interest. The relevance of such activities, such as the nature, timing and scope of the work by the law firm, should be reasonably considered in each individual case. The Working Group uses the term 'involvement' rather than 'acting for' because a law firm's relevant connections with a party may include activities other than representation on a legal matter.

(b) When a party to an arbitration is a member of a group of companies, special questions regarding conflict of interest arise. As in the prior paragraph, the Working Group believes that because individual corporate structure arrangements vary so widely an automatic rule is not appropriate. Instead, the particular circumstances of an affiliation with another entity within the same group of companies should be reasonably considered in each individual case.

(c) The party in international arbitration is usually a legal entity. Therefore, this General Standard clarifies which individuals should be considered effectively to be that party.

(7) Duty of Arbitrator and Parties

(a) *A party shall inform an arbitrator, the Arbitral Tribunal, the other parties and the arbitration institution or other appointing authority (if any) about any direct or indirect relationship between it (or another company of the same group of companies) and the arbitrator. The party shall do so on its own initiative before the beginning of the proceeding or as soon as it becomes aware of such relationship.*

(b) *In order to comply with General Standard 7(a), a party shall provide any information already available to it and shall perform a reasonable search of publicly available information.*

(c) *An arbitrator is under a duty to make reasonable enquiries to investigate any potential conflict of interest, as well as any facts or circumstances that may cause his or her impartiality or independence to be questioned. Failure to disclose a potential conflict is not excused by lack of knowledge if the arbitrator makes no reasonable attempt to investigate.*

Explanation to General Standard 7:

To reduce the risk of abuse by unmeritorious challenge of an arbitrator's impartiality or independence, it is necessary that the parties disclose any relevant relationship with the arbitrator. In addition, any party or potential party to an arbitration is, at the outset, required to make a reasonable effort to ascertain and to disclose publicly available information that, applying the general standard, might affect the arbitrator's impartiality and independence. It is the arbitrator or putative arbitrator's obligation to make similar enquiries and to disclose any information that may cause his or her impartiality or independence to be called into question.

PART II: Practical Application of the General Standards

1. The Working Group believes that if the Guidelines are to have an important practical influence, they should reflect situations that are likely to occur in today's arbitration practice. The Guidelines should provide specific guidance to arbitrators, parties, institutions and courts as to what situations do or do not constitute conflicts of interest or should be disclosed. For this purpose, the members of the Working Group analyzed their respective case law and categorized situations that can occur in the following Application Lists. These lists obviously cannot contain every situation, but they provide guidance in many circumstances, and the Working Group has sought to make them as comprehensive as possible. In all cases, the General Standards should control.

2. The Red List consists of two parts: 'a non-waivable Red List' (see General Standards 2(c) and 4(b)) and 'a waivable Red List' (see General Standard 4(c)). These lists are a non-exhaustive enumeration of specific situations which, depending on the facts of a given case, give rise to justifiable doubts as to the arbitrator's impartiality and independence; ie, in these circumstances an objective conflict of interest exists from the point of view of a reasonable third person having knowledge of the relevant facts (*see* General Standard 2(b)). The nonwaivable Red List includes situations deriving from the overriding principle that no person can be his or her own judge. Therefore, disclosure of such a situation cannot cure the conflict. The waivable Red List encompasses situations that are serious but not as severe. Because of their seriousness, unlike circumstances described in the Orange List, these situations should be considered waivable only if and when the parties, being aware of the conflict of interest situation, nevertheless expressly state their willingness to have such a person act as arbitrator, as set forth in General Standard 4(c).

3. The Orange List is a non-exhaustive enumeration of specific situations which (depending on the facts of a given case) in the eyes

of the parties may give rise to justifiable doubts as to the arbitrator's impartiality or independence. The Orange List thus reflects situations that would fall under General Standard 3(a), so that the arbitrator has a duty to disclose such situations. In all these situations, the parties are deemed to have accepted the arbitrator if, after disclosure, no timely objection is made. (General Standard 4(a)).

4.   It should be stressed that, as stated above, such disclosure should not automatically result in a disqualification of the arbitrator; no presumption regarding disqualification should arise from a disclosure. The purpose of the disclosure is to inform the parties of a situation that they may wish to explore further in order to determine whether objectively — ie, from a reasonable third person's point of view having knowledge of the relevant facts — there is a justifiable doubt as to the arbitrator's impartiality or independence. If the conclusion is that there is no justifiable doubt, the arbitrator can act. He or she can also act if there is no timely objection by the parties or, in situations covered by the waivable Red List, a specific acceptance by the parties in accordance with General Standard 4(c). Of course, if a party challenges the appointment of the arbitrator, he or she can nevertheless act if the authority that has to rule on the challenge decides that the challenge does not meet the objective test for disqualification.

5.   In addition, a later challenge based on the fact that an arbitrator did not disclose such facts or circumstances should not result automatically in either nonappointment, later disqualification or a successful challenge to any award. In the view of the Working Group, non-disclosure cannot make an arbitrator partial or lacking independence; only the facts or circumstances that he or she did not disclose can do so.

6.   The Green List contains a non-exhaustive enumeration of specific situations where no appearance of, and no actual, conflict of interest exists from the relevant objective point of view. Thus, the arbitrator has no duty to disclose situations falling within the Green List. In the opinion of the Working Group, as already expressed in the Explanation to General Standard 3(a), there should be a limit to disclosure, based on reasonableness; in some situations, an objective test should prevail over the purely subjective test of 'the eyes of the parties.'

7.   Situations falling outside the time limit used in some of the Orange List situations should generally be considered as falling in the Green

List, even though they are not specifically stated. An arbitrator may nevertheless wish to make disclosure if, under the General Standards, he or she believes it to be appropriate. While there has been much debate with respect to the time limits used in the Lists, the Working Group has concluded that the limits indicated are appropriate and provide guidance where none exists now. For example, the three-year period in Orange List 3.1 may be too long in certain circumstances and too short in others, but the Working Group believes that the period is an appropriate general criterion, subject to the special circumstances of any case.

8. The borderline between the situations indicated is often thin. It can be debated whether a certain situation should be on one List of instead of another. Also, the Lists contain, for various situations, open norms like 'significant'. The Working Group has extensively and repeatedly discussed both of these issues, in the light of comments received. It believes that the decisions reflected in the Lists reflect international principles to the best extent possible and that further definition of the norms, which should be interpreted reasonably in light of the facts and circumstances in each case, would be counter-productive.

9. There has been much debate as to whether there should be a Green List at all and also, with respect to the Red List, whether the situations on the Non-Waivable Red List should be waivable in light of party autonomy. With respect to the first question, the Working Group has maintained its decision that the subjective test for disclosure should not be the absolute criterion but that some objective thresholds should be added. With respect to the second question, the conclusion of the Working Group was that party autonomy, in this respect, has its limits.

1. Non-Waivable Red List

1.1. There is an identity between a party and the arbitrator, or the arbitrator is a legal representative of an entity that is a party in the arbitration.

1.2. The arbitrator is a manager, director or member of the supervisory board, or has a similar controlling influence in one of the parties.

1.3. The arbitrator has a significant financial interest in one of the parties or the outcome of the case.

1.4. The arbitrator regularly advises the appointing party or an affiliate of the appointing party, and the arbitrator or his or her firm derives a significant financial income therefrom.

2. Waivable Red List

2.1. Relationship of the arbitrator to the dispute

2.1.1 The arbitrator has given legal advice or provided an expert opinion on the dispute to a party or an affiliate of one of the parties.

2.1.2 The arbitrator has previous involvement in the case.

2.2. Arbitrator's direct or indirect interest in the dispute

2.2.1 The arbitrator holds shares, either directly or indirectly, in one of the parties or an affiliate of one of the parties that is privately held.

2.2.2 A close family member[4] of the arbitrator has a significant financial interest in the outcome of the dispute.

2.2.3 The arbitrator or a close family member of the arbitrator has a close relationship with a third party who may be liable to recourse on the part of the unsuccessful party in the dispute.

2.3. Arbitrator's relationship with the parties or counsel

2.3.1 The arbitrator currently represents or advises one of the parties or an affiliate of one of the parties.

2.3.2 The arbitrator currently represents the lawyer or law firm acting as counsel for one of the parties.

2.3.3 The arbitrator is a lawyer in the same law firm as the counsel to one of the parties.

2.3.4 The arbitrator is a manager, director or member of the supervisory board, or has a similar controlling influence, in an affiliate[5] of one of the parties if the affiliate is directly involved in the matters in dispute in the arbitration.

---

[4] Throughout the Application Lists, the term 'close family member' refers to a spouse, sibling, child, parent or life partner.

[5] Throughout the Application Lists, the term 'affiliate' encompasses all companies in one group of companies including the parent company.

2.3.5 The arbitrator's law firm had a previous but terminated involvement in the case without the arbitrator being involved himself or herself.

2.3.6 The arbitrator's law firm currently has a significant commercial relationship with one of the parties or an affiliate of one of the parties.

2.3.7 The arbitrator regularly advises the appointing party or an affiliate of the appointing party, but neither the arbitrator nor his or her firm derives a significant financial income therefrom.

2.3.8 The arbitrator has a close family relationship with one of the parties or with a manager, director or member of the supervisory board or any person having a similar controlling influence in one of the parties or an affiliate of one of the parties or with a counsel representing a party.

2.3.9 A close family member of the arbitrator has a significant financial interest in one of the parties or an affiliate of one of the parties.

3. Orange List

3.1. Previous services for one of the parties or other involvement in the case

3.1.1 The arbitrator has within the past three years served as counsel for one of the parties or an affiliate of one of the parties or has previously advised or been consulted by the party or an affiliate of the party making the appointment in an unrelated matter, but the arbitrator and the party or the affiliate of the party have no ongoing relationship.

3.1.2 The arbitrator has within the past three years served as counsel against one of the parties or an affiliate of one of the parties in an unrelated matter.

3.1.3 The arbitrator has within the past three years been appointed as arbitrator on two or more occasions by one of the parties or an affiliate of one of the parties.[6]

---

[6] It may be the practice in certain specific kinds of arbitration, such as maritime or commodities arbitration, to draw arbitrators from a small, specialized pool. If in such

3.1.4 The arbitrator's law firm has within the past three years acted for one of the parties or an affiliate of one of the parties in an unrelated matter without the involvement of the arbitrator.

3.1.5 The arbitrator currently serves, or has served within the past three years, as arbitrator in another arbitration on a related issue involving one of the parties or an affiliate of one of the parties.

3.2. Current services for one of the parties

3.2.1 The arbitrator's law firm is currently rendering services to one of the parties or to an affiliate of one of the parties without creating a significant commercial relationship and without the involvement of the arbitrator.

3.2.2 A law firm that shares revenues or fees with the arbitrator's law firm renders services to one of the parties or an affiliate of one of the parties before the arbitral tribunal.

3.2.3 The arbitrator or his or her firm represents a party or an affiliate to the arbitration on a regular basis but is not involved in the current dispute.

3.3. Relationship between an arbitrator and another arbitrator or counsel.

3.3.1 The arbitrator and another arbitrator are lawyers in the same law firm.

3.3.2 The arbitrator and another arbitrator or the counsel for one of the parties are members of the same barristers' chambers.[7]

3.3.3 The arbitrator was within the past three years a partner of, or otherwise affiliated with, another arbitrator or any of the counsel in the same arbitration.

3.3.4 A lawyer in the arbitrator's law firm is an arbitrator in another dispute involving the same party or parties or an affiliate of one of the parties.

---

fields it is the custom and practice for parties frequently to appoint the same arbitrator in different cases, no disclosure of this fact is required where all parties in the arbitration should be familiar with such custom and practice.

[7] Issues concerning special considerations involving barristers in England are discussed in the Background Information issued by the Working Group.

3.3.5 A close family member of the arbitrator is a partner or employee of the law firm representing one of the parties, but is not assisting with the dispute.

3.3.6 A close personal friendship exists between an arbitrator and a counsel of one party, as demonstrated by the fact that the arbitrator and the counsel regularly spend considerable time together unrelated to professional work commitments or the activities of professional associations or social organizations.

3.3.7 The arbitrator has within the past three years received more than three appointments by the same counsel or the same law firm.

3.4. Relationship between arbitrator and party and others involved in the arbitration

3.4.1 The arbitrator's law firm is currently acting adverse to one of the parties or an affiliate of one of the parties.

3.4.2 The arbitrator had been associated within the past three years with a party or an affiliate of one of the parties in a professional capacity, such as a former employee or partner.

3.4.3 A close personal friendship exists between an arbitrator and a manager or director or a member of the supervisory board or any person having a similar controlling influence in one of the parties or an affiliate of one of the parties or a witness or expert, as demonstrated by the fact that the arbitrator and such director, manager, other person, witness or expert regularly spend considerable time together unrelated to professional work commitments or the activities of professional associations or social organizations.

3.4.4 If the arbitrator is a former judge, he or she has within the past three years heard a significant case involving one of the parties.

3.5. Other circumstances

3.5.1 The arbitrator holds shares, either directly or indirectly, which by reason of number or denomination constitute a material holding in one of the parties or an affiliate of one of the parties that is publicly listed.

3.5.2 The arbitrator has publicly advocated a specific position regarding the case that is being arbitrated, whether in a published paper or speech or otherwise.

3.5.3 The arbitrator holds one position in an arbitration institution with appointing authority over the dispute.

3.5.4 The arbitrator is a manager, director or member of the supervisory board, or has a similar controlling influence, in an affiliate of one of the parties, where the affiliate is not directly involved in the matters in dispute in the arbitration.

4. Green List

4.1. Previously expressed legal opinions

4.1.1 The arbitrator has previously published a general opinion (such as in a law review article or public lecture) concerning an issue which also arises in the arbitration (but this opinion is not focused on the case that is being arbitrated).

4.2. Previous services against one party

4.2.1 The arbitrator's law firm has acted against one of the parties or an affiliate of one of the parties in an unrelated matter without the involvement of the arbitrator.

4.3. Current services for one of the parties

4.3.1 A firm in association or in alliance with the arbitrator's law firm, but which does not share fees or other revenues with the arbitrator's law firm, renders services to one of the parties or an affiliate of one of the parties in an unrelated matter.

4.4. Contacts with another arbitrator or with counsel for one of the parties

4.4.1 The arbitrator has a relationship with another arbitrator or with the counsel for one of the parties through membership in the same professional association or social organization.

4.4.2 The arbitrator and counsel for one of the parties or another arbitrator have previously served together as arbitrators or as co-counsel.

4.5. Contacts between the arbitrator and one of the parties

4.5.1 The arbitrator has had an initial contact with the appointing party or an affiliate of the appointing party (or the respective counsels) prior to appointment, if this contact is limited to the arbitrator's availability and qualifications to serve or to the names of possible candidates for a chairperson and did not address the merits or procedural aspects of the dispute.

4.5.2 The arbitrator holds an insignificant amount of shares in one of the parties or an affiliate of one of the parties, which is publicly listed.

4.5.3 The arbitrator and a manager, director or member of the supervisory board, or any person having a similar controlling influence, in one of the parties or an affiliate of one of the parties, have worked together as joint experts or in another professional capacity, including as arbitrators in the same case.

APPENDIX 40
CONTACT INFORMATION FOR VARIOUS INTERNATIONAL ARBITRAL INSTITUTIONS

AAA (www.adr.org)
Corporate Headquarters
1633 Broadway, 10th Floor
New York, New York 10019
Tel: +1 212 716 5800
Fax: +1 212 716 5905

ASIA
International Centre for Dispute Resolution
City Hall
3 St. Andrew's Road
178958
Singapore
Tel: +65 6334 1277
Fax: + 65 6334 2942
E-mail: BautistaM@adr.org

Australian Centre for International Commercial Arbitration
(www.acica.org.au)
Australian Centre for International Commercial Arbitration
Level 6, 50 Park Street
Sydney NSW 20
Tel: + 61 0 2 9286-3591
Fax: + 61 0 2 9267-3125

CENTRAL AND SOUTH AMERICA
International Centre for Dispute Resolution
1633 Broadway, 10th Floor
New York, New York 10019
Tel: + 1 212 716-5833
Fax:+ 1 212 716-5904
E-mail: MartinezL@adr.org

China International Economic and Trade Arbitration Commission
(www.cietac.org)
6/F Golden Land Building
32 Liang Ma Qiao Road
Chaoyang District
Beijing
P.R. China
Tel: + 86 10 646 46688
Fax: + 86 10 646 43500
E-mail: cietac@public.bta.net.cn
info@cietac.org

Dubai International Arbitration Centre (www.diac.ae)
Dubai International Arbitration Centre
Dubai Chamber of Commerce & Industry - 14th Floor
Dubai
United Arab Emirates
Tel + 9714 2280000 / 2028391
Fax + 9714 2273 247
E-mail centre@diac.ae / arbitrationcenter@dcci.gov.ae

EUROPE, MIDDLE EAST, AFRICA
International Centre for Dispute Resolution
14 Merrion Square
Dublin 2, Ireland
Tel: + 353-1-676-1500
Fax: + 353-1-676-1501
E-mail: AppelM@adr.org

German Institution of Arbitration (DIS) (www.dis-arb.de)
Beethovenstr. 5 – 13
50674 Köln
Tel: + 0221/28 55 2-0
Fax: + 0221/28 55 2-222
E-mail: dis@dis-arb.de

Hong Kong International Arbitration Centre (www.hkiac.org)
Hong Kong International Arbitration Centre
38th Floor Two Exchange Square
8 Connaught Place
Hong Kong S.A.R.
China
Tel: + 852 2525-2381
Fax: + 852 2524-2171
E-mail: adr@hkiac.org

ICC (www.iccwbo.org)
Secretariat of the ICC International Court of Arbitration
38 Cours Albert 1er
75008 Paris,
France
Tel: + 33 1 49 53 29 05
Fax: + 33 1 49 53 29 33

ICDR (www.adr.org)

LCIA
70 Fleet Street
London EC4Y 1EU
United Kingdom
Tel: +44 0 20 7936 7007
Fax: +44 0 20 7936 7008
E-mail: lcia@lcia.org

MEXICO AND CANADA
International Centre for Dispute Resolution
1108 E. South Union Avenue
Midvale, UT 84047
Tel: + 801 569 4618
Fax: + 801 984 8170
E-mail: AndersenS@adr.org

Netherlands Arbitration Institute (www.nai-nl.org)
Netherlands Arbitration Institute
Secretariat
Aert van Nesstraat 25 JK
3012 Rotterdam
Tel: + 31 10 281 6969
Fax: + 31 10 281 6968
E-mail: secretariaat@nai-nl.org

Permanent Court
Permanent Court of Arbitration
Peace Palace
Carnegieplein 2
2517 KJ The Hague
The Netherlands
Tel:+ 31 70 302 4165
Fax:+ 31 70 302 4167
E-mail:bureau@pca-cpa.org

Stockholm Chamber of Commerce (www.sccinstitute.com)
Arbitration Institute of the Stockholm Chamber of Commerce
P.O. Box 16050
SE-103 21 Stockholm
Sweden
Tel: +46 8 555 100 50
Fax: +46 8 566 316 50
E-mail: arbitration@chamber.se

Swiss Chambers' Court of Arbitration and Mediation
(www.sccam.org)
There are seven secretariats corresponding to each separate chamber of commerce. Details of the Zurich chamber are given here—the remainder are available on the website:

Zurich Chamber of Commerce (www.uncitral.org)
Bleicherweg 5
PO Box 3058
CH – 8022 Zurich
Tel : + 41 44 217 40 50
Fax : + 41 44 217 40 51
E-mail: direktion@zurichcci.ch

TABLE OF CASES

INDEX

A

AAA, 11, 559
AAA Code of Ethics, 55
AAA Commercial Arbitration Rules, 29-30, 41, 91, 179
AAA-ICSID Dispute Resolution Procedures, 445-476
Adjudication by an expert, 16, 18
ADR, 249-250
Advisory Committee Notes to the Federal Rules of Civil Procedure 2007, 128
Africa, International Centre for Dispute Resolution, 560
Agency, new parties, joinder, 33
American Arbitration Association. *See* AAA
American Bar Association Rules of Professional Conduct, 169
American Bar Association Standing Committee on Ethics and Professional
    Responsibility, 169
Amicus curiae, intervention as, 31-32
Answer to request for arbitration, 25-26
    Sample, 277-278
Arbitrability, 3, 4, 71
Arbitral independence, 37-42
Arbitral institutions, contact information for, 559-562
Arbitral tribunal. *See* index lines generally
Arbitration agreements or clauses, 1, 6, 7, 15, 16
Arbitrators
    Award, issuance, duty of, 45
    Due care, duty of, 44
    Due diligence, duty of, 45
    Fairness and impartiality, duty of, 43-44
    Independence and impartiality, 37-42, 44
    Party-appointed, 38, 40, 41
    Reference, completion of, 45
    Specific duties or international rules, 45
Arizona, 59
Arizona, State Bar of, 170
Asia, International Centre for Dispute Resolution, 560
Assignment, new parties, joinder, 34
Attorney-client privilege. *See* Legal professional privilege
Australia, 17, 27, 40, 105, 106, 138, 149
Australian Centre for International Commercial Arbitration, 559
    Rules, 224
Australian High Court, 138
Awards, 257-264

E